reflections
FOR MOVIE LOVERS

LIVING
INK
BOOKS
Writing Worth Reading

MATTHEW KINNE

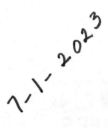

Reflections for Movie Lovers

Copyright © 2004 by Matthew Kinne

Published by AMG Publishers
6815 Shallowford Rd.
Chattanooga, TN 37421

ISBN 0-89957-146-8

First printing—October 2004

Cover designed by Market Street Design, Chattanooga, Tennessee
Interior design and typesetting by Reider Publishing Services,
    West Hollywood, California
Edited and Proofread by Eric Stanford of Stanford Creative Services, Dan Penwell,
    Carol Noe, and Rick Steele

Printed in the United States of America
09 08 07 06 05 04 –RO– 8 7 6 5 4 3 2 1

To my late father, Dr. Douglas G. Kinne,
a man who loved God and a good movie

"Every story or **movie** or song or poem that has ever stirred your soul is telling you something you need to know about the Sacred Romance."

- John Eldridge, *The Journey of Desire*

Please visit
www.matthewkinne.com
for more information on Matthew Kinne

CONTENTS

EXPLANATION OF TERMS

AFI: The American Film Institute (AFI) created a list of the 100 greatest American films of all time, as selected by a blue-ribbon panel of leaders from across the film community. The number listed here is the ranking of this film on that list. For more information on the American Film Institute, visit their web site at www.afi.com.

AA: Academy Awards: Some of the movies included won them, some didn't. This will tell you which movies did and what they won. Also included are the names of the recipients for the major categories including Best Director, Best Actor, Best Actress, Best Supporting Actor, Best Supporting Actress

MPAA RATING: The Motion Picture Association of America (MPAA) applied this rating to all movies created and released after 1968. Also included is a short list of the objectionable material found in the movie as given by the MPAA. If there is no list of objectionable material after the MPAA rating, than the MPAA didn't provide it. All listed ratings came straight from the MPAA website, www.mpaa.org. Movies created and released prior to 1968 are either not rated or have now been retroactively rated by the MPAA.

Actor names appear in parenthesis behind the name of the character. Voices of actors appear behind the names of their characters in animated films.

The date listed with each movie title is the original release year of the movie.

FOREWORD

© baehr, 2004
ZEITGEIST
By Dr. Ted Baehr, Publisher of *Movieguide*

"Yet to make such judgments on any question rather than trying
to examine the question properly, to discover what the full answers
might be, is coercive philistinism: it is to allow the mountebank
to triumph over the critic, the mob orator to drown the doubts of
the skeptic."

—Kevin Myers, "An Irishman's Diary," *Irish Times*, November 12, 1999

Someone who criticizes without a thorough analysis guided by clear standards is a charlatan or mountebank. In other words, their criticism is just hot air.

To criticize or to critique everything from a painting to a movie to architecture, one needs standards, just weights and measures that can determine the real value of the object being critiqued. Postmodern secular critics have abandoned standards, and, therefore, by definition, they are merely blowhards. Christians, however, have biblical standards, and should be able to judiciously apply them in every area of life, to discern the good from the evil and thus make wise judgments and decisions. If only it were so.

Without standards, where do ethics come from? Marxists say that poverty is unethical, but the Bible says the poor will be with us always and that we should care for the poor, the homeless, and the needy. Homosexuals say intolerance of homosexuality is unethical, but the Bible condemns homosexuality, while calling the faithful to love the sinner. One misguided, politically-correct minister said the real sin is war, not adultery, covetousness, lying, or anything that the Bible declares a sin, but where did he get this standard?

Of course, all this does not mean there aren't different types and approaches of applying those standards. An apologist looks at a movie, sees the sin and says that the movie shows why every man needs Jesus Christ. A teacher interested in discipling the viewer sees the sin in the movie and says that is why we should not conduct ourselves in that manner. A pastor concerned about his flock sees the sin in a movie and says, "I'm here to tell you not to see the movie."

On the other hand, the person who does not have standards derived from the Bible and who does not look at the movie exegetically, misses the sin in the movie, or the lack thereof, and his opinion is worthless. He is merely a blowhard or a mountebank. Such a person's approach to establishing his credibility is merely to bully, accuse, and promote himself.

Someone who takes a biblical approach, however, is there to promote the truth, applying just weights and measures so that people can develop discernment, wisdom, and understanding.

DOING THEOLOGY IN THE MASS MEDIA

The early church struggled with biblical interpretation. Allegorical interpretation led to theological anarchy where people read anything they wanted into the Scripture. Literal interpretation often brought out the inconsistencies in the text and created enormous stumbling blocks, sometimes producing the feeling that the Old Testament was a lesser testament. Eventually, sound biblical exegesis became the standard. Today, the real wrestling is not in terms of the biblical text, although that still occurs, but in terms of the mass media—namely movies and television programs.

Allegorical criticism reads the reviewer's views into whatever they're seeing, often so that the movie can be used as an apologetic device. Even morally repugnant movies such as KILL BILL: VOL. 1 have been interpreted to open the door to evangelistic discussion. The problem with this approach is the same problem with the early allegorical theology; it produces rampant confusion and leads people away from sound doctrine.

The same, of course, is true about literalism, where the only type of movie or television program that can claim to be Christian is one that paints by numbers the four spiritual laws.

A wiser approach is asking the right questions in terms of sound principles of theology. In this regard, a Christian worldview consists of the Christian doctrine of being, the Christian doctrine of God, the Christian doctrine of man, the Christian doctrine of salvation, and many other theological doctrines in the Bible that help to uncover truth.

Armed with the right questions and a comprehensive but easy to impart knowledge of Christian doctrine, one can do effective theology in the mass media that can help people understand the truth that will set them free without abandoning sound doctrine.

In *Reflections for Movie-Lovers*, former MOVIEGUIDE® reviewer and editor Matthew Kinne takes another approach. He uses movies to reflect on spiritual truths. He admits that some of the movies are not suitable for most audiences and focuses on the spiritual truth rather than analyzing the movie in question. If the reader will do the same, he or she will be inspired by *Reflections for Movie-Lovers*.

ACKNOWLEDGMENTS

'd like to give a special thanks to all who joined me at the movies: Anne, Karl, Hans, Matt, Laura, Angie, Holly, Chad, Christopher, Dave, Lainee, Kallie, and so many others.

A big thanks to mom——Jan Kinne——for her inspiration and love and the rest of my family including my grandparents, Harry and Lorraine, plus Rex, Tamara, Doug, and Brie (I love you, Brie).

I offer cheers to Rich Brauer who gave me an opportunity to work on a film with an Acadamy Award Winning Actor. I extend much appreciation to Dan Glass for jumping in the scary pool of filmmaking with me——you are a wisecracker. Good tidings to Glen Petersen and Bud Solem for taking me to Outlandish and inspiring me. I give respect and love to a visionary, the creator of Messenger Films and the one who gave me the first job in the film business—— Cristobol Krusen.

I have deep appreciation to Dr. Ted Baehr for his tireless work in Hollywood and I thank him for giving me a fine start in the movie business. And I thank God for the idea of this book and for inspiring Thomas Edison to make the movie camera.

And of course, a great thank you to my editor, Eric Stanford, my acquisition editor, Dan Penwell, and all those who placed their faith in me at AMG Publishers/ Living Ink Books. Cheers to my agent, Steve Laube.

Lastly, I praise Jesus who gave us so many wonderful parables.

INTRODUCTION

You begin to feel it while standing in line, an anticipation of excitement. It builds in your heart. You tell a neighbor, "I've been looking forward to this one for months." Your neighbor replies, "Me too." You smile at each other—knowing you'll both experience a marvelous event together. At the counter, you gladly depart with your hard-earned money because you are going to the movies and you are a movie lover.

The sub-Saharan explorer. The British spy. The autistic child. The single mom. The rebellious teen. And the army Captain who lost his entire platoon. All these movie characters speak to you. They tell you: "I know what your life is like. It's like mine. I know you struggle and fight for survival. I know you get beaten back but sometimes you find a nugget of grace and mercy in your life."

The lights dim and the projector flickers. The crowd quiets. You are transported to different locales, different times, and different cultures. You transcend your ordinary life. But somehow, these stories ring familiar. Somehow, they reflect the same stories you heard as a child. Stories of bravery, war, love and rebellion. Stories of sin and redemption. Stories that God has written since the beginning of time.

Image upon image, and word upon word washes over you in an audio/visual cascade of emotion. Truth and lies. Drama and conflict. Happy and terrifying moments. A problem solved for better or worse. A climax achieved and a worldview affirmed or denied. The end credits roll as you sit in your seat and take a deep breath. Your senses catch their breath. The story you just witnessed becomes a part of you. Compelled to tell others, you reflect on why this movie made a lasting impression on your heart and soul. Perhaps you didn't realize it, but God just spoke to you.

Movies reflect the image of man, and man reflects the image of God. God speaks to us through movies because he speaks to us through the stories of man. Your Bible is filled with such accounts of God reaching down into the short but incredible history of man with a message of love. Many movies illustrate the negative (the folly and sin of mankind), but some inspire us and point us to the divine. The best resonate in our minds and spirits long after the viewing experience is over, challenging our thinking and behaviors.

Jesus did that. He challenged the thinking and behaviors of his listeners. He told parables, little stories that (I'm sure) played like movies in the minds of his listeners. He mostly talked about the kingdom of God, a wonderful, spiritual reality that he wanted to see on earth as well as heaven. He illustrated the kingdom with common references that most everybody of His day understood: farming, eating, laboring, animals, and more. After Jesus spoke a parable, his listeners usually stood around and scratched their heads asking, "What does it mean? And "What does this mean to me?" Jesus then often took the time to explain what the parables were all about.

Reflections for Movies Lovers is my attempt to "explain" the spiritual and biblical truth behind many of our most beloved movies. Not all movies illuminate truth, but everybody can compare the "message" of the movie with God's truth.

That is what this book is all about. It is a chance to daily compare the "Reel" world with the "Real" world," that is, the life God wants for us—The kingdom of God. It is a chance to be reminded of a favorite cinematic parable and then relate that to a biblical parable. It's an exercise to probe your own spiritual walk as you journey forward in life with Christ.

Just because I write about a movie and use it as a devotional, doesn't mean I endorse it or agree with every little thing about it. Like all humanity, all movies portray sinners, usually depicting their sins. While, for the most part, I have steered clear of listing controversial movies, I have decided to comment on a few R-rated movies. This doesn't mean I recommend that all Christians see all R-rated movies, as I believe that some people probably shouldn't see any at all. Your choice of viewing is between you and God—and your parents if you are under 17. (It has been said that if the entire Bible were made into a movie, it would at least get a PG-13 rating. With wars, adultery, and drunkenness found within its pages, I don't doubt it.)

Finally, your interpretation of a movie, a movie scene, or a movie theme may be very different from my own. You may be reading one of the devotions found here and say to yourself, "I didn't get that at all from that movie." If you do find yourself saying this, I say "great." Just keep looking for God reaching out to you through story and film.

See you at the movies!

NEW BEGINNINGS

Movies That Root Our Identity in Christ

WEEK 1

January 1–7

BIG TOP GLORY
The Greatest Show on Earth (1952)
AA: Best Picture • MPAA: not rated
Read: Exodus 40:34–38

When Moses set up the tabernacle, he put the bases in place, erected the frames, inserted the crossbars and set up the posts. (Exodus 40:18)

Step right up to the greatest show on earth! The Ringling Bros. and Barnum & Bailey circus travels with clowns, trapeze artists, lion tamers, elephant trainers, midgets, and countless animals. They go from town to town, amazing audiences. The rings to the side are fun, but the real attraction lies in the center ring. It is here that the most amazing and daring stunts are performed, the playground for the star players of the circus. In this movie the Great Sebastian (Cornel Wilde) and Holly (Betty Hutton) compete for the distinction of center ring. Yet enemies of the show sabotage the circus train, and it collides with another train. Severely injured, circus boss Marc "Brad" Braden (Charlton Heston) displays the sawdust in his veins and demands that the show must go on.

In the Old Testament, God created his own "big top." He instructed the Israelites to construct a large tent, called the tabernacle. Made of fine blue, purple, and scarlet yarn, fine linen, goat's hair, ram skins dyed red, and the hides of sea cows, it was a remarkable structure to behold. The priests who entered it wore elaborate garments of ephods, breast pieces, and robes. This spectacle of the desert wasn't for the amusement of the desert dwellers, but it was very, very great. This tent, with its "center ring" called the holy of holies, was nothing less than the dwelling place of God himself. A cloud by day and a pillar of fire by night led this traveling caravan. No circus could compare with this awesome sight.

God calls himself the great I Am, and when he shows up, things happen. Lives are saved. Evil is thwarted. People are challenged, redeemed, instructed, and transformed. He is the great King over all the earth. His mercy is great. His love is great. His power is great. He calls his created people great and offers them great rewards. And he sits on a great white throne. He is the greatest being in the universe and his acts on earth, including establishing the tabernacle, are the greatest show on earth. No mere showman, he is a great communicator telling others of his greatness and bidding them to come to him. This new year, come and discover his greatness.

PRAYER IDEA: Ask God to show you his greatness today.

A BOSS OF LOVE

Cool Hand Luke (1967)

AA: George Kennedy, Best Supporting Actor
MPAA: PG for thematic elements
Read: Psalm 110

"Repent, for the kingdom of heaven is near." (Matthew 4:17)

What we have here is a failure to communicate," says the prison boss to Cool Hand Luke (Paul Newman). Picked up by the police for vandalism, Luke is convicted and sentenced to a few months of prison time. Day after day, he and the other prisoners cut weeds along the sun-scorched roads. But Luke decides he isn't going to conform to prison rules. He talks out of place, provokes a fistfight, challenges his prisoners that he can eat fifty hard-boiled eggs in an hour (and does), and runs off, not once or twice, but three times. The prison bosses try to break him with hard labor and beating, but he still doesn't get the message. In desperation the prison leaders resort to violence to cool Luke's wayward and rebellious ways.

Earlier in the story, the prison boss tells Luke that they will get along if he complies, but if he doesn't, things will get mighty uncomfortable. The boss tells Luke, "It's your choice." Many Christians think that God is sort of a prison boss who establishes arbitrary rules and then smacks down hard if we don't comply. While a system of cause-and-effect does exist on this earth, God is more interested in having a genuine relationship with us. The prison boss doesn't really want to know Luke; the prison boss only wants to control the prisoners. The prison boss isn't about love; he is about punishment. If you think God is nothing more than a prison boss, your God is distorted.

God is love, and his desire for us is communion and interaction. God is calling us to change our ways, but he isn't waiting to club us over the head if we mess up. (Often, though, we can beat up ourselves up or shoot our own feet through our sin.) The goal of God's call for repentance is neither to flex his muscle nor to produce soulless automatons. He wants us to choose him out of our own free will. God is communicating and is saying, "I love you." Are we listening to that, or do we hear "Straighten up, boy, or I'll smack you"? God wants to warm our hands and hearts by holding them close to his own.

PRAYER IDEA: Ask God to show you how loving his authority is today.

He set my feet on a rock and gave me a firm place to stand. (Psalm 40:2)

want to be where the people are," sings sixteen-year-old mermaid Ariel (Jodi Benson) in *The Little Mermaid.* Her life under the sea isn't exciting. She looks for a life above the ordinary, and when she sees a young human prince named Eric (Christopher Daniel Barnes), she knows she must somehow join him on dry land. She goes to meet Ursula (Pat Carroll), a wicked sea witch, to cut a deal. Ursula will give Ariel human legs for three days in exchange for Ariel's voice. If Prince Eric doesn't kiss Ariel by sunset of the third day, then Ariel will transform into a sea slug and for all eternity come under the possession of Ursula. When Ariel fails to kiss Eric by the proper time, her father, King Triton (Kenneth Mars), bravely takes her place. Eric fights off Ursula, frees Triton, and demonstrates that he is worthy of Ariel.

———————

ike Ariel, we humans desire something more out of life. We have a transcendental longing in our spirits. We were made to desire a home that is unlike anything we know here on earth. It was God's plan all along that we would enjoy fellowship with him in paradise for all eternity.

Also like Ariel, we humans sought change through wrong choices. Adam and Eve wanted to be like God. Satan as a serpent said, "Do you want to be like God? I can make you like God. Just eat this fruit and you'll be just like him" (see Genesis 3:1–5). This option looked good to Adam and Eve, and they ate the forbidden fruit, but in exchange they lost more than a pretty singing voice. They lost their souls. They lost their beauty and ability to praise God with a pure heart. God had to step in and take on the penalty for humanity's failure. The Son, Jesus, took our place and, with a demonstration of great love, vanquished evil by rising again and putting Satan underfoot. This act pulled us up to the dry ground, a beautiful land of redemption. God gave us legs to walk with him in the cool of the day—forever.

PRAYER IDEA: Ask God to give you firm footing as you live to stand for him.

TO BE YOUNG AGAIN

Disney's The Kid (2000)
MPAA: PG for mild language
Read: Psalm 37:25, 26

I will repay you for the years the locusts have eaten. (Joel 2:25)

Russ Duritz (Bruce Willis) doesn't like himself or anybody else very much. A nearly forty-year-old image consultant from southern California, Russ lashes out at his secretary, frustrates his assistant, refuses to help his own father, and rudely shuts up strangers. One day a little boy shows up in his home. Russ discovers that "the kid," named Rusty, is actually himself at age twelve. At first Russ treats Rusty like a hallucination. Then he loathes him for being real. Then he attempts to understand him. Russ realizes he must help Rusty go back to his home of 1968. To do so, Russ must embrace and love his former self and accept the child he once was. It is only when Russ learns to love himself that he can help Rusty go home and learn to love his neighbors, co-workers, and family as himself.

In one scene, when Amy is particularly frustrated with Russ, she tells him, "You could have been great." Russ lowers his head. He realizes he isn't great. He realizes that his cutthroat determination, rudeness, and moneymaking efforts only gave him heartache and loneliness. When he finally learns to love and welcome Rusty, the child he once was, he learns to step into greatness and become all he was meant to be.

In this coming year, learn to love yourself. Forgive yourself for past sins. Understand that many of your problems weren't even your fault. Come to Christ like a little child and let him give you his kingdom. Let him spoil you with his attention and love. Let him teach you lessons. Let him give you patience and wisdom and mercy. We are all God's children. We are all under the care of a loving heavenly Father. Let him place his hands on you and love you.

PRAYER IDEA: Ask God to give you child-like faith and behavior today.

FROZEN FRIENDS
Ice Age (2002)
MPAA: PG for mild peril
Read: Romans 5:6–8

A friend loves at all times, and a brother is born for adversity. (Proverbs 17:17)

Sid the dim sloth (John Leguizamo), Manfred the grumpy mammoth (Ray Romano), and Diego the conniving sabertooth tiger (Denis Leary) find a lost human infant in *Ice Age*. They try to return him to his tribe through ice, snow, danger, and cold. Little do Sid and Manfred know that Diego wants to eat the child. Diego plans to lead them to the tiger pack, where they'll be ripped to shreds. As they travel, Manfred risks his life for Diego and wins his trust and loyalty. When they finally meet the tiger pack, Diego returns the favor to Manfred and throws himself in front of the attacking beasts, now protecting his new, true friends.

By their nature, tigers and mammoths are enemies. Tigers eat mammoths, and mammoths don't like tigers. Through sin, people and God have also experienced a broken, shattered relationship. Yet Jesus demonstrated his love and friendship to us by laying down his life for us when we were still enemies with him. "Greater love has no one than this, that he lay down his life for his friends" (John 15:13). Self-sacrifice is the greatest form of friendship and generosity. Donating time and money can be generous acts, but the Lord set the standard for the greatest act of love.

Manfred didn't know that Diego was a foe. He thought Diego was a friend and acted kindly toward him because he thought Diego was "one of the herd." Every human on this planet is in the same herd. We might look different, eat differently, or come from different regions, but we are all, by nature, enemies of Christ. We are all in need of salvation. Happily for us, Christ died that we might live. And in doing so, he showed us ultimate love so that we could be friends with him forever. As a new year begins with the icy chills of January, remember to show the warmth of sacrificial love to others.

PRAYER IDEA: Ask God to show you how to live sacrificially for others today.

FINDING YOUR PURPOSE

The Jerk (1979)

MPAA: R for language and sexual situations
Read: Mark 12:28–34

Before I formed you in the womb I knew you. (Jeremiah 1:5)

Raised by a poor, black family in Mississippi, the jerk, Navin R. Johnson, leaves home at age thirty-five to go to St. Louis and discover himself and the world. Working as a gas station attendant, Navin (played by wild and crazy guy Steve Martin) jumps for joy when the new phone book arrives. He shouts, "The new phone book is here. I'm somebody now. I'm in print. Things are going to start happening to me now." Navin then joins a traveling carnival, where he discovers his "special purpose." Next, he strikes it rich with a strange invention called the Opti-grab. He marries Marie Kimble (Bernadette Peters) but loses both his money and his wife after he is sued. Out on the street, he regains luxury when his financially skilled parents and estranged wife find him and take him back in.

Each of us has a "special purpose" in God. Each of us is "somebody" even before our names are printed in ink. Some of us may never have our names printed anywhere but in the phone book, but all of us are special. Before we were formed, God had an accounting of us. He had our names recorded in his own book. He made us for his pleasure.

Many of us are looking for our purpose in life. Some people take up yoga, go back to school, travel to India, or take mind-expanding drugs to find their purpose. Others try to find meaning in endless work or service. But God says it's a lot easier than that. Basically, we are to love others as we love ourselves and to love God with all our strength, soul, and might. That's it. Lots of people can lose track of who they are when they pursue riches, fame, romance, or enlightenment. Many of us will never find riches or fame like Navin. But when we fulfill God's will for our lives through love, we'll enjoy a wealth of eternal blessings.

PRAYER IDEA: Ask God to show you his purposes for your life today.

MELTING THE ICE QUEEN

The Philadelphia Story (1940)

AFI: 51 • AA: James Stewart, Best Actor;
Best Original Screenplay • MPAA: not rated
Read: Galatians 6:1–3

Rebuke your neighbor frankly so you will not share in his guilt. (Leviticus 19:17)

Reformed playboy C. K. Dexter Haven (Cary Grant) is on a holy mission in *The Philadelphia Story*. He intends to break up the engagement of his former wife, Philadelphia heiress Tracy Lord (Katharine Hepburn), to wealthy George Kittredge (John Howard). It's not that Kittredge is a bad fellow. On the contrary, he's rather good and generous. But Kittredge wants to put Tracy on a pedestal, and what she needs is to be knocked down several notches. Dexter arrives at the Lords' mansion the day before the wedding with tabloid writer Mike Connor (James Stewart) and photographer Liz Imbrie (Ruth Hussey). Dexter tells Tracy, "You're prejudiced against weakness. You'll never be a first-class person or a first-class woman until you have some regard for human frailty." Faithful are the wounds of this friend, and Tracy eventually wises up about her haughty ways. As Dexter rebukes her and Mike romances her, Tracy repents and discovers the heart beneath her icy exterior.

Tracy couldn't find humility by herself. She needed help from friends. Though he thought he loved her, Kittredge and his praises only served to keep Tracy in sin. She kept absorbing his praises like a sponge, and she became more and more haughty. With friends like these, you don't need enemies. Beware of the person who feeds you flattery. It may do more harm than good.

What Tracy needed was a swat to the backside. She needed to be deflated and de-iced. Dexter came with the rebuke and Mike came to clean up the mess with genuine love. Sometimes haughtiness and other sin needs to be confronted with a tag-team assault of goodness. The Bible even supports this method. First, one goes in with a rebuke. Then, if the sinning party doesn't accept it, two are to confront him or her (Matthew 18:15–17). With a little help from our friends, we can all spur each other on to Christlikeness.

PRAYER IDEA: Ask God to help you accept a loving rebuke this year.

THE TEEN SCENE

Gen-X, Y, & Z and Wrestling with the Challenges of Youth

WEEK 2

January 8–14

IT'S ABOUT TIME

Back to the Future (1985)

AA: Best Sound Effects • MPAA: PG

Read: 2 Peter 3:8, 9

It is time to seek the LORD. (Hosea 10:12)

Take some plutonium, a DeLorean car, and a loony scientist named Doc Brown (Christopher Lloyd) and what do you get? You get a trip to the past and another trip back to the future. Marty McFly (Michael J. Fox) is your average slacker teenager from the 1980s, but he transports into the year 1955. There he stumbles upon a younger version of his parents, disrupts their meeting, and must find a way to get them together so they can marry and give birth to him! To Marty, time is of the essence because he has to show up at a precise location during a lightning storm to get back to the future.

Time is a funny thing. We know only a bit of the past and present, but God knows all time: past, present, and future. Lots of people think God is slow in answering prayer, and so we get impatient. But "with the Lord a day is like a thousand years, and a thousand years are like a day" (2 Peter 3:8). Think about it. If eternity means forever, then our lifetimes are like a dot on a line that never ends. Because Christians are going to spend eternity with God, we can relax about God's timing. It has been said that he is never late or early; he shows up right on time.

God tells us that there is a time for everything under the sun (Ecclesiastes 3:1). There is a time for planting and a time for reaping. Sometimes it's appropriate to cry, sometimes to laugh. There is a time to hug and a time to withhold from hugging. One thing is true: our times are in God's hands (Psalm 31:15). The best news about time is that at the appointed time Christ will return to take us with him into eternal joy. Time is short, so make the most of your time here on earth.

PRAYER IDEA: Ask God to help you make the most of the time you have on earth.

FINDING OUR PURPOSE
Reality Bites (1994)
MPAA: PG-13 for some language, drug content, and sensuality
Read: Jeremiah 17:7, 8

By him all things were created. (Colossians 1:16)

Reality bites for valedictorian college graduate Lelaina Pierce (Winona Ryder) and her friends, Vickie (Janeane Garofalo), Sammy (Steve Zahn), and Troy (Ethan Hawke). To them, life and jobs seem meaningless. Lelaina makes a video documentary chronicling their discontent. On tape Troy says, "There is no point to any of this. It's all a random lottery of meaningless tragedy and a series of near escapes. So I take pleasure in the details." Troy believes that life has no meaning or purpose and so must content himself with material pleasures like cheeseburgers and cigarettes. After Lelaina meets Michael (Ben Stiller), a video executive who takes her homemade video to his MTV-like station, she must decide what she values—the materialism and security of Michael or the philosophy of the poverty-stricken Troy.

A man named Agur says in Proverbs, "Give me neither poverty nor riches, but give me only my daily bread." (Proverbs 30:8) Apparently, Agur found purpose in God. Jobs come and go; friends and lovers come and go; but God and his love last forever. Troy thinks there is no point to this life and all we can do is enjoy the details of the material world before dying. Lots of people all around us think this is the best we can hope for. But God says he created you for his purposes.

You were made by God and for God. We can never find out what on earth we are here for by looking at the latest pop psychology or ourselves. God created you and thought of you even before you were born. When we know why he created us, then we can have perfect peace. Knowing our purpose gives our life meaning, simplification, focus, hope, and motivation. When we know that our life is but a pause before eternity, then we can live a life of meaning. Generation X, Y, and Z discontent doesn't have to linger in our lives. God has a wonderful purpose for us. We have the rest of our lives and eternity to discover and practice what that is.

PRAYER IDEA: Thank God for giving purpose to your life, even if you are still figuring it out.

AN INCORRECT JUDGMENT
Pretty in Pink (1986)
MPAA: PG-13
Read: Isaiah 11:1–5

Speak up and judge fairly. (Proverbs 31:9)

Phil ("Duckie") Dale (Jon Cryer) says of Andie, "I love that girl too much." Young Andie (Molly Ringwald) is one of the not-so-popular girls in high school, but she's cute, creative, and pretty in pink. When Duckie's friendship with Andie turns into devotion, and then devotion turns into obsession, Duckie can't think straight. He incorrectly judges Andie's new love interest, Blane (Andrew McCarthy), as an arrogant, insincere rich kid. But Blane's interest in Andie is genuine. In fact, because of Andie, Blane loses his friendship with his vain and materialistic friend Steff (James Spader). Steff calls Andie "low-grade trash"—a gross misjudgment indeed! After a few cries, a few honest discussions, and a visit to the prom by all, Duckie understands Blane, and the only loser who remains is Steff, hardened by his own sin.

The teenage years can be filled with cruel name-calling and misjudgments. How unfortunate, because lots of teens don't even know themselves, let alone others. Lots of grace, humility, understanding, and love are required to smooth over the damage of barbed insinuations and lies. When misjudgments occur between kids from opposite sides of the tracks, hearts are damaged. The goal for all of us, not just young people, is to love and understand one another, no matter how different we may be from each other.

The Bible says, "Do not judge, or you too will be judged" (Matthew 7:1). This doesn't mean we should never assess the character of another. It means we should never jump to conclusions about another and always take into consideration our own sins and errors. Correct judgment requires us to accept God's wisdom. It also requires a healthy fear of the Lord. It doesn't look at appearances, which can be deceiving, but at the heart of the matter, taking all things into consideration. Ultimately, correct judgment is about righteousness and faithfulness. It's righteous because it's fair. It's faithful because it aligns itself with the truth. Take time to get to know someone who is different from you. Resist the urge to judge someone by his or her appearance. Judge correctly.

PRAYER IDEA: Ask God to help you accept and give correct judgments.

Fathers, do not embitter your children, or they will become discouraged. (Colossians 3:21)

The quintessential 1980s teen angst "dramedy," *The Breakfast Club* reexamines high school stereotypes and the struggles (especially with adults) that teens face. Inside the Saturday morning detention hall are Claire (Molly Ringwald), the princess; Andrew (Emilio Estevez), the jock; John (Judd Nelson), the criminal; Brian (Anthony Michael Hall), the brain; and Allison (Ally Sheedy), the silent basket case. At first disdainful and venomous toward one another, they eventually talk to each other and expose their family challenges. Claire confesses that her parents don't understand her. Andrew says his father obsessively drives him to success. Brian likewise says his parents expect him to excel in academics. And John bitterly talks about receiving cigarettes for his birthday. Allison reveals that she has no reason to be in detention hall, but it is the only place where she feels a sense of normality. Clearly these kids are damaged goods, but all find brief commiseration and fellowship in their library prison.

These kids are not all right, because each of them has a troubled home with parents who just don't understand. A happy home is a two-way street: the children must obey their parents (Colossians 3:20) and the parents must not embitter the children (Colossians 3:21). Some of this, of course, is a vicious circle, with parents being firm, then the children rebelling, and then the parents coming down even harder. But some rebellion can be stopped with good communication and hugs. If children don't think their parents will understand them, then they might display their frustrations through inappropriate behavior. Already we know that kids from a one-parent home (who, hence, have half the love and discipline) are more likely to act socially irresponsible. They require lots of love and firm discipline so they won't rebel or become embittered.

Jesus asked for children to come to him. He wanted their fellowship. He didn't want them to grow up to become angry, embittered adults. He wanted them from a young age to have a good experience with matters of faith. If you are young and frustrated, take courage and talk to a trusted parent or adult. If you are an adult or a person in contact with youth, offer yourself to listen to their concerns. The teenage years are difficult. Don't put yourself or your loved ones into "detention hall."

PRAYER IDEA: Ask God to give you opportunity to love and minister to teens.

THE GREATEST MIRACLE

A Walk to Remember (2002)

MPAA: PG for thematic elements, language,
and some sensual material

Read: Luke 10:1–20

Though outwardly we are wasting away, yet inwardly we are being renewed day by day. (2 Corinthians 4:16)

Jamie Sullivan (Mandy Moore) writes in her yearbook, "I want to see a miracle." A poor dresser and the daughter of a conservative preacher, she's the brunt of jokes at school. At the same school, Landon Carter (Shane West) is the king of bad boys. When he pulls a prank that causes personal injury to another student, he is required to perform community service and participate in activities outside his circle of wild friends. Landon joins the school play and there meets Jamie. Slowly he begins to see her quiet spirit, faith, gentleness, beauty, and talent. They fall in love and begin "a walk to remember." Through their relationship, Landon is transformed. Past temptations and behaviors fall away. Strong character traits arise. When Jamie reveals to Landon that she has a terminal form of leukemia, he loves her even more. Jamie doesn't see her cancer go away, but she sees something far greater: a life transformed by love.

Like Landon, many teens love to test their limits. Their sports, behaviors, and talk frequently teeter on the edge of danger. When it comes to faith, it's the same thing. If their mother and grandmother's faith seems inauthentic, it's discarded. Lip service and pew sitting just won't do. What about the real thing? What about faith that's so real, so out there, so active and alive that it has the power to transform? What if there is a faith that can make you want to walk away from the past and live a better, transformed life in the future? This is the kind of faith that Landon saw in Jamie, and it is the kind of faith he adopted for himself.

Jesus is a radical, and his faith is contagious. When he said, "Come, follow me" (Mark 1:17), people left what they were doing and followed him. He spoke controversially, acted contrary to the religious leaders of the day, and loved powerfully. He sent people out to speak the good news and to cast out demons. But when questioned, Jesus said, "Do not rejoice that the spirits submit to you, but rejoice that your names are written in heaven." (Luke 10:20) The greatest miracle is a life transformed by love. It's great when we can do extreme sports and other fun activities, but it's even greater when God saves us and transforms us for all eternity.

PRAYER IDEA: Ask God to grant you extreme, transforming faith today.

THINK OUTSIDE THE BUILDING
Extreme Days (2002)
MPAA: PG for some thematic elements and crude humor
Read: Acts 2:42–47

J
A
N
U
A
R
Y

1
3

He [Paul] reasoned in the synagogue with the Jews and the God-fearing Greeks, as well as in the marketplace day by day with those who happened to be there. (Acts 17:17)

Four junior college graduates, Corey (Dante Basco), Will (A. J. Buckley), Brian (Ryan Browning), and Matt (Derek Hamilton) embark on one last road trip adventure together. They quit their jobs and explore the West Coast for the best in extreme sports. In Mexico, Corey gets word that his grandfather has died in Yakima, Washington. The four decide to turn their car north to pay their last respects. They meet Jessie (Cassidy Rae), a beautiful young woman with a broken-down vehicle bound for the University of Washington. They offer her a lift. Though Brian desires her as a conquest, Jessie's good nature and strong and reverent heart win them all over. When she tells Corey that God understands pain, Corey mocks her by shouting, "Hallelujah and amen!" Then he asks her, "So, Jessie, are you going to take me to church now?" Will replies, "She just did." By the time they arrive in Yakima, the guys understand that "church" can happen anywhere, anytime, as long as believers meet together and minister to one another——even during extreme days.

Church doesn't have to happen between four walls with a steeple on top. Church happens anywhere believers get together to fellowship, pray, teach, worship, and share with one another. The book of Acts presents a wonderful example of the Christian church in action. The followers of Christ in the early church met regularly together at the temple. They also met in each other's homes and ate together. They shared their money and food with anyone who had need. They were glad and praised God.

This is the kind of church experience that is attractive to those who are still searching, spiritually. This is the kind of Christian life that others want to be a part of. Corey, Will, Brian, and Matt experienced a fellowship of fun, pooling their money, looking for thrills. Their "church" became a little more holy when Jessie entered the picture and taught them lessons of self-control, conviction, and God's provision. Are you making "church" happen among your friends? Are you sharing, loving, and teaching about God wherever you are? The world needs a living, active experience of Christ right where we live——on the streets, on the ski hills, and at the beach.

PRAYER IDEA: Ask God to grant you opportunities to minister to others anywhere, anytime.

COMING OUT OF THE FOG

Clueless (1995)

MPAA: PG-13 for sex-related dialogue and
some teen use of alcohol and drugs
Read: Proverbs 17:21–28

Give your servant a discerning heart. (1 Kings 3:9)

Beverly Hills rich girl Cher (Alicia Silverstone) loves to play matchmaker. When her grades suffer, she orchestrates a love match between two of her lonely teachers. Impressed with herself and her own powers of persuasion, Cher also enjoys being the most popular girl in her school. But after Cher befriends a dowdy new girl named Tai (Brittany Murphy), her matchmaking skills go south. Cher matches Tai with a loser rich kid, but he rejects her. Tai likes a nice slacker skater boy, but Cher steers her away from him. Cher finds a well-dressed boy for herself, but he gives her the cold shoulder. Feeling low, Cher gets an extra dose of humility by flunking her driver's training. At rock bottom, Cher comes to her senses and sees the error of her ways. Tai finally hooks up with the now-responsible skater and Cher comes to find her true love: her square but cute "ex-stepbrother."

Discernment involves weighing choices based on facts, not feeling or trends. Discerning requires focus on the real issues. Discernment also requires choosing one's words carefully instead of speaking irresponsibly. Proverbs 28:11 says,

> A rich man may be wise in his own eyes,
> but a poor man who has discernment sees through him.

Cher trusted in her riches and popularity, and as a result her discernment skills stank. It wasn't until she experienced a little poverty that her discernment skills sharpened.

What's so important about discernment anyway? Sounds like it involves a lot of self-control. Well, life is too short to waste time pursuing people or activities that have no lasting value. To Cher, lasting value meant enjoying the company of the right people, despite social status or wealth. To you, it may be deciding among jobs, friends, churches, or even boyfriends (or girlfriends). God gave us all free will, and when we exercise it responsibly, we allow God to bring blessing into our lives. How can you be more discerning today? How can you apply wisdom to your dilemmas? Read what God says about it in his Word, pray, seek counsel, and collect the facts.

PRAYER IDEA: Ask God to give you a discerning heart.

THE MLK LEGACY

Defending, Accepting, and Liberating the Oppressed

WEEK 3

January 15–21

CREATED IN HIS IMAGE

Guess Who's Coming to Dinner (1967)

AA: Katharine Hepburn, Best Actress; Best Original Screenplay

AFI: 99 • MPAA: not rated

Read: Matthew 7:7–12

JANUARY 15

In the image of God ... he created them. (Genesis 1:27)

Before *Monster's Ball, Save the Last Dance,* and *Jungle Fever,* there was *Guess Who's Coming to Dinner.* Released during the height of racial tension and change in America, it is a landmark study of society's prejudices. White girl Joey (Katharine Houghton) returns home unexpectedly with her black fiancé, Dr. John Prentice (Sidney Poitier), to introduce him to her publisher father, Matthew Drayton (Spencer Tracy), and her patrician mother, Christina (Katharine Hepburn). Christina accepts her daughter's decision to marry John, but this interracial union shocks Matthew, and the doctor's parents are equally dismayed. Both families must sit down face to face and examine each other's level of intolerance.

Though we may never have to face the challenges of an interracial love affair within our family, we all must come to grips with racism and intolerance. Is accepting people of other races just some liberal Hollywood ideal, or does the Bible speak about it too? Many of us know that God asks us to love one another and also that we (humankind) are created in God's image, but how does that translate into daily interaction among the races?

When someone asked Mother Teresa why she helped poor Indian children, who would probably die anyway, she replied that she was doing it as unto the Lord. When we treat people as if they were Christ, we validate them, honor them, and bless God. This is nothing more than the Golden Rule: "Do to others what you would have them do to you" (Matthew 7:12). The parable of the Good Samaritan is the Golden Rule in action. The traveling Samaritan businessman could have gone along with society and treated the injured Jewish man poorly, but instead he cleaned him, bathed him, and even put him up at an inn (Luke 10:30–35). The old song says,

Red and yellow, black and white,
We are precious in his sight.
Jesus loves the little children of the world.

Treating everyone with dignity, respect, and love minimizes any racial differences and lets others know that we are all God's children.

PRAYER IDEA: Thank the Lord, for creating all nationalities and all peoples.

18

IGNORE THE DIFFERENCES

Stuart Little (1999)

MPAA: PG for mild language

Read: John 4:1–7

There is no difference between Jew and Gentile—the same Lord is Lord of all and richly blesses all who call on him. (Romans 10:12)

When you look at someone, do you notice the differences or the similarities between that person and yourself? Of even greater importance, do you let your differences stop you from showing Christian love to him or her? *Stuart Little* is a testimony to the value of loving someone who is very different from oneself. In fact, in the movie, such love doesn't merely extend to kindness but also to adoption, the giving of lavish gifts, unconditional acceptance, and a full-city search when Stuart is lost. Stuart, of course, is a talking mouse that is adopted into a human family, the Littles.

Mr. and Mrs. Little (Hugh Laurie and Geena Davis) go to an orphanage to find a new son. They want a little brother for their son George (Jonathan Lipnicki). When they see the orphans, they are instantly smitten with Stuart, and they make no issue whatsoever with the fact that he is a mouse. When they take him home, however, George sees the differences and wants nothing to do with the mouse. If George is indifferent to Stuart, then the cat, Snowbell (Nathan Lane), is hateful. It can't stand having a mouse as its owner. Mice are to be eaten, not to take orders from. The Littles' relatives come to visit Stuart and welcome him into the family. They call him adorable and give him gifts. Snowbell seeks help from his alley-cat friend Monty, who refers him to a bunch of gangster-type cats that decide that Stuart must be "scratched" out. But Snowbell later realizes what a mistake he has made and rescues Stuart from certain death.

When Jesus met the Samaritan woman at the well, he broke two taboos. First, he talked with a woman. Second, he talked with a Samaritan, a person from an undesirable people group, according to the Jewish people of the day. Jesus did not make it an issue that she was a woman and a Samaritan. He was there to give her "living water"—life eternal through faith in him. The Bible says there is neither Jew nor Gentile in Christianity (Galatians 3:28). All have sinned, and it is not our lineage or practice that makes us worthy of salvation and love, but God's grace alone. We are all made in God's image. Adopting a mouse is a silly, extreme example of ignoring differences. But among humans, we are all living under grace, equally needing love from one another.

PRAYER IDEA: Ask God to place his love for all people within your heart.

FAITH OF OUR FATHERS
Amistad (1997)
MPAA: R for scenes of brutal violence and related nudity
Read: Ephesians 6:19, 20

JANUARY 17

You have freed me from my chains. (Psalm 116:16)

In 1839 the Spanish slave ship *La Amistad* (Spanish for friendship) is captured off the coast of Connecticut by the U.S. Navy. On board, African slaves had previously killed all but two of their white oppressors. Back on land, a debate ensues as to what to do with these slaves. The queen of Spain wants the Africans extradited. The naval officers who picked them up want to claim them as salvage. Others want them tried and executed for murder. Yet abolitionists defend the Africans and claim they are not property but humans, forcibly kidnapped. After defense lawyer Roger Baldwin (Matthew McConaughey) wins the first case, the verdict is appealed to the Supreme Court. African leader Cinque (Djimon Hounsou) calls upon the memories of his ancestral fathers, which inspires his new lawyer, former president John Quincy Adams (Anthony Hopkins), to do the same. Adams recalls the Declaration of Independence and the Founding Fathers of America and gives a rousing speech. The Supreme Court accepts his wisdom and lets Cinque and the other Africans go free.

At the trial Adams reads, "We hold these truths to be self-evident, that all men are endowed by their Creator with the right to life, liberty, and the pursuit of happiness." Adams says that if these Africans cannot take part in this right, then the Declaration of Independence should be torn apart. Adams, a Founding Father in his own right, basically tells the court, "Uphold God's law or deny him." Thankfully, the court upholds the law. Cinque and Adams find solace and truth from their fathers. Righteous fathers protect, defend, save, and set their children free. Their law, judiciously and faithfully applied, brings justice and clarity to muddled situations.

Many times, in the Old and New Testament, the Jews appealed to "the God of our fathers, Abraham, Isaac, and Jacob." They knew that the God of their past would be the God of their present and future. They knew that God is the same yesterday, today, and always. His love endures forever (Psalm 100:5). His Word and law are unchanging. This is a great comfort to those of us who are parents. If fathers and mothers hold fast to the truth of our heavenly Father, then our children can find the strength to defend freedom and goodness when these are challenged in their lives.

PRAYER IDEA: Ask God how you can be a "father to the fatherless."

My people are destroyed from lack of knowledge. (Hosea 4:6)

Battered, old hound dog Sounder trees a coon in rural Louisiana in 1933. Belonging to a black sharecropper family, Nathan Lee Morgan (Paul Winfield) misses his shot, and the coon runs free. There will be no meat for breakfast in the morning. Yet come sunrise, a hearty roast cooks on the stove. No sooner have the children finished eating than Nathan is hauled off to prison for stealing. Mother Rebecca (Cicely Tyson) and oldest son David are left to take care of the sugarcane farm while the father spends a year in the labor camps. David travels on foot to look for his father but can't find him. Instead, he finds a school for black children and likes what he sees there. When Nathan is released early for sustaining an injury, he comes home. He finds out about David's journey and tells David to go to this school so that he can have a future out of the crops.

Through education, we can learn how to get out of old routines and into newer circumstances that offer greater opportunity. Nathan told his son David that he didn't want him getting too comfortable on the farm. At the end of the story, David and Nathan drive off to school in a wagon pulled by the family mule. David tells his father that he'll miss the farm but he won't worry about it. The Morgan family were poor and oppressed, but they exercised their will, made a choice to change, and used what little they had to move toward betterment.

Proverbs tells us that the "fear of the Lord is the beginning of knowledge" (Proverbs 1:7). Knowing that God made us for his purposes helps us to understand that our life is not our own and we must develop it as much as possible for his glory. In Scripture we learn that Joshua read *all* the words of the law (Joshua 8:34). Also, Jesus' parents found him in the temple courts, sitting among the teachers (Luke 2:46). Jesus grew in wisdom and stature and in favor with God and people (Luke 2:52). Even Paul told Timothy, "Devote yourself to the public reading of Scripture" (1 Timothy 4:13). Getting knowledge sometimes requires change and sacrifice. We shouldn't be content to remain ignorant.

Discover your gifts, then develop and use them for God's glory. He'll take care of you throughout the journey.

PRAYER IDEA: Ask God increase your knowledge for his Glory.

WORKING ON A BUILDING
Lilies of the Field (1963)
AA: Sidney Poitier, Best Actor • MPAA: not rated
Read: Luke 12:22–34

Seek first his kingdom and his righteousness, and all these things will be given to you as well. (Matthew 6:33)

Sometimes, whether you like it or not, you can be the answer to someone's prayer. Homer Smith (Sidney Poitier), an itinerant handyman becomes an answer to prayer for a group of impoverished nuns in *Lilies of the Field*. When Homer's car needs water, he stops at the nunnery. There, he fixes their roof. Despite his desire to leave, he agrees to build them a new chapel—for free! Homer frets because he is not working on paid jobs. Mother Maria (Lilia Skala) reminds him of the Bible verse that says, "Consider the lilies of the field, how they grow; they toil not, neither do they spin" (Matthew 6:28, KJV).

When Homer agrees to build their chapel, God steps in and not only provides the materials but also provides helpers who are more than happy to pitch in. God also gives Homer other part-time work. Hence, Homer doesn't have to eat at the nunnery but can eat the kind of meals he wants. In time Homer is even offered the job of foreman on a big highway construction job. But he refuses it. He knows his divinely appointed job is working on the nuns' chapel.

It has been said, "Believe in dreams so big that they are bound to fail if God isn't in them." The nuns dreamed and prayed for a builder to build a place of worship. When we trust in God for our needs, he provides. When we step out in faith, he will meet us at every step. Worrying doesn't help at all. The Bible teaches,

> Trust in the LORD with all your heart and lean not on your own understanding;
> in all your ways acknowledge him, and he will make your paths straight.
> (Proverbs 3:5, 6)

Homer Smith was receptive to the direction of God. Are you?

PRAYER IDEA: Ask God to grant you greater faith and trust in him.

LOVE YOUR NEIGHBOR

To Kill a Mockingbird (1962)

AFI: 34 • AA: Gregory Peck, Best Actor; Best Art Direction;
Best Adapted Screenplay • MPAA: not rated

Read: Luke 6:37, 38

Do not judge, or you too will be judged. (Matthew 7:1)

Kind and wise Atticus Finch (Gregory Peck) tells his daughter, Scout (Mary Badham), that it is a sin to kill a mockingbird. He tells her that when he was young he could shoot all the blue jays he wanted, but he couldn't kill a mockingbird, because all they did was make beautiful music. Scout learns that it is wrong to judge a quiet, supposedly crazy neighbor named Boo Radley (Robert Duvall in one of his first roles). She also learns that it is wrong to accuse a young man named Tom Robinson (Brock Peters) of raping a white woman simply because he is black. Prejudice rears its ugly head in the small town of Maycomb, Alabama, in 1932 in this terrific coming-of-age story.

After a near riot, Atticus tells his son, Jem (Philip Alford), "There are lots of ugly things in this world, and I wish I could keep you from them all, but that is impossible." When Atticus talks about ugliness, he is talking about sin. Ugliness toward others is prejudice. Loving one another means looking past skin color, ethnicity, and any other God-given attribute that makes us special. It means not jumping to conclusions based on faulty or scant evidence. The prejudice against Boo Radley and Tom Robinson was unmerited. Boo wasn't crazy; he just had shy ways. Tom didn't rape May Ella Ewell; she conveniently blamed him when her father beat and assaulted her.

What about tolerance? *Tolerance* is a highly charged, politicized word these days. It is not a word found in the Bible. Instead, love, patience, kindness, and favoring the unlovable and lowly are God's instructions to his church. Who are the outcasts and Samaritans of today? The poor? The uneducated? Racial minorities? How about those who have AIDS or are gay? Does God's love extend to them? Or to say it another way, are we to extend God's love to them? The answer is yes. "Love one another" has no exclusions. Tolerance is not the same as Christian love, because tolerance has no ability to transform the broken into wholeness, the sick into the well, or the sinner into a saint. Only Christ's love, salvation, forgiveness, and healing can do that. When we become Christ's hands, feet, mouth, and loving arms, we are encouraging songbirds to sing to their greatest potential.

PRAYER IDEA: Ask God for opportunities to love the unlovable.

**If a house is divided against itself, that house cannot stand.
(Mark 3:25)**

In 1971 the schools in Alexandria, Virginia, integrate for the first time. T. C. Williams High now has both black and white students, and so does its football team, the Titans. A black man, Herman Boone (Denzel Washington) is hired to coach, displacing longtime white coach Bill Yoast (Will Patton). Many white players threaten to sit out unless Coach Yoast is reinstated. But during training camp, the black and white players learn how to get along as friends and teammates. Back at T. C. Williams, tensions run high and the community continues to discourage the desegregation. Coach Boone is told that if he loses a single game, he's out and Coach Yoast is back in. With lots of tough love, Coach Boone tells his players to remember the Titans—Greek warriors who never gave up. When the team captain is injured in a car crash, doubts arise about the team's ability to win. But courage, strength, determination, and unity bring them victory at the state championship.

Any team effort requires unity. Character and ability far outrank skin color in their importance to team success. Business, sports, and the Christian church all thrive when the focus remains on the objective and not on the incidentals. Jesus prayed to the Father that his followers might have unity. He knew that if petty differences got in the way, the message of salvation and love would be compromised. Though the church is made up of many parts, it is one body. If Greek and Jew, rich and poor, fishermen, business people, and farmers could have unity (something never achieved before in all history), then the world would know that God had sent Jesus and created a true body of believers.

Sometimes unity must be preserved in spite of opposition. Boone and Yoast faced terrible prejudice, name-calling, unfair practices, and more injustices as they held up their example of unity. Boone and Yoast made a conscious decision to reject the dividing lies and stand fast in the uniting truth. Likewise, it is your responsibility to uphold unity and major on the majors. Every Christian must love God and love others and not get bogged down in squabbles and fights over style or fashion. Are you contributing to the unity of your church, or are you tearing it down?

PRAYER IDEA: Ask God to show you how you can promote unity in the Church.

SILENT FILM FEST
Quiet Movies with a Loud Message

WEEK 4

January 22–28

Let all who take refuge in you be glad. (Psalm 5:11)

Released in 1922, *Nanook of the North* was the first widely distributed feature-length documentary film. Nanook and his Inuit (Eskimo) family struggle to survive in the harsh conditions of Canada's Hudson Bay region. Nanook trades furs for supplies at an outpost, spears fish, hunts walrus, sleds with dogs, and traps arctic fox. When Nanook travels deep into the open snow with his family, it looks doubtful whether they will find shelter from the night and its brutal temperatures and snow. But Nanook takes his trusty walrus-bone snow knife, carves out blocks of snow, and builds an igloo big enough to sleep the whole family. Additionally, Nanook builds a smaller shelter for his dogs. When the winds howl, the temperature plummets, and the snows fall, all are safe and warm in igloos.

Many times God tells us in his Word that he is our refuge and our shelter. In him we find safety from the storms of life. When we are trying to make our way in a world full of dangers, we might not be able to see the solution to our problems. But when we seek God for a solution, he will answer sometimes in unexpected ways.

Before turning in for the night, Nanook adds one more necessary feature to the igloo: a window made of ice to let the light shine through. When God gives us shelter, he doesn't keep us in the dark but rather gives us guidance and direction. He is our refuge and our light (John 8:12), a place to rest our cold and weary bones. Will we seek God as a shelter from the storm? Will we let the light of Christ shine in our lives?

PRAYER IDEA: Ask God to give you courage when the storms of life come.

WORK AS UNTO GOD

Metropolis (1926)
MPAA: not rated
Read: Genesis 11

Whatever you do, work at it with all your heart, as working for the Lord, not for men. (Colossians 3:23)

A landmark achievement in early science-fiction filmmaking, Fritz Lang's *Metropolis* laid the foundation for camera work, special effects, and social commentary in motion picture production. Set around the year 2000, the aboveground city of Metropolis boasts grand architecture and refined cultural expression, though it was built by an oppressed crew of workers who live underground. One day Freder (Gustav Froehlich), the son of Metropolis mayor Fredersen (Alfred Abel), goes underground and sees the terrible conditions that exist there. He joins the workers as they plan a peaceful revolt. But Fredersen finds out about this scheme and employs an inventor named Rotwang (Rudolf Klein-Rogge) to create a robot that will confuse the workers and foil their plans. The robot is in the likeness of Maria (Brigette Helm), the benevolent spiritual leader of the workers. Rottwang kidnaps the real Maria, and the robot stirs up the workers. Machines fail and the workers revolt against Maria instead of the Metropolis mayor. Freder saves the real Maria, and the robot is burned. Finally Freder takes his father's hand and joins it with the hands of the workers—the beginning of understanding between employer and employee.

The mayor didn't understand or appreciate the workers because he saw them as soulless, slave-like underlings, meant to do his bidding. For years, the workers dutifully made monuments of stone, ruining their own human spirits while giving undue glory to the mayor and the people of Metropolis. This system emaciated the souls of above- and below-ground people alike, because the vanity of working for mere human glory takes its toll. When God is glorified in our work, on the other hand, our souls thrive through this expression of worship. The real Maria understood this fact and one day told the workers about the Tower of Babel. She said that because the tower was created for humankind's glory, God made it fall. She recognized that every act of labor should be an act of worship to God.

Some of us have difficult jobs and even more difficult employers. The work we do seems meaningless. But if we dedicate our work to the glory of God and work as unto him, we can endure difficult situations and people. If we dedicate our work to God and work for him, we can create even more wonderful works than if our scope were only of human origin.

PRAYER IDEA: Thank God for your work.

PURSUING RIGHTEOUSNESS

The General (1927)

MPAA: not rated

Read: 1 Timothy 6:11–16

He who pursues righteousness and love finds life, prosperity and honor. (Proverbs 21:21)

Long before Jackie Chan and the movie *Speed,* audiences cheered the comic moves of Buster Keaton on a train in *The General,* a 1927 silent classic. Keaton plays Johnny Gray, engineer of the General, a locomotive for the Western and Atlantic Flyer line. Pulling into the depot at Marietta, Georgia, in the spring of 1861, Johnnie visits his favorite woman, Annabelle Lee (Marion Mack). Word arrives that civil war has begun. Annabelle wants Johnny to enlist, but the recruiting office won't have him. They think he will serve the South better as an engineer. When Union soldiers steal the General and kidnap Annabelle, Johnny sets out to recover both. As the train speeds northward, Johnny leaps in, on, and around a borrowed engine and boxcars in fabulous choreography. When Johnny succeeds in his mission, he is promoted to lieutenant for the Confederacy.

Johnny pursues that which was stolen out from him. We too must choose to pursue things of value that have been stolen from us. Satan and sin destroy our lives and our relationship with God. God wants us to reclaim this relationship.

- "The LORD . . . loves those who pursue righteousness" (Proverbs 15:9).
- "Pursue righteousness, godliness, faith, love, endurance and gentleness" (1 Timothy 6:11).
- "Flee the evil desires of youth, and pursue righteousness, faith, love and peace, along with those who call on the Lord out of a pure heart" (2 Timothy 2:22).
- "Seek peace and pursue it" (1 Peter 3:11).

Righteousness is anything holy, correct, pure, and just—anything that fits firmly in God's kingdom. It isn't too lofty to obtain. It can be as simple as recovering stolen goods and kidnapped persons. The General and Annabelle did not belong in other hands; they belonged in the hands of Johnny. So Johnnie went after them. Go after what Satan has stolen from you. Go after your dignity, your peace, your faith in God, and your ability to love God and others. These things are within your reach. God says they can be pursued and apprehended. You do not have to play the victim and bellyache about what you have lost. Go on a wild spiritual chase filled with dangers and excitement. Enjoy the ride and claim the prize!

PRAYER IDEA: Ask God to challenge you to pursue righteousness.

RESTORING SIGHT

City Lights (1931)

AFI: 31 • MPAA: G

Read: Matthew 9:27–34

I was blind but now I see! (John 9:25)

In the last silent film by Charlie Chaplin, *City Lights,* the little tramp meets and falls in love with a blind flower salesgirl (Virginia Cherrill), who mistakes him for a wealthy duke. When the little tramp learns that an operation might restore her sight, he shovels horse manure and even becomes a boxer to earn the money she needs. But it isn't until he befriends an eccentric millionaire who gives him $1,000 that the tramp is able to help the girl. Through a wacky turn of events, the little tramp is arrested for stealing and sent off to jail. Months later, in a beautiful moment, the little tramp and the girl see each other for the first time.

The Gospels are full of records of Jesus restoring sight to the blind. His compassion to the blind and the infirm are clearly evident. When the blind reached out to Jesus in faith, he touched them and restored their sight.

Jesus performed these miracles, not only for the sake of the people, but also to display and prove his divinity. A man asked Jesus, "Are you the Messiah?" Jesus didn't answer the man directly. Instead, Jesus told the man that he did miracles, including healing the blind. Jesus wasn't trying to deceive the man, but he was giving a greater answer. He was saying, "I am God, because only God can do these things." Jesus was saying that because he healed the blind, he was in fact the Messiah. Our infirmities, including blindness, are opportunities for God's work to be displayed in our lives. He heals us or manifests his grace in as we bear the burdens of our disability. Either way, as we are healed or as we endure our plights, he is glorified.

PRAYER IDEA: Ask God to be glorified in your life through your infirmities.

OUT OF SLAVERY, A NATION
The Birth of a Nation (1915)
AFI: 44 • MPAA: G
Read: Exodus 6:5–8

Righteousness exalts a nation, but sin is a disgrace to any people. (Proverbs 14:34)

Reviled for its racist sympathies and positive depiction of the Ku Klux Klan, *The Birth of a Nation* forced America to revisit the aftermath of the Civil War. Released only fifty years after the end of the actual war, the events depicted in the movie were still vivid in the minds of America's elderly citizens. The story tells of two families. Representative Austin Stoneman (Ralph Lewis) and his son and daughter live in the North, while Dr. Cameron and his three sons and two daughters live in the South. The young men of these families go off to war and fight for their respective sides. Sadly, Dr. Cameron loses his two youngest sons. His eldest son, Colonel Ben Cameron (Henry Walthall), returns home wounded. After the war, Representative Stoneman visits the Camerons. Elsie Stoneman (Lillian Gish) develops a romance with Colonel Cameron. When she learns that her love is a member of the Ku Klux Klan, she rejects him. But her feelings change when she begins to witness hostilities from some of the Southern blacks. At the height of racial tensions, Elsie is kidnapped by a black leader and is nearly forced to marry him against her will. But dressed in the garb of the Invisible Guard, Colonel Cameron rides in and rescues her and they marry.

There is always pain during birth. A mother feels pain at the birth of her child, and a nation feels pain when it is born. The Civil War was only the beginning of America's pain. The South reeled at the sting of change in the aftermath of the great Rebellion. President Lincoln said, "Let the black people go and let the nation be preserved," and the South said, "No!" But the South did not prevail. Goodness triumphed eventually, though copious blood was shed.

Egypt also didn't want to free its slaves. But God established a leader named Moses who spoke, "Let Israel go so that it might be established as a nation," and Egypt said "No!" But Egypt did not prevail. God's goodness triumphed. Though copious Egyptian blood was shed, and though Israel occasionally rebelled and turned away from God, God established Israel as a nation. God gave birth to Israel and set them up as a chosen people.

Every day God births new Christians, and the enemy doesn't like it. The enemy fusses and tries to take the new convert back, often through painful trials. But God is building his church, and the gates of hell will not prevail against it!

PRAYER IDEA: Ask God to show you your part in birthing new Christians.

CAUSING A COMMOTION
Battleship Potemkin (1925)
MPAA: not rated
Read: John 2:12–19

They picked up stones to stone him, but Jesus hid himself, slipping away from the temple grounds. (John 8:59)

One of the landmark films defining motion picture composition and editing, *Battleship Potemkin* tells the story of the 1905 uprising in Russia, which paved the way for the Russian Revolution of 1917. Outraged by harsh conditions and the maggot-infested meat on the *Potemkin,* sailor Vokulinchuk (Aleksandr Antonov) stages a mutiny. Though he successfully overthrows the captain (Vladimir Barsky), he pays for it with his life. His shipmates take the boat into port at Odessa. Word quickly spreads of their rebellion, causing the locals to rise up against the tsarist Cossacks. On the massive steps of Odessa, the Cossacks brutally murder the rioting throng. The boat leaves port and sails out to sea, where it meets other ships in the tsar's navy. Anticipating a fight, the crew of the *Potemkin* are instead warmly greeted as brothers.

Like Vokulinchuk, Jesus rocked the boat. Wherever Jesus walked, he confronted religious leaders, exposing their rotten beliefs and doctrine. One day Jesus overturned the money changers' tables in the temple. Furious, Jesus said, "Get these out of here! How dare you turn my Father's house into a market!" (John 2:16). On several other occasions, Jesus and his disciples avoided dangerous, angry mobs who were armed with stones because they didn't like what Jesus had to say. Jesus caused commotions. The claims of a meek and mild Jesus just don't hold water.

Are you too nice? Are you nonconfrontational? If so, you aren't Christlike. "Woe to you when all men speak well of you" (Luke 6:26). You should rock the boat. You should ruffle a few feathers. Does this mean you become deliberately rude, arrogant, boastful, or proud? Of course not. The Bible condemns these attitudes. But there will come a day when the same passions that angered Jesus will well up in your heart and you will have an opportunity to express them. Will you shrink back or will you rise up? The choice is yours. Those who speak up for Christ will discover themselves among a rare band—spokespersons for truth.

PRAYER IDEA: Ask God to stir your heart with what stirs his.

BREAKING THE SILENCE

The Jazz Singer (1927)

AFI: 90 • MPAA: not rated

Read: Isaiah 62:1–5

When I kept silent, my bones wasted away. (Psalm 32:3)

Employing the revolutionary Vitaphone process, Warner Brothers took a chance with recorded musical numbers in an essentially non-talking film with their adaptation of the Samson Raphaelson Broadway hit *The Jazz Singer.* Entertainer Al Jolson plays Jakie Rabinowitz, the son of a Jewish cantor. Jakie turns his back on family tradition and transforms himself into cabaret entertainer Jack Robin. When Jack comes home to visit his parents, his mother warmly greets him, but his father does not. Stubborn Jack and his equally stubborn father (Warner Oland) try several times to reconcile but are unsuccessful. On the eve of his biggest show business triumph, Jack receives word that his father is dying. Out of respect, Jack ditches his opening night to attend Atonement services at the temple and sing in his father's place. In the end we are assured that Jack's father has at long last forgiven him.

Only twenty minutes or so of this movie have sound, but it wasn't the music that made this movie a classic but rather the ad lib comments from Jolson. Previous attempts at sound had failed because the performers sounded stilted and unnatural. But Jolson's conversational manner charmed audiences, and the movie became a great success. Warner Brothers became a leading film factory because they figured out how to break the silence.

Four hundred silent years passed from the writing of Malachi in the Old Testament until the birth of Christ. Christ's appearance broke the silence and forever bridged communication and fellowship between God and the human race. In his Word he encourages us to break the silence too. Now is the time to create a revolutionary, crowd-pleasing, joyful noise about our Lord. Let God speak through you and "let all the earth be silent before him" (Habakkuk 2:20). Join the prophet Isaiah as he says,

> For Zion's sake I will not keep silent, for Jerusalem's sake I will not remain quiet. (Isaiah 62:1)

The world needs to hear what you have to say. Open your mouth and speak of God's love to your city and region. Break the silence.

PRAYER IDEA: Ask God to fill your mouth with rejoicing and a testimony of his greatness.

MAKE 'EM LAUGH
Classic Comedy

WEEK 5

January 29–February 4

PART OF THE FAMILY
Arsenic and Old Lace (1944)
MPAA: not rated
Read: Genesis 4:1–8

I will give them an everlasting name. (Isaiah 56:5)

Depravity, sin, and bodies begin to stack deep in the odd, hysterical screwball comedy *Arsenic and Old Lace*. Mortimer Brewster (Cary Grant) rushes home to Brooklyn to tell his aunts that he has just gotten married to the sweet Elaine Harper (Priscilla Lane). Arriving at his aunts' home, he discovers bodies in the cellar, a crazy brother who thinks he is Teddy Roosevelt, another crazy brother who is wanted for twelve murders, and a whole lot of mayhem. In all the craziness, Mortimer decides that he must divorce so as to protect his wife from what he thinks is his own impending insanity. However, Brewster discovers that he was not born into the Brewster family but adopted, and so all is well.

Many people feel ashamed of family members who have mentally gone off the deep end. There is a reason for the term "skeletons in the closet" instead of "skeletons out in the open." Along with shame is the added fear that someone else in the family might be the next to snap. Mental illness is one unfortunate consequence of sin on earth. People don't necessarily become mentally ill from sin, but ever since Adam and Eve sinned, abnormalities and aberrations have been brought upon the minds and bodies of all mankind. We inherited calamity. As long as we are in the world, we may never completely escape physical and mental illness. But, we can escape our sin predicament and its consequences. We can be grafted into a new family that doesn't know sin.

Through Christ, we are all "sons of God through faith" (Galatians 3:26) and inheritors of his goodness, grace, and mercy. When we discover this, he changes us from fearful, outcast sinners to courageous, accepted saints. Mortimer rejoices at knowing his true lineage, and in the same way we can rejoice that our lineage is of God. Now that we are in Christ, do we reject our earthly family? Certainly not, but we love and pray for them so that they also may discover the love of a heavenly Father.

PRAYER IDEA: Thank God for taking away your sin and accepting you.

ESCAPE FROM DANGER
Some Like It Hot (1959)
AFI: 14 • AA: Best Costume Design • MPAA: not rated
Read: 2 Peter 2:19–22

A righteous man escapes trouble. (Proverbs 12:13)

How far will you go to escape danger? If you are a man, would you dress up in women's clothing, take a female name, and join an all-girl musical band? That's what Joe (Tony Curtis) and Jerry (Jack Lemmon) do when they witness the brutal killings of Chicago's 1929 Saint Valentine's Day massacre in *Some Like It Hot.* The girl group travels by train to Miami to put on a show, and for a while Joe and Jerry think they are out of harm's way. But more trouble occurs when Joe falls for Sugar Kane (Marilyn Monroe) but can't tell her about his true gender. Meanwhile, Jerry (now called Daphne) has a rich suitor who will not take no for an answer. When the mob goes to Miami to attend a "friends of Italian opera" convention, Joe and Jerry must plan one more frantic getaway.

Joe and Jerry weren't merely innocents at the wrong place at the wrong time when this mess got started. They were playing a gig at an alcohol-serving nightclub during Prohibition. By associating with illegal activities, they put themselves in danger.

Long life is promised to those who obey God and, in so doing, the laws of the land (1 Kings 3:14). But for those who tempt God's wrath with disobedience and flirtation with the world, safety is not so certain. Knowing the truth (James 1:22), choosing words carefully (Proverbs 21:23), not doing things you judge others for (Matthew 7:1), and discerning the times (Matthew 16:3) are other ways to escape calamity, according to God's Word. The ability to accept instruction and rebuke is still another way (Proverbs 15:31).

Why do clichés like "Keep your own nose clean" and "Early to bed, early to rise . . ." endure? They endure because they are true. Whether out of the mouths of our elders or wisdom from the Bible, no matter how cliché, each still carries powerful instructions that need to be heeded. They still protect, and still save us from lots of heartache and trouble. We must heed helpful guidelines. We must be obedient. We must be watchful. If we are not, we may have to go to extreme, ridiculous, and embarrassing lengths, like Joe and Jerry, to escape harm.

PRAYER IDEA: Ask God to forgive you for your disobedience.

HOODWINK ON THE TOWN

Ferris Bueller's Day Off (1986)

MPAA: PG-13 for language and thematic elements

Read: Psalm 10

The wicked freely strut about. (Psalm 12:8)

Ferris Bueller (Matthew Broderick) lies and manipulates to figure out a way to take a day off. First, he fakes an illness to his parents. Then he gets his girlfriend, Sloan (Mia Sara), out of school by calling the principal, Ed Rooney (Jeffrey Jones), and pretending to be her father. Next, Ferris cajoles his best buddy, Cameron (Alan Ruck), into letting him borrow his father's treasured Ferrari. Together, all three roam about Chicago, going to a Cubs game, dining at fine restaurants (with Ferris masquerading as Abe Froman, the sausage king of Chicago), and getting into mischief. All the while, sympathy grows for Ferris during his "illness." Just when Ed Rooney and Ferris's sister, Jeanie (Erin Gray), almost expose him at his ruse, Ferris races through the streets, reaches home, and jumps into bed, where his parents find him safe and sound.

The not-so-funny thing about this movie is that Ferris wins the sympathy of the audience by performing a series of cocky, smart-alecky deceptions. The audience cheers every time he gets away with another power play. To the consternation of Mr. Rooney and Jeannie, Ferris gets away with things tantamount to murder. All who toe the line with honest behavior know the frustrations of a beguiling hoodwink.

The psalmist David called deceivers "wicked." He prayed that their desires would not succeed, because he didn't want them to become even more proud than they already were. David asked God to break them. Mr. Rooney and Jeannie could never break Ferris because they were always trying to do it in their own strength and for their own vindication. They didn't seek justice with Ferris. To them, it was a personal vendetta. David, on the other hand, righteously appealed to God to bring victory over wickedness. Time and time again, God comes through. If Ferris were able to reach adulthood, he'd soon discover the harsh realities that his lifestyle would bring him. Live righteously, resist wickedness in Jesus' name, trust God to bring you victory, and let God handle the rest.

PRAYER IDEA: Ask God to give you a healthy fear his name.

TRY THE FISH

Airplane! (1980)

MPAA: PG

Read: Mark 1:14–20

Which of you, if his son asks for bread, will give him a stone? Or if he asks for a fish, will give him a snake? (Matthew 7:9, 10)

What's worse than a huge airplane crash? Answer: an airplane meal of bad fish that knocks out the pilots, putting hundreds of lives at risk. In the movie *Airplane!* troubled wartime pilot Ted Striker (Robert Hays) just got dumped by his longtime girlfriend, Elaine Dickinson (Julie Hagerty). She works as a stewardess at Trans American Airlines. In his quest to get her back, he follows her aboard the doomed plane. A bad meal of fish is served and the crew and passengers become seriously ill. Ted Striker finds himself to be the only healthy person aboard. Hence, only he can land the big bird safely. This gag-a-second joke fest proves that bad fish is no laughing matter.

What's worse than a gift of bad fish? Answer: a gift of a snake. Jesus knew that good fish was just about as good a gift as you could ever receive from someone in biblical times. Snakes are dangerous and they don't have much meat on them; fish are good eating. One time Jesus asked his disciples to let down their nets into deep water. They hauled aboard so many fish that their boat began to sink. Now, that is a blessing, pressed down, shaken together, and overflowing (Luke 6:38)! A whole batch of fish is a great gift.

And what was the disciples' response? Answer: astonishment. Simon Peter felt unworthy and said, "Go away from me, Lord; I am a sinful man!" (Luke 5:8). But Jesus encouraged them to not be afraid and they got up and followed him. God's blessing leads us to repentance and obedience. Great is his faithfulness, mercy, and love.

What is your fish wish? What do you need right now? Food? Success in business? Healing? *Airplane!* tells us through goofy gags what the terrors of bad meals can do. But God is longing to meet you at your place of need and *not* give you second or third best but the very best. How much more will our Father in heaven give good gifts to those who ask him (Matthew 7:11).

PRAYER IDEA: Thank God for blessing you so much that you just have to follow him.

REINCARNATION FRUSTRATION

Groundhog Day (1993)
MPAA: PG for some thematic elements
Read: Hebrews 9:22–28

I will redeem them from death. (Hosea 13:14)

In *Groundhog Day* weather forecaster Phil Connors (Bill Murray) is sent to Punxsutawney, Pennsylvania, to cover the official groundhog, Punxsutawney Phil, emerging from his hole. Phil Connors makes no effort to hide his boredom and bitterness, because he has done this gig for four years in a row. Snowed in, Phil and his producer, Rita (Andie MacDowell), and his camera operator, Larry (Chris Elliot), must stay the night. On awakening the following day, Phil discovers it's Groundhog Day again. In fact, again and again Groundhog Day repeats. Nothing Phil does can take him out of this endless cycle. Phil must learn how to be a better man before he can break the vicious cycle of this seemingly endless struggle.

Groundhog Day illustrates the fallacious and frustrating notion of reincarnation—living life over and over again. If we have to keep bettering ourselves with each new life, how do we know if we are better than we were in our previous life? How do we know how good is good enough for a promotion? Thank God we don't have to earn our promotion into a beautiful eternity.

God says a person is destined to die once, not die many times and each time come back as a different critter or person. God also says that after death we face judgment (Hebrews 9:27). To those who seek glory, honor, and immortality, he will give eternal life. Those who don't seek these things get eternal separation from God. Basically, we all get what we want for eternity: we get God and life or separation from him and death. We don't have to struggle to do good to earn salvation, because God has paid the ticket into heaven through Christ's death and resurrection. May God bless all humankind, weather forecasters, camera operators, producers, and more. And may groundhogs always predict an early spring!

PRAYER IDEA: Thank God that you don't have to earn a promotion to enter heaven.

"We're Going to War"

Duck Soup (1933)

AFI: 85 • MPAA: not rated

Read: Matthew 5:43–48

**Do not let the sun go down while you are still angry.
(Ephesians 4:26)**

In the zany 1933 comedy *Duck Soup,* Groucho Marx plays Rufus T. Firefly, the wisecracking dictator of the mythical country of Freedonia. After Groucho's political rival of neighboring Sylvania, the ruthless Ambassador Trentino (Louis Calhern), calls Groucho an "upstart," Groucho calls for war. Battle plans are drawn and Trentino hires Pinky (Harpo Marx) and Chicolini (Chico Marx) as spies to steal the war plans. Reconciliation is tried, but Groucho jokes his way into a tizzy where war is the only option. Shots are fired, bombs are dropped, and reinforcing troops in the form of apes, elephants, and dolphins are deployed for the rescue.

Often our biggest battles are started over the littlest issues, such as name-calling or insults. While these barbs can sting, they are no cause for battle. Time, talent, energy, and even lives are sometimes lost over the pettiest of concerns. (The feuding Hatfields and McCoys of the American South didn't even remember why they were fighting.) When we let problems with our neighbors simmer, they can sometimes boil over into dire consequences.

God doesn't want us to become consumed with hate and anger over our enemies. He wants us to love our enemies and he encourages reconciliation. Honest communication and apology often will provide a solution. God asks us to forgive those who sin against us and to even turn the other cheek. We can't stop problems from coming our way, but we can often prevent "war" through patience, kindness, and humble conversation. These acts of love can cover a multitude of human foibles.

PRAYER IDEA: Ask God to help you forgive your enemies.

A BONE TO PICK

Bringing Up Baby (1938)

AFI: 97 • MPAA: not rated

Read: Ezekiel 37:1–13

This is now bone of my bones. (Genesis 2:23)

Zoologist David Huxley (Cary Grant) wants nothing more than to receive a brontosaurus neck bone from a dig and get married to his assistant. But when he meets Susan Vance (Katharine Hepburn), one disaster after another happens in this madcap comedy called *Bringing Up Baby*. Susan accidentally spoils a golf match where David meets an important museum benefactor. Then she ropes David in to help manage a pet leopard named Baby. The dinosaur bone arrives, but Susan's dog runs off with it and buries it. All the while David's assistant/fiancée grows more and more impatient, and the whole motley crew end up in jail. Through zany, manic misunderstandings and lots of high jinks, Susan and David fall in love. The bone is recovered and one last mishap occurs in which the entire brontosaurus skeleton comes crashing down.

The first man on earth, Adam, knew all about the trouble a single bone can cause. God put Adam into a deep sleep, took out one of his rib bones, and created Eve from it. When Adam saw Eve for the first time, he said,

This is now bone of my bones and flesh of my flesh;
she shall be called "woman," for she was taken out of man. (Genesis 2:23)

Adam was impressed. But Eve ate the forbidden fruit and convinced Adam it was edible, and the two became the mother and father of a disobedient human race. Thank God for the prophet Ezekiel. He restored dignity to the bone.

Ezekiel prophesied of a great valley of bones that came together to form whole human skeletons. Then he saw flesh and blood cover these bones to form a vast army of living human beings. God can raise up bones, open graves, restore flesh, and empower people to fight for his righteousness and grace. Through Ezekiel, the human bone found glory. Next time you see a bone or a dinosaur skeleton or a mess of mishaps, don't think about sin and death. Think about God's restorative power. Susan and David fell in love over an old bone. What can God do with you and your old bones?

PRAYER IDEA: Ask God to use your old bones for his glory.

READY FOR ADVENTURE

Movies to Mobilize Us to Service

WEEK 6

February 5–February 11

TAKING CARE OF THE POOR

The Adventures of Robin Hood (1938)

AA: Best Art Direction; Best Editing; Best Score

MPAA: not rated

Read: Luke 18:18–21

This poor man called, and the LORD heard him. (Psalm 34:6)

Robbing the corrupt rich and giving to the poor—these are hallmarks of the hero in *The Adventures of Robin Hood,* a real movie classic. Robin Hood (Errol Flynn) stars as the rogue of Sherwood Forest, and Olivia de Havilland is his love interest, Maid Marian. In 1191 in merry old England, Prince John (Claude Rains) attempts to unjustly take the throne away from his brother, Richard the Lionhearted (Ian Hunter). Yet Richard is defenseless and must go into exile. Only Robin Hood and his merry men, including Little John (Alan Hale Sr.), Friar Tuck (Eugene Pallette), and Will Scarlett (Patric Knowles) will fight for the side of truth and justice. A protector of the people, Robin Hood defies Prince John at every opportunity, stealing from his caravans and giving to the impoverished people their rightful dues as they serve the rightful king. Through many trials, Richard eventually returns to England to sit upon the throne.

Blessed are you who are poor," declared Jesus, "for yours is the kingdom of God" (Luke 6:20). When we are poor, God has a chance to come in and provide. He will show up and provide for our needs in both conventional and creative ways. It is his joy and his nature to be our provider. When we are rich and self-sufficient, we have no need for God and can easily become full of pride. Riches also put us in a position of power, which can be abused. As Christians, we are to exercise the power and spirit of Christ to bless the poor— just as he did on earth two thousand years ago.

The Bible says we will always have the poor among us, but that doesn't exempt us from doing good to others and helping the poor. When we help the poor, we help Christ himself. "Whatever you did for one of the least of these brothers of mine, you did for me" (Matthew 25:40). Every community has poor people, and many communities in America have ministries that serve them. Consider helping out in a soup kitchen or evangelizing the homeless. These people are made in Christ's image, and many are helpless to change their circumstances on their own. When we give to the poor, we store up treasures for ourselves in heaven.

PRAYER IDEA: Ask God how you might give to the poor.

VENGEANCE IS HIS

Moby Dick (1956)

MPAA: not rated

Read: 2 Samuel 12:1–13

Get rid of all bitterness, rage and anger. (Ephesians 4:31)

'd strike the sun if it insulted me. All visible objects are but as pasteboard masks. Some inscrutable but reasoning thing puts molding among their features. The white whale tasks me. He is but a mask. It is the thing behind the mask I chiefly hate." These are the words of crazed, obsessed Captain Ahab (Gregory Peck) on his nemesis, Moby Dick. Behind these words is a fist raised in anger at God. Risking his crew, his ship, and even his own life, Ahab takes his ship, the *Pequod* (commissioned on a normal whaling mission), on an around-the-world chase to kill the thing that drives him mad. First Mate Starbuck (Leo Genn) warns Ahab that in doing so he is committing blasphemy and incurring the wrath of God, but Ahab turns a deaf ear to him. Even before the crew sets sail, a prophet named Elijah warns Ishmael (Richard Basehart), a kind and honest whaler, that this ship and crew are destined for destruction. When Ahab finds his quarry, the reign of death ensues.

---

erhaps one of the saddest tales to hear is that of a person who receives God's grace, forgiveness, and mercy, only to later reject God in anger and hate. Some turn away from God when a religious leader or respected elder commits an egregious sin. Others curse God when a natural disaster (or, as some call it, "an act of God") steals away home, family, or limb. Don't curse God. Rather, point the finger of blame at sin and its first practitioner, the evil one. When others sin against you, blame the sin within them. When nature or some terrific beast assails you, curse the evil one who comes to steal, kill, and destroy. And receive God's comfort, for he is with us always, even in the middle of our trials.

Human beings are fallible and nature is unpredictable. Both are bound to hurt us on this earth. Vengeance is not ours to take but is God's alone. When the righteous man Job had his family and home taken away from him, he was encouraged to curse God and die. But Job held fast. He did not place his righteousness before God's but instead humbled himself before his Maker. Later, Job was rewarded with twice as much as he had before. Bitterness is a rot that takes away life and joy. It paralyzes its owner. When tempted to exact revenge, avast! It is better to cast your cares on the crucified Christ than waste your time and energy on retribution. God is love, so let him fill you with himself.

PRAYER IDEA: Ask God to forgive you for your misplaced anger.

A LOVING KISS
Last of the Mohicans (1992)
AA: Best Sound • MPAA: R for violence
Read: Luke 7:36–50

Greet one another with a kiss of love. (1 Peter 5:14)

Despite being a fine adaptation of a classic James Fenimore Cooper novel, despite starring one of Britain's best talents in Daniel Day-Lewis, and despite the fantastic scenes of battle in colonial America, the most recent version of *Last of the Mohicans* is probably best known for its kiss between Cora Munro (Madeleine Stowe) and Nathaniel or Hawkeye (Day-Lewis). A budding romance between the British officer's daughter Cora and the independent Hawkeye, reared as a Mohawk, complicates things for the British officer, as the adopted Mohawk pursues his own agenda despite the wrath of people on both sides of the conflict. Ultimately, his feelings of love for Cora, no doubt enflamed by the war, culminate in one of the most romantic screen kisses of modern cinema.

One of the most tender acts performed for our Lord Jesus was a kiss. It was not his mother, a disciple, a close family member, or a friend who gave him this kiss; an adulterous woman kissed him. This woman learned that Jesus was nearby at the home of a Pharisee and brought an alabaster jar containing expensive perfume to anoint him. She wiped his feet with her hair, kissed them, and poured the perfume on them. No doubt Jesus' Pharisee host was incensed, but Jesus responded to the woman's kindness with an act far more precious and intimate than any kiss: he gave her forgiveness.

When we love much, we position ourselves for forgiveness. When we give others kisses, affection, time, hugs, smiles, help, instruction, care, and other acts of love, we welcome forgiveness. "He who has been forgiven little loves little" (Luke 7:47). Many New Testament books say, "Greet one another with a holy kiss." If people approach us with contrite hearts and kiss our smelly, dirty feet, we can't help but forgive them. Christian love always responds to an act of affection.

PRAYER IDEA: Ask God for opportunities to embrace those who need forgiveness.

MESSING WITH GOD'S LAW
Raiders of the Lost Ark (1981)
AFI: 60 • AA: Best Editing; Best Art Direction;
Best Sound; Best Visual Effects
MPAA: PG for action violence
Read: Exodus 25:10–22

**God struck him down and he died there beside the ark of God.
(2 Samuel 6:7)**

Jumping gaping holes, dodging poisonous darts, evading huge rolling rocks, and recovering ancient relics are all in a day's work for archeology professor Indiana Jones (Harrison Ford) in the movie *Raiders of the Lost Ark.* This classic film taught America about the Ten Commandments and their container, the ark of the covenant. After globe-trotting and thwarting snakes in pits, Indiana Jones recovers the famous biblical relic. Yet Nazis led by French archeologist Belloq (Paul Freeman) overpower Indy and seek to misuse the ark for their own selfish ends. They open the ark, and the power of God comes out and strikes them dead. Indiana and his girlfriend Marion (Karen Allen) are tied to a post nearby. They turn their eyes away, and their lives are spared.

Director Steven Spielberg didn't stray far from the truth in his depiction of the ark. Like the movie, the real ark had "cherubim with their wings spread upward, overshadowing the cover" (Exodus 27:9). Similarly, the movie correctly says that the insides of the ark held the remains of the tablets of stone on which were inscribed the Ten Commandments given to Moses by God (Deuteronomy 10:2).

When Jewish priests entered the Holy of Holies, where the ark stood, they tied a rope around their foot in case God struck them dead. Their bodies could then be pulled out by the rope. Biblical character Uzzah meant well when he tried to steady the ark with his hand, but God struck him down because he touched it (1 Chronicles 13:10). Thank God the ark isn't being toted around today! Since Christ's death and resurrection, there is a righteousness apart from the law through faith in Jesus Christ (Romans 3:21). The Bible has much to say about the law (old covenant) and grace (new covenant). This is perhaps the most important aspect of the Christian faith, and it is worth a closer study. Study it in your Bible and you'll further discover the richness of God's mercy.

PRAYER IDEA: Thank God for his Holy law.

VENGEANCE IS MINE

The Count of Monte Cristo (2002)
MPAA: PG-13 for adventure violence/swordplay
and some sensuality
Read: Nahum 1:1–8

The LORD takes vengeance on his foes. (Nahum 1:2)

There is nothing too dire, no place too grim, no situation too hopeless that God cannot bring redemption to it. Even the jealousy that festers in our hearts and grows over the years can be transformed by God's grace and love.

A job promotion, a loving girlfriend anxious to marry, and an exciting career lie ahead for young Frenchman Edmond Dantes (Jim Caviezel) in the early 1800s. But his jealous "friend" Fernand Mondego (Guy Pierce) steals it all away. Mondego frames Edmond as a traitor to France. Edmond is shipped off to the island home of the Chateau d'If prison and is placed in solitary confinement. Edmond pleads his innocence, but his words fall on deaf ears. In his cell he scratches on the wall, "God will give me justice," but in time he loses faith in God and he loses his self-dignity.

One day, years later, a miracle occurs when a fellow prisoner burrows up from under the floor, mistaking Edmond's cell for the outside. This older man is not only ambitious to escape but he is also educated and full of faith. Edmond tells him, "I don't believe in God." Abbé Faria (Richard Harris) tells him, "That's okay. He believes in you." Abbé Faria educates Edmond in exchange for help with the digging. Furthermore, Abbé Faria tells Edmond where to find a vast treasure on the outside. Through an accident, Edmond escapes from the prison, finds the fortune, reinvents himself as the Count of Monte Cristo, moves to Paris, and slowly and deliberately seeks revenge on those who conspired to put him away. Evil is avenged, but in the end Edmond takes Abbé Faria's words to heart and renews his faith in God, seeking to bless others with the good fortune he has found.

Justice and mercy, love and hate, forgiveness and vengeance—these are the things of life as well as this movie. Who among us hasn't had a friend betray us? Who hasn't lost faith when circumstances turned grim, when we felt alone and vulnerable? There are two options for dealing with jealous anger: give in to it and become poisoned in your soul, or throw it on the crucified Christ, who will accept it gladly and heal your heart. He is close to the brokenhearted and is rich in mercy. Jealousy may make great drama, but it's a lousy thing to carry around. Unload that baggage on Christ, and let him fill you with thankfulness and gratitude.

PRAYER IDEA: Ask God to let you not become jealous if you see things you want but don't have.

I'M TAKEN BY YOU

Twister (1996)

MPAA: PG-13 for intense depiction of bad weather
Read: 2 Kings 2:11–18

His way is in the whirlwind and the storm. (Nahum 1:3)

Oh, the elusive twister. Technology and study cannot predict when one will show up, how big it will be, or what path it will take. Two rival groups of scientists chase these windy behemoths in Oklahoma with the goal of launching high-tech, lifesaving tracking devices inside their tumultuous tunnels. Adventuresome TV weather forecaster Bill Harding (Bill Paxton) and his estranged tornado-hunter wife, Jo (Helen Hunt), lead their crew of brash, underfunded colleagues. Dr. Jonas Miller (Cary Elwes) tows along a state-of-the-art, corporate-sponsored team. They both discover several funnel clouds over two days, but Jonas gets too close to an F-5—a mile-wide, 300 mph monster—and is taken up to a windy death. Through risking their own lives and acting honorably, Jo and Bill deliver their package and collect the data that might help save storm-threatened lives in the future.

Like tornadoes, the Holy Spirit of God is unpredictable and all-powerful. "The wind blows wherever it pleases. You hear its sound, but you cannot tell where it comes from or where it is going. So it is with everyone born of the Spirit" (John 3:8). When God shows up ready to save, no human will can thwart him. The wind of God's Spirit goes where it chooses and takes all in its path. Anybody who has been to an evangelistic crusade can testify to how God sweeps over a crowd and pulls people out of their seats to new life.

Hundreds of years before Jesus was taken into the air to heaven following his resurrection, a man named Elijah was taken into heaven by a whirlwind. Elijah didn't face this terrible twister because of any sin. He faced this phenomenon after an act of obedience to God. Elijah spoke a rebuke to the messengers of the king of Samaria, and God saw fit afterward to give him an instant promotion. After Elijah was taken up, a search team looked for him, but they didn't find him.

The winds of the east, west, north, and south are at God's beck and call. Though twisters destroy, a whirlwind may be a blessing. Let the Spirit of God blow over you today.

PRAYER IDEA: Ask the Holy Spirit to whirl a passion in your heart to greater obedience.

FAITH TO MOVE MOUNTAINS
Everest (1999)
MPAA: not rated

Read: Mark 11:22–25

How beautiful on the mountains are the feet of those who bring good news. (Isaiah 52:7)

Awesome, *beautiful,* and *majestic* can only begin to describe the wonder that is Mount Everest. Towering over 29,000 feet, Everest is so tall that if a person were taken immediately from sea level to the summit, that person would black out and die in minutes from asphyxiation. Seventy-five percent of those who try to reach the top fail, and one percent die trying. The IMAX movie *Everest* documents three people who each have strong personal reasons for reaching the top, the ultimate in mountaineering. Ed Viesturs wants to summit without supplemental oxygen—a rare feat. Araceli Segarra wants to become the first Spanish woman to reach the top. Nepali Sherpa Jamling Norgay wants to summit because his father was one of two men to first reach the top. Brutally unforgiving, Everest claimed the lives of eight climbers during the making of this movie in 1996, casting a pall over those who continued on.

Why does Everest capture the imagination of the adventurous? Personal or national pride, competitiveness, and the chance to test one's own physical abilities rank high among the reasons for summiting this giant mountain.

Our Creator God, who fashioned this mountain, understands its allure and mystique. This pile of rock points to the majesty of God. Its incredible mass suggests immovability and steadfastness. Jesus said in Mark 11:23, "I tell you the truth, if anyone says to this mountain, 'Go, throw yourself into the sea,' and does not doubt in his heart but believes that what he says will happen, it will be done for him." If mountains can be moved, there is a corresponding temptation for great pride to settle in. The apostle Paul tempered Christ's statement in saying, "If I have a faith that can move mountains, but have not love, I am nothing" (1 Corinthians 13:2). Pride, failure to note signs of bad weather, and selfish crew members contributed to the disaster of 1996 on Everest. But when we lay down our pride and submit to God's leadership, we can move and conquer the mountains of doubt, despair, and troubling circumstances.

PRAYER IDEA: Ask God for the courage to confront the mountains you face.

VIVA' LOVE
The Many Expressions of Love

WEEK 7

February 12–February 18

TOO CRIPPLED TO LOVE?

An Affair to Remember (1957)

MPAA: not rated

Read: Luke 5:17–26

To the weak I became weak, to win the weak. (1 Corinthians 9:22)

Despite its title, *An Affair to Remember* is not about memorable adultery. It's about finding love despite obstacles. Handsome playboy Nickie Ferrante (Cary Grant) and beautiful nightclub singer Terry McKay (Deborah Kerr) experience a "love boat" cruise from Europe to New York. Despite being engaged to other people, they agree to reunite at the top of the Empire State Building in six months. After six months, they realize they are in love. However, as Terry desperately tries to make the date through city traffic, a vehicle strikes and cripples her. As weeks pass, Nicky fears that she married her fiancé or does not love him anymore. In actuality, Terry doesn't want to be seen as the lame woman she has become. She doesn't think she is worthy of Nicky's love. Through some persistence and straight talk, Nicky discovers Terry's malady and takes her into his arms, vowing to love her always despite her physical imperfections.

Many people think they are beyond love because of a physical imperfection. Some don't even have a debilitating disease to blame. People look at their flabby thighs, crooked nose, or buckteeth and say, "Who could ever love a face like mine? Who could ever love a body like mine?" Are you crippled to the idea of love? Is there something holding you back, some excuse that is preventing you from receiving the heavenly Father's loving embrace?

Nicky Ferrante didn't look at Terry's legs and walk out the door. When he saw Terry's condition, he loved her all the more. Similarly, God is close to the brokenhearted, the overweight, the malformed, and the outcasts. Christian love strives to bring the lame to Jesus despite obstacles. Helping others find divine love is a good remedy for our own self-pity. Remember the Bible story of the friends who lowered a crippled man through a hole in the roof so that Jesus could see him? That's the kind of activity that God wants us to undertake, bringing the lame and downcasts to him.

Nobody is beyond love. There is no excuse for denying anyone to come to Christ. He loves the down-and-out, the up-and-out, and the up-and-in. Loving him and being loved by him is a divine love affair to remember.

PRAYER IDEA: Give God praise despite your deformities.

ROUGH TALK

It Happened One Night (1934)

AFI: 35 • AA: Best Picture; Frank Capra, Best Director;
Clark Gable, Best Actor; Claudette Colbert, Best Actress;
Best Adapted Screenplay • MPAA: not rated
Read: Zechariah 8:16, 17

Faithful are the wounds of a friend. (Proverbs 27:6, KJV)

Lots of "its" happened in *It Happened One Night*. A few of those "its" were firm rebukes by down-on-his-luck newspaperman Peter Warne (Clark Gable) to rebellious socialite Ellie Andrews (Claudette Colbert). A few days earlier, the stuck-up Ellie married King Westley (Jameson Thomas), but her wealthy father had the marriage annulled. Tired of her father's control, she runs away from Miami for New York. On the bus, she meets Warne and they end up traveling together. Warne shows her kindness, but Ellie could not care less about it. Warne says, "Why, you ungrateful brat," and he continues to call her "brat" and brings her down a notch or three every chance he gets through the rest of the story. Eventually these rebukes soften Ellie and she begins to see Warne as someone she can love and trust.

When truth is spoken out of love, it is a powerful weapon. Warne could have let Ellie walk all over him. He could have let her carry on in ignorant pride. But he didn't. Proverbs says,

Better is open rebuke than hidden love. (Proverbs 27:5)

This isn't about using harsh, mean, careless, or cruel words. Instead, it is about using strong, loving words that speak to the root of the matter.

Today lots of people mollycoddle one another and placate wrong thinking. "Don't rock the boat"; "Don't want to ruffle any feathers"; and "tolerance" are the buzzwords of this attitude. So, while Christians are quietly keeping mum and being "nice," they watch their friends continue to rot in sinful thinking, words, and attitudes. This isn't about the right to complain or fuss. Jesus really only made a fuss to the self-righteous Pharisees. It's about loving others and demonstrating the right to speak honest, sometimes painful truth into their lives. The words you use are a double-edged sword and they can pierce the thickest skin and the hardest hearts. God's Word, which equals truth, which equals Christ, which equals love, has a powerful effect, because it is life giving and it is powerful.

PRAYER IDEA: Ask God to give you the courage to give and accept a rebuke.

THE SACRED ROMANCE

Serendipity (2001)

MPAA: PG-13 for a scene of sexuality and mild language

Read: John 3:16

God is love. (1 John 4:16)

s there someone out there whom you are destined to romance—your one true love? Englishwoman Sara (Kate Beckinsale) believes in serendipity, and she's willing to prove it by leaving her love life to fate. Though she is dating another man, she serendipitously meets John (John Cusack) when they both try to buy the same gift during the holiday shopping season in New York City. John is dating someone else too, but he falls hard for Sara and wants to see her again. Sara asks John to write his name and phone number on a five-dollar bill and give it to her. She spends it and says that if it comes back to her, they were destined to be together. Likewise, she picks out a used book and writes her name and number on the inside cover. If John finds the book, that will further add to their manifest destiny. In charming but predictable fashion, years pass and the two become engaged to their different partners, but fate brings the "signs" back into their lives.

Many young people today are in love with love. They hold to the philosophy that "You were meant for me and I was meant for you."

The problem in all of this is that chance can be cruel. If the years are piling on and you still haven't found your special someone, did you somehow miss him or her a few years back? Wake up! Life is not like it is in the movies. Romance doesn't work this way. True love is not that cruel.

There is a greater love than serendipitously finding that certain someone. God wants to have a romance with you, a sacred romance. He's always ready to forgive you, love you, free you, and give to you. "How great is the love the Father has lavished on us!" (1 John 3:1). Lots of people may think that God doesn't love them or that God wouldn't love them because they are so bad. Nothing could be further from the truth. "God is love" (1 John 4:16), and when we trust in him as our eternal lover, we will quickly find that all of our spiritual and emotional needs are met in him.

You can hope to randomly meet someone who would love you unconditionally, or you can trust in the God who is always there, ready to extend his perfect love to you. His love is greater than any other you will find on this planet.

PRAYER IDEA: Ask God to help you believe that he is the greatest love of all.

THE PROMISE OF PAIN

Shadowlands (1993)
MPAA: PG for thematic elements
Read: 1 Peter 4:12–19

My joy in unrelenting pain—that I had not denied the words of the Holy One. (Job 6:10)

In the early 1950s, C. S. ("Jack") Lewis (Anthony Hopkins), author of the Narnia books, teaches at Oxford in England. A man of measured words, he carefully lives his life as a bachelor. One day an American woman named Joy Gresham (Debra Winger) visits him. Her brutal honesty surprises Jack and astounds his colleagues. Months later she divorces her abusive and alcoholic husband and moves to England permanently. Then Joy asks Jack to marry her for convenience, so that she can stay in England. Jack agrees, but then the more time he spends with Joy, the more he falls in love with her. When Joy falls ill from cancer, Jack marries her for love. Now they live in the "shadowlands," not knowing the future. Surprisingly, her cancer goes into remission and the two enjoy some of their happiest moments in life together. Eventually Joy's cancer returns and Jack must come to grips with her death and his own grief.

Twice during the movie Lewis says, "Pain is God's megaphone to rouse a deaf world." From a natural perspective, Lewis deserved a long and happy relationship with his wife. After all, he had sacrificed many years to live as a bachelor while writing some of the greatest works of fiction and Christian apologetics of all time. The contribution that Lewis made to the world was enormous, and it seems, he should have earned special favor with God and received wonderful blessings. Instead, Lewis found suffering.

Did God let Jack suffer hopelessly? No! First, God gave Joy a much longer than expected reprieve through the remission of her cancer. Then God gave Jack words to share with the world that have encouraged and strengthened many others who have experienced grief. In the movie Lewis says, "I pray because the need flows out of me. It doesn't change God; it changes me." He wouldn't have been able to share such profound and true words without a personal experience of suffering.

God shapes all things, including pain, to point us to his glory. Jesus endured suffering all the way to the cross. If God didn't spare his own Son from suffering, would he guarantee that you will not experience it? The only guarantee of freedom from suffering is in the eternal life that lies beyond this one—if we accept Christ's death on the cross for our sins.

PRAYER IDEA: Ask God to show you how to learn obedience through suffering.

FREEDOM FROM SCHEDULE

Roman Holiday (1953)

AA: Audrey Hepburn, Best Actress; Best Writing;
Best Costume Design • MPAA: not rated

Read: Luke 10:38–42

The work of God is this: to believe in the one he has sent. (John 6:29)

Princess Anne (Audrey Hepburn) tirelessly tours Europe performing her royal duties—attending diplomatic functions, greeting dignitaries, gesturing kindly to crowds, and living as a princess should. Secretly, though, her spirits are tiring. One night she goes hysterical, demanding freedom from her demanding schedule. Her aides inject her with a sedative, but Princess Anne escapes to the Roman streets for a holiday and meets newspaper reporter Joe Bradley (Gregory Peck). Bradley lets the princess (who now calls herself Anya) sleep on his couch. The next day the papers say the princess has fallen sick and can't attend her appearances. But Joe discovers that his houseguest is no average girl and hopes to get a scoop by trailing her around the city. The next day Joe and Anne hit the town and have all sorts of fun. In fact, they fall in love. Realizing that love and relationship far outweigh empty works, Anne nevertheless returns to duty, wiser and happier for her experiences.

All work and no play made Anne a dull girl. The same can be true for all of us. Endless obligations and repetitive tasks take their toll on our spirits, making us lifeless and stir-crazy. Jesus tells us many times throughout the Gospels that relationship is what really counts in life. Someone once asked Jesus what were the works God required. He responded, "The work of God is this: to believe in the one he has sent." Jesus was really saying that the question shouldn't be about works. Resting at the feet of Jesus, listening to his words, learning from him, letting him speak to you, and growing in faith—that really is the work of God. We should not be focused on meaningless acts that give the appearance of holiness but have no power or substance.

The princess had a duty to fulfill, so she returned. But Joe didn't have a duty to print a story on the fun day out. Because he fell in love with Anne, he set aside news reporting for something far better—personal pride and the wonderful memory of a daylong date. We can get so busy doing God's work that we forget to enjoy his company. Spend a day talking with Jesus. Tour a city or a park and fall in love with him all over again. Don't let work choke you off from experiencing the best part of Christianity. Faith in God is nothing more than trusting in a very good friend. Sometimes we need to stop what we are doing and just have a holiday with him.

PRAYER IDEA: Ask God to forgive you for letting works crowd you out from knowing him.

GET REAL WITH OTHERS
How to Lose a Guy in 10 Days (2003)
MPAA: PG-13 for some sexually-related material
Read: Matthew 7:21–23

If you really knew me, you would know my Father as well. (John 14:7)

In New York, Andie Anderson (Kate Hudson) wants to be a serious journalist. Meanwhile, she is languishing as the writer of how-to columns for a vapid woman's magazine called *Composure*. In order to get favor with her boss, Andie agrees to attract a man and drive him away in ten days, then write about it in a story called "How to Lose a Guy in 10 Days." At a bar she meets advertising agent Ben Berry (Matthew McConaughey). Little does she know that Ben has also made a deal with his boss. Ben bets that he can get a girl to fall in love with him in ten days. If he wins the bet, he lands a lucrative advertising account. So, after Andie and Ben meet, she tries to repel him while he tries to win her over. Both are totally disingenuous with the other because both have false motives. On the brink of collapse, their relationship seems doomed until they take a day trip to see Ben's parents. In the presence of Ben's father, Andie relaxes, and her real personality emerges. At that moment she begins to develop true feelings for Ben. When Ben's bet is exposed, Andie realizes it was all a crock. Andie tries to run away, but Ben chases after her. They both realize that a seed of real attraction exists between them.

These days, authentic relationships are hard to find. Everybody has a mask or a side or a complete fabrication that they are putting forward. Some people, after getting married, discover that their spouse isn't the same person they knew when they were dating. Some people put on church faces and attitudes on Sunday but live like the devil during the week. When we discover the true personality of people we thought we knew, it hurts.

Imagine what Jesus feels when people only give him lip service. Jesus talks about a day when people will say, "Hey, didn't I do all these wonderful things in your name, Jesus?" But Jesus will reply, "I never knew you. Away from me, you evildoers!" (Matthew 7:23). It's not enough to "do" things for Jesus. That's not what he wants. He wants to know you—the real you, warts and all. Be real before God, and he'll be real with you. Spend time in prayer and fellowship with God the Father, and he'll show you his Son. Don't be a faker. It's so much easier just to be real. If you are earnest to know God, he will reveal himself to you—a beautiful, honest, genuine, and liberating relationship.

PRAYER IDEA: Ask God to forgive you for the fakery you've displayed toward others.

YOU BELONG TO ME
Breakfast at Tiffany's (1961)
AA: Best Score; Best Song • MPAA: not rated
Read: Hosea 3:1–5

We belong to the Lord. (Romans 14:8)

In *Breakfast at Tiffany's*, Holly Golightly (Audrey Hepburn) will not settle down with any man unless he's a rich, older gentleman. As a high-priced escort, she sees many rich men but can't land a single one. In Holly's apartment building an aspiring young writer named Paul (George Peppard) discovers Holly and finds her fun, kooky, and irresistible. Yet Paul is in the clutches of his keeper, an older female editor (Patricia Neal). Eventually Paul finds the courage to break free from his editor, and he asks Holly out on a date. Full of playful fun, their morning date takes them to the upscale department store, Tiffany's. In the end Paul declares his love to Holly, but she won't have any of it. It isn't until Holly is homeless and standing out in the soaking rain that she realizes her idealized hopes and dreams were all a sham.

God's Word contains a wonderful story about a call girl who is plucked out of her routine to be the beloved of a good suitor. God tells Hosea to take Gomer as his wife. Hosea does, but Gomer keeps going back to her adulterous, licentious lifestyle. Any normal man might give up on Gomer and throw up his hands in surrender. But Hosea doesn't. God tells him to try again. Hosea goes down to where Gomer is being sold by her pimp and buys her. Then Hosea gets firm with Gomer. He says, "You are to live with me many days; you must not be a prostitute" (Hosea 3:3). You can almost see Hosea shaking Gomer out in the rain and telling her to wise up.

Our God is loyal even when we are not. He pursues us even when we go back to sin. He follows us into the rain to tell us to love him and leave our life of sin. God made us, he loves us, and we belong to him even if we would rather sell ourselves to a counterfeit lover. Holly wanted extremes. She wanted to pursue a playgirl lifestyle, and she wanted to settle down with a rich man. But there was error in her aspirations. Paul cared nothing for riches, but he knew that the false love of his female editor didn't satisfy. So Paul reached out, beyond hope, beyond Holly's comprehension, to give her real love. Eventually they found that they could love one another. Our God is our keeper, our provider, and our beloved.

PRAYER IDEA: Thank God that he isn't counterfeit and that he is your true beloved.

HAIL TO THE CHIEF

A Salute to Our Presidents

WEEK 8

February 19–February 25

CLING TO CHRIST

Escape from New York (1981)

MPAA: R for violence and language

Read: Psalm 68

How shall we escape if we ignore such a great salvation? (Hebrews 2:3)

In 1997 the crime rate of the United States of America rises four hundred percent. Manhattan has become a walled-off maximum-security prison filled with the country's worst criminals and lunatics. Then one day Air Force One crash-lands inside the city and the president (Donald Pleasence) is held hostage by a crime lord, called the Duke of New York (Isaac Hayes). In exchange for a promise of freedom, mercenary Snake Plissken (Kurt Russell) is given twenty-four hours to go in, find the president, and escape from New York with him. Without being given any option to negotiate by government official Bob Hauk (Lee Van Cleef), Plissken is injected with mini-bombs that will explode in his neck and kill him in twenty-four hours. The antidote lies just outside the city, if Plissken is successful. So Plissken takes the job and glides into New York, landing on top of the World Trade Center. A taxi driver named Cabbie (Ernest Borgnine), a go-to guy called Brain (Harry Dean Stanton), and Brain's gal Maggie (Adrienne Barbeau) aid him, sometimes unwillingly. All the while, the clock ticks and danger lies behind every broken brick wall and burning trash heap.

There was only one way that Snake Plissken could escape New York with his life—he had to take the president with him. Nothing else would satisfy. If Snake came up empty-handed, the time bombs inside him would explode and he would die. Psalms 68:20 says,

> Our God is a God who saves; from the Sovereign LORD comes escape from death.

Snake's real agenda wasn't to escape from New York; it was to find a way to escape death. Likewise, our goal on this planet isn't to escape dangers and corrupt Dukes and double-crossing Brains. It's to find the one leader who can lead us out and give us life. The president himself is the one who shoots Duke dead and gives Snake life. Finding Christ, our one true leader, always leads to life. In fact, there is no life without him. Imitation leaders, like the Duke of New York, can at best provide some temporary protection. But when the Duke dies, who is left? Who can provide us with our escape? Do whatever you can to find Christ, and once you find him, never let him out of your sight. Only he can navigate you to safety.

PRAYER IDEA: Praise God that he is your only hope of escape from corruption.

PRAY FOR OUR LEADERS

All the President's Men (1976)

AA: Jason Robards, Best Supporting Actor; Best Art Direction;
Best Sound; Best Adapted Screenplay • MPAA: PG

Read: Romans 13:1–7

FEBRUARY 20

The authorities are God's servants. (Romans 13:6)

America has had many great and noble presidents, but in 1973 it was discovered that Richard Nixon was involved in the Watergate scandal, a cover-up that eventually led to his resignation. *All The President's Men* tells the story of *Washington Post* reporters Carl Bernstein (Dustin Hoffman) and Bob Woodward (Robert Redford) as they investigate a seemingly minor break-in at the Democratic Party national headquarters. The more they explore, the closer the White House comes into view as playing a major role. With the approval of executive editor Ben Bradlee (Jason Robards) and the help of mystery source Deep Throat (Hal Holbrook), the pair follow the money all the way to the top. Caught, Nixon has no other choice but to step down.

Scandal and sin are nothing new to leaders of nations. King Saul tried repeatedly to hunt down and kill David. As king, David committed adultery with Bathsheba and sent her husband, Uriah, to the front lines to be killed in battle. The Egyptian pharaoh during the time of Moses was stubborn and tyrannical. Jesus himself had to evade King Herod's thugs sent out to murder the newborn Redeemer. These authorities distinguished themselves as imperfect men, to say the least.

Unless our leaders instruct us to act contrary to the Word of God, we are to obey them (Hebrews 13:17). Why? Because "there is no authority except that which God has established" (Romans 13:1) We are to pray for our rulers, for their protection, and for God's wisdom to be given them, so that we might lead quiet and peaceful lives (1 Timothy 2:2). And one day, like the rest of us mortals, "all rulers will worship and obey [God]" (Daniel 7:27). We might not like our current governmental leaders, but we can do more than complain about them. We can pray for them and respect their office.

PRAYER IDEA: Thank God for the president and all our national leaders.

OUR GENTLE RULER
13 Days (2000)
MPAA: PG-13 for brief strong language
Read: Proverbs 25:15

A gentle answer turns away wrath. (Proverbs 15:1)

For thirteen days in October 1962, war seemed imminent. The U.S.S.R. had begun building medium- and long-range nuclear missiles in Cuba. America had a loaded gun pointed at its head. Within weeks, if not days, our Communist foes would be able to launch deadly force against the United States. President John F. Kennedy (Bruce Greenwood), his brother Bobby (Steven Culp), and his personal adviser Kenny O'Donnell (Kevin Costner) took counsel from American military leaders who wanted to launch preemptive strikes. But President Kennedy would not accept a military solution. Through blockades, secret talks, hardball United Nations confrontations, and gentle but firm negotiations with representatives of Khrushchev, the U.S.S.R. stood down and nuclear war was thwarted.

If the bully comes into your backyard and threatens to fight, there are options for dealing with him. The unwise man could go right up to the bully and bop him on the nose. But what would that lead to? The bully would punch back, a brawl would ensue, and somebody would be injured. When tension kept ratcheting up minute by minute in 1962, Kennedy kept a cool head and orchestrated a political solution. Evil sometimes must be stopped by force, but the Russians ultimately didn't want to get hurt by the U.S. any more than we wanted to get hurt by them.

Our president exercised fruit of the Spirit such as patience, goodness, gentleness, and self-control. If he had practiced impatience, evil, harshness, or rashness, the outcome of the Cuban missile crisis might have been quite different. Fruit of the Spirit must also guide our own personal crisis situations. God, our true guard, stands ready to issue these fruit as weapons of spiritual warfare. We wrestle not against flesh and blood but against principalities, powers, and rulers of this dark world (Ephesians 6:12). Defense by physical force isn't necessarily wrong, but if we understand that battles are rooted in the spiritual world, then we can employ these spiritual weapons in some of our most difficult contests.

PRAYER IDEA: Ask God to show you how to use gentle words to turn away wrath.

POINT OF NO RETURN

*Dr. Strangelove or How I Learned to Stop Worrying
and Love the Bomb* (1964)

AFI: 26 • MPAA: PG

Read: Matthew 12:30–32

Do not grieve the Holy Spirit of God. (Ephesians 4:30)

Concocting a cockamamy conspiracy that the Communists are ruining our body fluids by fluoridating U.S. waters, Air Force General Jack D. Ripper (Sterling Hayden) goes completely mad and sends B-52 bombers to drop nukes on key U.S.S.R. targets. U.S. president Merkin Muffley (Peter Sellers) meets with his advisers in the war room. There the Soviet ambassador tells him that if the U.S.S.R. is hit by nuclear weapons, it will trigger a doomsday device that will destroy all of earth. British Group Captain Lionel Mandrake (also Peter Sellers) tries to wrestle the abort code out of General Ripper, but Ripper kills himself. Former Nazi scientist Dr. Strangelove (Peter Sellers yet again) can't help but display perverse enjoyment at these turns of events. Eventually Mandrake unravels the code, and all but one plane turns back. Major T. J. ("King") Kong (Slim Pickens) rides a nuke, bronco-style, down to the earth, triggering the dreaded doomsday device.

The point of no return. It's a concept of great importance both in war and in personal spirituality. Eternity is a very long time to be wrong. Are we willing to believe and act in ways that have irreversible consequences? General Ripper made the biggest blunder of his life and, in so doing, destroyed humankind for all time. The biggest blunder a person can do, spiritually, is commit the unpardonable sin—blaspheming the Holy Spirit. Jesus says in Luke 12:10, "Everyone who speaks a word against the Son of Man will be forgiven, but anyone who blasphemes against the Holy Spirit will not be forgiven."

Much debate has taken place as to the exact nature of "blaspheming the Holy Spirit," but Jesus made it clear that "he who disowns me before men will be disowned before the angels of God" (Luke 12:9). God is continually reaching out to all people by his Holy Spirit, and those who deny the Holy Spirit deny the call of God. If we disown God, we have no right to join him for eternity but only deserve destruction. General Ripper's crazy move reminds us that we might not have the time we think we have. Don't be caught dead blaspheming the Holy Spirit!

PRAYER IDEA: Thank the Holy Spirit for leading you to salvation.

THE WARRIOR KING

Air Force One (1997)

MPAA: R for violence

Read: 2 Samuel 5:17–25

I come against you in the name of the Lord Almighty, the God of the armies of Israel. (1 Samuel 17:45)

Traveling on Air Force One, the U.S. President James Marshall (Harrison Ford) flies to Moscow and gives a stirring speech outlining America's new zero-tolerance policy on terrorism. On the flight home, terrorists disguised as journalists and led by Ivan Korshunov (Gary Oldman) take over Air Force One. They take the passengers (including the president's wife and daughter) hostage. The terrorists plan to execute one hostage every half hour until their demands are met. However, our commander in chief knows how to fight back. President Marshall uses his skills as a former Medal of Honor winner from the Vietnam War, and in so doing, he deals terror to the terrorists.

The irony of hijacking Air Force One is surpassed only by the idea that a U.S. president would himself "go to war" against the aggressors. This president personally defends his family, his plane, himself, and America too. That premise is silly, right? Not necessarily so. The Bible commonly depicts national leaders as warriors. David, a fierce warrior, first fought for Israel by defeating the Philistine warrior Goliath. As king, David would again defeat the Philistines, the Moabites, Zobah, the Arameans, and the Ammonites. David's predecessor, King Saul, was also a fierce, armored warrior.

Why did these leaders fight? Shouldn't executives of God's chosen people have been ruling somewhere in a well-protected room? No. God wanted them to have a hands-on approach to leadership. Their job was to take and then defend the land that God had promised Israel since the time of the Exodus. Today our president is called the commander in chief, and he calls the shots for protection of our land and country. God empowers his servants, including national leaders, to fight back against evil when it strikes. These leaders protect and defend us. May God's justice and goodness prevail. And may God protect, defend, and bless our president.

PRAYER IDEA: Ask God to give our President wisdom as he defends our country.

PROTECT THE NAME

In the Line of Fire (1993)

MPAA: R for violence and strong language

Read: Matthew 26:31–35

You are Peter, and on this rock I will build my church, and the gates of Hades will not overcome it. (Matthew 16:18)

When the situation demands it, a Secret Service agent must place himself in the line of fire. Failure haunts Secret Service Agent Frank Horrigan (Clint Eastwood) after he fails to protect President Kennedy, slain in the streets of Dallas. Stunned and humiliated, Horrigan goes off protection detail for decades. He has no confidence in himself and his abilities to use himself as a human shield for the sake of the president's life. But thirty years later Horrigan returns to service when a man calling himself Booth (John Malkovich) threatens the current president. Horrigan accepts the assignment, then relentlessly hunts down Booth and interrupts his evil plans.

God is our Commander in Chief. Are we his Secret Service Agents? Do we protect and defend him and his name? Are we champions of the Lord? God is all-powerful, and nothing can kill him, but his reputation and desires on earth are challenged and thwarted every day. That is why he asks us to pray, "Thy will be done, on earth as it is in heaven." His reputation is preserved when we worship him and speak truth about him. His desires on earth are fulfilled when we obey him. When we do these two things, he is very pleased.

Peter the disciple denied Christ. When challenged by a mere servant girl, Peter said, "I don't know the man!" (Matthew 26:72). Three times Peter dodged a bullet and denied the Lord. Afterward, Peter wept bitterly over his failures. Peter could have left the "force" (that is, the faith), but he did not. Christ could have kicked him off the team, but Peter had a job to do. Jesus ordered Peter to build the church. Even before Peter denied Christ, Jesus knew that Peter was up for the job as chief defender and propagator of the church. Our failures do not determine our fitness for the kingdom. If God appoints us for a job, even if we fail, we are to keep that appointment and do our work for his glory.

PRAYER IDEA: Ask God to forgive you for failing to protect and defend his name.

STEALING STEALS SO MUCH

The Bicycle Thief (1948)

AA: Honorary Best Foreign Film • MPAA: not rated

Read: Proverbs 30:7–9

Restore our fortunes, O Lord. (Psalm 126:4)

Neorealist film *The Bicycle Thief* has been hailed the world over as one of the greatest movies of all time. An honest but impoverished man, Antonio (Lamberto Maggiorani) goes out to buy a bicycle, which he needs for a good job. On the first day of work, his bicycle is stolen. He and his son Bruno (Enzo Staiola) go to the police to file a report, travel all over Rome to look for it, ask for help from his friends, and even go to see a pseudo-spiritual counselor for help. But no luck. Antonio finds the man who he thinks stole the bike, but he does not find the bike. In his desperation and anguish, he himself steals a bike, only to be captured and then released out of pity by the owner. The anguish Antonio feels is acute.

Stealing steals so much more than property. It steals the owner's dignity and, sometimes, even the owner's livelihood. The simplest of commandments, "Do not steal," carries so much meaning. Time, intellectual property, talent, and other intangibles can also be stolen. The greatest thief is Satan, who has stolen souls away from God since the dawn of history. Those who steal out of evil motives will have to face God.

Audiences connect with Antonio's pain because they, too, have felt the pain of loss. Indeed, in this sin-wracked world, goodness and its evidences are sometimes hard to find. Sorrow is all too common. Humans have pity on the thief who steals out of need:

Men do not despise a thief if he steals to satisfy his hunger. (Proverbs 6:30)

Christ had pity on the thief who hung beside him on the cross and told him, "Today you will be with me in paradise" (Luke 23:43). Thank God that he restores our soul and buys back what the devil steals.

PRAYER IDEA: Praise God for restoring to you what Satan has stolen.

FOREIGN FILM FEST
Gems from Overseas

WEEK 9

February 26–March 4

ANGELIC CONFUSION
Wings of Desire (1985)
MPAA: PG-13 for brief nudity and thematic elements
Read: Psalm 91:11–13

Are not all angels ministering spirits ... ? (Hebrews 1:14)

Like any modern city, Berlin is filled with discontented, lonely people desperate for love. In *Wings of Desire,* angels Damiel (Bruno Ganz) and Cassiel (Otto Sander) fly about Berlin to observe and record the affairs of humanity. Able to provide some comfort with a touch or a whisper in the ear, they are powerless to influence individual choice. A suicide leaps from their arms to his death below. Damiel sees a beautiful circus performer named Marion (Solveig Dommartin) and longs to experience love and the mysteries of humankind. Forsaking his nature, he becomes flesh and blood to love and be loved, to experience all the bumps and bruises that Cassiel can only vaguely comprehend.

Angels are God's created beings, lower than himself but a little above the human race. Sent to provide messages of God to people, sent to protect people and herald the coming of God, they can sing but cannot be redeemed. When Satan sinned against God, he took a third of the angels with him, and these are known as fallen angels or demons. Booted out of heaven because sin and righteousness cannot coexist, Satan and his throng scour the earth, looking for those they can persuade to spend eternity separated from God in hell.

The angels in *Wings of Desire* are not like real angels. In reality, angels cannot become human beings, though some have temporarily taken on human likeness when they needed to make an announcement to people. Similarly, angels are not independent agents or mini-gods. They are servants of God who fulfill his orders, but they can be sped into service through the prayers of men and women. Finally, angels are not, nor will they ever be, spirits of the dead. Some people say that a deceased relative watches over them, but this is wrong. Angels are wonderful, and they are worthy subject matter for books, television, and movies, but as you learn the truth about them, you will appreciate them even more.

PRAYER IDEA: Ask God to teach you more about the role of angels in his kingdom.

KEEPERS OF THE SWORD
Crouching Tiger, Hidden Dragon (2000)
AA: Best Foreign Language Film; Best Cinematography;
Best Art Direction; Best Score
MPAA: PG-13 for martial arts violence and some sexuality
Read: Ephesians 6:13–20

FEBRUARY 27

I did not come to bring peace, but a sword. (Matthew 10:34)

In *Crouching Tiger, Hidden Dragon,* the Green Destiny is no ordinary sword. Though it shines beautifully, it has bled countless opponents. When its owner, Master Li Mu Bai (Chow Yun Fat), decides to leave his life as a warrior, he gives the sword to his friend, the elder and great protector Sir Te (Sihung Lung). Yet Sir Te's houseguest, Jen Yu (Zhang Ziyi), secretly steals the Green Destiny to use it for selfish purposes with her master teacher and murderer Jade Fox (Cheng Pei-Pei). Master Li and the beautiful Yui Hshu Lien (Michelle Yeoh) continually show Jen Yu mercy as they track her down in relentless pursuit. They want not only to recover the Green Destiny but also to provide Jen Yu an opportunity to repent of her rebellion and become a student of the Wudan under the kind Master Li.

With its double blade and sharp point, the sword is an offensive weapon. It is able to penetrate and cut, "even to dividing soul and spirit, joints and marrow; it judges the thoughts and attitudes of the heart" (Hebrews 4:12). There is no turning one's back on God's sword, his Word. If you do, you are in danger of a fatal blow. No wonder Jesus said that he did not come to bring peace but a sword (Matthew 10:34). His words are not merely nice teachings or pleasant platitudes but are life-changing, life-giving truths. Christ's disciples became sword wielders or Word bearers for Christ.

We are keepers of God's sword. The apostle Paul admonishes us, "Take … the sword of the Spirit, which is the word of God" (Ephesians 6:17). Are we to keep it in a box like Sir Te, mishandle it like Jen Yu, or handle it skillfully and correctly like Master Li? This sword comes standard issue when we sign up to fight in God's army. But remember, the sword is not made of metal. God's sword is made of truth. His sword is invisible and can be kept quietly on the tongue until it is necessary to unsheathe it. Then, with a blow of love, the sword is released with an exacting thrust to make its mark on the souls and minds of those who feel its precious sting.

PRAYER IDEA: Ask God to always let you carry the sword of his Word as you serve him.

THE PHANTOM DO-GOODER

Amélie (2001)

MPAA: R for sexual content

Read: Psalm 66

Let her works bring her praise at the city gate. (Proverbs 31:31)

A divine moment of happenstance and a yearning for a life of significance drive the cute French ingénue Amélie (Audrey Tautou) to demonstrate unusual acts of kindness to those around her. In 1997, on hearing that Princess Di was killed, Amélie drops a perfume bottle top, which rolls under a piece of bathroom tile. Behind the tile she discovers a small metal box filled with youthful trinkets from the early 1950s. She tracks down the owner of the box, now a man in his fifties, and blesses him by secretly returning the box to him. In time Amélie secretly encourages her father to travel, sets up romance for a lovelorn coworker, stages a situation in which an underappreciated fruit-stand worker can advance in his career, and more. For her efforts, she is rewarded with romance.

Though this movie has been billed as a modern fairy tale, it is not magic that gives joy to Amélie and to those around her or even the audience; rather, it is pure goodness to others—a trait often lacking in movies and in real life. Despite Amélie's apparent lack of faith in God, she operates out of a spiritual principle: "Give, and it will be given to you" (Luke 6:38). She also understands not to flaunt her good deeds and does them secretly.

The Bible says, "When you give . . . , do not let your left hand know what your right hand is doing" (Matthew 6:3). We are created by God to do good works, which he has prepared for us. These good works have been given to us as a gift from God, so we shouldn't boast about how good we are at doing them. In fact, these works don't give us salvation or make us any better than anybody else in God's eyes. They can give us joy and rewards, and hopefully they give others joy too. Discover a way where you can secretly do good for others.

PRAYER IDEA: Ask God to grant you opportunities to express kindness.

GIVE THANKS IN ALL THINGS

Life Is Beautiful (1997)

AA: Roberto Benigni, Best Actor;
Best Foreign Language Film; Best Score
MPAA: PG-13 for Holocaust-related thematic elements
Read: 1 Thessalonians 5:16–18

Be joyful always. (1 Thessalonians 5:16)

Those who dismissed *Life Is Beautiful* as an unrealistic portrait of Nazi concentration camps have missed the point. This movie doesn't try to be "realistic" but rather says that happiness is not based on circumstances but on attitude. In 1930s Italy, Jewish bookkeeper Guido (Roberto Benigni) pursues and marries a lovely woman named Dora (Nicoletta Braschi, Benigni's real-life wife). They have a son, Giosué (Giorgio Cantarini), and live happily until German forces invade and occupy Italy. The Nazis force Guido and his family into a concentration camp. In an attempt to help his son survive the horrors of forced imprisonment, Guido pretends that the Holocaust is a game and the grand prize for winning is a tank. The son plays along and in the end finds his reward.

Compared to the horrors of the Holocaust, the saying "When life gives you lemons, make lemonade" seems terribly trite. However, the principle remains true. It is easy to become discouraged in the face of death and brutality, but realize that nothing goes beyond God's watchful eye. When we cry, he cries. When we suffer, he suffers. Sin and death were never a part of his plan. We were designed to live forever in paradise with him. Yet God, in his goodness, designed an escape plan for evil. Evil doesn't have to finish its course and bring ultimate suffering and separation from God. Evil and its effects can be stopped and even redeemed. What Satan has meant for evil God has meant for good.

"Give thanks in all circumstances, for this is God's will for us in Christ Jesus" (1 Thessalonians 5:18). When we hold on to our joy, despite evils, our spirits cannot be defeated. Many testimonies are recorded of people who, while facing death at the hands of an enemy, exhibited perfect peace. Without Christ, impending death (whether from concentration camps or terrorism) seems grim and hopeless. But with Christ, all things, even joy and hope, are possible (Matthew 19:26).

PRAYER IDEA: Give God thanks in all things, even in the face of terrible evil.

You prepare a table before me. (Psalm 23:5)

What a meal it was! *Babette's Feast* is set in a Danish seaside village in the mid-nineteenth century. Philippa (Bodil Kjer) and Martina (Birgitte Federspiel), two young daughters of a beloved minister, devote their lives to the service of God. Their father dies, but they continue the work. Decades later, a French friend sends a woman named Babette (Stéphane Audram), who has lost her family in an outbreak of civil war, to live with the sisters. She turns out to be an excellent cook, housekeeper, and shopper. Babette wins a lottery and prepares a sumptuous feast coinciding with a memorial to the reverend minister's one-hundredth birthday. Friends, townsfolk, and former lovers gather to eat this meal, which is discovered to have cost all of Babette's winnings.

Feasting and celebrating go hand in hand in God's world. In the Old Testament alone, we see how the Israelites enjoyed the Feast of Tabernacles, the Feast of Weeks, the Feast of Unleavened Bread, and many more feasts, including the Passover. These were eaten out of obedience and recognition of God's marvelous provision for the Israelites. When Jesus celebrated the Last Supper with his disciples, he said, "Take and eat; this is my body. ... This is my blood" (Matthew 26:26, 28). He was telling them and subsequent disciples that he was offering his own body as a feast, that we should enjoy it out of remembrance of him.

Eating and drinking are necessities of life. Without them we die. When we eat and drink out of celebration to God, we nourish not only our bodies but also our spirits. When we come by faith to Christ, he promises that he will "come in and eat" with us (Revelation 3:20). Every time we lift a morsel to our mouths, let us thank God that he is our delicious sustenance.

PRAYER IDEA: Thank God for the gift of good food and drink.

CHRIST ON EARTH TODAY

The Seventh Seal (1957)

MPAA: not rated

Read: Acts 5:12–16

As you sent me into the world, I have sent them into the world. (John 17:18)

Swedish filmmaker Ingmar Bergman broods in this haunting, allegorical drama. The Black Death sweeps across Europe in the fourteenth century, killing a third of all its inhabitants. Crusader Antonius Block (Max Von Sydow) returns from the Holy Land and is visited by Death. The knight challenges the Grim Reaper to a game of chess in order to buy more time on earth. Antonius seeks answers to life's most difficult questions and poses them bluntly, as no film character has done before or since. He asks, "Can it really be so terrible to want to know God with the senses? Why must he always hide behind unseen miracles and promises and hints about eternity? I want knowledge, not faith or blind acceptance. I want him to give me his hand and show me his face." Antonius enjoys fleeting moments of happiness while befriending a traveling actor family, but eventually he loses his game of chess.

Antonius never finds the answers to his questions, and that's a tragedy to be sure, but the fact that he asks them resonates with viewers even today. For a scant thirty-three years, Christ walked the earth as a man and offered himself to humankind, but then he ascended into heaven, never again to appear in physical form. What assurances can we offer those who wish to believe in a God they cannot see? Where is Christ today?

The answer isn't "blowing in the wind" or in warm-fuzzy fad religions. While the "heavens declare the glory of God" (Psalm 19:1), the church is the hands and feet of Christ. Filled with the Holy Spirit, ordered by God to love, and obedient to that call, the church represents a physical manifestation of God on earth. That is why it is so important to love one another and give glory to our Father in heaven. If we don't love others and champion the kingdom of God, who will? Where will the inquisitors find their answers? Without Christ, all will meet a meaningless death. Eternity is too long and death too permanent without the hope of salvation through faith in Jesus Christ. We must represent Christ to all who haven't found him yet.

PRAYER IDEA: Ask God to use you as an instrument of his love.

PURSUING HIS PASSION

Cinema Paradiso (1989)

AA: Best Foreign Language Film • MPAA: PG

Read: Acts 1:6, 7

No eye has seen, no ear has heard, no mind has conceived what God has prepared for those who love him. (1 Corinthians 2:9)

Young Salvatore ("Toto") Di Vita (Salvatore Cascio) loves the movies. In his little Italian town, Salvatore constantly pesters film projectionist Alfredo (Philippe Noiret). At the Cinema Paradiso, Toto steals clips of film (usually kissing scenes cut out at the demand of the local priest) and asks Alfredo how to run the projector. Eventually Alfredo teaches Toto the ropes. One day the cinema burns down and Alfredo loses his vision. Toto becomes the operator. When Toto is a young man, he dreams of making his own movies. Alfredo tells him to go to school and not come back. Alfredo tells Toto, "Life is not like the movies. It's harder." Thirty years later, Salvatore is now a successful film director in Rome. He receives a call from his mother telling him that Alfredo is dead. Toto returns to his hometown and receives an unexpected, beautiful gift——a film reel of one kiss after another.

Why must people find romance, passion, excitement, and thrills only in the movies? Is real life too difficult? Wouldn't it be great to go on great adventures, battle fierce foes, share love with the needy, and find the great romance of your life——a romance that never ends but keeps getting bigger and better? Wouldn't it be great to tell your own fantastic stories instead of watching someone else's? Wouldn't it be great live a passionate life? But life here on earth is difficult, isn't it? Bills, obligations, mundane jobs, and our fear of the unknown hold us back in bland lifestyles.

God wants excitement and adventure for you. He originally made humankind to run free and naked in a garden. He took the Israelites on a forty-day road trip through the desert and then through the Red Sea. (Talk about a hike!) Through Christ, God talked about living in a kingdom. Through Christ, God talked about going into all the world to preach the gospel. That includes over seas, through jungles, across deserts and over mountains. God is no couch potato. He's all the cinematic heroes rolled into one——and then some! Next time you get a thrill from the movies, realize that God gave you that capacity and that he longs to fulfill it in you. Pick up a few stories from missionaries and read about their adventures as they went into the world to preach. God has an adventure for you. It may start small, but it is fueled with passion.

PRAYER IDEA: Ask God to give you the courage to go on an adventure for him.

THE SPORTING LIFE

How Competition Shapes Our Lives

WEEK 10

March 5–March 11

How Deep and How Wide

A River Runs Through It (1992)

AA: Best Cinematography

MPAA: PG for momentary nudity and some mild language

Read: John 4:1–10

There is a river whose streams make glad the city of God. (Psalm 46:4)

L iving vastly different lifestyles, one thing brought them all together: fly-fishing. One son, Paul (Brad Pitt), rebelled against their father, the Reverend Maclean (Tom Skeritt), while the other son, Norman (Craig Sheffer), lived responsibly. Paul liked to drink and brawl, while Norman read literature and wooed a country girl named Jessie (Emily Lloyd). Two lives traveled on separate courses, but a river joined them in common activity to achieve a common goal. Though they might have stood yards apart, not saying a single word to each other, they fished with flies for trout and were momentarily unified in purpose.

J esus is our River of Life. His living water makes our hearts glad. He brings rebels and the faithful together. Rebels come to quench the desires that rumble deep within their stomachs. They seek satisfaction for their thirsty souls. The faithful come to be renewed and refreshed. They come back to the well in faith because they know that he is faithful to pour out his love and redemptive power once again. When Jesus gave water to the woman at the well, he knew her sinful past. She drank and was refreshed. Yet this same well was also available to those who followed him daily. They drank and were likewise refreshed.

The words of an old worship song claim that a River of Life flows out of you, healing others and setting them free. The wonderful thing about this River of Life is that it flows. It doesn't puddle in our souls but comes into our lives and flows out. Love begets love. Life begets life. When we let the love of Christ dwell richly in our hearts, it can't help but pour out to those around us. Love doesn't stop but keeps on rolling through fields, hills, cities, and wherever people need a drink. Jesus, our River, runs through our lives to others. Let him flow through your life today.

PRAYER IDEA: Ask God to let his living water flow through you to thirsty souls.

KEEPING THE SABBATH HOLY

Chariots of Fire (1981)

AA: Best Picture; Best Original Screenplay;
Best Costume Design; Best Score
Read: Deuteronomy 5:12–15

MARCH 6

Observe the Sabbath, because it is holy to you. (Exodus 31:14)

Many Christians applaud *Chariots of Fire*. They appreciate the example of Scottish missionary Eric Liddell (Ian Charleson) when he says, "I believe God made me for a purpose, but he also made me fast. And when I run I feel his pleasure." Conversely, the movie demonstrates the vanity of running for one's own glory in the depiction of Liddell's competitor Harold Abrahams (Ben Cross). A major theme of the movie, however, is keeping the Sabbath holy. Liddell does not run his best event in the 1924 Olympics because it is held on a Sunday. The Olympic committee cannot make Liddell change his mind. Liddell runs and wins a different event, keeping his vows to God and demonstrating his excellence.

Is Sunday really the Sabbath? And is it more holy than other days? The Sabbath, by definition, is "the seventh day of the week observed from Friday evening to Saturday evening as a day of rest and worship by Jews and some Christians" (*Merriam-Webster's Collegiate Dictionary*). Christians have called Sunday the Sabbath and worshiped on that day probably out of recognition of Easter Sunday, the day of Christ's resurrection. Some Christian denominations still worship on Saturday.

Jesus rebuffed some Pharisees and told them, "It is lawful to do good on the Sabbath" (Matthew 12:12). The apostle Paul clarified the law and said, "One man considers one day more sacred than other; another man considers every day alike. Each one should be fully convinced in his own mind" (Romans 14:5). The bottom line is that whatever we do in observance of days and practices, we should do it as unto the Lord. In doing so, we give honor to God.

PRAYER IDEA: Thank God for every day including the Sabbath.

TRAINED TO WIN
The Karate Kid (1984)
MPAA: PG
Read: Hebrews 12:7–13

Everyone who is fully trained will be like his teacher. (Luke 6:40)

New Jersey born and bred Daniel (Ralph Macchio) moves to southern California with his single mother. Daniel falls in love with a rich girl, Ali (Elisabeth Shue), but her former boyfriend Johnny (William Zabka) can't stand it. Johnny and his friends often beat up Daniel. One night the kind, old Mr. Miyagi (Pat Morita) karate-chops Johnny and his friends until they stop bullying Daniel. Impressed, Daniel asks Mr. Miyagi for karate lessons. Mr. Miyagi agrees and orders Daniel to perform all kinds of chores. Daniel doesn't think this is training but rather cruel and unusual punishment. But Mr. Miyagi shows Daniel how this discipline is helping him develop his karate skills. Mr. Miyagi puts Daniel through more training until Daniel is ready to go to the All-Valley Karate Tournament. Though he has never participated in a formal karate competition before, Daniel fights his way to the final match. Through hard work, training, and discipline (and a few ancient Japanese moves like "the crane"), Daniel beats Johnny, preventing any more schoolyard or streetside attacks.

Discipline is passed down from teacher to student. Mr. Miyagi learned karate from his father, and now Mr. Miyagi passes his knowledge to Daniel. When we experience the discipline of our heavenly Father, we sometimes lose heart and don't understand what is happening. But "the Lord disciplines those he loves" (Hebrews 12:6). When God disciplines us, he is showing us his love. When Mr. Miyagi disciplines Daniel, he is acting like a true father. Daniel becomes good at karate because he learns how to be like Mr. Miyagi. When God disciplines us, he is training us to be like him: holy. Training and discipline are often painful, but the result is success. Those who train physically find success in competition. Those who train spiritually find a "harvest of righteousness and peace" (Hebrews 12:11).

Isn't *disciple* another form of the word *discipline*? As Christ's disciples, we must conform to his likeness through matching our thoughts and behaviors with his. We learn from Christ through his Word. We are empowered to be like Christ by his Holy Spirit, and we walk in obedience to him. The more we put his commands into practice, the more like him we become.

There are no black belts in Christianity, but there are levels of maturity and Christlikeness. Don't be afraid to let Christ take you to the next level. Submit to God's discipline and grow!

PRAYER IDEA: Ask God to grant you a willing heart to submit to his discipline.

A SECOND CHANCE
Seabiscuit (2003)
MPAA: PG-13 for some sexual situations and
violent sports-related images
Read: 1 Corinthians 1:26–31

MARCH 8

He has sent me to bind up the brokenhearted. (Isaiah 61:1)

You don't throw a whole life away because he's banged up a little," says millionaire businessman Charles Howard (Jeff Bridges), echoing the reserved horse trainer Tom Smith (Chris Cooper). So Howard buys failed, short, sleepy, knob-kneed, ornery Seabiscuit and gives him a failed boxer named Red Pollard (Tobey Maguire) for a jockey. Together, all three men form a bond and nurture the horse to become the greatest sensation of the late 1930s. Failing to win the Santa Anita Handicap, Seabiscuit nevertheless tears up the track all the way to Baltimore to have a head-to-head match race against the bigger, stronger War Admiral. Just days before the race, Pollard breaks his leg. Alternate jockey George Woolf (Gary Stevens) steps in and Seabiscuit makes War Admiral eat his dust. Not long after, Seabiscuit breaks his ankle in a race. Doctors say the horse will never ride again. But with love, patience, and slow rehabilitation, both Red and Seabiscuit mend and ride together to win the elusive Santa Anita Handicap.

Second chances—we all need them. Third and forth chances, too. God made us for greatness, but along the way, we all got banged up and lost our races. Some of us found hope and soldiered on through the pain. But many others buckled under the whipping sting of sin. As in the story of Seabiscuit, the wearisome toll of battle makes us feel like we are good for nothing but the pasture. Sometimes we feel like it would be better if somebody just "put us down." If we haven't been this low, we probably know someone who has been. What is the solution? What was Seabiscuit's solution? Love—patient, hopeful, nurturing, and encouraging love from men who knew pain but also perseverance.

Jesus gives us a second chance when he forgives us and binds our brokenness. Jesus gives us a second chance when he sends friends our way to help us heal and get back on our feet. Peter failed and denied Christ, but Jesus forgave him and set him up as the head of the church. Paul persecuted the church and even killed Christians, but Christ struck him with blindness and rebuilt him into the greatest missionary ever. Throughout the Bible and throughout history, God takes the foolish things of the world to shame the wise (1 Corinthians 1:27). Let God heal you. Let God use you to heal others. Give yourself and others a second chance.

PRAYER IDEA: Ask God to use you to heal others and give them a second chance.

THE LEAST OF THESE
Radio (2003)
MPAA: PG for mild language and thematic elements
Read: Matthew 19:13–15

Whatever you did for one of the least of these brothers of mine, you did for me. (Matthew 25:40)

In Anderson, South Carolina, Harold Jones (Ed Harris) coaches football and is considered a celebrity by the locals. He regularly puts winners on the gridiron. So, naturally, folks get upset when Coach Jones takes in a fatherless, mentally disabled black boy named Radio (Cuba Gooding Jr.) as a sort of assistant coach and mascot. Some think Radio is a distraction. Others criticize his effect on the game when the team finishes at only .500. But Coach Jones won't budge. He loves Radio and punishes others who make fun of him or play tricks on him. When the pressure to kick Radio out of Hannah High gets too great, Coach Jones defuses the tension and steps down as the coach, saying, "It's never a mistake to care for someone." Today, Radio still coaches and encourages athletes at Hannah High.

Caring for the downtrodden. It seems simple enough, but often it's not. Sometimes others stand in the way of our fulfilling the Christian mandate to help the needy. Jesus faced this sort of obstacle when he called little children to himself. The disciples thought the children were a distraction to his ministry. But Jesus said, "This *is* my ministry." Jesus also lets us know in no uncertain terms that when we care for the sick, the lowly, the downtrodden—and the mentally challenged—we are in fact caring for him. We are the hands and feet of Christ ministering to Christ himself in the form of a person with a deficiency.

Coach Jones goes on to say, "Radio teaches us as much as we teach him." Indeed, that is the hidden blessing of loving the unlovable. When we come out of our comfort zone to reach out to those who are socially undesirable, we grow as persons and learn that love has no limitation because of social standing or mental or physical health. Love others and, in so doing, love Christ. Reach out to one of the "least of these" and discover a world of joy.

PRAYER IDEA: Ask God to help you love "the least of these."

THE WEAK ARE STRONG

Hoosiers (1986)

MPAA: PG

Read: 1 Samuel 17:45–50

It is God who arms me with strength and makes my way perfect. (2 Samuel 22:33)

Nobody loves basketball quite like the people of Indiana. But in 1952, at the start of the basketball season, the high school Hoosiers from Hickory look terrible. New coach Norman Dale (Gene Hackman) has a mysterious, spotty past. Assistant coach Shooter (Dennis Hopper) has a problem with booze. Lots of parents and other adults don't like Coach Dale's manner. Only six players show up on opening day, and by the end of the day, one quits. But in time the players begin to trust in the coach, and a few more players are added to the team. They begin to improve and win games. At the season's end, they squeak by district and regional finals. Next stop: Indianapolis for the state championship. Nobody had predicted that the little team from Hickory could top the taller, stronger contenders from South Bend. But with grit, determination, and a few prayers, this little team rallies and wins the big game!

The underdog beating the big dog is a story as old as David and Goliath. Lots of people didn't believe in David's "coach," the one true God of Israel. Most soldiers, from both the Israelite and Philistine armies, scoffed at David's belief that he could best Goliath. Goliath taunted David and called him a "boy." Goliath predicted that he would feed David's flesh to the birds. But David called on God, and God heard his prayers.

In *Hoosiers,* just before the tip-off of the championship game, one player drops to his knees and prays. The coach looks at him a moment and then whispers into the boy's ear, "God wants you out on the floor." The boy smiles, rises to his feet, and defeats his foe. Victory over adversity requires a willingness to face it, knowledge that our preparation has made us ready, and a humble understanding that God ultimately receives the glory. Through David's previous contact with God in prayer, David was already assured of the outcome. David knew he was going to win. We can place that sort of confidence in God too. He is faithful to his promises.

PRAYER IDEA: Thank God for the blessed assurance that He is faithful to his promises.

BLESSINGS FOR OBEDIENCE

Jerry Maguire (1996)

AA: Cuba Gooding Jr., Best Supporting Actor

MPAA: R for strong language and sexuality

Read: Deuteronomy 11:13–17

Summon your power, O God; show us your strength, O God, as you have done before. (Psalm 68:28)

One night Jerry Maguire writes a mission statement on quality sports management, including ideas of personal attention and not focusing exclusively on the bottom line. Jerry copies it and delivers it to everyone at his work, Sports Management International. He gets summarily fired. Going into business alone, he is able to hold on to only one client, NFL player Rod Tidwell (Cuba Gooding Jr.), and he is able to gather only one employee, secretary Dorothy Boyd (Renée Zellwegger). Rod asks one thing of Jerry: "Show me the money." But the harder Jerry tries, the more he fumbles the ball. The leaders of Rod's team, the Arizona Cardinals, see Rod as a hothead and a complainer, someone who is not a team player and is uninspiring on the field. Rod holds on to Jerry by a thread, but after Rod catches the game-winning pass in an influential game, both Rod and Jerry get the attention, respect, and salaries they crave.

Rod asks Jerry to deliver the paycheck, but it isn't until Rod delivers on the field that Jerry can "show him the money." Likewise, God isn't a vending machine or a panic button we can push and automatically get something in return. Sometimes God can't answer our prayers because we aren't in a position to receive them. Sometimes we can't receive God's blessing because our sins gets in the way. Sometimes there are things we must do in order to see God move in our lives.

The clearest and simplest way that we can receive God's blessings is through obedience to him. If we love and serve him with all our heart, God promises rain, providing us with grain, new wine, and oil (Deuteronomy 11:13, 14)—all the things we need. God also says that if we turn away from him, he will shut the heavens so that it won't rain, and that brings death (Deuteronomy 11:17). Sound harsh? Well, God made us, and he can do anything to use us for his glory or shake us to get our attention. Works can't earn our salvation. That comes through grace alone, received by faith. But works and acts of obedience to God, such as praying, loving God and others, evangelizing, and following him, bring lasting and definite rewards.

PRAYER IDEA: Ask God how you can be more obedient to him.

"I DO"
Movies about Marriage

March 12–March 18

LET HIM GO

My Best Friend's Wedding (1997)

MPAA: PG-13 for one use of strong language
and brief sex-related humor

Read: James 3:13, 14

Love . . . does not envy. (1 Corinthians 13:4)

In *My Best Friend's Wedding,* Jules Potter (Julia Roberts) doesn't want her best friend, Mike O'Neal (Dermot Mulroney), to marry Kimmy (Cameron Diaz). As teens, Jules and Mike decided that, if they weren't already married to other people by age twenty-eight, they would marry each other. Jules has remembered that vow and has secretly been in love with Mike ever since. Now, weeks before Jules's twenty-eighth birthday, Mike calls. Jules thinks he is going to propose marriage, but instead he tells her that he has found another woman. Jules bristles. Secretly, she vows to break up the wedding. Through false charm, devious plans, and downright lies, she tries to drive a wedge between Mike and Kimmy. Finally, on the day of the wedding, Jules tells Mike that she loves him and kisses him. Kimmy sees the kiss and runs away. Mike chases Kimmy, and Jules chases Mike, but in the end Jules confesses her sin of envy and blesses the marriage.

Many of us fall into the sin of envy. We fret, moan, and complain that we don't have something we desperately want. We even plot and scheme to unfairly take the object of our desire. Lots of times, what we want isn't even what we really need. The desire to win something consumes us to the point of obsession, which in turn becomes idolatry. This, of course, is condemnable. When we hold so tightly to something we think we want or need, we lose the ability to receive into our hand the blessing that God wants to give us.

Jules's friend George tells her, "Do you really love him, or is it just about winning?" Jules sighs and realizes that her romance with Mike is just a game. While her feelings for him were honest, she wasn't honest with herself about his feelings for Kimmy. She gives up and, in so doing, wins back her pride and self-esteem. Rock musician Sting sings, "If you love someone, set them free." God doesn't cajole or arm-twist you into loving him. He gives himself for you and is patient with you, and you love him for it. Because of his sweet and wonderful love, practice the same character with others. Let God be your sufficiency. If you love someone who doesn't love you back, don't blame God. Ask him to give you a better option. Let go and let God.

PRAYER IDEA: Ask God to forgive you for your envy and idolatry.

HATING YOUR FAMILY

My Big Fat Greek Wedding (2002)

MPAA: PG for sensuality and language

Read: Luke 9:57–62

If anyone comes to me and does not hate his father and mother, his wife and children, his brothers and sisters—yes, even his own life—he cannot be my disciple. (Luke 14:26)

Poor Toula (Nia Vardolos). Her Greek family is always embarrassing her. They're loud, easily offended, always bickering, always eating, and can't understand anyone who isn't Greek. Her big, fat Greek wedding almost never comes to pass because her beloved fiancé, Ian (John Corbett), is not—heaven forbid—of Greek descent. For years, Toula feels trapped in a lifestyle she never wanted: the lonely life of a hostess at her family's Greek restaurant. Her father and mother smother her with their effusive comments and rules for living. But Toula wants more. First she wants to go to college, then to learn the travel agency business, then to date and marry a non-Greek. When her father, mother, and other family members flip out, she must decide whether to toe the family line or go out on her own.

When the love of our life, Jesus Christ, calls us to leave family and friends for a greater cause, will we follow? Will we be able to stand up to their snide comments, taunts, and jeers? They might think we have gone off the deep end by "getting religion." Taking a stand for Christ in a family of non-Christians can be very difficult. Even taking a stand for Christ in a Christian family can sometimes be troublesome.

Once a middle-aged man decided to leave a stable career for overseas missions. His elderly mother went ballistic. She fretted, worried, and complained. Finally the man said, "Mom, why did you send me to Sunday school and take me to church? Didn't you want me to embrace all of Christ?" She finally agreed and stopped the bellyaching.

Following Christ can sometimes put a wedge between us and the ones we love the most: our family. Christ doesn't want us to hate our families, but he wants us to have the right priorities. He comes before family. Our family should never come in the way of our following him. If our family pulls us back from what we know we need to do for him, there may be a time when we have to take a stand.

PRAYER IDEA: Ask God to help you love your family in proper balance to your love for him.

HIS LOVE IS TRUE

Runaway Bride (1999)

MPAA: PG for language and suggestive dialogue

Read: Ephesians 4:22–25

My lover is mine and I am his. (Song of Songs 2:16)

You've heard the expression "Always a bridesmaid but never a bride." In the movie *Runaway Bride,* Julia Roberts plays a woman named Maggie who is always a bride but never a wife. Three times she becomes romantically involved to the point of agreeing to marriage and even walking down the aisle in a white dress. But when the moment comes for her to finally commit to holy matrimony, she runs away. It isn't until she meets a newspaper columnist named Ike (Richard Gere), who challenges her on her patterns, that she realizes who she really is and what she really wants.

Lots of people stumble through life not really knowing who they are or what they stand for. They will fall for anyone because they stand for nothing. They will fall for anyone because they're looking for identity and perfect love from imperfect people who can offer nothing more than attention and activities. People join groups and clubs for the same reason: to feel like they belong to someone. But they don't know true communion and fellowship. When we commit ourselves to Christ and let his Spirit indwell us, we receive perfect love and discover our true identity in him.

When we face God and he asks us to be his bride, do we say, "I do"? Or do we merely give the appearance of being in his fold? When the pressure is on, do we run away to other spiritual suitors? Christ is the perfect suitor because he completes us. Only he is able to help us become all we were intended to be. As the bride of Christ, we are challenged to give up false thoughts and activities by which we identify ourselves. But his commitment to us is unsurpassed. His love is everlasting and his transforming power in our lives is eternal.

PRAYER IDEA: Ask God to prepare you as his bride.

"AS YOU WISH"
The Princess Bride (1987)
MPAA: PG
Read: Mark 11:20–25

**He answered their prayers, because they trusted in him.
(1 Chronicles 5:20)**

A kindly grandfather tells a fairy tale to his bedridden grandson (Fred Savage). In the fairy tale, a beautiful commoner named Buttercup (Robin Wright) orders around her farm boy, Westley (Cary Elwes). With every command, he replies, "As you wish," and does the thing she demands. Eventually they declare "true love" for one another and he goes off to make his fortune. When news comes that Westley has been killed by the dread Pirate Roberts, the pompous Prince Humperdinck (Chris Sarandon) forces Buttercup to marry him. Before the wedding, though, she is kidnapped. A masked stranger orders a Spanish swordsman (Mandy Patinkin), a giant (André the Giant), and a pseudo-intellectual (Wallace Shawn) to rescue the princess bride. While Buttercup appreciates the rescuing, she doesn't care for the masked stranger and shoves him down a steep hill. As he falls, he yells, "As you wish," revealing himself to be Westley. Reunited, they again declare their love for one another and face fire swamps and torture to disarm Humperdinck and his devious plans once and for all.

N ow, here is a curious story. A woman discovers that a man will do anything she wants and so she falls in love with him. The man is so smitten with the woman that every time she barks an order, he says, "As you wish." If this is true love and we are the bride of Christ, shouldn't we be able to command Christ to do anything for us and expect him to comply and gently say, "As you wish"? Not exactly. Anybody who has had a relationship with Christ soon realizes that not every prayer is answered with enthusiastic acquiescence. Many times God answers with a "no."

But God longs to bless us. He longs for us to be full of faith in him. He longs to be the answer to our prayers, but he also wants us to say, "Thy will be done. Thy kingdom come." In other words, God is not a vending machine that will spit out treats when we pop in prayers. When our lives and hearts are lined up with God's, when our will becomes his, he is more than happy to say yes to our prayer requests. True love is God and humankind in harmonious agreement. The asking, seeking, and knocking verses of Matthew refer to knowing God himself, not getting goodies from his hand. God is a providing God, but he also asks us to love him with all our heart, mind, soul, and strength (Matthew 22:37, Deuteronomy 6:5).

PRAYER IDEA: Ask God to help you never confuse his hand with his heart.

PLANNING GOODNESS

The Wedding Planner (2001)

MPAA: PG-13 for language and sexual humor

Read: Proverbs 14:22

In his heart a man plans his course, but the Lord determines his steps. (Proverbs 16:9)

What a conundrum! The wedding planner Mary (Jennifer Lopez) falls in love with a pediatrician named Steve (Matthew McConaughey), but he's the groom for the next wedding she is organizing. It all starts when Mary accidentally gets her shoe stuck in a manhole cover and a runaway garbage bin rolls toward her. Steve spots Mary and whisks her and her shoe away to safety. They go out for one evening on a date and almost kiss, but the rain stops them. The next day Mary meets Fran (Bridgette Wilson-Sampras), a beautiful businesswoman who wants no expense spared at her own wedding. But Mary also meets Steve, Fran's fiancé. As a series of humorous conflicts unfolds, Mary must also fend off the advances of Massimo (Justin Chambers), a young man fresh off the boat from Italy. At her worst moment, Mary meets her ex-fiancé while a background singer croons, "Answered prayers come in unexpected ways." Steve and Fran realize they aren't right for each other. Massimo lets Mary go, and Mary and Steve become available to discover the love they have for each other. The wedding planner finally plans her own wedding.

In true Hollywood fashion, this romantic comedy has our two young lovers facing and overcoming many obstacles on their way to the altar. Hollywood calls them plot points. In real life we call them challenges—unpredictable surprises that get in the way of our plans. Mary prides herself on planning every element of her weddings, down to the last detail. Imagine her surprise when she discovers that Steve is already engaged! She also has to deal with Massimo, a man she does not love. He pines for her and tells people she is going to be his wife. How can she manage that?

Like Mary, many of us plan well. We try to bring order into our lives and we offer advice to help others bring order to their big events. Assuring words come from Proverbs: "Those who plan what is good find love and faithfulness" (Proverbs 14:22). We can plan well, and sometimes obstacles will come our way, but ultimately God will provide all our needs, including love and faithfulness. Many wait for true love to arrive, but God promises these things if we plan and practice good.

PRAYER IDEA: Thank God that he plans blessings and goodness for you.

A WOMAN WORTH FIGHTING FOR

The Quiet Man (1952)

AA: John Ford, Best Director • MPAA: not rated

Read: Psalm 19:1–5

. . . prepared as a bride beautifully dressed for her husband. (Revelation 21:2)

Emerald-green hills, horses, thatched-roof cottages, and a little wearing o' the green all can be found in a gem of a movie called *The Quiet Man.* After years of negotiation and toil, director John Ford (whose real name is Sean O'Feeney) finally created his quiet celebration of his native Ireland with this endearing movie. In it Sean Thornton (John Wayne), an American boxer, swears off fighting after accidentally killing a man in the ring. Sean returns to Ireland to buy and live in the home of his birth in the little town of Inisfree. There he meets and falls in love with the fiery redhead Mary Kate Danaher (Maureen O'Hara). They marry, but her tempestuous brother refuses to pay Sean a dowry. In turn Mary Kate, a true loyalist to tradition, doesn't recognize the marriage, and it isn't consummated. When Mary Kate tries to leave town on a train, Sean takes matters into his own hands. He pulls her off the train and accepts a fist-fight with her brother in what was then the longest brawl ever filmed.

God fights for us, too. Our God is our bridegroom, and we are his bride. The Bible, in the Old and New Testaments, continually reminds us of this. And our God is a jealous God. When he is ready for his bride, he will come for us. Revelation speaks of him showing off his bride, spotless and clean (Revelation 21). We are clean because he has fought our battles, won, and wiped away our every tear and stain. God is relentless in knocking out the competition when he is ready to take us as his bride. Satan tries to steal us away, but God triumphed over him on the Cross.

St. Patrick understood the grace that can be ours and so dedicated his life to sharing this good news with the people of Ireland. Thank God that this good news applies to us today, too.

PRAYER IDEA: Thank Jesus for fighting for you with his shed blood.

TRUE LOVE WAITS

Four Weddings and a Funeral (1993)

MPAA: R for strong language and sexuality

Read: Revelation 19:7–9

**Do not arouse or awaken love until it so desires.
(Song of Songs 2:7)**

Serial wedding attendee Charles (Hugh Grant) lives in merry old England. Terrible at keeping relationships, he is in awe of anyone who marries. At one wedding he meets a woman named Carrie (Andie McDowell) and is instantly attracted to her. The feeling is mutual, but another wedding later, Charles discovers that Carrie is engaged to a powerful Scotsman. Deeply saddened, he nevertheless attends Carrie's wedding, and there a tragedy strikes. His good friend Garath (Simon Callow) dies. Charles reunites with a former girlfriend and, on his wedding day, Carrie returns to say that she and the Scotsman have broken up. From the pulpit, the priest states these words: "Holy matrimony, instituted of God in the time of man's innocence, represents the mystical union between Christ and his church and therefore is not by any means to be enterprised nor to be taken into hand lightly, inadvisably or wantonly, but reverently, discreetly, soberly, and in the fear of God." After four weddings and a funeral, Charles cancels his own wedding so that he can spend the rest of his days with Carrie.

The priest was right. Marriage is holy. It is a representation of Christ and the church. Therefore, it shouldn't be debased with false love. Love cannot be forced, rushed, or cajoled into existence. It either exists or it does not. Those who try to force the hand of love find it won't be there when it is needed most. Edward tried to resurrect love with an old girlfriend, but when he was honest with himself, he realized that he loved Carrie and not his bride-to-be. He did the right thing and broke off the marriage. He kept the marriage act sacred by leaving it alone.

Are you about to get married? Make sure it is for the right reasons and with the right person. Are you now married and have found that the spark of love is gone? Get back to your first love. Rediscover what made you fall in love with your spouse. Pray to God for help and do and say the things you once did that represented your true love. Are you single? Then cheer on every marriage to be like Christ and his love for the church. Every marriage that goes on loveless and dry is a marriage that falls short of God's plan. May God bless you with a love so great that you'll prepare to be his bride for his wedding day.

PRAYER IDEA: Ask God to guard your heart so that you may be prepared to be his spouse.

COSTUME
EPICS
Sweeping Stories of
the Ancient World

WEEK 12

March 19–March 25

LET GO AND LET GOD
The Ten Commandments (1956)
AA: Best Special Effects • MPAA: G
Read: Exodus 2:1-3

Oh, that their hearts would be inclined to fear me and keep all my commands always, so that it might go well with them and their children forever! (Deuteronomy 5:29)

The gospel has been called "the old, old story," but a still older story tells of God's liberation of the masses. The Exodus of the Israelites dramatically comes to life in epic proportions through Cecil B. De Mille's *The Ten Commandments*. Pharaoh Rameses (Yul Brynner) oppresses the Israelites through ruthless and brutal slavery. Adding to this misery, Pharaoh decrees that all Hebrew boys are to be killed. Moses (Charlton Heston) is spared when his mother sends him down the river in a basket and he is adopted by Pharaoh's daughter to be raised in the royal courts. Yet, when Moses becomes a young man, God tells him something extraordinary: "I am sending you to Pharaoh to bring my people the Israelites out of Egypt." Through persistence, plagues, the Passover, and plunder, Egypt relents and the Israelites flee to the desert. On Mount Sinai, God gives Moses the Ten Commandments.

These rules are the moral framework for living. As sin began to abound, the law was given to provide direction for healthy living under God and with each other. The law, though powerless to change the heart of anyone, stood firm as a moral compass to give its adherents the best possible life, both now and eternally.

This story is as much about the grace of God as it is about the law of God. Before Adam and Eve sinned, they continually fellowshipped with God in the garden. It was perfect. Later the Israelites grumbled in the desert, needing direction in their lives. Without the law, they were well on their way to abandoning their faith in God and practicing self-destructive acts. We can't operate a car or appliance for long without consulting a manual. Likewise, our lives need a manual. When we follow this manual, our lives run optimally. Long before Spock of *Star Trek* fame said, "Live long and prosper," God told us how we can enjoy these blessings. "Walk in all the way that the Lord your God has commanded you, so that you may live and prosper and prolong your days" (Deuteronomy 5:33). Long life and prosperity: it happens through obedience to God's law!

PRAYER IDEA: Ask God to show you how you might prosper through greater obedience.

TALE OF TWO KINGDOMS

Spartacus (1960)

AA: Peter Ustinov, Best Supporting Actor; Best Art Direction;
Best Cinematography; Best Costume Design
MPAA: not rated
Read: John 3:1–8

My kingdom is not of this world. (John 18:36)

Roman slave Spartacus (Kirk Douglas) envisions a day of freedom for all Roman slaves. Skillfully trained as a gladiator, he condemns the practice of fighting to the death. Disgusted by the tyranny of Rome, Spartacus turns on his owners and leads the other slaves in rebellion. Two senators, the republican Gracchus (Charles Laughton) and the militarist Crassus (Laurence Olivier), are humiliated by the slave rebellion. The pride of Rome cannot stand under such flagrant disobedience. Something must be done about Spartacus. As the two statesmen struggle to gain greater power in the name of preserving Rome, Spartacus and his followers advance on the capital in their pursuit of freedom.

Gracchus and Crassus both believe in the grandeur of Rome. Both are in love with its size and power over the Western world. While Gracchus believes in a political solution to the problem of Spartacus, Crassus believes in the mechanisms of force, might, intimidation, control, and fear. Both Gracchus and Crassus are wrong. Though they eventually beat Spartacus, they cannot beat his goals. Rome eventually will fall. Its failed infrastructure of control through brutality could not stand up to the true ideals of freedom and love.

Like Spartacus, Jesus challenged Roman authority. Jesus came to earth to establish the kingdom of God, not a kingdom of force or political power. Throughout the Gospels, Jesus teaches of this kingdom—a kingdom marked by sacrifice, humility, childlikeness, righteousness, and love. This radical concept flew in the face of Roman leaders who knew nothing of such concepts. Ultimately, they sided with the Jews and crucified him. But Jesus could not be kept down and rose again to continue his kingdom and rule on earth. Christ's kingdom is not reserved for heaven alone. God wants to establish his rule and reign in your life today. Are you letting him? Or are you flirting with the power of Rome, so to speak? A person cannot belong to both a lasting kingdom of light and a doomed kingdom of darkness.

PRAYER IDEA: Ask God to teach you more about his kingdom reign.

A Rich Garment

The Robe (1953)

AA: Best Art Direction; Best Costume Design • MPAA: not rated

Read: Revelation 12:10, 11

He has clothed me with garments of salvation and arrayed me in a robe of righteousness. (Isaiah 61:10)

It's bewitched!" says Roman tribune Marcellus Gallio (Richard Burton) about the robe of Christ. After nailing Christ to the cross, Marcellus puts on the homespun robe of Jesus, but its touch stings his skin and soul. Tormented by guilt and suffering over putting an innocent man to death, Marcellus seeks out the identity of this so-called "king of the Jews." The more Marcellus talks to those who met Jesus, including a crippled girl, a poor boy, and a disciple named Simon Peter (Michael Rennie), the more Marcellus is convinced that Jesus is the Son of God. Marcellus joins the cause of Simon Peter and declares himself to be a Christian. Returning to Rome, the new emperor Caligula (Jay Robinson) considers Marcellus a traitor to the rule of Rome and sentences him to death. Marcellus and his faithful woman Diana (Jean Simmons) proudly march off to meet their heavenly King.

What broke the spell of guilt and suffering that Marcellus experienced? It wasn't finding the robe and destroying it. The simple piece of cloth had no power in and of itself. Marcellus was transformed from mental illness to spiritual clarity and peace through nothing less than a personal encounter with Christ. The crippled girl, the poor boy, and Simon Peter all carried Christ in their hearts. All showed Marcellus forgiveness and unconditional love.

Christ heightened the guilt and suffering of Marcellus. Through love, the power of the witnesses, and the forgiveness provided by Christ's own shed blood, Marcellus found relief through a spiritual encounter. Today, Christ continues to change lives through these same methods. Let Christ use you to put his robe on others. Love others deeply. Tell them of Christ's love and forgiveness. Let the risen Lord speak loud and clear in your heart. If Christ can forgive the man who nailed him to the cross, he can forgive you and others.

PRAYER IDEA: Ask God to fill you with his light and forgiveness to clothe others with Christ.

"I KNOW THIS MAN"

Ben-Hur (1959)

AA: Best Picture; William Wyler, Best Director;
Charlton Heston, Best Actor; Hugh Griffith, Best Supporting Actor;
Best Cinematography; Best Editing; Best Art Direction; Best
Costumes; Best Score; Best Special Effects; and Best Sound

MPAA: G

Read: Matthew 28:16–20

Peter answered, "You are the Christ." (Matthew 16:16)

One of the most acclaimed and awarded movies of all time, *Ben-Hur* is subtitled *A Tale of the Christ*. It is a tale of denying, meeting, receiving from, and then being saved by the Christ. For almost two thousand years since his ascension, people have come to know Christ. But how did people meet and come to belief in Christ when he walked the earth? *Ben-Hur* says how.

Judah Ben-Hur (Charlton Heston) lived as a rich Jewish prince in Jerusalem. As a young adult, he met a boyhood friend, now a Roman centurion named Messala (Stephen Boyd). Yet Judah and Messala quickly discover their political differences. When Judah accidentally hurts the new governor, Quintus Arrius (Jack Hawkins), Messala sends Judah to the galleys. As Judah walks to the ships, Jesus gives him water. When Judah's ship sinks after an attack, Judah rescues the governor and is freed. Judah returns home and discovers that his mother and sister are lepers. On his way to the leper colony, Judah sees Jesus again. Jesus is on his way to the cross. Judah tries to give Jesus some water but is thwarted in this by Roman guards. Judah's love interest, Esther (Haya Harareet), tells Judah wonderful stories about Jesus. Judah meets Jesus a final time and believes in him as he dies on the cross. As the blood trickles down the cross in the rain, it reaches Judah's mother and sister and cures them of leprosy.

How does Judah meet and come to faith in Christ? The same way we do: by personal encounters with him. How do people encounter Christ? By meeting him through his church. We are the hands and feet and mouth of God, and if we don't carry Christ into the world, who will? *Ben-Hur* is one of the most celebrated and treasured movies of all time, winning eleven Academy Awards. It is a tale of the Christ because it is a tale of a man coming to know and believe in Christ. Share your own tale of how you met Christ and, in so doing, win awards in heaven.

PRAYER IDEA: Ask God to make greater in your heart his tale of how he rescued you.

KNEEL BEFORE ME
Gladiator (2000)
MPAA: R for intense, graphic combat
Read: Daniel 6:10–12

Whoever does not fall down and worship will immediately be thrown into a blazing furnace. (Daniel 3:6)

I n *Gladiator,* nearly all the Western world has been conquered by Rome. After murdering his father, Caesar's wicked son Commodus (Joaquin Phoenix) unjustly assumes the emperor's throne. Commodus offers his hand to request the loyalty of Roman general Maximus (Russell Crowe), but Maximus does not accept it. Enraged, Commodus kills Maximus's wife and child and sends Maximus off to be executed. Maximus escapes but is captured and forced to fight as a gladiator in the Roman Coliseum. For the rest of his life, Maximus faces pain and hardship because he took a stand and did not bow to an evil ruler.

W hat leader is demanding your allegiance? Whom will you serve? Many Americans might laugh at these questions because we elect our officials. In our democracy, we have the freedom to pledge our allegiance to no person. But today these questions may not necessarily apply to political leaders or even religious leaders. Better ways to phrase the question might be these: "Who rules the throne of your heart? Who rules your thoughts and deeds? Who rules your life?" Sure, we have duties to our job and family, but for whose pleasure do we live and move and have our being? Our own? Satan's? God's?

In Daniel's time, three Hebrew men were to be thrown into the fire because they did not worship false gods. They told the wicked King Nebuchadnezzar, "Even if [God] does not [rescue us], we want you to know, O king, that we will not serve your gods or worship the image of gold you have set up" (Daniel 3:17). What guts they had, what bravery! God blessed them for their obedience and saved them from the fire. The Word of God hasn't changed. God commands us to "have no other gods before [him]" (Exodus 20:3). If we are enslaved to our addictions, our work, or even our duties, then the throne in our hearts has been usurped. When we kick God off the throne of our lives, he cannot bless us when we face the lions and tigers in the arenas of life.

PRAYER IDEA: Ask God to grant you the resolve to let no one else rule over your life.

ALL FOR YOU

The Passion of the Christ (2004)

MPAA: R for sequences of graphic violence

Read: Isaiah 53:2–6

He took bread, gave thanks and broke it, and gave it to them, saying, "This is my body given for you; do this in remembrance of me." (Luke 22:19)

Mired in controversy and dripping with blood, *The Passion of the Christ* opens a window in time so the viewer sees every excruciating detail of the suffering of Christ. From the beatings, scourging, flaying, and ridiculing by the Roman soldiers to the crown of thorns, the long walk to Skull Hill, and the crucifixion, Jesus offers himself up for the sins of the world and is brutalized until he dies. Then, triumphantly, he rises again! Not so much a study in the character of Christ and of those who followed him as an unflinching look at what he went through for you and me, this film endeavors to remind people to never forget the cruel indignities that Jesus endured to take away our sins.

But why would anyone want to see so much bloodletting? Why torture yourself by seeing someone else being tortured for two hours, even if it is a depiction of our Lord? Director Mel Gibson knows that our culture today is jaded and anesthetized to violence in film. It seems he wants to rattle our cages and place indelible images in our minds and hearts about the suffering of Christ. Two hours of depicted torture of anyone else would be merely cruel and sadistic, but we are reminded that these wounds mean everything. These wounds have no less power than to save the entire world from all its sins for all time. These wounds are worth considering and contemplating for two hours because these wounds sustain us every day of our lives.

Isaiah 53:5 says,

He was pierced for our transgressions,
he was crushed for our iniquities;
the punishment that brought us peace was upon him,
and by his wounds we are healed.

"By his wounds." Let us never forget these wounds. Many will watch this movie and say, "I never knew what he went through for me." Through Holy Communion we are reminded that Christ broke his body and spilled his blood for our sins. Christ asks us to "do this in remembrance of me" (Luke 22:19). Do you remember that he broke his body and spilled his blood for you? Do you appreciate the cost he paid to heal you of your wounds? The remembrance of it ought to cause us all to fall on our knees and worship. It has made all the difference in the world.

PRAYER IDEA: Fall on your knees and worship him for what he did for you.

LIVE AS FREE PEOPLE

Braveheart (1995)

AA: Best Picture; Mel Gibson, Best Director;
Best Cinematography; Best Sound Effects; Best Makeup
MPAA: R for brutal medieval warfare
Read: Genesis 2:16, 17

It is for freedom that Christ has set us free. (Galatians 5:1)

William Wallace (Mel Gibson) is Braveheart, a bold Scotsman who used the strength of his arms and the fire of his intellect to rally his fellow citizens to liberation. In the 1200s Scotland is ruled by a wicked imperialist king of England, Edward I Longshanks (Patrick McGoohan). The king's men abuse their power, rape women, and pillage Scottish villages at will. When Wallace's wife, Murron (Catherine McCormack), is attacked and killed, his fiery vengeance turns into a freedom crusade. He tells his Scottish charges, "Every man dies. Not every man lives." Consumed with a passion for freedom, Wallace pushes back the English armies, often with far fewer troops at his disposal. Though he is eventually captured, tortured, and killed, Wallace inspires Robert the Bruce (Angus MacFadyen) and others to continue the pursuit of liberation.

Defending freedom is one of the great privileges and challenges of the Christian faith. God is in the business of setting people free from sin and hell through faith in Christ. God himself, through Christ, provides the way for people to be free from the chains with which the armies of sin would enslave their soul. It often isn't until we realize how enchained we are that we can appreciate the freedom Christ brings through forgiveness and personal liberation. Oh, that you may know the riches of his mercy!

Despite the prevailing idea of many modern people that Christianity is a list of rules or a constraint on freedom, God loves freedom and loves to give it to his people. The first command given by God to human beings, even though it contained a condition, started with the words "You are free to eat from any tree" (Genesis 2:16). What an awesome statement—"You are free"! God wants people to focus not on the restrictions of faith in their lives but on the near-limitless freedoms it provides, yet to realize there are conditions with those freedoms. The disciples, the apostle Paul, and Jesus himself offered themselves as living sacrifices in defense of freedom. Freedom isn't free. It has conditions, but it is wonderful. The blessing of having it is worth fighting for. May you always have a brave heart to proclaim the wonders of freedom in Christ.

PRAYER IDEA: Thank God for the freedom and joy found in Christ's salvation.

OSCAR
WATCH
Best Picture Winners

WEEK 13

March 26–April 1

HE STANDS WITH US

On the Waterfront (1954)

AFI: 8 • AA: Best Picture; Elia Kazan, Best Director;
Marlon Brando, Best Actor; Eva Marie Saint, Best Actress;
Best Original Screenplay; Best Cinematography;
Best Editing; Best Art Direction • MPAA: not rated
Read: 1 Corinthians 16:13

MARCH 26

Stand firm . . . and do not let yourselves be burdened again by a yoke of slavery. (Galatians 5:1)

Washed-up boxer Terry Malloy (Marlon Brando) is in big trouble with his boss, Johnny Friendly (Lee J. Cobb). Johnny and his mob of thugs run the shipping and dockworkers union with an iron fist. After Terry inadvertently participates in the murder of a fellow longshoreman, he develops a conscience. After this murder, Father Barry (Karl Malden) encourages the surviving longshoremen to expose and defeat Johnny. Father Barry says of the ships and docks, "This is my parish, and Jesus stands here with you." Terry takes these words to heart. When his brother, Charlie (Rod Steiger), is rubbed out, Terry has no choice but to expose Johnny in court and defy him by showing up for work at the docks. In flexing his spiritual muscle, Terry stands up as a contender for truth and justice.

Like Father Barry says, Jesus stands with us in the middle of the most ugly and difficult of situations. He stands there with us when it would be dangerous if we exposed sin and corruption. He stands there with us when our jobs, our relationships, and even our lives are on the line. Situations can be ready to explode, but because Jesus stands with us, we can have perfect peace and stand up for truth and justice.

God was with Daniel and protected him in the Lion's den. God was with the Hebrew children and protected them in the fiery furnace. God was with Noah and Noah's family in the ark, protecting them from the raging waters over the earth. Jesus was in the boat with his disciples when the seas raged. As ambassadors for Christ, our job is to be the hands and feet of Christ to our friends who are in trouble. The whole world is our mission field, and we are the delegated representatives. Christ's love, truth, and justice need to be taken to the mean streets and evil mob circuits of this world. Stand up for truth and justice because God stands up for you.

PRAYER IDEA: Ask God to give you the mean street as your mission field.

STAND BY YOUR MAN

A Beautiful Mind (2001)

AA: Best Picture; Ron Howard, Best Director; Jennifer Connelly,
Best Supporting Actress; Best Adapted Screenplay
MPAA: PG-13 for intense thematic material,
sexual content, and a scene of violence
Read: Hebrews 3:1–6

MARCH 27

God, who has called you into fellowship with his Son Jesus Christ our Lord, is faithful. (1 Corinthians 1:9)

A Beautiful Mind is a portrait of courage and faithfulness in the midst of a seemingly endless horror: schizophrenia. Alicia Nash (Jennifer Connelly) meets her man, John Nash (Russell Crowe), brilliant math and physics scholar, at Harvard. After they marry, Alicia discovers that John is mentally ill. He believes in people and situations that do not exist. Though John is hospitalized, fired from his job, and even endangers the life of his family members, Alicia tells John, "I need to believe that something extraordinary is possible." Though John is not totally cured of his malady, his extraordinary wife and his old colleagues make it possible for John to live a productive life and go on to win the Nobel Prize.

Faithfulness is more than loyalty; it is being "full of faith." At their darkest hour, Alicia expresses that she needs more faith and hope, and through the years she finds the strength to hold on to hope. Her love helps conquer the worst symptoms of schizophrenia, and John eventually emerges from his fog as a functioning, fulfilled person.

God demonstrates his faithfulness continually. Testimonies of his faithfulness can be found throughout the Scriptures. He is the same today, yesterday, and forever, and his word is true. He rewards and recognizes faithfulness to his people. When you face a dark time, cry out, "God, show yourself faithful." He will be there even if you can't sense his presence. In this age He doesn't always thwart the plans of evil, but you can be assured that in the midst of trouble he is there with you. Like David said in Psalm 23:4,

Though I walk through the valley of the shadow of death,
I will fear no evil, for you are with me.

He is faithful to you. Are you faithful to him?

PRAYER IDEA: Thank God that he is always near and faithful.

NEVER TOO OLD

Marty (1955)

AA: Best Picture; Delbert Mann, Best Director; Ernest Borgnine,
Best Actor; Best Original Screenplay • MPAA: not rated

Read: Genesis 21:1–7

MARCH 28

There is surely a future hope for you, and your hope will not be cut off. (Proverbs 23:18)

Whatever it is women like, I ain't got it," says Marty (Ernest Borgnine), a lonely thirty-four-year-old Italian-American butcher living in the Bronx. Every Saturday night he says to his buddy Angie (Joe Mantell), "What do you want to do tonight?"

Angie replies, "I don't know." And the endless circle starts.

Marty's mother (Esther Minciotti) gives him grief, saying, "Why don't you get married? You should be ashamed of yourself." Marty *is* ashamed. He knows the embarrassment and pain of being single all too well. When Marty goes to a dance, he meets a plain but intelligent young woman named Clara (Betsy Blair). Despite their insecurities, Marty decides to take a chance and see if something beautiful can happen for their future.

When Abraham was old, God told him that he was going to have a son who would father a whole nation, Israel. Abraham was amused and waited, but no son came. Abraham's wife, Sarah, said to Abraham, "What are you going to do about it?"

Abraham said, "I don't know. What are you going to do about it?"

Sarah told him, "I tell you what you are going to do. You are going to sleep with my handmaiden Hagar and have a son with her."

Eighty-one-year-old Abraham slept with Hagar, and Ishmael was born. But this was not God's plan. Nineteen years later, at one hundred years of age, Abraham fathered a son through his wife, Sarah. They were so amused and over-joyed that they named their son, Isaac, which means "laughter."

Lots of people think they are too old to have something beautiful happen to them. Thirty-somethings and older people give up on love, opportunity, and the blessings of God because their past looks less than stellar. They resign themselves to life-less routines. God doesn't want your old bones in a rut. He wants to use your wisdom, experience, and strength for his glory. He wants to do something wonderful with your old bones, and you can enjoy the ride. Many people these days are retiring early and pursuing second careers in volunteer work for God. Others are finding new love. Seek God and find out what new blessing or direction he wants to give you.

PRAYER IDEA: Ask God to keep you always faithful and looking for new opportunities.

OFFICE AFFAIRS
The Apartment (1960)
AFI: 93 • AA: Best Picture; Billy Wilder, Best Director;
Best Original Screenplay; Best Art Direction; Best Film Editing
MPAA: not rated
Read: Genesis 39

[Wisdom] will save you also from the adulteress. (Proverbs 2:16)

C. C. ("Bud") Baxter (Jack Lemmon) knows that the quickest way to the top is through the bedroom. It's his bedroom, all right, but his bosses are the ones doing the bedding. In *The Apartment,* Baxter provides a rendezvous point for his philandering superiors, including his callous boss J. D. Sheldrake (Fred MacMurray), and earns a series of quick promotions. But things get out of hand when he falls in love with elevator operator Fran (Shirley MacLaine), Sheldrake's mistress. Eventually Bud must choose between a swanky office and a one-way ticket out the door.

Adultery never pays. It always ends in ruin. The Bible warns us about the dangers of adultery. The adulterer of Proverbs says,

I have come to the brink of utter ruin in the midst of the whole assembly. (Proverbs 5:14)

Joseph had an opportunity to have a liaison with Potiphar's wife, but Joseph did the right thing: he refused her. That earned him a one-way ticket to jail. Some promotion, eh? But thankfully the story continues and Joseph not only becomes second in command over the whole prison; he eventually takes charge of all Egypt. Now, that's getting ahead God's way!

Adultery, or any kind of cheating, might get you ahead in the short term, but dire consequences are sure to come. Ultimately, it isn't the consequences we face on earth that count; it's facing God that really matters. Our actions have eternal consequences. Each person will have to give an account of his or her sins before God, adultery included. Marriage is the only approved context for sexual expression—that's God's way. When we play by God's rules, we experience his kindness and favor. It's the surest way to the top in his kingdom.

PRAYER IDEA: Ask God to give you strength to resist sinful temptations.

ARE YOU ON GOD'S LIST?

Schindler's List (1993)

AFI: 9 • AA: Best Picture; Steven Spielberg, Best Director;
Best Adapted Screenplay; Best Cinematography; Best Editing;
Best Art Direction; Best Score

MPAA: R for language, some sexuality, and war violence

Read: Romans 10:9, 10

MARCH 30

, , , names are written in heaven. (Hebrews 12:23)

To get your name on someone's list is usually not a positive thing, but Schindler's list was wonderful. "The list is life," declares Schindler's faithful Jewish accountant Itzhak Stern (Ben Kingsley). A member of the Nazi party, Oskar Schindler (Liam Neeson) is a womanizer and war profiteer. But as he sees the devastation that his fellow Germans are wreaking on the Jews, his heart turns toward their plight. He makes a list of "essential workers" for his enamelware manufacturing plant and rescues more than eleven hundred Jews from certain death, many times buying them from his Nazi friends, who kept them as slaves. At war's end he becomes a fugitive because of his alliance to the Nazi party, but his Jewish staff know he is a hero because of the list he made.

God wants you on his list. He wants to give you eternal, abundant life—a life of hope, joy, and peace in him. His list is called the "book of life," as explained in the book of Revelation. (Chapters 13, 17, and 20) Unfortunately, however, if our names are not written in this book, we will be cast into a lake of eternal fire forever, without the blessing of communion with God.

In light of that, a question emerges: "How do I get on his list?" Though Schindler grieved that he couldn't add more people to his list, the Bible says that God wants everybody on his list (1 Timothy 2:4). To get on God's list, all it takes is an act of faith on our part. "If you confess with your mouth, 'Jesus is Lord,' and believe in your heart that God raised him from the dead, you will be saved" (Romans 10:9). With this simple but profound act, declaring our allegiance to Christ as Lord and Savior of our lives, we can start our eternal life with him. And what's more, there are no added charges, because Jesus paid the price!

PRAYER IDEA: Thank your Heavenly father for writing your name in the book of life.

WE ARE A PECULIAR PEOPLE
Forrest Gump (1994)
AFI: 71 • AA: Best Picture; Robert Zemeckis, Best Director;
Tom Hanks, Best Actor; Best Adapted Screenplay;
Best Film Editing; Best Visual Effects
MPAA: PG-13 for drug content, some sensuality,
and war violence
Read: 1 Corinthians 1:18–25

MARCH 31

We are fools for Christ. (1 Corinthians 4:10)

"Stupid is as stupid does," says Forrest Gump (Tom Hanks). To say the least, this man is peculiar. Odd, dumb, and even plain foolish are other ways of putting it. But for the most part, life is just fine for this southern simpleton. He goes to a good school, becomes a football hero, and is decorated as a Vietnam War hero. He meets presidents and becomes a shrimp tycoon. He invents the smiley face logo and starts the fitness craze. He goes to church, helps his disgruntled friend Lt. Dan (Gary Sinise) come to faith and peace, and marries his lifelong sweetheart, Jenny (Robin Wright Penn). Though Jenny eventually dies of AIDS, Forrest is glad to enjoy life with his son, Forrest Jr.

Many might think that God can only use important, smart, and educated people in his kingdom. We see teachers, preachers, writers, and leaders doing great exploits, and we think that only those who are wise can really do something important for God. The Bible says this isn't true. In fact, God says,

The wisdom of the wise will perish, the intelligence of the intelligent will vanish. (Isaiah 29:14)

Peculiar means not only "strange" but also "chosen, selected, and unique." The King James Bible calls Christians peculiar in Titus 2:14 and in 1 Peter 2:9. Like Forrest Gump, we have been selected for great and marvelous works. In his simplicity, Forrest shames the wise. His goodness affects all those around him for good, and the audience treasures him for it. Why not become a fool for Christ and show your own peculiarity to those around you?

PRAYER IDEA: Praise God for creating you to be unique.

FOOLING TO EXCESS
April Fool's Day (1986)
MPAA: R for language, sexual situations, and violence
Read: Ephesians 5:1–4

Like a madman shooting firebrands or deadly arrows is a man who deceives his neighbor and says, "I was only joking!" (Proverbs 26:18, 19)

Gotcha. April fool." A rowdy group of college kids embark on a weekend voyage to an island mansion belonging to classmate Muffy (Deborah Foreman). What looks like a fun time is quickly spoiled as one by one the youths are murdered. One is run over by a boat, another stabbed, another hung. Or are they? Eventually only Rob (Ken Olandt) and Kit (Amy Steel) are left, and just when they are about to burst out of their skins in fear and panic, Muffy reveals that it was all a joke. Wanting to create a special murder mystery bed-and-breakfast out of the island home, Muffy concocts a gruesome, gore-filled house of horrors that's sure to have guests running for the doors.

April Fool's Day pranks are usually good fun and cause only temporary embarrassment or anxiety. But when does joking go too far? Is there a level of joking that becomes inappropriate for Christians? The apostle Paul says there is: "Nor should there be obscenity, foolish talk or coarse joking, which are out of place, but rather thanksgiving" (Ephesians 5:4). Was Paul trying to be a killjoy? Of course not. But he *was* saying that some things shouldn't come out of a Christian's mouth, and the best way to experience fun is through joy and thanksgiving.

In your joking, celebrate life, don't put it down. Every pun, joke, riddle, practical joke, or act of silliness you do should have an underlying attitude of joy and peace behind it. When we gently tease our friends, we cherish them, especially when done with a smile. But a straight-faced, abusive, emotionally jarring prank can go too far. It you try to laugh it off and say, "I was only joking," your friends may soon pack their bags and say, "I was only leaving." Joking is a spontaneous outburst of merriment. Train your sense of humor to be aware of fun making instead of making fun of others.

PRAYER IDEA: Thank God for giving you joy and humor.

PLAY BALL

Movies about America's Pastime

WEEK 14

April 2–April 8

SECOND CHANCES

The Rookie (2002)

MPAA: G

Read: Luke 23:39–43

I tell you, not seven times, but seventy-seven times. (Matthew 18:22)

A rookie who joins the highest level of professional sports is usually in the nineteen- to twenty-three-year-old range. In *The Rookie,* thirty-five-year-old high school baseball coach Jim Morris (Dennis Quaid) makes his dream come true by joining a major league baseball team in a wonderful tale of second chances. Having tried and failed to get into the majors after an injury at twenty years of age, Jim Morris goes on to teach and coach at Big Lake (Texas) High School. After a team loss, Coach Morris tells his team to dream bigger. They tell him to do the same and ask him to agree to try out for the big leagues if they win divisionals. When they do win, Coach Morris keeps his word, throws ninety-eight mph fastballs, is drafted into the Tampa Bay Devil Ray farm team, and is called up to the majors three months later.

God is always ready to give people a second chance. Think about the prodigal son who took off and squandered his father's money. The father welcomed the returning son with open arms and a party. Think about the thief on the cross. The man was taking his last breaths when Jesus said, "Today you will be with me in paradise" (Luke 23:43). Think also about Peter. Jesus told Peter that when somebody sinned against him, he should forgive that person not twice, not seven times, but seventy-seven times. Actually, what God was saying here was not that we should forgive seventy-seven times but that we should forgive an infinite number of times! God gives people as many chances as they are willing to run back to him for forgiveness.

When you've been up to the plate a few times and struck out, realize that God will always keep you in the game if you keep asking him for his help. You may never get to play in the big leagues or even have your dreams come true, but God will never give up or back out on you.

PRAYER IDEA: Thank God that he continually forgives you of your sins.

He who cherishes understanding prospers. (Proverbs 19:8)

I n 1962 Scotty Smalls (Tom Guiry) moves to a new neighborhood with his mom and new stepdad. Scotty doesn't have any friends and doesn't get along well with his stepdad. Soon, though, Scotty is accepted by a group of baseball-playing kids. At first Scotty's baseball skills are terrible, but he learns to bat, catch, and throw as well as the rest of them. At the sandlot baseball diamond, a fence divides the outfield from the junkyard of old, mean Mr. Mertle (James Earl Jones). On the other side of the fence, the boys fear an enormous, hungry dog simply called the Beast. Rumor says this super-sized dog eats baseballs and kids. After Scotty hits a Babe Ruth–signed baseball over the fence, the gang must figure out a way to retrieve it without getting killed by Mr. Mertle or the Beast. In time the boys discover that Mr. Mertle is kind and that the Beast is nothing more than a friendly Saint Bernard.

T he truth sets Scotty and his friends free from fear. Scotty fears that he and his stepdad will never get along, but in time they do. Scotty fears he will never learn baseball, but that changes. Everybody fears old Mr. Mertle, but they love him after they discover he knew Babe Ruth, the great Bambino. Finally, the Beast is cut down to size when they learn he is an average-size Saint Bernard that would more likely lick you than bite you. Understanding the truth of a situation eventually shoots down every lie that Scotty and the gang believed.

When we understand the truth, our imaginations are put to rest. We know the pros and cons of a situation and can make rational assessments about how we ought to respond. In many cases, the truth of a matter minimizes feared risks. Proverbs encourages us to "get understanding" (Proverbs 4:5), because when we do, it will guard us. A person who has understanding delights in wisdom because he knows that wisdom will protect him. A person unafraid is a person who knows the facts and has assessed a situation with all the information available. Scotty and his friends grow up that summer because they obtain wisdom and are set free from their fears. If something is binding you with fear, get all the information and understanding you can about it (including the fact that God always loves you). This will help you live in peace.

PRAYER IDEA: Praise Jesus for relieving your fears with wisdom and understanding.

THE LUCKIEST MAN
The Pride of the Yankees (1942)
AA: Best Film Editing • MPAA: not rated
Read: Psalm 100

Give thanks in all circumstances. (1 Thessalonians 5:18)

Growing up in New York, Lou Gehrig (Gary Cooper) dutifully obeys his mama. She nurtures and protects him and has plans for him to be an engineer. But Lou loves baseball. As a teen, he transfers from Columbia College to Hartford to play the game. From Hartford, Lou joins the New York Yankees and plays regularly, never missing a game. He falls for Eleanor (Teresa Wright), the daughter of the Chicago White Sox owner. Eleanor and Lou marry, and Lou continues to play baseball every day. In 1939 Lou begins to slump and thinks he is losing his ability. Sadly, Lou's doctor confirms the worst. He has ALS, a deadly nerve disease that now bears his name. After 2,130 consecutive games, Lou tells the crowd at Yankee stadium that he is "the luckiest man on the face of the earth," endearing him to the American people forever as an example of thankfulness and grace.

Lou had every reason to be discouraged and angry. He lived a moral, exemplary life and yet was given a death sentence in his prime. Many of us complain, fret, and become sour when facing much less. The dog barks one too many times or you spill juice on your favorite dress, and that ruins your whole day. Why? Perhaps because you see the faults in your life instead of your blessings. When Lou gives his farewell speech, he lists his blessings. He speaks of his teammates, managers, parents, and wife, choosing not to focus on the pain and struggles that were to come. He faces his fears with courage and dignity.

Thankfulness is a developed skill; it doesn't come naturally. But God asks us to work at it. He knows this sin-wracked world can dish out its share of pain and sorrow, but he says, "Take heart! I have overcome the world" (John 16:33). God is our healer, provider, and friend. He has given us everything we need for life. Even when sickness comes to steal our life away, we know that "to live is Christ and to die is gain" (Philippians 1:21). On this earth we rejoice and live in him, and if we die, we join him in a sinless, wonderful heaven. There is no room for bitterness with a perspective like that. Like Lou, we are "lucky."

PRAYER IDEA: Ask God to help you develop an attitude of gratitude.

Be strong and courageous. (Deuteronomy 31:6)

From World War II through the mid 1950s, women had a league of their own. After many of the professional baseball players were drafted and sent off to the front lines, owners got together and formed the All-American Girls Baseball League. They wanted the game to go on. Sisters Dottie (Geena Davis) and Kit (Lori Petty) joined up in spite of their fears of the future. Would America accept them? Would their countrymen come home safely? Perhaps their biggest challenge was taking guff from manager Jimmy Dugan (Tom Hanks), who yelled at them like they were some of the guys. He caused one player to cry. When Dottie's husband returns from war, honorably discharged due to injury, she tells Dugan that she's quitting. Dugan asks her why and she says, "It's too hard." He replies, "If it was easy, everybody would be doing it." Dottie conquers her fears and returns to her position as catcher for the Rockford Peaches in the first-ever Women's World Series.

When we say yes to Christ, he doesn't give us a field of daisies but a battlefield. God wants us to step up to the plate, batter up, and run the bases. He promises to love us and never leave us, but our journey in him is liable to get us laughed at, dirty, and bruised. Some may scoff at us and tell us we don't belong on the team. Our own leaders may chastise us and hold us accountable to a higher standard. What is our response? Should we cry or should we press on?

If we should fall or get bruised, God will pick us up and wipe away our tears. Jesus doesn't say there's no crying in Christianity. He says, "If you cry, I'll be there to take care of you and send you back into the game." Yes, he wants us to be courageous, but that doesn't mean fear disappears. It means we start believing in God's promises, stepping out in faith and operating in the Spirit of God. The All-American Girls Baseball League was special because they did something nobody had ever done before. They broke the mold of what baseball was like, and it earned them a spot in the Baseball Hall of Fame. Take courage and break the mold. Let Christ shape you into a winning player for his team.

PRAYER GOD. Thank God for wiping away your tears and shaping you into an all-star on his team. Amen.

THE COMEBACK KID

The Natural (1984)

MPAA: PG

Read: Judges 16:23–31

They called Samson out of the prison, and he performed for them. (Judges 16:25)

As a high school youth, Roy Hobbs (Robert Redford) excels at baseball so much that his father calls him a "natural." When his father dies early, Roy decides to pursue baseball in the big leagues. He jumps a train and takes along his favorite baseball bat, called "Wonderboy," a bat he made out of a tree struck by lightning. On the train Roy meets a mysterious woman and follows her back to her room. Joyful anticipation turns to terror when the woman pulls a handgun on him and shoots him in the gut. Sixteen years later, when most men his age retire from the pros, Roy joins the New York Knights. Corrupt owners and gamblers despise him. In the playoffs, Wonderboy breaks apart. Now, without his special bat and with a bleeding gut caused by the gunshot wound, Roy experiences one more miracle. He hits a home run, smashing the floodlights of the field. Sparks rain down and the evil hopes of those who bet against him come to ruin.

In the Old Testament, the Israelite Samson experienced a similar fate. He was born with incredible strength, overcame obstacles as a youth, and became a respected leader. Yet as a middle-aged man Samson lost his special possession: his hair. Samson's strength was in his hair. As long as it was long, he was strong. If it was shaved off, he was weak. A wicked woman cut his hair and the Philistines overtook him. They blinded him and taunted him and had him play games for them. With one final prayer to God, Samson asked for his strength to return. God honored this prayer, and Samson destroyed a pagan temple and vanquished his enemies.

Roy Hobbs comes back to show the naysayers that it wasn't Wonderboy that gave him his talent; it was his own God-given abilities. Even with the disadvantages of age and injury, Roy brings victory for his team and defeat for his enemies. God is a God of second chances. If you ever think you're washed up and your strength is gone, go to God in prayer and see what he can do. It's never too late. God honors even the eleventh hour opportunity. In spite of our sins, such as mistakenly trusting in wicked women, God can redeem our failures.

PRAYER IDEA: Thank God for eleventh-hour miracles.

GUIDED BY VOICES
Field of Dreams (1989)
MPAA: PG
Read: Numbers 22:27–31

God called to him from within the bush, "Moses! Moses!" (Exodus 3:4)

Ray Kinsella (Kevin Costner) bought the farm—a cornfield in Iowa, that is. However, his dreams of successful farming are as good as dead when he responds to a voice in his head that speaks, "If you build it, he will come." Ray plows down his field and builds a baseball diamond, and profits plummet. Despite his brother-in-law's offer to bail him out with a sale, Ray takes a chance to meet Shoeless Joe Jackson (Ray Liotta) and other White Sox players of old as well as his deceased father at the baseball field. Ray exhibits insane behavior, such as driving across the country to meet strangers and welcoming hundreds of people who show up at his farm to watch baseball without even knowing why. At the final hour, his premonitions bear out a wonderful reality. He is rewarded for obedience to the voices in his head.

Christians often talk about that still, small voice. It is the voice of God who leads and directs our thoughts according to Scripture. That voice also comes in the form of hunches, songs, confirmations, wisdom, and sometimes even audible speech. God spoke to Moses from a burning bush, to Balaam through a donkey, and to Paul with a blinding light. He speaks to us today through the record of his Word, the teaching of his Son, and the witness of his Holy Spirit. Even "the heavens declare the glory of God" (Psalm 19:1), confirming to us that God is here. God speaks to us in many ways. Are we listening?

"Come, follow me," Christ says to the sinner (Matthew 4:19). "Go and make disciples," he says to his flock (Matthew 28:19). God hasn't retracted these radical statements. They still ring throughout the churches, the streets, and even to nature itself. Through the centuries, many have responded to these commands. Many continue to implore God to speak to them for guidance. Not every voice claiming to be God is God's. He will not contradict his Word, but he still speaks, directs, teaches, and leads. Testimonies of his glorious guidance resonate throughout the church. Ask God to speak to you today and quiet your spirit to hear his voice. What do you think he wants to tell you today? "Repent"? "Trust"? "Understand"? "Be still"? Or simply "I love you"?

PRAYER IDEA: Ask God to help you discern his voice from all the others.

A COUNTERFEIT DIAMOND
Eight Men Out (1988)
MPAA: PG
Read: Malachi 1:6–14

Love the Lord your God with all your heart and with all your soul and with all your mind and with all your strength. (Mark 12:30)

In 1919 the Chicago White Sox were the greatest ballplayers in the American League. With a lineup including Hap Felsch (Charlie Sheen), Buck Weaver (John Cusack), and "Shoeless" Joe Jackson (D. B. Sweeney), they were a seemingly unstoppable baseball team. Facing off against the Cincinnati Reds in the World Series, the Sox were considered the favorites to win. But many of the Sox were unhappy with their salaries. So eight men out of the lineup decided to let up on their play and "lose" the series for $10,000 apiece. When this scandal was exposed, the offending players ruined both their careers and the innocence of children who looked up to these heroes of the diamond.

Cheating disrespects and dishonors all involved. In this case it disrespected the owners (who then asked for a commissioner to enforce fair play), the fans (especially the impressionable young who counted on a good, clean battle), and the players themselves (who didn't give their best). Baseball is a great game with great tradition and great integrity. To purposefully "throw" the World Series is contemptible. Many of the players blamed the team owner for his stinginess, but this was no excuse for their dishonesty. Reason cannot excuse sin.

God wants us to give our all. He doesn't want us to hold anything back. He doesn't want burnt offerings or a half-hearted sacrifice. He wants us to give *all* of ourselves in whatever we do. God calls this commandment the most important one of all. When we give all of ourselves, God is impressed and others are too. Loving God all the way is an effective witness. When we hold back on giving our all, we not only cheat God but in addition we tell others that God really isn't worth it. We also settle for a reward that is much less than what God wants to give us. No amount of money is worth losing the glorious riches of grace, mercy, love, and eternal rewards that God intends to give to his "team."

PRAYER IDEA: Ask God to forgive you for settling for less than His best.

SHIP SHAPE
Adventure & Tragedy at Sea

WEEK 15

April 9–April 15

SAILOR, TAKE WARNING
The Perfect Storm (2000)
MPAA: PG-13 for mild language and scenes of peril
Read: Matthew 8:23–27

APRIL 9

**Put out into deep water, and let down the nets for a catch.
(Luke 5:4)**

Ignoring history, weather reports, current conditions, and reprimands from crew and fellow captains, Captain Billy Tyne (George Clooney) drives his boat farther and farther out to sea. His objective is the Flemish Cap, home of many a swordfish and ground zero for the perfect storm. Disappointed by his empty hold, the captain fools himself into thinking that he can catch a mess of fish and return safely, riding out the towering waves. When the waves rise even higher and a whopper upends his tiny craft, the captain finally realizes his fatal mistake.

At least twice Christ defied the raging sea, not caring what others said about the lethal waves about him. On one occasion, he slept soundly under deck. His shipmates said, "Don't you care if we drown?" (Mark 4:38). Jesus said, "You of little faith" and with a word calmed the sea (Matthew 8:26). Thus he demonstrated his divinity. On another occasion Jesus surfed the waves barefoot. Peter saw him and said, in effect, "Hey, Jesus, if that's you, ask me to come out and join you." Jesus didn't blink and replied, "Come on." The crew gasped, but Peter climbed out and started walking on water. When he saw the waves, he became afraid and began to sink. Jesus again said, "You of little faith, why did you doubt?" (Matthew 14:31).

On our own voyages in life, when we ignore the signs of storm, we act in foolishness and pride. We present an opportune time for God to administer personal humbling. But when we have Christ on board our voyages in life, we are on the safest spot on the planet, no matter what assails us. Jesus takes Bible smugglers safely into countries that ban his Word. Jesus protects weaklings who walk into gang territory. Jesus silences kings bent on his destruction. Woe to us who float our own boat for selfish gain. But when we get on board his ship to do some serious work for him by his calling, we can be sure he's with us on every wave crest and valley.

PRAYER IDEA: Ask God to be a crewmember on his boat.

Wisdom is better than weapons of war. (Ecclesiastes 9:18)

Traveling twenty thousand leagues under the sea, the brilliant but eccentric Captain Nemo (James Mason) operates a high-tech submarine during the late 1860s. It is the only one of its kind—a futuristic craft called the Nautilus, which Nemo built with his own hands. Under the South Seas, Nemo pilots the Nautilus into warships and cargo ships transporting nitrates and phosphates, the substance of explosives and weapons of war. When the Nautilus rams a ship bound for Asia, the only survivors come aboard: a naturalist, Professor Pierre Aronnax (Paul Lukas), his assistant Conseil (Peter Lorre), and a professional whaler, Ned Land (Kirk Douglas). While the professor tries to understand Nemo, Ned seeks to pillage the Nautilus of its booty and escape. Nemo continues to ram ships into oblivion, justifying his murder by saying he is avenging evil by stopping the shipping of destruction. When Nemo's base island of Volcania comes under attack, Nemo voluntarily destroys it and the Nautilus, determined that no warring people should ever understand his technological achievements.

Like most people, Nemo sees war and is disgusted by it. But Nemo misplaces his anger and uses the Nautilus as an instrument of death. Nemo demonstrates hypocrisy, condemning war while at the same time causing the deaths of the crews of war and cargo ships. Nemo justifies himself as a peacekeeper, but his methods result in his own destruction. Those who live by the sword die by the sword. His beliefs ultimately cause his own ruin.

The apostle Paul says, "The weapons we fight with are not the weapons of the world" (2 Corinthians 10:4) We don't use guns, swords, or ramming ships to kill evil, but we have divine power, demolishing arguments and pretentious threats from those who seek to bring ruin and evil into the world. Satan tried to kill Christ and keep him in the ground, but Christ didn't strike back with violence. He struck back by rising from the dead! That's Holy Spirit power, and it's stronger than any man-made weapon. Whether we face evil on a personal, family, community, or national level, it can be thwarted and overcome by the power of God. Pray to be delivered from evil. Speak truth when lies abound. Call on God's Holy Spirit and expect God to move. He is our ultimate weapon.

PRAYER IDEA: Thank God for giving you divine power to demolish strongholds.

It's Curses for You, Matey

Pirates of the Caribbean:
The Curse of the Black Pearl (2003)
MPAA: PG-13 for action/adventure violence
Read: Galatians 3:13, 14

Now you are under a curse. (Genesis 4:11)

Shiver me timbers! Captain Jack Sparrow (Johnny Depp), former helmsman of the notorious ship the *Black Pearl,* languishes in a prison somewhere in the Caribbean. Meanwhile, new captain Barbossa (Geoffrey Rush) and his salty crew attack a colonial English village, looking for the last piece of missing Aztec gold, now in the possession of the governor's daughter, Elizabeth (Keira Knightley). Previously, the crew of the *Black Pearl* stole Aztec gold and fell under its curse, becoming skeleton-like members of the living dead when the light of the moon falls upon them. If all the gold is recovered, the curse will lift and the crew will resume lives of flesh and blood. Barbossa kidnaps Elizabeth to take her to the chest of Aztec gold, but her boyfriend, Will Turner (Orlando Bloom), busts Jack Sparrow out of jail and together they chase the *Black Pearl.* Through swashbuckling, derring-do, and a little trickery, Elizabeth is rescued, Barbossa is thwarted, and Jack once again commands the ship he loves.

Curses aren't just fanciful myths found in gypsy, witch, and pirate stories. They actually exist, and we are all affected by a big one right now. When Adam and Eve fell through disobedience, God cursed the snake and the ground, making people toil for their food. When Cain killed Abel, God told Cain he was under a curse. A curse is a divine retribution upon a person or item for a sin or shortcoming. In the case of the pirates of the Caribbean, the curse of the *Black Pearl* is a living death. The pirates look like real men in the sunlight, but when the moon falls on them, they become like skeletons. They became dead men because they stole Aztec gold. But the curse will be removed when the violation is corrected. When the gold is brought back to its rightful place, the people will come alive.

Jesus corrected our sin by dying on the cross. He took upon himself the curse that fell upon the world. Anyone who hangs on a tree is under God's curse (Deuteronomy 21:23). Through his death, we can receive eternal life. Revelation tells us that one day "no longer will there be any curse" (Revelation 22:3). Oh, what a great day that will be! But in the meantime, let God lift the curse and penalty of your sin.

PRAYER IDEA: Thank God that one day there will no longer be any curse at all.

RISKING OTHERS
U-571 (2000)
AA: Best Sound Effects • MPAA: PG-13 for war violence
Read: Acts 5:27–42

For your sake, we face death all day long; we are considered as sheep to be slaughtered. (Romans 8:36)

Lieutenant Andrew Tyler (Matthew McConaughey) desperately wants to captain an American submarine during World War II. When a special mission arises, his superior, Lieutenant Commander Mike Dahlgren (Bill Paxton), chooses not to give him the appointment. Tyler complains about this decision and says, "I'd give my life for any one of my men."

Dahlgren replies, "What about their lives? Would you be willing to sacrifice their lives? Are you willing to lay their lives on the line? As a captain, you can't hesitate. If you do, you put the entire crew at risk. If you aren't prepared to make that decision without pause, then you have no business being a submarine captain."

The special operation goes awry and Dahlgren is killed. Now Tyler captains a German U-boat, U-571, and its encoded radio, the Enigma. When fired upon, he asks a sailor to make the ultimate sacrifice so the rest of the crew and the Enigma can be saved.

Being willing to give your life for another is admirable and difficult. But being willing to give lives under your command for the lives of other people is even more difficult. Yet that is what a boat captain or a foot soldier captain must be prepared to do. It is also what all Christians must be prepared to do. Jesus tells his disciples to go into *all* the world and spread the gospel. He doesn't say, "Go to only the safe places." Many areas of the world today have a Christian presence because brave missionaries dared to risk their lives for the cause of Christ.

The apostle Peter risked other lives by leading ministry in the temple courts. Peter and his fellow apostles were brought before the Sanhedrin for questioning. These men were flogged and released. In days and years to come, they would be constantly persecuted and put in harm's way for the sake of preaching Christ. Many of them would become martyrs. Being willing to die was part of their job requirement. Today, likewise, missionaries evangelize and serve God in places where the name of Christ is hated. If you are considering leading a mission team, count the cost. You might find the tally is high, but its reward is great, because if God is for you, then who can be against you?

PRAYER IDEA: Ask God to let you risk others and yourself for his sake.

HELP ME UP

The Poseidon Adventure (1972)

AA: Best Visual Effects; Best Song • MPAA: PG

Read: Proverbs 4:10–19

If one falls down, his friend can help him up.
But pity the man who falls and has no one to help him up!
(Ecclesiastes 4:10)

Before the movie *Titanic,* the greatest shipwreck movie was *The Poseidon Adventure.* At midnight on New Year's Eve, the Greece-bound *S.S. Poseidon* was struck by a ninety-foot tidal wave, turning it upside down. Casualties mount, but when the ship comes to rest, an officer encourages the survivors to wait for rescue. A disgruntled preacher named Reverend Scott (Gene Hackman) thinks otherwise and persuades a small party to join him on a climb toward the hull of the ship in hopes of meeting a rescue team there. As they journey, dangers like hot steam, fire, and rising waters take their toll on the frightened group. At their final roadblock, Reverend Scott makes the ultimate sacrifice so that others might live. At the hull, a rescue crew cuts through the inch-thick metal bottom and pulls out the remaining tired but grateful survivors.

When our lives turn upside down and it looks like we will not come out alive, friends can lead us to safety. Friends help us climb over the chaos, past gruesome casualties, through fire and raging waters, and up and out into the clear blue sky. Reverend Scott teaches us we have to accept blessings we are given. In the movie, those who choose to wait and remain in the ballroom are offered salvation but refuse it and die. The blessing of life is offered to the passengers, but they have to seize it through effort.

The Old Testament records that to gain the life God had planned for them, Israelites often had to battle the Philistines. Before these battles, the Israelites had to walk out of Egypt and across the hot, danger-filled Sinai desert. Life—spiritual and physical life—isn't necessarily gained by waiting around for salvation. God gives us the free gift of salvation but asks us to walk it out. That's where friends can encourage, lead, and guide us. On this walk, real fellowship, discipleship, testing, and refinement can occur.

Help others out of the dark, deadly waters. Lead others to the light. Be prepared to sacrifice and face dangers along the way. And, oh, what a journey you'll have!

PRAYER IDEA: Ask God to show you how to be a friend to those lives that have been turned upside down.

ANCHORS AWEIGH

Master and Commander:
The Far Side of the World (2003)
AA: Best Cinematography; Best Sound Editing
MPAA: PG-13 for intense battle sequences and mild language
Read: Psalm 119:85–88

APRIL 14

Christ is the head of the church, his body, of which he is the Savior. (Ephesians 5:23)

Captain Jack Aubrey (Russell Crowe) masterfully commands his crew of the battleship *Surprise* in 1805, during the Napoleonic wars. Sailing the waters off the coast of Brazil, they encounter the immense, well-armed French ship *Acheron*. The *Acheron* pummels the *Surprise,* and if it weren't for the fog, the *Surprise* would have never escaped to restore itself and fight another day. Fight again it does. The *Surprise* goes all the way around Cape Horn, chasing the *Acheron* to the waters around the Galapagos Islands. Just when they think they have lost the French ship, the ship's doctor spots it anchored on the other side of the island. Captain Jack commands his crew to disguise the *Surprise* as a whaling vessel and, inspired by Captain Jack's master plan, they fool the *Acheron* and take it.

Christ is our Master and Commander. He leads us, guides us, provides for us, studies our needs and meets them, assigns us a role in his kingdom, and encourages us to be all we can be. Christ is a perfect Captain, and we are his crew. Sometimes Christ leads us across heavy seas, and sometimes we ride upon glass. As we work with him, for him, and beside him, we take a journey of adventure and love. We also stand for truth, justice, and mercy against a foe that would seek to dominate us through tyranny.

No force or social group has ever been as world changing and powerful for truth, justice, and mercy as the Christian church led by our Captain, Jesus Christ. Every Christian who ever let the life of Christ live within him or her and took a stand for Christ is a crew member. We surprise our friends with joy and our enemies with a sure hand despite our weakness. We show mercy and treat all with love. We sing songs and work together. We belong on the side of right.

If you haven't found a church to join, ask your friends if you can join them at theirs. If you are already active in a church, ask others to join you. Seek your marching orders from the great Commander, Jesus Christ, and set sail for a new life of adventure, truth, and love.

PRAYER IDEA: Ask God to assign you a place on his mission.

PARADISE LOST
Titanic (1998)

AA: Best Picture; James Cameron, Best Director;
Best Cinematography; Best Editing; Best Art Direction;
Best Costume Design; Best Score; Best Song; Best Sound,
Best Sound Effects; Best Special Effects
MPAA: PG-13 for disaster-related peril and violence,
nudity, sensuality, and mild language
Read: 1 Thessalonians 4:16–18

A man's pride brings him low. (Proverbs 29:23)

The ship is beautiful. Filled with the finest furniture, fixtures, and food, it is a floating palace. Few hotels can match its opulence. Equaling the depth of its riches is the height of arrogance among its makers. One says, "God himself cannot sink the *Titanic*." Well, we all know what happens during the night of April 14, 1912. The sin, pride, and arrogance fade into dread and death when the floating paradise strikes an iceberg and sinks. God didn't author this tragedy; the sin and miscalculation of human beings did.

Adam and Eve lost paradise also. A beautiful place called Eden disappeared when the two decided they knew better than God. We, in turn, inherited their sin nature. Try as we might, we cannot overcome it with good works, and we cannot just ignore it. Our sin nature must be dealt with before God.

God could have left it there so that we'd all be sunk in the same boat. But he found a way to resurrect us by sinking and resurrecting his own Son. At the end of the movie *Titanic*, Rose (Kate Winslet) once again imagines the opulence of the *Titanic*. She imagines her beloved Jack (Leonardo Dicaprio) on the grand staircase, beckoning her home. We, too, will see our beloved Christ return, and the dead in Christ will rise to rule and reign with him forever in paradise, where sin and death are no more.

PRAYER IDEA: Ask God to forgive you of your pride and thank Jesus for rising again.

GO WEST
Movies That Define the Pioneer Spirit

WEEK 16

April 16–April 22

FINISHING THE JOB
The Magnificent Seven (1960)
MPAA: not rated
Read: 2 Timothy 4:6–8

Jesus said, "It is finished." (John 19:30)

Based on Japanese director Akira Kurosawa's *The Seven Samurai, The Magnificent Seven* demonstrates what seven gunmen can do in finishing a dirty job——ridding a Mexican town of bandits. Three Mexican townspeople go north of the border to find a solution. At first they seek to buy guns, but after they see Chris (Yul Brynner) disarm a group of thugs, they want to hire him. Chris interviews several characters to join him for the job. Though the pay is low, six other shooters join in and go south to run off the bandit Calvera (Eli Wallach) and his band of men. Just when the magnificent seven seem to have Calvera on the ropes, Calvera tricks them and runs them out of town. But Chris doesn't leave a job unfinished. He and his comrades return to the Mexican village and finish the job they started——with guns blazing from both sides.

Chris and his partners could have tucked tail and said, "Well, Calvera won. Guess we should go home." But for honor, pride, and the good of the people, they go to face the enemy again and battle on until the job was done. Christ could have buckled on several occasions in the face of evil, but he returned to the battleground to have guilt put upon him so that others might live. The job of forgiveness, reconciliation, and restoration of peace with God and humanity wasn't finished until Christ said it was.

Until the day you die, there is no retiring from Christianity. There is no hanging up your gun belt when it comes to your relationship with Christ and your service to him. It's an ongoing process. Though there are times when you have to strategically retreat for refueling or supplies, your job is to always live in Christ, letting Christ use you for his glory in the battlefields of this earth. Christ is mighty to save. When you let his power manifest itself in your life, you will live victoriously, even if you get shot up. If God has started a work in you, see it through to completion. Get back in the arena and enjoy the triumph of God in your life as you serve him by serving others.

PRAYER IDEA: Ask God to fill you with his strength so that you may persevere in the arena of life.

ABANDONMENT AND ACCEPTANCE

Dances with Wolves (1990)

AFI: 75 • AA: Best Picture; Kevin Costner, Best Director;
Best Adapted Screenplay; Best Cinematography;
Best Film Editing; Best Score; Best Sound • MPAA: PG-13
Read: Psalm 68:6

A P R I L

1 7

Accept one another. (Romans 15:7)

The suicidal Lt. John Dunbar (Kevin Costner) requests a post on the western frontier after he accidentally leads Union troops to a victory during the Civil War. He reaches the post by prospector wagon, finds the fort deserted, and decides to stay. Little does Dunbar know that relief is not coming. Indians kill the prospector, and Dunbar's commissioning officer commits suicide. Thus nobody knows that Dunbar is out there alone. In time Dunbar befriends a curious wolf. Then he befriends a local Sioux Indian tribe and they rename him "Dances with Wolves." Dunbar/Dances with Wolves falls in love with a Sioux-raised white woman named "Stands with a Fist." They marry, and Dunbar is accepted into the tribe. He sheds his white man's ways—a changed man with a new name. Later Dunbar visits his old post. On arrival he meets many despicable people. They aren't an opposing tribe but members of the U.S. Army. Ridiculed, beaten, and even condemned to death by those he formerly served, Dunbar now represents a traitorous threat.

Like Dunbar, lots of us want a life of adventure on the range but instead feel abandoned in the wilderness. Lots of us feel lonely at our post, unsure of what our next move should be. We might have had celebrated moments in our earlier years, but now our only friend is our dog. Those we ran with before don't care if we are alive or dead. When we are in this low state, God is able to come in and love us and give us a family. He longs to change our name from Lonely, Outcast, and Afraid to Loved, Accepted, and Secure.

Many Christians who dabble in their former pursuits discover that they are no longer accepted. Former partners in sin and crime don't want to be with people who are different from them. So it's very important that we keep on loving, supporting, and accepting new Christians. Evangelism to the lost begins with love and acceptance. And becoming more like Christ (a process called discipleship) continues through love and acceptance. We are transformed into Christlikeness by love. Those who know deep love and acceptance in Christ will discover that their old life is a stark contrast to their new one.

PRAYER IDEA: Ask God to show you how to love the abandoned and lost.

THE VALLEY OF DEATH

Stagecoach (1939)

AFI: 63 • AA: Thomas Mitchell, Best Actor; Best Score

MPAA: not rated

Read: Isaiah 40:1–5

Even though I walk through the valley of the shadow of death, I will fear no evil, for you are with me. (Psalm 23:4)

In the star-making movie for John Wayne, the outlaw Ringo Kid (Wayne) joins the marshal, the driver, a drunk, a whiskey runner, a gambler, a prostitute, and a refined pregnant woman traveling through Apache territory on a stagecoach. The going's fine for a while, especially when the small transport receives a cavalry escort. But the deeper they go into Monument Valley, the less protection they have. Hot, dirty, thirsty, and crowded, the travelers come under attack by Geronimo and his warring band. The Kid makes good use of a rifle while the other men shoot it out. But just when things seem bleak, the cavalry rides in with swords raised and bugles blaring. Geronimo gets a licking and the stagecoach arrives a little bruised and broken but safe. The Ringo Kid guns down a worse criminal than he and makes an honest woman out of Dallas (Claire Trevor), the prostitute traveler.

Traveling alone through dangerous territory——it's a mythic theme in literature and film. Just where does the anguish come from in this scenario? Journeying isn't so bad. Dangerous territory isn't really insurmountable either. If it were, travelers wouldn't venture into it. The real risk lies in doing it alone. Vulnerability to a force greater and fiercer than yourself is the actual danger.

The Ringo Kid and his fellow passengers find relief in the cavalry, who rally together and fight back the Indian threat. Each of us will enter into what seems to be a lonesome valley, the valley of death, but God promises to be our traveling companion. He will be right there with us. But God has another weapon in his holster——he levels the playing field. In Isaiah 40:4 God says,

Every valley shall be raised up, every mountain and hill made low.

When everything is flat, the glory of the Lord will be revealed. The power, majesty, splendor, and greatness of God is revealed out in the open. And that's a great place to be. Ride out to the valleys, watch God raise them up, and see his glory ride to your aid!

PRAYER IDEA: Thank God for riding with you in the dark and rugged places.

GOD RODE IN
Shane (1953)
AFI: 69 • AA: Best Cinematography • MPAA: not rated
Read: John 12:12–16

See, your king comes to you, righteous and having salvation, gentle and riding on a donkey, on a colt. (Zechariah 9:9)

A cowboy ain't complete without a horse. On a horse, the cowboy rides into town, shoots the man in the black hat, and then rides off into the sunset. Shane (Alan Ladd) is a mysterious ex-gunslinging stranger who rides into a valley, where he discovers a bitter feud going on between homesteaders and ranchers. The ranchers eventually hire a gunman to impose their will on the settlers. But Shane straps on his six-shooters and rides into town to settle the matter with a gunfight against the evil hired gun, Jack Wilson (Jack Palance).

C ountry singer Johnny Cash called Jesus Christ "the greatest cowboy of them all." On Palm Sunday, Jesus rode into town, not on a black stallion or golden palomino, but on a donkey, a beast of burden. His power wasn't displayed with a flashy gunfight but by getting back up after taking a deadly punch. Jesus demonstrated his authority and divinity by rising from the dead. In that way he shot down the enemy ultimately, defeating him. His sentence will come at the end of time.

When the man in the black hat (Satan) steals your joy or tries to run you off your rightful inheritance, call in Christ. We have a Man in White to fight our battles. His name is Jesus Christ. Did the little shepherd boy David have the natural strength to kill the Philistine Goliath? No, but God arrived and fought through David and won. Did the Israelites stand a chance against the Egyptians, who charged behind them on horseback? No, but God opened up the Red Sea and created a safe passage for the Israelites. This same passage created a trap for their enemy. The waters closed down on the Egyptians, and the Israelites escaped. When the evil one comes with threats and weapons, take courage. The battle belongs to the Lord.

PRAYER IDEA: Believe in God to fight your battles when the enemy threatens.

Those who seek me find me. (Proverbs 8:17)

In *The Searchers* plays Ethan (John Wayne) an emotionally complex Civil War vet in search of himself and his kidnapped niece, Debbie (Natalie Wood). After the war, Ethan returns to his brother's home and delights in a family reunion. For a moment life is good. But joy turns to sorrow when Comanche Indians attack while Ethan is away on business. They kill everyone in Ethan's family and steal little Debbie away. Determined to find her, Ethan and his adopted nephew, Marty (Jeffrey Hunter), mount horses and search Texas and the West to find her. Despite more Comanche attacks, thieves, and would-be murderers, they finally find Debbie and in the process mature as men.

Just as Ethan pursued Debbie, so God pursues us. He follows us wherever we go. He longs to take us back home to the safety of his care. He'll go through storms, high water, and dangerous territory just to hear us say we recognize and love him. He searches our hearts to see if we have faith. He tries to get our attention through circumstances, his Word, and other people. Even when we are disobedient and seemingly far from God, he is really never more than a prayer away. "He rewards those who earnestly seek him" (Hebrews 11:6).

God is the hound of heaven, a dog relentlessly searching until it finds what it is looking for. One of the most beautiful parables of the Bible is about a shepherd looking for a lost sheep. When the sheep wanders off, the shepherd leaves the flock to find it. When he finds the lost sheep, he is happier over it than he is over all the ones that remain. If someone tells you that he or she doesn't believe in God, you can reply, "Well, He believes in you." God continually pursues us with his love.

PRAYER IDEA: Thank God for his continually pursuing love.

NEVER FORSAKEN

High Noon (1952)

AFI: 33 • AA: Gary Cooper, Best Actor; Best Film Editing;
Best Score; Best Song • MPAA: not rated

Read: John 6:60–71

Never will I leave you; never will I forsake you. (Hebrews 13:5)

As three outlaws assemble at the train station of a small western town, Tex Ritter sings,

Do not forsake me, oh my darling, on this our wedding day.

In town, retiring lawman Marshal Will Kane (Gary Cooper) weds pacifist Amy (Grace Kelly) and plans to leave town for good. At high noon Frank Miller (Ian MacDonald) will be arriving on the train and joining his three friends to go into town and shoot Will Kane dead. Will decides to stays and face Frank Miller, whatever the consequences. Will tries to recruit deputies from the streets, bar, and church, but the fearful townspeople turn their back on their former marshal. Even Amy tells Will that she won't stick around to see him die. As high noon arrives, the train rolls into town. Off steps Frank Miller and on steps Amy. Hearing shots, though, she steps off to join Will. Will shoots down two of the criminals but is trapped by the third. As he is facing certain death, Amy raises a firearm and comes to her husband's aid in the fight. Amy and Will survive because she did not forsake him.

In Will's greatest time of need, only Amy stood beside him. He asked many men to join him, but nobody who could do the job agreed. When the pressure mounted, the bravest men tucked and ran. Jesus faced deserters too. Jesus gave some difficult teaching, saying, "The bread is my flesh," and this freaked out many of his disciples. They no longer followed him. Jesus turned to those closest to him and asked, "You do not want to leave too, do you?" Simon Peter (who would later deny him to but also go on to lead the church) answered, "Lord, to whom shall we go? You have the words of eternal life" (John 6:67, 68).

What compels you to stay with Christ? Why do you follow him? You might have grown up in the church. Do you follow Christ because your parents did? Have you discovered deep down in your soul and understood for yourself that Christ alone has the words of eternal life? There are many other options out there. Christianity isn't necessarily the most glamorous lifestyle. But it is the only true one. Christ is the only one who can rid this town and all towns of the evil ones. Christ is our Marshal, our only Savior, and he deserves to not be forsaken.

PRAYER IDEA: Declare to Christ that you'll follow Him because he alone has life.

Pleasant words are a honeycomb, sweet to the soul and healing to the bones. (Proverbs 16:24)

Grace MacLean (Scarlett Johansson) and her horse Pilgrim experience deep pain. On a winter horseback ride Grace's friend Judith is struck by a truck and killed, while Grace and her horse Pilgrim are seriously injured, both physically and emotionally. In an attempt to bring Pilgrim back from his monstrous condition, Grace's mother, Annie (Kristin Scott Thomas), takes them to Montana in search of Tom Booker (Robert Redford). Tom is a "horse whisperer," a cowboy with the ability to communicate with horses. Tom uses patience, kind words, trust, and incremental exercises to bring Grace and Pilgrim out of hurt and despair and into wholeness and healing.

This beautiful movie is filled with examples of God's grace. How appropriate that the lead character would be named Grace and the horse, an animal of transportation, would be named Pilgrim. We all travel on a pilgrim's progress toward God and his wonderful grace. God often speaks to us in a still, small voice. Never rude, he whispers in our ear, "Come, follow me." Even his rebukes and corrections are filled with love.

All of us are damaged goods in need of tender treatment. As the story of the horse whisperer progresses, the audience discovers that Annie needs love and gentle words as much as her horse does. Tom provides these important needs. Then her husband, Robert (Sam Neill) shows her love. She returns home a changed woman, wiser and with a calm spirit. When we are full of wrath at the damage of sin in our lives, God's gentle answer calms our spirits. Even the wind and the waves obey him, and he doesn't need to shout. He stills the storm with a whisper (Psalm 107:29). Let us offer quiet, gentle words to those who are in pain. Then let the healing begin.

PRAYER IDEA: Ask God for the opportunity to present quiet and gentle words to someone in pain.

BEAUTIFUL MUSIC
Musicals That
Make You Sing

WEEK 17

April 23–April 30

. . . the unfading beauty of a gentle and quiet spirit. (1 Peter 3:4)

Do you put mousse or gel into your hair to make you look better? How about grease? In the movie *Grease*, a tribute to the 1950s, Danny Zuko (John Travolta) puts a ton of the goop on his hair to look as cool as he can. He can't run, play football, or wrestle, but he sure can wear a slick pompadour and sport a shiny black jacket. Summer was great with his demure sweetheart, Sandy (Olivia Newton-John), but back at Rydell High School his glam and standoffish ways repel her. She receives further scorn when the leader of the Pink Ladies, Rizzo (Stockard Channing), says Sandy is "too pure to be Pink." When Sandy realizes that Danny does everything he can to win her over, she makes herself into a frizzy-haired, leather-panted cool chick.

It's okay to look our best, but today's image-crazy society often demands that we spend and do more to our appearance to get ahead and be sexually attractive. The plastic surgery business is growing by leaps and bounds. Cosmetics, beauty salons, tanning booths, gyms, and clothing retailers all profit from our need to look cool.

Looking cool may get you ahead in this world, but remember where true beauty lies. It is on the inside. "Man looks at the outward appearance, but the LORD looks at the heart" (1 Samuel 16:7). All the clothes and plastic surgery and makeovers cannot change one's inner character, and when that is destroyed, all that is left is a pretty face on an empty shell. Next time you grease your hair, remember to grease your soul and character too.

PRAYER IDEA: Ask God to help you remember that your true beauty is on the inside.

LONGING FOR HOME
The Wizard of Oz (1939)
AFI: 6 • AA: Judy Garland, special award for screen juvenile;
Best Score; Best Song • MPAA: G
Read: John 14:1–4

You know the way to the place where I am going. (John 14:4)

Who doesn't know the words to this enchanting song?

Somewhere over the rainbow, way up high,
there's a land that I dreamed of once in a lullaby.

Dorothy (Judy Garland) sings this song and longs for a place of her dreams, a fantastic place to call home. Conked out during a tornado, she finds herself trapped in Oz, a strange land with a talking scarecrow (Ray Bolger), tin man (Jack Haley), and lion (Bert Lahr), along with munchkins, flying monkeys, and wicked witches. Dorothy follows a yellow brick road in search of a wizard (Frank Morgan) whom she hopes can help her get back to Kansas and the home she loves. But in the end she learns that with her magical ruby slippers she could have gotten home all along.

It is not unusual for a Christian to be restless in this world. Jesus says we are not of it (John 15:19). Over thousands of years of sin's effects, the world today is quite different from the one God made. Tired of ugliness, disease, sin, and death, we often sigh and wish for God to make things right. The witches of our own Oz make life difficult. We want an almighty God to wave a wand and take us to his home.

Well, take heart. There is good news. First, God says that, though there is going to be trouble in the world, he has overcome it (John 16:33). Second, he says that "the one who is in you [the Holy Spirit] is greater than the one who is in the world [Satan]" (1 John 4:4). God tells us these things so that we can have peace. Jesus is also preparing a home for us in heaven, a place to call our own (John 14:1–4). God wants to give us peace right now—and eternal peace too! And we don't need ruby slippers to get it.

PRAYER IDEA: Thank God for His peace and for preparing a place for you in Heaven.

"LAUGHING AT CLOUDS"
Singin' in the Rain (1952)
AFI: 10 • MPAA: G
Read: James 1:2–8

He will rejoice over you with singing. (Zephaniah 3:17)

The *Saturday Review* says that *Singin' in the Rain* has "just about everything you could ask of a musical." These include laughs, charm, romance, history, fourteen hit songs, and those dance numbers ranging from the hilarious to the fantastical to the famous puddle-sloshing, umbrella-toting title number indelibly recorded by Gene Kelly. The time period is the late 1920s. Sound has just entered the motion picture industry. Screen hero Don Lockwood (Kelly) is ready to make his big break into "talkies." The problem is that his leading lady, Lina Lamont (Jean Hagen), talks with a whine, squeak and a squawk. Troubles mount when his longtime fan, the talented Kathy Selden (Debbie Reynolds), enters the scene. Careers are threatened as Kathy steals Don's affections, prompting jealousy from Lina. But despite it all, Don keeps a dance in his step and a song in his heart.

Life doesn't always work out like it does in the movies, but nobody can steal our joy. In the Psalms, David often spoke of rejoicing in God, even when he was discouraged and beset by enemies. The apostle Paul asked us to "rejoice in the Lord always" (Philippians 4:4). In fact, he went on to say that, when we rejoice, the peace of God will guard our hearts (verse 7). Don Lockwood could have given in to discouragement, but instead he sang in the rain. He rejoiced even in the midst of trouble.

When we develop an attitude of gratitude and give thanks in all things, we can learn the secret to contentment. Though clouds may come, rains fall and waters flood, our marching orders are to "count it pure joy" (James 1:2).

PRAYER IDEA: Sing a song of praise to your Heavenly Father when the tornado hits.

SOOTHING THE SAVAGE CAPTAIN
The Sound of Music (1965)
AFI: 55 • AA: Best Picture; Robert Wise, Best Director;
Best Editing; Best Score; Best Sound • MPAA: G
Read: Psalm 150

APRIL 26

**They ministered with music before the tabernacle.
(1 Chronicles 6:32)**

Perhaps no musical is more beloved than *The Sound of Music*. In addition to its brilliant cast, spectacular Alpine locations, and gripping story, it has those wonderful songs, including "Do, Re, Mi," "A Few of My Favorite Things," and "Edelweiss." These songs not only win the audience over but they also win over the heart of the stern, retired naval captain, Georg von Trapp (Christopher Plummer). Maria (Julie Andrews) leaves her convent to care for the widowed captain's seven children. She finds their quiet, regimented household stifling and soon teaches the children music while romping through the hills. Despite the captain's protests, he soon warms to their music and his hard heart is melted. In time he not only joins his children in public performances but also marries Maria before fleeing the Nazis.

An old saying claims that "music soothes the savage beast." God knew what he was doing when he invented music. The Bible is filled with references to making music for our betterment. In 1 Samuel 16 we read how David was charged by King Saul to play the harp. The king figured that God would come through the music and not only lift his spirits but also rid him of evil spirits. Later, when David was king of Israel, he appointed ministers of music with specific duties and regulations.

Perhaps you think that you are all thumbs on an instrument or that your voice has all the beauty of a water buffalo's bellow. No matter. God asks you to sing and shout and make music unto him (Psalm 150). He doesn't care if you are out of tune. Lots of music dishonors God, but God wants to be blessed, and to bless us, with song. So belt out a tune of praise to God. When you do, your heart can be cheered, and that "is good medicine" (Proverbs 17:22).

PRAYER IDEA: Say to God, "Let the music I sing and listen to give you glory. Amen."

OUR INTERCESSOR
Chicago (2002)
AA: Best Picture; Catherine Zeta-Jones, Best Supporting Actress;
Best Art Direction; Best Costume Design; Best Editing; Best Sound
MPAA: PG-13 for sexual content and dialogue,
violence, and thematic elements
Read: Romans 8:33, 34

APRIL 27

He is able to save completely those who come to God through him, because he always lives to intercede for them. (Hebrews 7:25)

In *Chicago*, jazz singer Roxie Hart (Renee Zellwegger) gets away with murder. She shot and killed a lover who promised her an audition with a stage show manager. Her lover lied. He really wanted to get her into bed. So capping him a few times with a pistol, she figured he had it coming. Through questioning, she confesses to the crime and is hauled off to a women's correctional facility. Another jazz singer, Velma Kelly (Catherine Zeta-Jones), is also in prison. Roxie and Velma hire trial lawyer Billy Flynn (Richard Gere), a man who has never lost a case, to defend them. Velma's and Roxie's cases come to trial and both are found innocent thanks to lots of lies and compelling performances by Flynn, who intercedes on the behalf of his clients.

Like Roxie and Velma, we have gotten away with murder. Our sin, and the sin of all humankind, killed Jesus. When we sinned, God said a punishment must be issued. But instead of convicting us to death and eternal separation for him, he passed his conviction down to his only Son, Jesus Christ. Jesus took the punishment for our sins. He died so that we don't have to. Sure, we probably haven't literally murdered anybody, but any sin is worthy of condemnation and punishment by God. After all, Adam and Eve got kicked out of Eden for the seemingly small disobedience of eating a piece of fruit.

Thank God for grace. Thank God for Jesus, who comes to our defense. But unlike Billy Flynn, Jesus doesn't mince words about our sin. He doesn't whitewash who we really are. He just tells the Father that the punishment has already been completed. There is no condemnation for those who are in Christ Jesus (Romans 8:1, 2). God is the final judge on right and wrong. Thank God that Jesus took a bullet for our sins. He is the greatest defense attorney ever, and everybody who accepts his plan gets off free.

PRAYER IDEA: Thank Jesus for making a way so that you don't have to pay the penalty for your sins.

CRY FOR HER LEADERSHIP

Evita (1997)

MPAA: PG for thematic elements, images of
violence, and some mild language

Read: Hebrews 10:1–7

**If [one's gift] is leadership, let him govern diligently.
(Romans 12:8)**

From playwright Andrew Lloyd Webber comes this movie musical, reviving the genre for a new generation. An illegitimate daughter from Argentina dreams of a better life. As a teenager, Evita (Madonna) boards a train bound for Buenos Aires. Making herself available to men, she quickly finds work on stage, screen, and the pages of magazines. In 1943 a military coup occurs in Argentina with Colonel Juan Perón (Jonathan Pryce) in close succession for the presidency. In 1944 Perón meets Evita and they marry. Juan steps in as "the people's dictator" and lets Eva charm the hurting commoners. Driven by self-aggrandizement, Eva dresses to the nines and wows international heads of state on a world tour. To her own people, she offers tokens of money toward fixing problems instead of providing real solutions. Just when her star begins to dim and her vanity is exposed, Evita wins back the sympathy of her fellow citizens when she reveals the truth about her health. She is dying of cancer. At her state funeral, thousands mourn a figure that brought beauty but little change.

Though loved and respected as a "spiritual" leader of her country, Evita ultimately represents a tragic figure of power. A true leader is a servant. Evita thought her glamorous appearance would bring some joy to poor Argentines. While providing fodder for the gossip and fashion pages, it didn't serve the people's needs. People whispered, "Why does she go around in such fancy clothes while I have holes in mine?" Evita told the press that her charitable foundation would justify her selfish actions, but her money never fixed any long-term problems. Her gifts helped people for a few days or weeks, but unemployment rose. Her leadership epitomized flash but no substance.

More than ever, today's volatile international climate demands quality leaders. Hebrews 10 lists the stuff of good leaders. They speak the word of God (truth), they are faithful, they are not carried away by strange teachings, they are sacrificial, they do good, they share with others, and they keep watch over their charges. True leaders are accountable to their country, to their staff, and to God. Christ exemplified the ultimate in leadership by not only teaching truth and meeting the needs of others but also giving his all—his very life. A true leader works hard to make sure that people around him will succeed not only in the short term but also eternally.

PRAYER IDEA: Ask God, "Let your leadership be evident in my life for those who work under me."

135

╔══╗

BOILED BLOOD
West Side Story (1961)
AFI: 41 • AA: Best Picture; Jerome Robbins and
Robert Wise, Best Director; George Chakiris, Best Supporting Actor;
Rita Moreno, Best Supporting Actress; Best Cinematography;
Best Art Direction; Best Film Editing; Best Costume Design;
Leonard Bernstein, Best Score; Best Sound • MPAA: not rated

Read: Ezekiel 35:1–6

A P R I L 2 9
╚══╝

Away from me, you bloodthirsty men. (Psalm 139:19)

The tragic tale of Romeo and Julie is retold in *West Side Story*. In New York City a gang of white thugs called the Jets hate a Puerto Rican gang called the Sharks, and vice versa. One young man, Tony (Richard Beymer), recognizes the madness and wants to get out. A former leader of the Jets, he doesn't see skin color or ethnicity as a reason to fight. In fact, he falls in love with Maria (Natalie Wood), the sister of the Sharks leader Bernardo (George Chakiris). A fight commences. The two-person match becomes a rumble when Tony steps in to call it off. Tempers flair, limbs flail, and in the mayhem Tony accidentally stabs Bernardo to death. Second in charge of the Sharks, Chino (Jose de Vega) vows revenge, and with gun in hand, he searches for Tony. Tony hears a false story that Maria has been killed, and he calls for Chino to kill him. Chino find Tony and pulls the trigger. Maria shows up while her beloved lies dying in a pool of blood.

It's true: "Bloodthirsty men hate a man of integrity" (Proverbs 29:10). In fact, they seek to kill the upright. The Sharks and Jets never mean to kill each other, but with long-harbored hate simmering just beneath the surface, no controls for murderous acts are put into place. Holding on to hate and hostility creates fertile ground for the spirit of death and destruction to work its evil ways. Tony and Maria call for a truce, but their brothers, sisters, and friends won't have it. The desire to hurt the other group is too strong. Bloodlust leads to bloodshed, and innocent lives are destroyed.

It's true: "Those who sow trouble reap it" (Job 4:8). Likewise, those who sow to please the Spirit reap eternal life (Galatians 6:8). Unfortunately, Tony also gets in the way of trouble when it is at its breaking point, and though his heart is good, he pays a price for the wickedness of those around him. Put aside your anger. Forgive those who seek to do you harm. Create an environment where everyone can live in peace. These things please God, according to the scriptures:

> When a man's ways are pleasing to the LORD, he makes even his enemies live
> at peace with him. (Proverbs 16:7)

PRAYER IDEA: Ask God to show you how to sow in peace in the midst of trouble.

I GET AROUND

Movies about Getting from Here to There

WEEK 18

April 30–May 6

JOINING CHRIST FOR THE JOURNEY
Around the World in Eighty Days (1956)
AA: Best Picture; Best Adapted Screenplay;
Best Cinematography; Best Film Editing; Best Score • MPAA: G
Read: Matthew 4:18–22

APRIL 30

I hope to visit you while passing through and to have you assist me on my journey there. (Romans 15:24)

Few people have ever had a first day of work quite like the Spaniard Passepartout (Cantinflas). English nobleman Phileas Fogg (David Niven) wagers at his gentlemen's club that that he can travel around the world in eighty days. Wasting no time, Fogg hires Passepartout as a butler, and the two immediately depart. First, they travel to Paris. Then they inadvertently balloon to Spain. There Passepartout fights a bull, which earns them a boat ride east. In the deep jungles of India the butler rescues Princess Aouda (Shirley MacLaine) from a fiery death. Then the three travel together on elephant back, then by Chinese junk, then by steam liner, and then by a train across America. Arriving in England just in time, Fogg wins his bet, but because of Passepartout's faithful obedience, Fogg wins something far greater than money: a bride!

When he was hired, Passepartout didn't expect to follow Fogg around the world, but he did so willingly and dutifully. Passepartout didn't complain but made the best of every situation. He obeyed without hesitation. It is not right to ask God to join us on our journey. We must follow Christ on *his* journey. Christ's journey is to go about the globe and look for a bride. Will we help him find a bride? Will we risk danger in foreign lands and rescue others to bring them to the feet of Christ?

When Jesus called his disciples, he said, "Come, follow me." At once they left what they were doing and followed him (Matthew 4:19, 20). They would never return to the same old routines again. First, they followed Jesus around Judea. Then they dispersed into the world and found the bride of Christ, through witnessing and discipleship. Following Christ isn't easy, but it should never be boring. It's a trip of faith, danger, and great reward. Fogg has deep pockets for his journey, and God has endless resources too. We should never be afraid of being uncared for or neglected. God is the master tour guide.

PRAYER IDEA: Ask God to take you around the world on a journey in search of his bride.

LIFE IS A HIGHWAY

The Incredible Journey (1963)

MPAA: G

Read: Deuteronomy 1:32–36

Go in peace. Your journey has the Lord's approval. (Judges 18:6)

A bull terrier named Bodger, a Siamese cat named Tao, and a Labrador retriever named Luath embark on an incredible journey. These three family pets travel two hundred miles through the Canadian wilderness to get back to the home they love. Thinking that their caretaker abandons them, the three animal friends cross fields and streams. They endure hunger, near drowning, and peril by a gunman, a bear, and a lynx. Bodger is the oldest and he has to rest frequently, but the others stop and wait for him. Their family cannot believe that they could travel such a distance, but just when they give up all hope, the three animals arrive at their beloved home.

It is almost too easy to compare the Christian life to a journey. Christian classics like *Pilgrim's Progress* and *Hind's Feet on High Places* have confirmed the analogy for many contemporary Christians. Throughout history, our literary heroes have embarked on a journey.

Let's take a closer look at what a journey entails. There is a starting point and a destination. There is a map to our route. There is preparation and gathering of the supplies we will need. There is an assessment of the dangers and of the benefits. Then there are the first steps, the middle steps, and the last steps.

Our faith *is* a journey. But the Christian walk lasts for eternity. We start by accepting Christ, but there is no final destination. Heaven isn't our last stop. It's merely a stepping stone to an eternal relationship with our God. We pray, "On earth as it is in heaven." And so, our quest starts with a desire to see heaven in our lives more every day. It's a journey of eternal glory that can start now. Best of all, we are not alone. Christ walks with us as we walk for him and in him.

PRAYER IDEA: Thank Jesus for taking you on a journey from glory to glory.

COME HOME
Trip to Bountiful (1985)
AA: Geraldine Page, Best Actress • MPAA: PG
Read: Hebrews 11:13–16

Return home, my daughters. (Ruth 1:11)

All that the aged Carrie Watts (Geraldine Page) wants to do is go home. But she's trapped in an apartment in 1940s Houston, Texas, with a controlling daughter-in-law, Jessie Mae (Carlin Glynn), and a henpecked son, Ludie (John Heard). Her fondest wish—just once before she dies—is to revisit Bountiful, the small Texas town of her youth. Ludie is too concerned for her health to allow her to travel alone, and Jessie Mae insists they don't have money to squander on bus tickets. Mama Watts finally escapes on a bus to a town near Bountiful. Then the town sheriff takes her the rest of the way to where she sees her childhood home and is swept away by memories. Though her home is now rundown and abandoned, nothing can take away her joy, not even Ludie and Jessie Mae, who have arrived to take her back to Houston.

When we crave a home, we are really craving God's eternal security and love. Heaven is our eternal home, and we will live there far longer than in any earthly home. The Bible says that our life here on earth is fleeting (Psalm 144:4). Our bodies waste away in our home of flesh, which is a mere tent (2 Corinthians 4:16). But our heavenly home is a mansion (John 14:2).

It has been said that, if you aim for earth, you get neither heaven nor earth. But if you aim for heaven, you get both. People will try to convince you that thoughts of heaven are of no earthly good. People will try to tell you that your desires for heaven are unnecessary or even wasteful. Don't believe them. You were designed for a wonderful eternal home. You were designed for lasting fellowship with God in a mansion in an everlasting city. Crave to be with Christ in your heavenly home and encourage others to also crave a heavenly home. Our heavenly home is filled with love and fellowship.

PRAYER IDEA: Thank your Heavenly Father for making a home for you in heaven.

ARE YOU IN HIM?

Fantastic Voyage (1966)
AA: Best Art Direction; Best Visual Effects
MPAA: PG for mild violence and language
Read: Ephesians 4:1–6

In him we live and move and have our being. (Acts 17:28)

Some voyages travel across outer space. Others require travel in inner space. *Fantastic Voyage* takes five travelers inside the body of an injured diplomat (Jean del Val). Aboard the submarine Proteus, Grant (Stephen Boyd), Cora (Raquel Welch), and the others are shrunken to microbe size and injected into the bloodstream. They begin their voyage to repair the injury, when it becomes clear that there is a saboteur on board. Now they must repair the injury and stop the saboteur before time runs out.

The term Christian literally means "of Christ" A Christian lives in Christ and for Christ, doing his or her all for Christ's benefit and glory. It is in his strength, his wisdom, and his power that we live. Furthermore, we are his body, performing different functions for God's kingdom, just as our different tissue systems perform their unique services to make our own physical body function properly. Some are called to preach, others to teach, others to serve, and so on. When Christ was offering his body and blood for us during the Last Supper, he rooted out a saboteur named Judas.

As we live in Christ, let us be mindful of our own thoughts and actions so that they do not run contrary to Christ's will. Let us not inadvertently become saboteurs to his body. Temptations may come to sell our allegiance to Christ for a sum of money, but let us stand firm. The body of Christ is God's bride, and she is the testimony of his glory. The church is to be protected, preserved, and made strong by our diligence and mindfulness to its health. When we live for God's purposes, ours is a fantastic voyage.

PRAYER IDEA: Ask God to never let you be a saboteur to his purposes.

THE FALLACY OF FATE
Detour (1945)
MPAA: not rated
Read: Matthew 10:26–31

In all things God works for the good of those who love him, who have been called according to his purpose. (Romans 8:28)

New York City lounge pianist Al Roberts (Tom Neal) thumbs his way to Los Angeles to meet up with his nightclub-singer girlfriend, Sue (Claudia Drake). Near Phoenix, Roberts is picked up by gambler Charles Haskell, Jr. (Edmund MacDonald). Unexpectedly, Haskell dies. Roberts panics. He knows the cops will never believe that he did not kill Haskell. So Roberts hides Haskell's body, steals his car and money, and assumes Haskell's identity. Just over the California line, Roberts picks up a hitchhiker named Vera (Ann Savage), a venomous-tongued vixen who knows that Roberts isn't Haskell. Vera forces Roberts to continue in his pose as Haskell so that she can collect from Haskell's millionaire father. All plans come to a halt when Roberts accidentally strangles Vera with a telephone cord. Stunned at his bad luck, Roberts thumbs his way back east, merely waiting for the moment when he will be picked up by the police for double homicide.

Roberts narrates to the audience, "Fate can put the finger on you for no good reason at all." But is there such a thing as fate? Did the powers-that-be or God have it out for Roberts? Scripture tells us that all of the hairs of our head are numbered by God and that not a sparrow falls without God's knowing it (Matthew 10:29, 30). If we are Christians, we are not to fear the future, even when calamity comes our way. God knows what's going on.

If there is no such thing as bad luck and happenstance for the Christian, then there is nothing to fear. "Do not be afraid of those who kill the body but cannot kill the soul" (Matthew 10:28). Even Job was blessed beyond measure after losing his house and family in what looked like a random, freak accident. God made you, and he can do what he wants with you. But he also loves you and refines you and lets trials come your way. If God takes you on a detour in life, go along for the ride. There's nothing to fear.

PRAYER IDEA: Tell God, "Your watchful eye is always on me. I trust in you."

THREE WAYS TO REWARDS

Chitty-Chitty Bang Bang (1968)

MPAA: G

Read: Philippians 3:8–11

Be strong and do not give up, for your work will be rewarded. (2 Chronicles 15:7)

English children Jemima (Heather Ripley) and Jeremy (Adrian Hall) love an old, beat-up racecar. When a scrap-metal worker vows to take it away, the children rush to their inventor father, Caractacus Potts (Dick Van Dyke), and ask him to buy the car. Embarrassed because he is poor, he goes to a candy manufacturer to try to sell his musical candy, Toot Sweets. He doesn't make the sale, but he does meet the confectioner's daughter, a beautiful woman named Truly Scrumptious (Sally Ann Howes). Caractacus dances and earns a few nickels to buy the hunk of junk, then transforms it into the magnificent car called Chitty-Chitty Bang Bang. The children, Father, and Truly jump into Chitty and go to the beach for a picnic. There Father tells a story about pirates who wish to steal Chitty-Chitty Bang Bang and take it to a land called Vulgaria, where children are rounded up and sent off to prison. When the fantastic tale is finally told, Caractacus is informed that a buyer wants to manufacture Toot Sweets. Caractacus and Truly decide to marry, and the children take joy in their new car and new mother.

Everybody but the king of Vulgaria receives rewards in this movie. These treasures include a spiffy-looking car, riches, a husband, a wife, a mother, and security. Three principles are at work to yield such wonderful results. First, righteousness. Truly Scrumptious and the Potts family act honorably, with goodwill and fairness. In business and in life, God recognizes such honest ethics. Proverbs 13:21 says, "Prosperity is the reward of the righteous." Second, the four individuals acted with wisdom. Proverbs 9:12 says, "If you are wise, your wisdom will reward you." Third, they were persistent. Caractacus kept creating until he found a winner. He didn't stop after the first try. He also relentlessly pursued the confectioner, even when the candy maker initially passed on the Toot Sweets.

Are righteousness, wisdom, and persistence daily habits in your work and life? If not, is there any reason to believe you'll be rewarded? As an old saying puts it, "If you go on doing what you have always done, you'll go on getting what you've always got." Discover how you can fold these habits into your life—and then discover the rewards.

PRAYER IDEA: Ask God to show you how to add righteousness and wisdom to your life.

HURRY HOME
Planes, Trains, and Automobiles (1987)
MPAA: R for some strong language
Read: Ephesians 1:3–6

God sets the lonely in families. (Psalm 68:6)

Neal Page (Steve Martin) takes planes, trains, and automobiles and travels nearly three days to get from New York to his home in Chicago for Thanksgiving dinner. In a comedy of continuous errors, Neal battles blabbermouth and shower-curtain-ring salesman Del Griffith (John Candy) for a taxi to their airport. Then Del is seated next to Neal on the plane. Due to foul weather in Chicago, the plane lands in Wichita, Kansas. From dirty motels to nonexistent rental cars to breakdown trains and rides in the back of a semi truck, Neal endures Del's boorish ways along the whole route. After finally arriving in Chicago late on Thanksgiving Day, Neal realizes that Del doesn't have a family. So despite the horrors of the last few days, Neal takes Del home to meet the family and eat a turkey dinner.

God sets the lonely in families and asks us to do the same. In fact, in Christ, we are all lonely people adopted into the family of God. Without salvation, we are estranged from our heavenly Father. We are alone. At salvation we have all the joys, benefits, and responsibilities of becoming his child.

Think back to the times when you were lonely and without family. Didn't feel so good, did it? Think back to the time when you might have acted out of line because you wanted attention. That didn't feel so good either.

Loving others like family doesn't mean you have to like them. Love is a choice, based not on feelings but on choice. God asks us to love our enemies, even those lesser enemies who assail our sense of dignity, good taste, and humor (like Del). God asks us to reach out to these folks and bring them into the family of God. Boorish, loud, obnoxious, irritating, and annoying people are probably that way because they haven't had the love they so desperately needed. If you are having a difficult time reaching out to these people (so-called EGRs for "extra grace required"), do what Jesus did: retreat to the lonely places, seek God for that extra measure of grace, and then go to the lonely faces.

PRAYER IDEA: Ask God for strength to go to the lonely people and give them love.

IN PRAISE OF WOMEN
Celebrating the Feminine Mystique

WEEK 19

May 7–May 13

BE ALL YOU CAN BE!

Little Women (1994)

MPAA: PG for two uses of mild language

Read: Matthew 25:22, 23

Some of the Jews were persuaded and joined Paul and Silas, as did a large number of God-fearing Greeks and not a few prominent women. (Acts 17:4)

Louisa May Alcott's beloved *Little Women* comes alive on the big screen again with Winona Ryder playing Jo, one of four March sisters. The other three are Meg (Trini Alvarado), Beth (Claire Danes), and Amy (Kirsten Dunst and Samantha Mathis). While their father is off fighting the Civil War, their mother, Marmee (Susan Sarandon), encourages the girls to be all they can be. The girls hold amateur theatrical plays in the attic and write a newspaper called *The Pickwick Society*. Jo, in particular, has dreams of becoming a writer. After Jo refuses a marriage proposal from her kindly neighbor, Laurie (Christian Bale), she travels from Concord to New York and there finds success as an article writer for magazines. When she returns home to Concord, she pens a novel, accepts a marriage proposal, and finds a publisher!

Like Marmee, the Bible encourages women to be all they were meant to be. Why would Luke, the author of Acts, use the word "prominent" to describe some women who joined the faith unless they had indeed achieved some position of note? Throughout Scripture we find stories of women who worked hard, married, raised families, and performed great exploits for God. We also see women who achieved greatness through small acts, such as the widow who put two small coins into the temple treasury (Luke 21:1–3) and Mary, who took the time to be with her Lord (Luke 10:40–42).

God put talents, skills, and dreams inside each one of us. All we have to do is develop them. God put dreams in you, and if you seek him first, he will give you the desires of your heart. The March family is a Christian family, and Marmee prays with her girls and for her girls and believes in them and their abilities. Christ believes in you, too. He wants to see you prosper, even as your soul prospers. If you like to write, write. If dance, then dance. If play sports, then play sports. When you use your talents for God, you will be blessed. Those who witness your talents will be blessed, and God will also be blessed.

PRAYER IDEA: Ask God to help you encourage women to be all God has for them.

NOT INTO TEMPTATION
His Girl Friday (1940)
MPAA: not rated
Read: James 1:12–18

Each one is tempted when, by his own evil desire, he is dragged away and enticed. (James 1:14)

A fast-talking, wisecracking screwball comedy, *His Girl Friday*, directed by Howard Hawks, made stars out of Cary Grant and Rosalind Russell. Walter Burns (Cary Grant) is a manipulative Chicago newspaper editor, ex-husband of former reporter and bride-to-be Hildy Johnson (Rosalind Russell). When Hildy comes into Walter's office to tell him she is quitting the newspaper business and settling down to become a respectable woman with dullard Bruce Baldwin (Ralph Bellamy), Walter plots not only to win her back to her job but also to win her heart back for himself. The answer to Walter's goal is a hot news story of a man on death row awaiting a pardon. When the man escapes from prison and hides out in the prison pressroom, Hildy and Walter conceal him in a desk and create an exclusive story for themselves. Meanwhile, Ralph and his mother try hard to get Hildy on a train bound for Albany, New York. The more Hildy and Walter bicker and plot, the more she realizes that her place is with Walter at the newspaper.

For all its zany fun, *His Girl Friday* is basically a story of temptation and giving in to it. Walter lies to Hildy, tries to stop her train from leaving, gives her counterfeit money, and fools Ralph. Hildy knows the newspaper business is a temptation, but she flirts with it to the point where she collapses her own will and better judgment. She abandons a family life for a career life with a man of questionable character.

Like Walter against Hildy, Satan knows our weak spots and keeps sticking us there until we break. Nobody should blame God for temptation. And nobody should focus on temptation but rather turn away from it. Hildy broke her will because she didn't get out of the fire. Walter dangled a few carrots in front of her nose, and she bit—and that was it. Know your weaknesses and stay away from them. Refuse to talk to some people if they wish you harm. Whatever your skills are—journalism, editing, or business, for example—do them as unto the Lord and keep your practices ethical and honest. We are his every day of the week.

PRAYER IDEA: Ask God to lead you not into temptation.

THE ROT OF CORRUPTION
All about Eve (1950)
AFI: 16 • AA: Best Picture; George Sanders,
Best Supporting Actor; Best Screenplay; Best Costume Design;
Best Sound Recording • MPAA: not rated
Read: Ecclesiastes 7:1–7

Flesh and blood cannot inherit the kingdom of God; neither doth corruption inherit incorruption. (1 Corinthians 15:50, KJV)

Garnering as many Academy Award nominations as *Titanic, All about Eve* dramatizes with razor-sharp wit the folly of fame, the jealousy of jaded players, and the lies of lowly understudies ravenous for the spotlight. Young Eve Harrington (Anne Baxter) waits outside a Broadway playhouse to meet her idol, aging stage veteran Margo Channing (Bette Davis). With seeming humility, Eve tells Margo about her difficult past, and Margo takes her on as a personal assistant. Eve meets other Broadway greats, including critic Addison DeWitt (George Sanders), director Bill Sampson (Gary Merrill), and playwright Lloyd Richards (Hugh Marlowe). While Eve appears to be the image of gratitude and modesty, she connives to take over the town as the queen of the stage. While the audiences and acting community fawn over Eve's demure manner and stellar performances, Margo seethes, rants, raves, and becomes undone with jealousy. Eve gains the starring role in Lloyd's next play, but it comes at the cost of losing her friends and her self-respect. In the end an equally ambitious and undoubtedly immoral young woman shows up at Eve's door, adoring her as an idol.

What corrupts people today? The obvious come to mind—money, fame, power. Desiring these things over God brings ruin to many. Eve gains the spotlight, the limelight, and the adoration of many, but at what cost? She loses her friends and her self-respect. Proverbs tells us,

He who plots evil will be known as a schemer.
The schemes of folly are sin, and men detest a mocker. (Proverbs 24:8)

Were the ambitions of Eve evil? Not necessarily. Any ambition is holy if is it inspired by God and done for his glory. But Eve lied, pretending to be somebody she was not in order to become somebody she shouldn't have been—a vain glamour queen without a heart.

Watch that you do not become corrupted by the temptations of this world. Don't fool yourself into thinking that lying, cheating, and pretensions are anything that will ultimately bring you job satisfaction. Be real. Be holy and scheme to do good.

PRAYER IDEA: Ask God to keep you from corruption and to keep you ambitions pure.

FAITH AND DOUBT
The Song of Bernadette (1943)
AA: Jennifer Jones, Best Actress; Best Cinematography;
Best Art Direction; Best Score • MPAA: not rated
Read: Mark 9:14–24

MAY 10

Stop doubting and believe. (John 20:27)

The Song of Bernadette begins with this statement: "For those who believe in God, no explanation is necessary. For those who do not believe in God, no explanation is possible." In 1858 in Lourdes, France, Bernadette (Jennifer Jones), a sickly peasant girl, has a vision of "a beautiful lady" in the city dump. Only Bernadette can see her. Intrigued, others join Bernadette on her visits. One day the lady tells Bernadette to dig in the ground for a spring. Bernadette does, and waters begin to flow. A few people touch or drink the water and are healed of their diseases. This touches off a frenzy of faith throughout France, and Lourdes becomes a pilgrimage destination. Town lawyers, doctors, and clergy state their skepticism and try to get Bernadette to renounce the visions. But Bernadette never wavers in her belief in the vision of the "lady" and the healing power she brings.

We may never know if "the lady of Lourdes" had divinity behind her appearances, but there was a time when Christ clearly showed up for all to see. He claimed divinity and proved it with miracles and by forgiving others. Yet many of his contemporaries denied him. On occasion, even our Lord's own disciples fell short in their belief in him. Many of the most religious and educated men denied the divinity and healing power of Christ. Even if Jesus exposed doubt, condemned it, or became frustrated with those who had it, he always remained loving. Jesus countered doubt by one of four responses: (1) proving his divinity through a miracle; (2) correcting the naysayers with the truth of Scripture; (3) preempting doubt by predicting it, as with Peter (Matthew 26:31–35); or (4) asking people to come to belief.

The apostle James said that the person who doubts is like a wave of the sea, tossed by the wind (James 1:6). This isn't a threat; it's an observation. Doubters don't know what to believe. As an old saying has it, "If you don't believe in something, you'll fall for anything." Today we have the added benefit of history to observe how God has taken care of his followers. When we immerse ourselves in Scripture and hear the testimony of God's people through the ages, we build up our faith and combat doubt.

PRAYER IDEA: Tell God, "I do believe; help me to overcome my unbelief!"

Repent, for the kingdom of heaven is near. (Matthew 4:17)

Just one year before Scarlett O'Hara vamped in *Gone with the Wind,* Bette Davis starred as Julie Marsden, an angry, jealous, and sinful not-so-gentle woman of the South in *Jezebel.* During the 1850s in New Orleans, Julie bucks social convention and wears a red dress at the Olympus Ball. She embarrasses her banker fiancée, Preston Dillard (Henry Fonda), so much so that he breaks off their engagement and moves north. Three years later, when Preston arrives at Julie's plantation, she is ready to repent and mend her ways. That is, until she sees Preston's new wife, Amy (Margaret Lindsay), from New York. Julie goes back to her wicked ways, causing strife and even, inadvertently, the death of a family friend and onetime suitor, Buck Cantrell. During a yellow fever epidemic, Preston is stricken and Julie finally wakes up, morally. She vows to nurse him at a yellow fever colony, jeopardizing her own life in the process.

Sometimes it takes extreme circumstances, such as the death or near-death experiences of friends and loved ones, for bullheaded people to change their lives. Repentance is not necessarily easy, but the alternative to repentance can be even more difficult. People don't always realize the consequences of a heart set on sin until it is too late. Often the only obstacle to repentance is human pride. Humility is a bitter pill to swallow.

The Jezebel of the Bible took advantage of her high position as a daughter of a king to perform murder and malice. Her many sins included promoting idol worship, killing off the Lord's prophets, opposing the prophet Elijah, and in general being rude to others. Tempestuous folly may make entertaining Bible stories and Hollywood movies, but it doesn't fly when dealing with real flesh-and-bone people and a real, holy God. Young women may enjoy trash talk and backstabbing deeds, but these do great damage and will not go unnoticed. Repentance includes contrition and a change of character. Repentance can do great wonders and open doors for God's forgiveness, but the effects of some sins can never be rectified here on earth. You reap what you sow. So next time the temptation comes to act like a prima donna, remember the soiled Southern belle, Jezebel.

PRAYER IDEA: Ask God to forgive you for your words and deeds that have hurt others.

A SUSPICION OF ROYALTY

Anastasia (1956)

AA: Best Actress, Ingrid Bergman • MPAA: not rated

Read: John 20:24–30

After his suffering, he showed himself to these men and gave many convincing proofs that he was alive. (Acts 1:3)

She looked like her. She claimed to be her. Could this former insane asylum inmate really be the daughter of the murdered Russian czar Nikolai, the Grand Duchess Anastasia? Most would say no, because the czar and his entire family were reportedly killed in the Russian Revolution of 1918. Ten years later, General Bounine (Yul Brynner) plucks a street girl from obscurity in Paris, dresses her, feeds her, teaches her, and convinces her that she is the princess. Why? Bounine knows that the czar ferreted away piles of money, and hence, if he can convince the public that his Anastasia (Ingrid Bergman) is the real Anastasia, then maybe he can get his hands on the cash. Russian society does not accept her, so he takes her to Copenhagen to meet the czar's mother, the Dowager Empress (Helen Hayes). However, the empress will not receive Anastasia, even for inspection, because many impostors and money-grubbers have already troubled the empress. Eventually, though, the Empress meets Anastasia and accepts her as her own granddaughter, even as the general rejects his own initial greed.

After Christ died on the cross and was buried, many doubted his resurrection. Many thought the disciples invented the Resurrection story to keep their "revolution" alive. But mounting evidence increased the validity of his post-death appearances. Christ revealed himself to many people over a period of forty days before his ascension into heaven, speaking to them about the kingdom of God. He told Thomas to put his fingers in his side and commanded him to believe. Christ also performed many miracles after his death to prove his own divinity.

It has been said that Christ must be a madman, a fool, a liar, or none other than the Son of God. Which option will we believe? Most of the disciples died a martyr's death, proclaiming the good news of Jesus Christ. Would they have died for a lie? Many people, even many Christians, live like Christ is still in the grave. They believe in Jesus and his teachings, all right, but they don't act like Christ is alive. Yet he lives! He still saves, still heals, still moves in the hearts and lives of people, and still convinces the doubters of his existence. Know that he's alive. Accept his grace and live full of faith.

PRAYER IDEA: Ask God to live in your life more strongly than ever before.

TO BE UNDERSTOOD
What Women Want (2000)
MPAA: PG-13 for sexual content and mild language
Read: Hebrews 4:14–16

The LORD knows the thoughts of man. (Psalm 94:11)

After a freak accident, advertising executive Nick Marshall (Mel Gibson) acquires the rare ability to hear what women are thinking. He listens in on the secret inner voice that goes on in their heads every single day. Raised by a Vegas showgirl mother, Nick mostly sees women as sex objects. But after he receives his "gift," he realizes that women are complex, interesting creatures who have definite needs to be loved and accepted. Initially Nick wants to crush his new boss, Darcy McGuire (Helen Hunt), and in fact successfully gets her fired. But as he hears her thoughts, he falls in love with her. After electricity hits him, Nick loses his ability to hear women's thoughts. But because he has learned to appreciate what women want, he helps Darcy regain her job and restores their relationship.

In this fantasy, one man is able to hear all the thoughts of every woman he encounters. In reality, God is able to hear and understand every thought of every person on the planet. Unbelievable? Sure, but God made every one of us, and his Word says that he can handle and process all that thinking. In fact, God understands not only our every thought but also our every need. Unlike Nick, however, he doesn't need a crash course in sensitivity training. God knows that we are made of clay and that we have weaknesses.

You might be a little frightened to realize that God knows your every thought, but this is actually quite comforting. If God knows our every thought and need, he is never surprised by our prayers. If God knows our every thought, we don't have to explain ourselves, because he already knows. We can cut to the chase in prayer and have instant intimacy with our Maker. Explanation and misunderstanding do not apply. What joy to have instant access to an understanding Maker! God knows what women (and men) want, and he is quick to meet our need and demonstrate to us his abounding love.

PRAYER IDEA: Thank your, heavenly Father, for knowing your every need.

HOOKED ON HITCHCOCK

Movies from the Master of Suspense

WEEK 20

May 14–May 18

MADE IN HER IMAGE
Vertigo (1958)
AFI: 61 • MPAA: PG

Read: Colossians 1:15–20

Cursed is the man who carves an image or casts an idol. (Deuteronomy 27:15)

San Francisco police detective Scottie Fergusson (James Stewart) develops a bad case of vertigo in the movie with the same name. An old friend, Gavin Elster (Tom Helmore), hires Scottie to watch his wife, Madeleine (Kim Novak). This woman thinks a nineteenth-century woman, who committed suicide at age twenty-six, possesses her. Scottie follows Madeleine around town, rescues her from drowning, and falls in love with her. Madeleine climbs the bell tower of an old Spanish mission and throws herself to her death. Unable to help her because of his fear of heights, all Scottie can do is watch. Later, Scottie finds a woman named Judy who looks like Madeleine. Scottie transforms her image to be just like Madeleine's. Judy willingly agrees to this because all she wants is Scottie's love. When Scottie manipulates Judy to obsessive lengths, terror and death strike a second time.

Real transformation isn't cosmetic; it's deep. When God transforms you, he'll change you to look like him. If someone else tries to change you, it won't have any lasting value. Personal trainers want to change your body, beauticians want to change your skin and hair, and self-help gurus want to change your attitude. Friends may try to change your tastes or habits. But these provide only temporary solutions. Self-actualization is found only in the loving arms of Christ. Real change is from within.

Christ is the image of the invisible God. Christians are too. We carry Christ and reflect his glory to the world. When people look at the church, they shouldn't see egos but Christ alone. Every talent, every smile, every act of love by the church is like a facet of a giant diamond that sparkles and shines the brilliance and majesty of God. Don't try to make people into little versions of yourself. Point them to Christ and let Christ transform them from the inside out. Discipleship isn't your will imposed on another. It's asking, "Lord, your will be done in this life as well as my own." Let the image of God dwell richly in you.

PRAYER IDEA: Ask God to forgive you for trying to change people for your own selfish ends.

BAD MEMORIES

Rebecca (1940)

AA: Best Picture; Best Cinematography • MPAA: not rated

Read: Psalm 72:12–14

Do not oppress the widow. (Zechariah 7:10)

Ghosts need not be present to haunt the living. The deceased former Mrs. de Winter, Rebecca, strikes fear and trembling into the current Mrs. de Winter (Joan Fontaine) at their English castle home. In Monaco, Max de Winter (Laurence Olivier) meets the lovely but demure Joan. After a short romance, Max asks Joan to marry him. She agrees and they move to England, to Max's home of Manderley. Joan can't quite get used to the home, filled with artifacts and memories of the former Mrs. de Winter. Head housekeeper Mrs. Danvers (Judith Anderson) particularly loved Rebecca and holds disdain for Joan. Max broods, tensions ratchet up, and the new de Winter marriage is challenged. Eventually Max cracks and tells Joan that Rebecca was not the golden girl that everybody makes her out to be. In fact, Rebecca was so cruel and calculating that foul play contributed to her untimely drowning. One final police investigation clears Max of suspicion, and finally he is able to enjoy life with his new wife and rid himself Rebecca's oppressive memory.

Wicked events and people who have attacked us in the past can oppress us today if we let their memory do so. Time doesn't necessarily heal all wounds, especially if the wounds get reopened. All too easily we entertain thoughts that aren't healthy or godly. We think about problems of the past and make them problems of today, forgetting that God has given us a new heart and new strength. At one point in the story, the demonic Mrs. Danvers tells Joan, "You've nothing to live for. Why don't you jump? Don't be afraid." The housekeeper needed cleaning out. She carried with her an oppressive spirit of death that eventually caused her own destruction.

Jesus tells us to be alert because our enemy "prowls around like a roaring lion" (1 Peter 5:8). When we are conscious of oppression, we can combat it when it comes to call against us. Oppression is a deliberate attack by the enemy, but God is our defender. God calls us to take captive every thought and make it obedient to Christ. Oppressive thoughts need not haunt us. As Christians, we actually have God's authority to confront such attacks through the name of Christ, proclaiming his Word and just plain resisting. Against such defense, our oppressive enemy must flee.

PRAYER IDEA: Thank God that he gives you weapons of war against oppression.

UNCOVERING MYSTERIES
Rear Window (1954)
AFI: 42 • MPAA: PG
Read: Colossians 1:25–27

They may know the mystery of God, namely, Christ, in whom are hidden all the treasures of wisdom and knowledge. (Colossians 2:2, 3)

What's a photographer to do all day when he's confined to a wheelchair and stuck in a small New York apartment? If he is L. B. ("Jeff") Jeffries (James Stewart), he becomes a voyeur and stares out of his rear window and into the homes of his neighbors. Jeff sees strange things and begins to construct scenarios for the people whom he observes. Directly across from him, a neighbor (Raymond Burr) has knives, newspapers, and arguments with his wife. When this man's wife mysteriously disappears, Jeff and his girlfriend, Lisa (Grace Kelly), suspect murder. Are they correct, or are they snooping into business not their own? Do the distance and the glass deceive them?

Sometimes, if we look long and hard enough toward heaven, we can unravel some of the mysteries of God. On this earth, understanding God is like looking through a dark glass. When we look through this glass, it is difficult to qualify the details of what we are observing. Many find God inscrutable and unreachable, yet he implores us to look for him with all our might. One day, when we join him in heaven, we'll be able to unravel his mysterious ways.

God wants us all to be detectives. He wants us to discover the clues of his majesty and love. What do you see in the world? Calamity of the faithful? War? Pestilence and disease? Do they cause you to say, "There is no God" or "Where are you God?" Or do you see these same things and say, "God must be so grieved." When you see the beauty of creation, do you say, "Wow, God, you sure did some fantastic work"? To those who have eyes to see and ears to hear, the truth of the gospel is apparent. The Bible says, "Seek and you will find; knock and the door will be opened to you" (Matthew 7:7). If the best we can do to comprehend God on earth is like looking through a dark glass, how much greater will it be when he is fully revealed?

PRAYER IDEA: Thank God for the intrigue of his mysteries and the excitement of the search.

MISTAKEN IDENTITY

North by Northwest (1959)

AFI: 40 • MPAA: not rated

Read: Luke 22:54–62

All men will know that you are my disciples, if you love one another. (John 13:35)

Why wouldn't international spies think Roger Thornhill (Cary Grant) was a government agent? After all, Thornhill fits the profile and he mistakenly answers to the name of intelligence officer George Kaplan. So the goons of spy leader Phillip Vandamm (James Mason) kidnap Thornhill right out of a New York City bar, interrogate him, and then get him drunk when he doesn't talk. Naturally, Thornhill disagrees with this treatment and tries to flee, north by northwest, all the way to Rapid City, South Dakota. Along the way, Thornhill is wanted for murder, chased by police, seduced by a beautiful blonde agent, dive-bombed by a crop-dusting plane, and hired by the actual FBI to finish a job. The climax takes him to a fight atop Mount Rushmore as Thornhill attempts to unravel this case of mistaken identity.

If it looks like a duck and quacks like a duck, then it is a duck." "Don't judge a book by its cover." "What you see is not necessarily what you get." These platitudes don't apply in every circumstance. Thornhill actually is an advertising executive who, as he puts it, deals in "expedited exaggerations." He is in the business of pushing unnecessary product on pushover people. He sells lies. His impersonation of George Kaplan further involves him in the FBI busting of the spy ring.

If we join Christianity by putting our faith in Christ, are we willing to be identified with Christ? Or do we merely wish to give the appearance of being one of the fold? Peter the disciple denied Jesus three times. He said, "I'm not with him." But those who observed Peter saw the signs. They had observed the moments when he was with Jesus. They had seen him love like Jesus. They knew that he was a disciple. There was no mistaken identification. Are you acting like a disciple of Christ? If others observed you, would they think you were a Christian? Or would they think you worked for some other boss? Don't fool others or let them be fooled by you. Make yourself known by your love.

PRAYER IDEA: Ask God to let your love for him and others be evident always.

CARE FOR THY MOTHER

Psycho (1960)

AFI: 18 • MPAA: R

Read: John 19:25–27

Honor your father and your mother. (Deuteronomy 5:16)

Norman Bates (Anthony Perkins) is a mama's boy of the worst kind. Together, he and his mother supposedly run the Bates Motel, a dilapidated, mostly defunct place off an old Arizona highway. Beautiful thief Marion Crane (Janet Leigh) checks in, but she doesn't check out. After arriving, Marion thinks she hears Norman's mother give him a tongue-lashing about bringing her into the house for dinner. Then the audience watches Marion being killed in the shower, apparently by Norman's mother. Later we learn the awful truth. Norman's mother has been long dead, and Norman has been perversely "honoring" his mother by dressing as her, speaking as her, and performing murders as her. In short, he is a psycho. Thankfully, investigators and police link the clues together and stop Norman from repeating his crazy mommy act.

The movie *Psycho* depicts mother worship in the worst extreme. Of course, the Bible's admonition to honor your father and mother doesn't involve murderous jealousy and role-playing. It considers more healthy and respectful obligations. Love is called for when honoring our mothers. Sometimes this requires great patience. Sometimes it includes a period of personal sacrifice in which you have to give up fun time or even career time to care for her when she is sick. Sometimes it involves hiring others to care for her so that you can go about other business.

When Jesus hung on the cross, he looked down and saw his weeping mother at his feet. Taking pity on her, Jesus saw his beloved disciple John beside her and said to his mother, "Dear woman, here is your son." And to the disciple he said, "Here is your mother" (John 19:27). From that time on, John took her into his home. Jesus set up his mother in a home health care program of the best kind. Jesus honored his mother by making sure she was going to be taken care of during his death, resurrection, and ascension. When we care enough to give our moms the very best, God is pleased and honored too.

PRAYER IDEA: Thank God for your mother and grandmothers.

MEN IN
UNIFORM
Tales from the
Front Lines

WEEK 21

May 19–May 27

NEVER ABUSING HIS POWER

Paths of Glory (1957)

MPAA: not rated

Read: Joshua 5:13—6:7

Put Uriah in the front line where the fighting is fiercest. (2 Samuel 11:15)

Colonel Dax (Kirk Douglas) faithfully serves in the French trenches during his search for paths of glory, General Paul Mireau (George Macready) challenges General George Broulard (Adolphe Menjou) for the need to take the "anthill," a complex network of trenches and bunkers occupied by German forces. General Mireau commands Colonel Dax to do the dirty work and overtake the "anthill" by force. Colonel Dax and his men barely make it out of the trench before being battered back by heavy German gunfire. Some men don't leave the trenches at all. Deeply disturbed, General Mireau secretly orders French troops to fire on Dax's men in order to motivate them to get out onto the battlefield. When the French troops ignore these orders, Dax doesn't move and the "anthill" remains in German hands. Blinded by their own arrogance, the generals order Dax to pick three men for trial, judgment, and execution under charges of cowardice. Dax obeys but recognizes the complete inhumanity and error of his superior officers.

Following orders into harm's way is one thing, but following orders to probable death for an uncertain result is just plain foolhardy. King David of the Bible and General Mireau both acted foolishly. David wanted to protect his own pride. He killed off Uriah so that he could steal Uriah's wife, Bathsheba. This wasn't command; this was abuse of power.

God will never commit you to danger without promising to back you up. When you battle for him, you can be sure that he won't be shooting bullets *at* you but rather *with* you. He might ask you to do strange things, like the times he had his people march around a city seven times or sent a boy out to battle a giant, but these assignments are only to test your faith. He wants you to trust in him and his victorious power.

He doesn't risk his warriors recklessly or needlessly. He is a trustworthy Commander in Chief who knows everything about our strengths and weakness and those of our enemies. He demonstrates his strength in our weakness so that we will give him all the glory when victory comes. He doesn't guarantee that we won't fall in service for him, but he does guarantee to always be with us, loving us and imparting his strength to us.

PRAYER IDEA: Thank God that he never asks you to do or say anything without giving you the strength to do it.

UNFULFILLED PROMISE

All Quiet on the Western Front (1930)

AFI: 54 • AA: Best Picture; Lewis Milestone, Best Director

MPAA: not rated

Read: Psalm 89

Does he promise and not fulfill? (Numbers 23:19)

A landmark antiwar movie, *All Quiet on the Western Front* compares the differences between the promises of war and its actualities. The story follows a group of German schoolboys who are talked into enlisting into World War I by their patriotic and enthusiastic teacher. In the trenches, life balances precariously. All of the schoolboys suffer. Some face injury. Others die. The few who live often cry or go crazy, unable to handle the pressure. One schoolboy, Paul (Lew Ayres), begs a Frenchman to forgive him. But the man is dead, a victim of Paul's own hand. Back home on leave, Paul visits the teacher who encouraged him to join the war. The teacher wants to hear tales of bravery and heroism, but Paul cannot muster any enthusiasm. The horrors of war are too great. Sent back to the front lines, Paul reaches out for a butterfly in the midst of battle, only to be struck down by a French sniper.

D isappointment. Discouragement. Disenfranchisement. These are the answers to false promises. The German youths joined the war for a sense of purpose, patriotism, or personal pride but found the battlefield to be a place of anguish and pain. They discovered that "hope deferred makes the heart sick" (Proverbs 13:12). Who can be enthusiastic about war when it delivers so much pain? Who can be enthusiastic about life when it likewise offers up frustration and disappointment?

The answer to this pain is in placing one's hope appropriately. Never blindly accept a promise. Consider the source. Only accept a promise from someone you can trust. God is such a person. He is not a personality that can lie (Numbers 23:19), but a rock and a firm foundation.

The words "faithful" and "faithfulness" appear in the Bible over 140 times. Since God is truth, he cannot be anything but faithful. God doesn't promise to spare us from war, but he promises to be with us in the middle of it. He promises to love us always as we walk through the valley of the shadow of death. This Memorial Day season, be faithful in respecting our veterans. Express your gratitude to them—and mean it. Honor their service on the battlefields by letting them see God's faithfulness in you.

PRAYER IDEA: Ask God to help you be faithful to all who have served in war.

KEEP ON KEEPING ON

Men of Honor (2001)
MPAA: R for strong language
Read: Luke 11:5–8

**Let us run with perseverance the race marked out for us.
(Hebrews 12:1)**

Men of Honor is about a man of perseverance. Carl Brashear (Cuba Gooding Jr.) perseveres to become the first African-American Navy diver ever, then he later strives to become the first amputee Master Chief Diver in America. When he is a young man, his father encourages him to go out into the world and be the best. As a cook in the Navy, Carl is promoted to rescue swimmer, then sets his sights on Master Chief Diver. Against fantastic odds of racism, grueling training, lack of recognition, dives that take him to near-death situations, and a foot amputation, Carl achieves his goal through dogged persistence.

As with Carl, running to win is normal behavior in the Christian life. We are to count the cost and then we are to run with perseverance the race marked out for us. What is our cost? Everything, including our very lives. We must be prepared to meet opposition and ridicule and even family strife. What is our race? Fixing our eyes on Jesus and continually running to him, letting our all be for his glory. "Whatever your hand finds to do, do it with all your might" (Ecclesiastes 9:10).

We cannot run the race and face terrible odds in our own strength. We need our heavenly Father to encourage us to achieve. God imparts his strength to our hearts. So with Christ, all things are possible. If you should fall on the way, fall forward to Christ. He will pick up you up and keep you going toward victory.

PRAYER IDEA: Thank Jesus for calling you to win and for giving you the tools to do it.

SPEECH REVEALS CHARACTER
A Few Good Men (1992)
MPAA: R for very strong language
Read: Matthew 12:33–37

Woe to those who call evil good and good evil. (Isaiah 5:20)

The few, the proud, the Marines. In *A Few Good Men* the Marines protect American interests with uncompromising determination. At Guantanamo Bay, Cuba, Col. Nathan Jessup (Jack Nicholson) doesn't allow any foul-ups, especially from Marines who lag behind in drills, such as PFC Santiago (Michael DeLorenzo). One night two Marines—Dawson (Wolfgang Bodison) and Downey (James Marshall)—go into Santiago's room, stuff a rag down his throat, and tie him up with duct tape. A few hours later, Santiago dies. Three Navy lawyers—Lt. Daniel Kaffee (Tom Cruise), Cmdr. JoAnne Galloway (Demi Moore), and Lt. Sam Weinberg (Kevin Pollak)—attend to the case, representing Dawson and Downey. The legal team learns of the term *code red,* referring to an illegal and often brutal method to teach a wayward recruit a lesson. They also learn that Jessup unofficially approves of code-red events. Kaffee brings Col. Jessup to the stand and demands the truth about what happened to Santiago. Jessup barks back, "You can't handle the truth," but in a match of wills, Jessup cracks and eventually admits to ordering the illegal and murderous code red on Santiago.

A Few Good Men asks, what is good behavior? Is it following orders, regardless of how extreme they may be? Or is it protecting and defending the innocent? Or both? Jessup has power but no goodness. Dawson and Downey obey Jessup and have honor, but they aren't being good either. Through a court of law, Jessup, Dawson, and Downey are exposed as having evil within them. Kaffee pulls it out of them. "The good man brings good things out of the good stored up in him, and the evil man brings evil things out of the evil stored up in him" (Matthew 12:35). Your sins will find you out.

What do the words of your mouth reveal about your character? Eventually—someday, somewhere—you'll reveal yourself, warts and all, to an inquisitor. You will be tested and the quality of your character will come out of your mouth. You will also have to give an account before God about your words and behaviors. "By your words you will be acquitted, and by your words you will be condemned" (Matthew 12:37). Let Christ's life dwell in you so fully that your words will be his and you won't be ashamed when Judgment Day arrives. Be a tree of good fruit.

PRAYER IDEA: Declare God's goodness and ask him to display his goodness in your life.

No Small Beginnings

Sergeant York (1941)

AA: Gary Cooper, Best Actor; Best Film Editing • MPAA: not rated

Read: 1 Samuel 17:34–37

Give, and it will be given to you. A good measure, pressed down, shaken together and running over, will be poured into your lap. (Luke 6:38)

Tennessee citizen Alvin C. York (Gary Cooper) ain't nothing but a hillbilly. A rifle-packing drinker, he just wants to buy some land, start a farm, and marry Gracie Williams (Joan Leslie). But Alvin realizes that if he wants to win the girl, he must clean up his act. So he finds Jesus through Pastor Rosier Pile (Walter Brennan) and becomes a man of peace. When the First World War commences, Alvin's domestic plans are thwarted. He desires exemption from military service through conscientious objection. But his church has no formal creed against war, so Alvin's case doesn't stand and he goes off to basic training. When Alvin is deployed to France, Gracie worries for his safety. Alvin's mother says, "The Lord takes care of those who fear him." In France, Sergeant York single-handedly captures a German troop using the same strategy he used in a turkey shoot back home. The U.S. government hails Sergeant York as a hero and restores to him all the things he lost when he went off to war: land, home, and fortune.

Lots of people think they can't be effective for God because of their limitations. Some of Alvin's superior officers think he won't fight in battle. Some of Alvin's fellow soldiers think he won't know how to shoot. But Alvin knows how to shoot turkeys and uses that same skill in war. Alvin doesn't despise his humble beginnings but utilizes them for national purposes and achieves great exploits in the war against the evil oppressor.

When King David was just a boy, he wasn't afraid to stand up to Goliath. David told King Saul, "When a lion or a bear came and carried off a sheep from the flock, I went after it, struck it and rescued the sheep from its mouth. . . . This uncircumcised Philistine will be like one of them" (1 Samuel 17:34–36). Because David trusted God and used his skills for God, he successfully challenged Goliath. Lots of us think that we are too simple or uneducated to be of any use in God's army. But each of us has unique experiences and knowledge. When we make ourselves available to God, we each have our own role to play as we fight the good fight. And when we give to God, he will give to us.

PRAYER IDEA: Ask God to keep you from despising small beginnings.

FOR GOODNESS'S SAKE

Saving Private Ryan (1998)

AA: Steven Spielberg, Best Director; Best Cinematography;
Best Editing; Best Sound; Best Sound Effects

MPAA: R for very strong language and
graphic sequences of war violence

Read: Romans 5:6–8

MAY 24

No one is good—except God alone. (Mark 10:18)

In *Saving Private Ryan* the elderly James Ryan (Harrison Young) visits a memorial garden in northern France. He looks at a white cross with a name inscribed: Captain John Miller (Tom Hanks). Overcome with emotion, James Ryan asks his wife, "Am I a good man? Have I lived a good life?" She says yes, trying to comfort him, but he is inconsolable. During World War II, Private Ryan (Matt Damon) loses all of his brothers in battle. So Captain John Miller is sent with a band of soldiers under his command to search the French countryside for Private Ryan. The objective: to send him home. In a momentous battle, a mortally wounded Captain Miller says to Private Ryan, "Earn this. Earn this." Years later, Private Ryan is still haunted by these words.

What a tremendous burden Captain Miller puts on Private Ryan! For more than fifty years, Ryan doesn't know if he has "earned" his salvation or not. He must have asked himself constantly, *How good is good enough? How do I measure goodness? Have I lived a good life?* These questions also bother Captain Miller's team. They ask, "How many lives are worth losing to save one life?" In Miller's quest to save Ryan, U.S. casualties mount higher. Many wonder if saving Private Ryan is worth it.

The bad news is that Ryan is not worth it. He—and all of us—are *not* good. We never have been and never will be. Ryan is a sinner and unable to earn his spiritual salvation; so are we. The greatest of saints, like Mother Teresa and Billy Graham, haven't even earned their salvation. Compared to Christ, "our righteous acts are like filthy rags" (Isaiah 64:6). The good news is that Jesus put himself into harm's way and died so that we might live. And when Jesus died, he didn't say, "Earn this." He said, "Whoever *believes* in me shall not perish but have everlasting life" (John 3:16, emphasis added). Salvation is a free gift; it is not earned. All we need to do is accept it by faith.

PRAYER IDEA: Thank God that your salvation is based on his grace alone.

EAGER TO EDIFY

Glory (1989)

AA: Denzel Washington, Best Supporting Actor;
Best Cinematography; Best Sound • MPAA: R for war violence
Read: 1 Corinthians 14:1–13

Jesus Christ . . . gave himself for us to redeem us from all wickedness and to purify for himself a people that are his very own, eager to do what is good. (Titus 2:13, 14)

All they want to do is fight. During the Civil War, black citizens of Massachusetts sign up for the 54th Division, ready to preserve the Union and abolish slavery. After intense and thorough training by young Colonel Robert Gould Shaw (Matthew Broderick), this unit is as sharp and prepared as any in the Union. But because they are black, they are overlooked. Mostly they perform physical labor, such as clearing land. Conditions are so bad that Colonel Shaw has to harangue fellow officers just to get his men new shoes. After repeated appeals to his superiors and even to President Abraham Lincoln, the 54th not only receive new shoes but are given the honor of attacking a Confederate fort on the South Carolina seashore. Knowing that casualties will be high, the 54th nevertheless valiantly advance, ready to show North and South their training and glory as soldiers.

Eagerness isn't often looked upon as a Christlike characteristic, but it is commended in God's Word, especially with regard to spiritual gifts. Paul encourages us to "eagerly desire spiritual gifts, especially the gift of prophecy" (1 Corinthians 14:1). Prophecy is encouraged because it strengthens, encourages, and comforts those who hear it. Prophecy edifies the church. The soldiers of the 54th are eager to fight because they want to strengthen the cause of the Union. They see white soldiers bringing glory to their country, and they want the same.

Prophecy also compels the unbeliever to God. Prophecy, like a weapon, pierces the heart and lays it open. This prompts the unbeliever to fall down and worship God. Eagerly desire spiritual gifts (1 Corinthians 14:1). They are our weapons of warfare. Some said the 54th couldn't fight, and may scoff at you for wanting spiritual gifts, but don't be discouraged by them. Be eager to edify. God can use you even if you haven't fought in his army before. God can use you to bring glory to his name through building up the church.

PRAYER IDEA: Ask Jesus to grant you greater zeal for spiritual gifts.

THEY WERE NOT FORSAKEN

We Were Soldiers (2002)

MPAA: R for language and graphic war violence

Read: Psalm 23

The LORD your God goes with you; he will never leave you nor forsake you. (Deuteronomy 31:6)

We were soldiers once," reflects Lt. Colonel Hal Moore (Mel Gibson), who leads four hundred young fathers, husbands, brothers, and sons into bloody battle against some two thousand North Vietnamese soldiers in the first combat the U.S. sees during this infamous war. Lt. Colonel Moore tells his men that he will be the first to set foot on foreign soil in this battle and he will be the last to leave. He also tries to comfort them by reciting Psalm 23:4,

Even though I walk through the valley of the shadow of death, I will fear no evil, for you are with me.

When Lt. Colonel Moore is radioed to come back to Saigon for debriefing, he refuses and says he won't leave his men.

Lt. Colonel Moore walks with his men in the battle and so will God with us. When Jesus hung on the cross, he sensed that God had left him. He cried out to God, "My God, my God, why have you forsaken me?" (Matthew 27:46). Indeed, since Jesus took on the sins of the whole world at his death, he must have at least momentarily been separated from God. But the good news is that Jesus took our punishment so that we would never have to be separated from God. Jesus took the "bullet" in our place so that God can forever be with us in battle.

Perhaps you have experienced the horrors of war yourself or have a family member or friend who did. Or perhaps you have witnessed firsthand a fatal accident or a terminal illness. These dark days and moments sometimes seem too terrible to bear. But God promises to be with us in the middle of them, loving us as he always has. We may not understand what is happening, and we may not see his goodness displayed, but he promises to never leave us nor forsake us. He's the first to show up and he never leaves.

PRAYER IDEA: Thank Jesus for taking your place on the battlefield of life.

THE FIGHT AFTER THE WAR
The Best Years of Our Lives (1946)
AFI: 35 • AA: Harold Russell, Honorary Oscar; Best Picture;
William Wyler, Best Director; Frederic March, Best Actor;
Harold Russell, Best Supporting Actor; Best Original Screenplay;
Best Film Editing; Best Score • MPAA: not rated • Read: Psalm 144

MAY
27

Then the land had rest from war. (Joshua 11:23)

Three American servicemen return to their hometown, Boone City, after World War II to find their lives irrevocably changed by their military experience. Navy man Homer Parrish (Harold Russell) lost his hands and is now afraid to love his fiancée, Wilma. As he struggles to overcome his disability, Wilma repeatedly tells him that she loves him and still wants to marry him. Al Stephenson (Frederic March) returns to a family in which the children are now grown. Despite objections by his superior, Al finds it difficult as a loan officer to turn down veterans who haven't any collateral. Decorated airman Fred Derry (Dana Andrews) finds himself stuck in a lousy job and a loveless marriage while at the same time falling in love with Al's daughter, Peggy (Teresa Wright). Together, the three veterans must find a way to move on with their lives.

It still happens today. Military personnel return home from active duty and find that their loved ones and their lives have changed. Many service people adjust well, but some have nightmares, reliving horrors they have seen on the battlefield. Some find solace in the bottle or in shutting down emotionally. Many find it difficult to relate to others who haven't undergone the experiences of war.

Psalm 144:1 says,

Praise be to the LORD my Rock, who trains my hands for war.

A right and true sentiment, but after the war is over, is the Lord still a Rock and does he train the hands of veterans for peacetime? This is an important question. God answers the question about life after war as Psalm 144:12, 13, 15 continues:

Our sons in their youth will be like well-nurtured plants,
and our daughters will be like pillars carved to adorn a palace.
Our barns will be filled with every kind of provision. . . .
Blessed are the people whose God is the LORD.

One thing is certain: God takes care of his sheep and makes sure they have purpose and occupation. This Memorial Day, remember the living veterans as well as the war dead. Pray that God would grant our veterans provision and give them purpose and peace.

PRAYER IDEA: Ask God how you can remember the living veterans.

EPIC PROPORTIONS
Sweeping Stories
of Massive Scale

May 28–June 3

THE PRICE OF FORGIVENESS

To End All Wars (2001)

MPAA Rating: R for strong war violence and strong language

Read: Matthew 5:38–48

Greater love has no one than this, that he lay down his life for his friends. (John 15:13)

They thought they were fighting to end all wars. Instead, they battled a war raging inside their hearts. Members of the 92nd Division of the Argyll & Sutherland Highlanders are captured by the Japanese and placed in a POW camp. All POWs ask, "How should I respond to my enemy?" Rage, reflection, remorse, and true religion become the answer in this movie. Chief Japanese officer Ito (Sakae Kimura) uses sticks, shovels, and pistols to enforce respect and discipline under the Bushido code. When the POWs are ordered to make a railway, Major Ian Campbell (Robert Carlyle) begins to plan an escape. Captain Ernest Gordon (Ciarán McMenamin) launches a jungle university, and Dusty Miller (Mark Strong) begins a "church without walls." When Major Campbell is caught trying to escape, Dusty tells Ito he will take the punishment instead. Ito literally crucifies Dusty outside the camp while the other POWs look on. This begins a spiritual transformation throughout the camp as the prisoners display love and forgiveness toward their captors.

To members of the 92nd Division of the Argyll & Sutherland Highlanders, the price of peace and forgiveness is nothing less than complete self-sacrifice. Fighting and plotting against their human enemies brings them only more scorn and punishment. When Christ and his Word enter the camp through Dusty's preaching and example, morale rises and the men perform their work as unto the Lord. They became such good workers that Ito gives them rewards of food and provisions. Ito sheds tears when he witnesses Dusty's offer to take Major Campbell's place. The spirit of love and forgiveness continues when Captain Gordon leads a group of his fellow POWs to treat and care for wounded Japanese soldiers. This example becomes too much for Ito to bear and he breaks, emotionally and spiritually.

The power of forgiveness overpowers even the most controlling, brutal forces. It weakens the will of oppression because forgiveness doesn't recognize the power of oppression. Forgiveness says, "I shall not be broken." The burning coals of hate have nowhere to go but back onto the oppressor. If these starving, overworked POWs can forgive their captors, who can you forgive today? Who can you release from having a power of control and brutality over you?

PRAYER IDEA: Ask Jesus to fill you with his spirit so that you may not be overcome by evil.

A MARGINALIZED KING
The Last Emperor (1987)
AA: Best Picture; Bernardo Bertolucci, Best Director;
Best Adapted Screenplay; Best Cinematography;
Best Art Direction, Best Editing, Best Costume Design;
Best Score; Best Sound • MPAA: PG-13
Read: John 19:16–24

MAY 29

Then a new king, who did not know about Joseph, came to power in Egypt. (Exodus 1:8)

The last emperor of China, Pu Yi (John Lone), never gets a chance to rule his people. Crowned at age three, he can never leave the confines of the Forbidden City. The People's Republic of China keeps him as a mere symbol while they elect a president to control the people through communism. Pu Yi marries Wan Jung (Joan Chen) and emerges from the Forbidden City. Outside, he becomes a pawn to the emperor of Japan. Then, after being imprisoned by the communists for crimes against the new Chinese government, he is finally released to a dissolute lifestyle in an obscure existence as just another peasant worker in the People's Republic.

This sad tale of rejecting one's leader is all too common in this world. One king replaces another, often by force or dubious means. Spiritually speaking, America has marginalized its Emperor too. Founded on the Christian principles of "life, liberty and the pursuit of happiness," as endowed to us by our Creator, America has replaced Christ as its spiritual and moral head. Through neglect, forgetfulness, and downright rebellion, our nation has placed the unjust ruler of materialism and greed in Christ's place. While giving lip service to our trust and faith in Christ, we have chosen to follow pluralism and individuality.

It's strange that Pilate placed a sign reading "King of the Jews" over Jesus as he hung on the cross. Pilate recognized the Lord's position but mocked his power and authority. Those who killed Christ are like those who marginalize him today. They may attend church and say, "Oh, yeah. Christ is a good teacher." But they don't live like he makes a difference. They don't live like he is the final authority. Jesus himself said, "Not everyone who says to me, 'Lord, Lord,' will enter the kingdom of heaven" (Matthew 7:21). Is Christ your Emperor, or have you locked him up in a forbidden city?

PRAYER IDEA: Ask Jesus to forgive you when you marginalize him.

RAGE AGAINST A NATION
The Last Samurai (2003)
MPAA: R for violence and battle sequences
Read: Psalm 2

Why do the nations rage and the peoples plot in vain? (Acts 4:25)

Disaffected and lost, Civil and Indian War veteran Captain Nathan Algren (Tom Cruise) accepts a job as a military adviser for the Japanese emperor Meiji (Shichinosuke Nakamura) in 1876. The emperor wants to modernize, but the samurai, led by a renowned soldier named Katsumoto (Ken Watanabe), rebel. Unprepared for battle, the emperor's soldiers fight the samurai and are slaughtered. Captain Algren is taken captive by Katsumoto and led away to a remote mountain village. There Captain Algren learns the way of the honor-based samurai and switches his loyalties from the emperor to Katsumoto. In a final confrontation between the samurai, armed with swords, and the army, holding modern rifles, Captain Algren becomes the last samurai when his comrades fall dead one by one.

Though Algren has fought for the U.S., a country that represents freedom and democracy, he has become disaffected and callous after a brutal massacre in the Indian wars. Algren has lost faith in the American dream. Despite the false religion of the samurai, the brutality of their existence, and their preoccupation with shame and suicide, Algren finds among them a serenity and peace that he lost on the killing fields of the American plains. Though the samurai are an imperfect people, Algren switches loyalties to them because he feels let down and betrayed by his own people.

National pride and loyalty are qualities that seem to be slipping every day in America. Lawlessness and socialistic attitudes are replacing biblical ideals for how we should function as a nation. No doubt, our country has committed atrocities in the past, but the ideals of truth, justice, and equality under God remain our goal. No matter how flawed we are, America celebrates life, liberty, and the pursuit of happiness under God. To Captain Algren, modernization equals disingenuousness. But modernity isn't the issue. Sin is. Any society, be it ancient Japan or modern America, must conduct itself upon godly principles if it is going to offer the pursuit of happiness and national pride. Dissidents will come (and perhaps Algren would have found any reason to be one), but woe is us if we abuse our freedoms under God.

PRAYER IDEA: Ask God to keep America a godly nation in all that it does.

DIVISION OR UNITY

Gettysburg (1993)

MPAA: PG for language and battle scenes

Read: 1 Corinthians 12:12–31

How good and pleasant it is when brothers live together in unity! (Psalm 133:1)

The unity of a young nation, the United States of America, was never more severely tested than during the four-day battle near Gettysburg, Pennsylvania, in 1863. This faithful recreation of that turning point in our history comes alive with thousands of Civil War re-enactors marching over the same hallowed ground where the federal army of the North and the Army of North Virginia marched almost 150 years ago. Colonel Joshua Lawrence Chamberlain (Jeff Daniels) valiantly defends the Little Round Top on one day, and on the next, Major General George Pickett (Stephen Lang) loses his entire division. Throughout it all, brother fights brother, friend fights friend, and the nation battles itself. As Brigadier General Lewis A. Armistead (Richard Jordan) lies dying, he asks a Northern Lieutenant, "Will you tell [Northern] General Hancock that General Armistead sends his regrets? Will you tell him how very sorry I am?" Over fifty thousand casualties later, the nation still toils over the question of unity.

Two sides square off and fight to the death, yet both cherish the same God, language, culture, and history. When objectives diverge, unity is strained. The cost emerges as something more than the soldiers anticipate. Regret sets in when friend murders friend. Looking at a wake of dead bodies strewn behind, the folly of division becomes clear.

Perhaps this is why Paul concluded the book of Romans with this stern warning: "I urge you, brothers, to watch out for those who cause divisions and put obstacles in your way that are contrary to the teaching you have learned" (Romans 16:17). Tearing apart a nation—a church, a marriage, or a family—is like tearing apart a body. It is painful and sometimes causes death. Unity of purpose, not just language, culture, and history, is essential to spiritual and physical health. That is why, if it is in our power, we should "make every effort to keep the unity of the Spirit through the bond of peace" (Ephesians 4:3). For if peace fails, then what else is left? Ephesians continues and summarizes our position: "You were called to one hope . . . one Lord, one faith, one baptism; one God and Father of all, who is over all and through all and in all" (Ephesians 4:4–6).

PRAYER IDEA: Ask God to keep unity in the body of Christ.

A RING OF FIRE
The Lord of the Rings:
The Fellowship of the Ring (2001)
AA: Best Cinematography; Best Visual Effects; Best Makeup;
Best Score • MPAA: PG-13 for epic battle sequences
and some scary images
Read: Genesis 3

J
U
N
E

1

Be strong and courageous. (Joshua 1:6)

The great trilogy by J. R. R. Tolkien, *The Lord of the Rings,* has finally been visualized on film. Audiences give it resounding praise. Tolkien, a friend and fellow Christian writer with C. S. Lewis, has had his work scrutinized, criticized, and praised since it was published in the mid-twentieth century. *The Fellowship of the Ring,* the first story in a trilogy, tells of the "one ring" that destroys its wearer while giving him evil power. By a stroke of fate, a hobbit named Frodo (Elijah Wood) protects the ring as he and his companions travel great lengths to destroy it in the fires of Mount Doom so the enemy Sauron cannot use it against them. Through mountains, snow, darkness, forests, and danger at every corner, the fellowship of the ring march on. They must succeed or forever live under the evil of the dark lord Sauron.

———————

A ring has no beginning and no end; it is continuous by virtue of its shape. Human beings were created by God to continually enjoy fellowship with him on earth for all eternity, but sin and evil entered the world and brought death. However, the ring of everlasting joy with God was broken. What the first humans had hoped for was a delicious experience of eating forbidden fruit. Instead, it turned to bitter poison. Adam and Eve voluntarily placed a ring in their own snouts to be led off to death (Proverbs 11:22). God, in his righteous mercy, banished them from a garden paradise because sin and holiness cannot coexist.

Centuries later God provided the ultimate solution to the endless ring of sin and death. Christ came, battling doubt, disbelief, persecution, and more, to rid the world of the devil's reign. Christ's toilsome journey ends at a point of ultimate testing—death on the cross. Christ had to die alone and sacrifice himself for our sake, taking the penalty of sin and death upon himself for all time and all humankind. The epic story of Christ is sometimes called the monomyth, the one great, majestic story that isn't a mere legend but a true story of ultimate spiritual importance, transcending the ages for the ages. It is the greatest story ever told, filled with battles for our souls. And Christ is victorious!

PRAYER IDEA: Thank God for entering human history through his son Christ.

WATCH YOUR WORDS

Gone with the Wind (1939)

AFI: 4 • AA: Best Picture; Victor Fleming, Best Director;
Vivien Leigh, Best Actress; Hattie McDaniel,
Best Supporting Actress; Best Adapted Screenplay;
Best Cinematography; Best Editing; Best Art Direction;
Technical Achievement Award • MPAA: G • Read: Proverbs 21:23

J
U
N
E

2

**Do not let any unwholesome talk come out of your mouths.
(Ephesians 4:29)**

In *Gone with the Wind* the vain, shallow Southern belle Scarlett O'Hara (Vivien Leigh) moans to her frustrated husband, Rhett (Clark Gable), "If you go . . . where shall I go? What shall I do?"

He replies, "Frankly, my dear, I don't give a d——"

Rhett's response (perhaps the most famous and quoted movie line of all time) flabbergasted audiences around the world. Never before had they heard such language on the big screen. Debates began on acceptable and unacceptable language in movies. Officials charged with enforcing the Motion Picture Code defended their decision to let it stand. Controversy surrounded the picture for months.

Though *Gone with the Wind* had one offensive word in it, many movies before and after it are considered the cleanest, most wholesome movies of all time. Why? Because until 1966 members of the Roman Catholic Church and the Protestant Film Office read every script from every major studio to compare it to the high moral standards of the Motion Picture Code. If the film passed the code, it was distributed; if it didn't, theaters would not screen it. The code essentially adapted the Ten Commandments to the motion picture industry. It states in one line, "Obscene speech, gestures or movements shall not be presented." In 1968 the MPAA's rating system was formed when the church withdrew from monitoring the Motion Picture Code.

Today lots of people bemoan, "They don't make movies like they used to." Perhaps it is because the church doesn't monitor movie scripts anymore. God's people aren't holding up a standard in Hollywood. The MPAA rating system is powerless to enforce decency and goodness in the movies. It doesn't respect religion or religious views. It doesn't wash out the mouths of filmmakers and actors who use dirty language. Morality always follows a standard. With regards to language, we are to monitor our own mouths. We are to police our own families. Unwholesome talk isn't just using obscene words; unwholesome talk includes lying, slander, complaining, gossip, and curses. So don't be like Rhett—watch your mouth!

PRAYER IDEA: Ask God to let the words of your lips always be pleasing in his sight.

GIANTS IN THE LAND
Giant (1956)
AFI: 82 • AA: George Stevens, Best Director • MPAA: G
Read: Deuteronomy 1:19–28

The Emites used to live there—a people strong and numerous, and as tall as the Anakites. (Deuteronomy 2:10)

Rancher "Bick" Benedict (Rock Hudson) marries Maryland horsewoman Leslie (Elizabeth Taylor) and sets up his home on a 500,000-acre ranch in central Texas. Leslie quickly challenges Bick on tradition and lifestyle. She shows kindness to the local Mexican hands. She befriends hired wrangler Jett Rink (James Dean), a man who later challenges Bick's pride by becoming a very wealthy oilman. She even throws tantrums when she can't join the men in political and business conversation. After the children are raised, she supports their individual career choices. Bick thinks it is all nonsense. He says, "You just don't fraternize with the hired help." He also believes a "woman's place is not among the men." As the years pass, Bick learns to face these giant obstacles, ultimately fighting for a Mexican woman who marries into the family.

To Bick, male chauvinism, racism, and Jett Rink represent giants in the land. Bick avoids these looming threats because his forefathers avoided them. Bick isn't entirely comfortable in Texas, because three obstacles keep poking at him, but his wife keeps after him until he confronts these threats and overcomes them. By standing up to Jett Rink, who constantly mocks him, and by caring for Leslie and the Mexicans in respectful ways, Bick is able to fully enter the land and inhabit Texas.

When Israel was about to enter the Promised Land, spies were sent ahead to check it out. They came back and reported that giants lived in the land: Emites, Amorites, and Anakites. These spies were terrified and were never able to fully go up and possess the land. They did not enter the land because they would not change their hearts and believe in the truth of God. Is God asking you to change and enter into a new position? Are you able to fully inhabit the land God is giving you, or are you afraid and unbelieving, holding on to obstacles that shouldn't matter, despite their fierce appearance? Boldly step forth and enter into that which God has reserved for you.

PRAYER IDEA: Ask God to forgive you for doubting his protection.

THE GAMBLERS
Taking a Chance
at the Movies

WEEK 23

June 4–June 10

CONNING THE CON MAN

The Sting (1973)
AA: Best Picture; George Roy Hill, Best Director;
Best Original Screenplay; Best Editing; Best Art Direction;
Best Costume; Best Score • MPAA: PG
Read: Matthew 26:47–56

**You intended to harm me, but God intended it for good.
(Genesis 50:20)**

Double crosses, switchbacks, and robbery are par for the course in *The Sting*, a tale of two con men who plan and pull off the biggest con of their lives, worth a whopping $500,000! Johnny Hooker (Robert Redford) is a man with ambition but a lack of experience. When mob boss Doyle Lonnegan (Robert Shaw) kills a friend and coworker of Hooker, Hooker teams up with seasoned veteran Henry Gondorff (Paul Newman) to soak Lonnegan for his money. Gondorff shows Hooker the ropes while baiting Lonnegan, and just when it looks like the hit is foiled, a "trick ending" reveals that it's all part of the sting.

Like Hooker and Gondorff, Satan thinks he's got everybody fooled. It has been said that the greatest con Satan ever pulled is convincing most people that he doesn't exist. While he has fooled some of the people all of the time, he doesn't fool all of the people all of the time. Some escape his clutches and are called the redeemed: God's church.

Two thousand years ago, Satan thought he had pulled the ultimate job. He filled a man named Judas with greed, and Judas ratted on his boss: Jesus. Jesus was cuffed, brought in, accused, and sentenced to death. Satan thought he could kill off God and make a mockery of what he was doing. What he didn't realize was that God had an ace up his sleeve. In fact, God was holding all the cards. After Jesus was killed and buried, he rose again on the third day, escaping the confines of hell and flabbergasting Satan and all his thugs. So in the end, who conned whom? This world is God's house, and the house always wins.

PRAYER IDEA: Thank God for pulling a fast one on the devil.

LET LOVE RULE
Guys and Dolls (1955)
MPAA: not rated
Read: Colossians 2

Such regulations indeed have the appearance of wisdom, with their self-imposed worship, their false humility and their harsh treatment of the body, but they lack any value in restraining sensual indulgence. (Colossians 2:23)

Street evangelist Sarah Brown (Jean Simmons), at the Save a Soul Mission in New York City, discovers that it takes more than drums, bugles, and condemnatory preaching to bring sinners into the fold in the musical *Guys and Dolls*. She discovers it also takes honesty and a little love. All the wheeler-dealers are in town, and they're depending on Nathan Detroit (Frank Sinatra) to set up this week's version of "the oldest established permanent floating crap game in New York." Unfortunately, he needs $1,000 to get the location. Sky Masterson (Marlon Brando) accepts Nathan's $1,000 bet that he can't get Sarah Brown to go with him to Havana. Sky succeeds, but his conscience bothers him and he gives Nathan the $1,000. Yet Sky also succeeds in another bet, bringing all the gamblers into the Save a Soul Mission. Throughout it all, Sarah learns that rules and strict behavior don't motivate people; straight talk and love are what work. In the end she marries Sky, and Nathan marries his longtime love, Miss Adelaide (Vivian Blaine).

Sarah Brown and her partners had no power in restraining the sensual indulgence of Sky Masterson or the gamblers of New York. All that the gamblers saw in them was condemnation and a boring lifestyle. Although Sky initially charms Sarah so that he can win the bet with Nathan, he soon sees that his behavior was a sham. He claims to have lost the bet, pays Nathan, and becomes an honest man. His honesty, his knowledge of holy Scripture (yes, he really did know the Bible), and his understanding of grace and love affect Sarah deeply. She runs back into his arms and marries him. She becomes a changed woman, full of grace because she encountered grace.

Christ scoffed at human rules and regulations. He healed (worked) on Sunday and ate with sinners (like the gamblers). He didn't merely come to bring order and discipline to the world; he came to save the world from sin and make a way so that sinners and God could be reconciled. Jesus brought us to the purest love. Jesus brought us to genuine relationship. Jesus took away our self-imposed, self-important rules and said, "The Son gives life to whom he is pleased to give it" (John 5:21).

PRAYER IDEA: Ask God to help you discern the difference between man-made regulations and his precious law.

ORGANIZING A STEAL

Ocean's Eleven (2001)

MPAA: PG-13 for language and sexual content

Read: Luke 10:1–20

Let the water under the sky be gathered to one place, and let dry ground appear. (Genesis 1:9)

Released convict Daniel Ocean (George Clooney) has his next hit completely organized. First, he assembles a crack team of ten specialists. Ocean himself is the idea man. There's the bankroll (Elliott Gould), the high roller (Carl Reiner), the pro (Brad Pitt), the rookie who is good at small-time picks (Matt Damon), twin brothers as the getaway drivers, and a bomb expert named Basher (Don Cheadle). Rounding out the group are an "eye in the sky" (a surveillance expert), an insider, and a "grease man" (an acrobat who can flip and twist through the tightest of situations). Together they form Ocean's eleven. These bandits plan to rob three Las Vegas casinos: the Bellagio, the Mirage, and the MGM Grand. The three casinos all belong to Terry Benedict (Andy Garcia), who is dating Danny's beautiful ex-wife, Tess (Julia Roberts). Deep under the Bellagio lies more than $160 million in a state-of-the-art safe. Through extensive research, planning, and organization, the vault is penetrated and relieved of its contents.

Daniel Ocean successfully robs one of the most secure locations on earth because of one thing: organization. Since the creation of the world—when God told the earth, water, sun, stars, and sky to go to their rightful places—organization has brought order, righteousness, and holiness. But because Satan rebelled, disorder has plagued planet earth. Satan has been largely successful in taking people to hell with him because he's been able to keep his rule of evil secure. Jesus came to upset Satan's rule and to "steal" back the lives and souls of all humankind.

Jesus formed a small group of twelve, followed by a larger group of seventy-two, and gave them a surefire plan to crack Satan's safe and get at the goods. In Luke 10, Jesus stated the goal: "Go out into the fields and reap the harvest." Jesus talked about luggage: "Do not take a purse or bag or sandals." He talked about social protocol: "Do not greet anyone on the road." He talked about the measure of success: "He who listens to you listens to me; he who rejects you rejects me." And he talked about the final result: "that your names are written in heaven." This plan to steal back from Satan continues to work today. Are you in?

PRAYER IDEA: Thank God for taking back what the devil steals.

FATE OF THE SWINDLER
The Hustler (1961)
AA: Best Cinematography; Best Art Direction • MPAA: not rated
Read: 1 Corinthians 5:9–13

Neither the sexually immoral nor idolaters nor adulterers nor male prostitutes nor homosexual offenders nor thieves nor the greedy nor drunkards nor slanderers nor swindlers will inherit the kingdom of God. (1 Corinthians 6:9, 10)

Fast Eddie Felson (Paul Newman) loves to shoot pool. A Californian, he travels from state to state and shoots pool for money. At first he pretends he's no good, but when the stakes are high, he lets his opponents have it. He is a hustler. In New York, at Ames Billiards, Eddie meets legendary pool player Minnesota Fats (Jackie Gleason) and challenges him to a match. For over twenty-five hours, Eddie and Fats play, until Eddie collapses from exhaustion. Defeated, Eddie runs into the arms of a lonely alcoholic named Sarah (Piper Laurie). Gambler Bert Gordon (George C. Scott) hustles Eddie to go into business together. Bert gets seventy-five percent of the take! Sarah joins the men in Lexington, Kentucky, but can't stand the corruption and lies that go with hustling. Undone, she commits suicide. Eddie leaves Bert's employment and rushes back to beat Minnesota Fats at Ames.

Eddie, Bert, and Sarah all live lives of degradation, regularly practicing at least one of the sins listed in 1 Corinthians 5. On earth, though they might experience momentary thrills, most of their life is not defined by any real meaning. To say nothing of the next life, they are missing the kingdom of God on earth. The statement above from 1 Corinthians is as much a fact as it is a promise. God isn't just threatening a lack of inheritance for sin; he's saying, "If you live this way, this is what you're going to get." Sarah finds life so dark and unrewarding that she tries to find relief through suicide. Unfortunately, this was not the answer.

Sometimes it takes a big event, like the suicide of a friend, to wake up a sinner from his or her ways. When Sarah dies, Eddie doesn't stop playing pool, but he exposes Bert for his selfishness. Eddie also decides to play wisely (not to exhaustion) and challenges Fats to another game. If you practice any of the above sins from 1 Corinthians 5, don't wait for catastrophe to change. Repent now. If you know people outside the faith who practice these sins, don't judge them but lead them to Christ and let Christ convict them and clean them up. Swindlers only waste their own spiritual health.

PRAYER IDEA: Repent to God of your sins and thank him for cleaning you up.

LYING FOR MONEY

Waking Ned Devine (1999)

MPAA: PG for nudity, language, and thematic elements

Read: 1 Timothy 6:1–10

Do not deceive one another. (Leviticus 19:11)

I n Tullymore, Ireland, a town of fifty residents, Ned Devine wins the lottery and dies from shock. Ned's old friends, Jackie O'Shea (Ian Bannen) and Michael O'Sullivan (David Kelly), discover his body and agree that Ned would have wanted them to benefit from his good luck. So they create a scheme—waking Ned Devine from the dead. First, Michael convinces the lottery authority that he is Ned Devine. Second, Jackie gathers everyone from the town and asks them to point to Michael if the lottery authority comes around and asks, "Who is Ned Devine?" Through this delicate and elaborate ruse, a young pig farmer is able to marry the woman he loves, the town curmudgeon is killed, and Jackie and Michael raise a glass to their dear departed friend.

D espite the humor, warmth, and charm of this movie, the two friends and the rest of the town of Tullymore lie for money. When the amount of the lottery winnings is discovered to not be a mere 500,000 pounds but a whopping 7 million pounds, the townsfolk are more determined than ever to get Ned's money. Objections from Jackie's wife and the fear of life in prison do not deter Jackie and Michael and this town full of liars. While their eventual lot in life may have temporarily improved, the ends do not justify the means.

The pig farmer in *Waking Ned Devine* could have looked for a different, better-paying job. Jackie and Michael could have said, "We are content with what we have." The curmudgeon could have lived another day to learn joy. "Godliness with contentment is great gain" (1 Timothy 6:6). Contentment brings satisfaction and a sense of fulfillment. Contentment disarms arguments, quarreling, and suspicions. Do you need more money? Pray for opportunities and work hard. Do you need contentment? Pray and give thanks to God for what you have. Do you want to marry a stinky pig farmer? Help him to get a new job so that he doesn't smell. God wants to bless you, but even more he wants you to live above reproach.

PRAYER IDEA: Ask God to show you how to be content with the blessings he has given.

PRAYING GOD'S WAY

How Green Is My Valley (1941)

AA: Best Picture; John Ford, Best Director; Donald Crisp,
Best Supporting Actor; Best Art Direction; Best Cinematography

MPAA: not rated

Read: Matthew 6:5–15

JUNE 9

Let us draw near to God with a sincere heart in full assurance of faith. (Hebrews 10:22)

In the early 1900s a Welsh miner, Mr. Morgan (Donald Crisp), runs his home with a firm hand but a kind heart, teaching his six sons and one daughter about prayer, respect, and hard work. The youngest son, Huw (Roddy McDowell), wants to join his father in the colliery, but his father hopes to make an academic out of him. One winter day Huw falls through ice and becomes crippled. For months Huw recuperates, hoping to walk again someday. Come springtime, the village preacher, Mr. Gruffydd (Walter Pidgeon), takes Huw out onto the flowering hillside and teaches him, "As your father cleans his lamp to have good light, so clean your spirit."

Huw asks, "How?"

Mr. Gruffydd replies, "By prayer. By prayer, I don't mean shouting and mumbling and wallowing like a hog in religious sentiment. Prayer is only another name for good, clear, direct thinking. When you pray, think. Think well about what you are saying. That way your prayer will have strength."

Huw does walk again and learns more life lessons from his father and fellow villagers in the classic *How Green Is My Valley*.

Jesus wants us to talk straight with our heavenly Father. After all, Christianity is all about a relationship between God and people. If communication isn't genuine and sincere, it is a waste of time. Lots of people think they need to "pray hard," babbling on and on, believing they will be heard for their many words. Jesus said this isn't necessary. In fact, God knows what we need even before we ask him. God wants us to pray continually, but this should be a natural, ongoing conversation, not begging.

Jesus also tells us to pray in secret. God wants to have quality time alone with us. If we take time to be alone with God, Jesus promised, God will reward us. How do you pray? Not at all? Then start. God is waiting to hear from you. Openly and fervently? Then perhaps you need to ask yourself why you are praying—to please people or to please God. Quietly, privately, and sincerely? Then good for you; keep it up. God loves your fellowship. Think about what you are praying and pray about what you are thinking.

PRAYER IDEA: Ask God to show you how to pray more sincerely and effectively.

BREAK TRADITION
Fiddler on the Roof (1971)
MPAA: G
Read: Galatians 1:14–17

Why do your disciples break the tradition of the elders? (Matthew 15:2)

Life in the small Ukrainian town of Anatevka is like a fiddler on a roof, beautiful but precarious. As the communists threaten political change, the younger generation threatens social change. Matchmaking, in particular, is under question. Traditionally, the matchmaker matches and the father approves. But Tzeitel (Rosalind Harris), the eldest daughter of Tevye (Topol), gives a pledge to her tailor boyfriend that they will marry. Tevye sings of tradition but gives his blessing anyway. Tevye's second daughter falls in love with a teacher and freedom fighter named Perchik (Paul Michael Glaser). This daughter doesn't even ask for her father's blessing or permission. When Tevye's third daughter runs off and marries a Russian, he disowns her, ashamed that she has married outside the faith. To top it all off, the communists clean out the town of Anatevka and demand that the Jews leave their home.

Jesus challenged tradition, and the Pharisees were quick to point it out. Jesus didn't skip a beat, asking the hypocrites, "Why do you break the command of God for the sake of your tradition?" (Matthew 15:3). Jesus was telling them that obedience to the rules of God is more important than obedience to man-made rules. Tradition isn't necessarily bad, but if it gets in the way of true worship and service to God, it should be discarded. Tevye's daughters broke tradition because they wanted to marry the men they loved, not the ones assigned to them.

When we are rooted and built up in Christ, we discover freedom from human regulations. Human traditions don't create holiness. They don't create life and happiness. They might provide temporary satisfaction in knowing that we have done something that is time honored, but they have little real chance of captivating us with their hollow, shallow philosophy that gives the appearance of godliness but is in fact merely constrictive.

Question tradition. See if it lines up with the Bible. It may look good, but it might be unduly restrictive. Following the law of the land is right and proper, but following man-made religious rules may not be. "It is for freedom that Christ has set us free" (Galatians 5:1); we are not to be placed under a man-made yoke. Celebrate your freedom in Christ with joy, thanksgiving, and honor to him.

PRAYER IDEA: Thank your Heavenly Father for setting you free from man-made traditions.

DEAR
OLD DAD
Films of Our Fathers

June 11–June 17

AND IN THE SON

In the Name of the Father (1993)

MPAA: R for language and politically generated violence

Read: John 5:19–30

I and the Father are one. (John 10:30)

Troubled Belfast teen Gerry Conlon (Daniel Day-Lewis) never got along well with his father, Giuseppe (Pete Postlethwaite). After Gerry skirmishes violently with police on the streets in the early 1970s, Giuseppe sends Gerry and his buddy Paul Hill (John Lynch) away to London, hoping that his son will find stability and employment. Instead, Gerry and Paul become homeless petty thieves. They rob an apartment one night, and since they are momentarily rich, they return to Belfast. After the pair barely unpack, police burst into the Conlon residence and arrest Gerry, Paul, and other Irish youths for the bombing of a London pub. Incredibly, Gerry's father and other family members are also arrested as accessories to the crime. Quickly convicted, these innocents find themselves inside a maximum-security prison. As the years pass, Gerry becomes his father's greatest advocate, especially when Giuseppe's health fails. Their case goes to trial again, but for Giuseppe, it's too late. He dies in prison. The Irish innocents are released. Outside the courthouse, Gerry vows, "In the name of my father and of the truth, I will fight on until the guilty are brought to justice."

Jesus constantly defended the Father. As a mouthpiece for God, he took the attention off himself and put it on another. He reminded the Jewish community that the Father he served was the God of Abraham, Isaac, and Jacob. And he challenged those who doubted his relationship with the Father. By equating himself with the Father, he inspired both faith and hatred.

While standing up for God the Father can be dangerous, it is also one of the most fulfilling activities we can do. Today, more than ever, God and his Word are challenged in the public arena. When we serve as God's advocates and defenders, our message is of utmost importance. If we keep silent about God, others may use the law to silence us. We don't have to fear defending God, because the tougher the world gets against God, the more the gospel is advanced. The apostle Paul said the chains of prison encouraged him to speak the word of God more courageously and fearlessly (Philippians 1:14).

The unchurched need to see fearless defenders of God. Desperate times call for courageous leadership. Will you defend God the Father in the courts of public opinion?

PRAYER IDEA: Ask your Heavenly Father how you may defend him and his Word more.

HIS DETERMINED WILL

National Lampoon's Vacation (1983)

MPAA: R for language and sexual situations

Read: Jeremiah 29:11

He determines the number of the stars. (Psalm 147:4)

Clark Griswold (Chevy Chase) determines to take his family on a vacation to Wally World in Los Angeles. Flying there from their home city of Chicago would be too easy. Clark looks at his new station wagon and says to his wife, Ellen (Beverly D'Angelo), "We're taking the whole tribe across country." One hilarious disaster after another ensues as the Griswolds head west. From gas-pumping foibles to getting lost in St. Louis to enduring a zany visit with relatives in Kansas, Clark intends to get to Wally World or bust. When the family runs off the road in Arizona, a repair shop takes them for all their cash. Exhausted and stir-crazy, they arrive in California and discover that Wally World is closed. Undaunted, Clark forces an employee to take his family on all the rides.

Yesterday, today, and tomorrow, God sets his mind in firm determination to carry out his master plan. He organized matter into all the planets and stars and called it creation. He determined to create humankind and gave us a free will so that we would voluntarily love him. When humankind sinned, God determined to make a way of salvation for us through Christ's death and resurrection. Jesus didn't want to die, but he determined to obey the Father. In the future, God will make a new heaven and a new earth and throw Satan forever into a lake of fire. It's his determination.

Determination is nothing more than a firm, unwavering will. Though some might be frightened of God's will, we can take great comfort in his determination. God is the same today as he was yesterday, so we can predict his character and trust in his promises. He is not a man that he should lie; he is divine, and so nobody, not man nor Satan nor principalities nor powers, can thwart him on his crusade of love. We might feel that God is like Clark Griswold, creating havoc as he blindly stumbles forward with his agenda. But unlike Clark, God knows all, sees all, loves all, and has the power to get things done right.

PRAYER IDEA: Confess to Father God that you haven't figured it all out.

A TALE OF TWO DAY CARE CENTERS

Daddy Day Care (2003)

MPAA: PG for language

Read: Psalm 8:1, 2

Since my youth, O God, you have taught me. (Psalm 71:17)

Product developer Charlie Hinton (Eddie Murphy) can't convince his employer at a large food company to pick up his new brand of cereal, Veggie-Ohs. So Charlie and his partner, Phil (Jeff Garlin), are fired. Days turn into weeks, and weeks turn into months, and still Charlie cannot find a new job. Bills stack up, especially those from Chapman Academy, a prestigious preschool and day care center run by the stern Mrs. Gwyneth Harridan (Angelica Huston). There Charlie's son, Ben, learns five languages and is bored to tears. Charlie and Phil see the oppressive manner in which Chapman Academy is run and decide to open their own day care center and call it Daddy Day Care. At first the kids run wild and no order exists, but as the men bring the center up to code and genuinely love the children, the day care center thrives. Mrs. Harridan does all she can to stop Daddy Day Care, but eventually Chapman Academy closes its doors. Parents and kids agree that Daddy Day Care is better because it meets kids at their level and gives them what they really need: love and support.

Often children are pushed to perform beyond their developmental abilities. Patient, caring instruction may be absent, and all that's left is the lashing of a harsh taskmaster. The children get frustrated. The parents get frustrated. And everybody suffers. What's needed is age-appropriate instruction with lots of hugs, creativity, and room to explore. Great male role models help too. Child care is a noble and wonderful profession, even for men.

Our Father in heaven is our Creator. He knows exactly what we need and when we need it. How do you treat God's children? Like a person made in the image of God? Each of us is a unique creature. Each has special needs. The educational goal of the church is not academic intelligence but divine usefulness. We are to be skilled at loving God and loving others. Education is merely a tool to help us become more like Christ. Our Daddy in heaven cares for us every day. Let us do unto others the same.

PRAYER IDEA: Thank your Heavenly Father for loving you at a level you can understand.

OH, GROW UP!
Father of the Bride (1991)
MPAA: PG
Read: Hebrews 5:11—6:3

Perseverance must finish its work so that you may be mature and complete, not lacking anything. (James 1:4)

Father of the bride George Banks (Steve Martin) can't seem to let his daughter, Annie (Kimberly Williams), leave the nest. When twenty-two-year old Annie returns from a study session abroad, she announces to her family that she is engaged. George goes ballistic. First, he searches the list of America's most wanted to see if Annie's fiancé is among them. Then he makes a fuss about meeting the in-laws. Then he contorts his face and grimaces when the costs mount. Then he lands himself in prison for stealing hot dog buns because of all his pent-up rage. Finally, on the wedding day, Dad is able to face the inevitable and accept that his young daughter is now a young woman. Except for a few little mishaps, such as snow and parking problems, the wedding goes off without a hitch.

In this comedy about growing up, it's the dad who has the most maturing to do. Dragging his feet, kicking, and screaming, George resists with all his ability through every difficult step toward Annie's wedding day. In the end, he knows he must change and therefore gives in to the inevitable. He abandons the false notion that his daughter is still a little girl and finally accepts the truth that she is old enough to marry and start a family of her own.

In Hebrews the author chastises slow learners (like George). The author tells his readers that they should be teachers by now, not going over the same information again and again. (George's long-suffering wife keeps after him about his silly resistance to change until he finally relents.) How does one mature? According to the author of Hebrews, the mature are those who "by constant use have trained themselves to distinguish good from evil" (Hebrews 5:14). George's school of hard knocks eventually brings him around. He realizes it is good to let his daughter go. Have you trained yourself to distinguish good from evil? Or have you kept yourself in a fog, resistant to change and acting immaturely for your age and training? Wise up. Learn to discern what is good and true and what is not. Don't be content to be a baby in matters of faith. Grow up!

PRAYER IDEA: Ask God to forgive you for being content in immaturity.

LISTEN TO GOD

Frequency (2000)

MPAA: PG-13 for intense violence and disturbing images

Read: Deuteronomy 6:1, 2

Listen to his voice, and hold fast to him. For the LORD is your life. (Deuteronomy 30:20)

Can a ham radio transmit signals back and forth over a period of thirty years? They can in the movie *Frequency*. John Sullivan (Jim Caviezel) is a thirty-six-year-old police officer living in contemporary New York City. He finds his father's old ham radio and turns it on. Because of some strange solar activity, he hears a voice from thirty years in the past—that of his own father, Frank (Dennis Quaid)! At first they doubt each other, but when John accurately tells the outcome of the 1969 World Series, Frank believes. Their joyous conversation turns sober when John warns his father not to go a certain way in a warehouse fire the next day. Frank obeys and lives, changing the course of history. But now this turn of events causes a mass murderer to kill John's mother. John uses the ham radio to tell his father to stop the murder before it is too late. As the two talk, victims are saved, lives are protected, and John reunites with both his parents in a happier version of the present.

Hindsight is always 20/20, isn't it? If we knew what was going to happen in the future, we could order our lives accordingly to maximize our benefit and minimize our risk. God has the advantage of being able to see all of history, but unfortunately we don't. Wouldn't it be great to talk to someone who knew the future so that he or she could warn us and guide us about our actions today? Well, God knows the past, present, and future and we can talk with him anytime we want. Since God is all knowing, wouldn't it make sense to follow his way?

Lots of the trouble in our lives could have been avoided if we had only listened to those who knew better. The great leaders of the Bible have all said, "Listen to God." Moses, Isaiah, Christ himself, and the apostle Paul all broadcast this message. When the broadcasting on your radio is bad and you can't hear your favorite program, don't you bang on the radio and fidget with the dial so that you can hear? When God calls, do you have him tuned out, or are you dialed in to some other voice? Tune in to God, and he will speak to you. Listen to what he has to say and live.

PRAYER IDEA: Thank your Heavenly Father for speaking to you through his word.

Fathers, do not embitter your children, or they will become discouraged. (Colossians 3:21)

Football coach Thomas Baker (Steve Martin) and his wife, Kate (Bonnie Hunt), have twelve children, none adopted. Tom and Kate want to improve the quality of life for their family and so move from the country and into a colossal house in a Chicago suburb. There Tom picks up a head coaching job for his alma mater team, the Stallions. At the same time, Kate picks up a publishing deal for her book, *Cheaper by the Dozen,* and embarks on a two-week book tour. Tom must fend for himself with his rambunctious teams on the gridiron and at home. But Tom can't cope. Children cry, get into trouble, rappel off the roof, get sick, and disobey. Not only do the children miss their mother, but their father seems too busy with the football team to pay them the attention they need. After near-total chaos ensues, Tom decides to resign as coach so that he can pursue a greater dream: being the dad he needs to be at home.

Fatherhood is an incredibly rewarding and awesome responsibility. Though at times the challenges may seem too hard to bear, a little love and a lot of patience go a long way. Tom loves his children, but he doesn't have time for them with his demanding job. This lack of attention embitters them, and a good number of them decide to purposefully disobey their dad to get his attention. Even though they are grounded, these children leave home and go across the street to a birthday party. Dad calls Mom back home and admits to his family that his job choice was selfish. A change of schedule brings time for proper fathering. The children become happy once again and order is restored to the house.

If you have children, are you giving them the time they need? They don't necessarily need a lot of it, just enough quality moments. If you don't have that kind of time for your children, why not? What is taking away so much of your time? What is of greater importance? They don't need every modern convenience that a good salary can give them; they need love and attention. If you are thinking of becoming a father, keep all these things in mind. Children aren't little monsters. Rather, they are little human beings in need of love and direction. Will you give that to them?

PRAYER IDEA: Ask God for time and opportunities to show love to children.

REMEMBER THE KING

The Lion King (1994)

AA: Best Score; Best Song • MPAA: G

Read: Ecclesiastes 12

Remember the wonders he has done, his miracles, and the judgments he pronounced. (1 Chronicles 16:12)

Young Prince Simba (Matthew Broderick) is the pride of the African Serengeti. One day he will be king, but now Simba's father, King Mufasa (James Earl Jones), reigns over all land that the sunlight touches. From the dark shadows prowl Simba's wicked Uncle Scar (Jeremy Irons) and his hyena hoodlums. They scheme to usurp the throne from Mufasa and succeed. Mufasa is killed in a wildebeest stampede and Scar leads Simba to believe that he is at fault. Simba flees the kingdom in shame, trying to forget all that has happened. When Simba matures, a wise baboon named Rafiki (Robert Guillaume) helps him to remember who is he. Simba realizes that his father lives inside him and thus Simba is encouraged to face Scar and take back the throne.

Like Simba, we are children of the King, meant to rule. We are a royal priesthood. But also like Simba, many of us have forgotten who we are. We have experienced shame and have hidden ourselves away from our responsibilities. Others take the throne and destroy that which God wants to give to us. But in God's world it is never too late to reclaim that which is ours and be restored to our rightful place.

The first step in repentance and restoration is knowing where we came from and who we are. Ecclesiastes 12:1 says,

Remember your Creator in the days of your youth, before the days of trouble come.

Simba forgets who he came from, and so the land becomes dark and gray under the tyrannical rule of Scar. Days of trouble come to the pride lands, while the prodigal son tries to forget his place. Remember where you came from and what God has done for you. Keep a record of God's blessings and answers to prayer. Thank him often for what he has done and what he is still doing in your life. If you remember him, he will remember you, bless you, and keep you in his grace so that you can seize the land he has called you to possess.

PRAYER IDEA: Continually remember God's blessings and answers to prayer.

STIFF
UPPER LIPS
Brit Lit on Film

WEEK 25

June 18–June 24

Those whom I love I rebuke and discipline. (Revelation 3:19)

Poor Emma Woodhouse. Though she means well in the movie adaptation of Jane Austen's *Emma*, the title character (Gwyneth Paltrow) can't stop erring in the sins of presumption, assumption, misinterpretation, and manipulation while performing her favorite sport: matchmaking. Her friend Mr. Knightley (Jeremy Northam) scolds her, "Vanity working on a weak mind produces every kind of mischief. Better to be without sense than misapply it as you do." When Emma ridicules a talkative poor neighbor, Mr. Knightley rebukes her again: "How could you be so insolent, Emma? Badly done." In time Emma confesses her sins, and her friendship with Mr. Knightley deepens into romance.

As children, we are often scolded by our parents. As adults, we might feel that we can get away from watchful eyes. But God asks us to hold our friends accountable when they sin. Proverbs tells us that "faithful are the wounds of a friend" (Proverbs 27:6, KJV). Jesus said to his disciples, "If your brother sins, rebuke him" (Luke 17:3). He also said, "Those whom I love I rebuke" (Revelation 3:19).

It is important to understand, however, that Jesus also asks us to take account of the sin and error in our own lives before taking others to task (Luke 6:41, 42). That way we won't fall into the trap of self-righteousness or pharisaical thinking. The bottom line is that we all mess up once in a while and we all need each other to help us out on our sometimes-difficult journey in Christ. When we sin, a rebuke is nothing more than a helping hand to pull us back onto the right path.

PRAYER IDEA: Ask God to help you give and receive a loving rebuke.

THE LAME WALK
The Secret Garden (1993)
MPAA: G
Read: Mark 2:1–12

"Get up, take your mat and go home." (Matthew 9:6)

Thank God for new seasons, springtime, flowers, and regrowth. *The Secret Garden* tells a tale of such things and lets the audience know that in their own lives they can see miracles. Ten-year-old Mary Lennox (Kate Maberly) was born and reared in India. When her neglectful parents die in an earthquake, she is sent to live at her uncle's castle in England. There she is neglected once again. Her uncle is emotionally distant after having lost his wife ten years ago, and the head housekeeper, Mrs. Medlock (Maggie Smith), is uptight, rude, and no company at all. In time Mary befriends a neighbor boy named Dickon (Andrew Knott), and together they discover a secret garden, restore it to life, and also help restore Mary's lame cousin, Colin (Heydon Prowse), to health and wholeness.

Gardens, growth, life, healing, and restoration are the stuff of Jesus' life, teaching, and mission. Jesus was buried in the ground, yet three days later he came out to new life. He gave sight to the blind and told the lame to walk. He calls us all to follow him, and he says that he has come that we "may have life, and have it to the full" (John 10:10).

Mary Lennox could have fretted and complained about her troubles. She could have said, "Nobody loves me. I guess I'll go eat worms." But she takes a step of faith to go outside into the cold, damp English countryside and explore what is there. The garden she finds is no ordinary garden. It used to be her deceased aunt's garden. Her uncle wanted it closed off forever, but Mary knows that roses and other flowers might again bloom there, where now there are only weeds and dead plants. She also knows that the fresh air and flowers will bring encouragement and hope to her lame cousin, Colin.

Tend and nurture the new life that God has put within you. Take hold of all the healing and growth that he wants to give you. Bring yourself and others to him and his touch, and discover what miracles he can do for you.

PRAYER IDEA: Ask God to heal you of all your infirmities and bring healing to others.

TRANSFIGURED BY LOVE
A Room with a View (1986)
AA: Best Adapted Screenplay; Best Art Direction; Best Costume

MPAA: not rated in the U.S.; PG in the U.K.

Read: 1 Samuel 10:6, 7

JUNE 20

We will all be changed. (1 Corinthians 15:51)

There is nothing like God's good, green earth and a room with a view to stir the soul. When a proper young Edwardian Englishwoman, Lucy Honeychurch (Helena Bonham Carter), holidays in Italy, her passion for life is awakened. While walking through a square, Lucy sees a violent act and faints. A traveling companion named George Emerson (Julian Sands) revives her and says, "Something tremendous has happened." Indeed, something tremendous has happened. Lucy discovers passion and love for the first time. Her heart turns toward George despite her better judgment and her stuffy aunt's attempts to discourage the attachment. Later, George unexpectedly kisses Lucy. Even though her head tells her no, Lucy cannot change the momentum of her heart. She tries to fall in love with a proper, well-behaved suitor back in England, but she eventually denies him.

One of the most wonderful moments of Christ's life on earth was his Transfiguration. Matthew, Mark, and Luke speak of Christ's face and clothes brightening as a flash of lightning (Matthew 17:1–8; Mark 9:2–8; Luke 9:28–36). No doubt, those who looked upon him shining bright, were enraptured by the beauty and wonder of the moment. Jesus glowed with God's blessing. He became the literal "light of the world" (John 1:9; 8:12). His countenance pierced the darkness.

When we are apprehended by the wonderful beauty of Christ, and when we accept the meaning of his violent death in our lives, we will be changed. We will say in our hearts, "Something tremendous has happened." Snatched away from a dour, death-dealing suitor, the devil, we are transfigured into the bride of Christ. God makes us glow and awakens us to new life.

PRAYER IDEA: Ask Jesus to help you see his beauty everywhere.

A REVERSAL OF FORTUNE

Sense and Sensibility (1995)
AA: Best Adapted Screenplay
MPAA: PG for mild thematic elements
Read: Colossians 1:9–14

Surely I have a delightful inheritance. (Psalm 16:6)

Sensible Elinor Dashwood (Emma Thompson) and passionate Marianne Dashwood (Kate Winslet) live in opulent comfort with their mother and father. When Mr. Dashwood dies, however, all his fortunes pass to his eldest son from a previous marriage. In *Sense and Sensibility* Elinor, Marianne, and their mother are left with almost nothing and are forced to rent a small cottage in the country. Further embarrassment heaps upon Elinor and Marianne when their promising romances take a turn for the worse. But their faith and good character, coupled with the goodness of true friends, wins out in the end. The sisters discover an inheritance far greater than money can buy: true love to exemplary suitors Edward Ferrars (Hugh Grant) and Colonel Brandon (Alan Rickman).

God's Word says, "Hope deferred makes the heart sick" (Proverbs 13:12). If an expected inheritance falls through or another tragedy visits us, it's hard to believe that there is someone watching out for us with a grand inheritance in hand. God has an inheritance of everlasting peace and fellowship with him. We acquire this at salvation, when we are adopted into his family. And God has no half-daughters or stepsons. We are all his rightful children with access to his riches.

We cannot earn this divine inheritance. It is not a wage, lest the workers boast of their exploits. It is a free gift given from our Father to his offspring. It is a reward for submission and respect. Those who don't know the Father do not share in this inheritance. The inheritance is for those who recognize that all good gifts are from God and God alone.

PRAYER IDEA: Thank God for counting you as one of his children, eligible for his inheritance.

DO NOT BE DECEIVED

Much Ado about Nothing (1993)

MPAA: PG-13 for momentary sensuality

Read: Matthew 24:4–11

Watch out that no one deceives you. (Mark 13:5)

It all seems such a mess, but it's really much ado about nothing. Benedick (Kenneth Branagh) scorns Beatrice (Emma Thompson), and Beatrice spars with Benedick. The two bicker and fight like nipping dogs. Young lovers Hero (Kate Beckinsale) and Claudio (Robert Sean Leonard) are to be married in one week. To pass the time, they conspire with Don Pedro (Denzel Washington) to set a "lover's trap" for Benedick and Beatrice. Meanwhile, the evil Don John (Keanu Reeves) conspires to break up the wedding by accusing Hero of infidelity. The wedding is ruined; Claudio shuns Hero; Hero is perceived dead; and Beatrice asks Benedick to murder Claudio. However, in the end, lies are exposed, Don John is brought to justice, and loves and lives are mended once again, bringing not one, but two couples to the marriage altar.

This Shakespearean story warns against lies and deception. But it also warns against jumping to conclusions. Claudio does see a woman fornicating with a guard, but she is not Hero. Instead of questioning the guard and Hero, he assumes the worst and damages the reputation of his wife-to-be, who has indeed saved herself as a maid. Likewise, Benedick and Beatrice think the worst about each other. They insult each other, never stopping to realize that they are perfect for each other, until Don Pedro and Claudio take the veil off their eyes through a little fun.

Deception causes all sorts of trouble. Almost every book in the Bible warns about deceit and its dangers. Deceit was first recorded when the serpent tricked Eve into eating the forbidden fruit. Much ado has been created in the world because of that mess, yet the consequences are far from nothing. When deceit is thwarted through searching out and in upholding by the truth, we can often avoid terrible consequences. But woe to us who fall under its evil spell. Some trouble really is nothing, but when deceit and lies are mixed in, someone is bound to get hurt.

PRAYER IDEA: Ask God to help you to expose deceit when it comes to visit.

WILLFUL UNTO DEATH

Wuthering Heights (1939)

MPAA: not rated

Read: Romans 8:5–11

**Set your minds on things above, not on earthly things.
(Colossians 3:2)**

Adopted son and former gypsy beggar Heathcliff (Laurence Olivier) deeply loves his adopted sister, Cathy (Merle Oberon). They reside in their home, Wuthering Heights, nestled within the heather-filled English moors. Cathy's blood brother treats Heathcliff unmercifully, so Cathy and Heathcliff often escape to the rocky crags and there pretend to be sophisticated royalty. As they mature, all Heathcliff wants to do is marry Cathy. But Cathy wants more: she wants a privileged life like that which she and Heathcliff imagined. But Heathcliff can't deliver it. So she develops a relationship with their neighbor Edgar Linton (David Niven) and marries him. Heathcliff leaves Wuthering Heights and years later returns as a wealthy man of distinction. He marries Edgar's sister, Isabella (Geraldine Fitzgerald), for spite. Going mad with regret for marrying Edgar instead of Heathcliff, Cathy dies in Heathcliff's arms. Heathcliff prays that the ghost of his beloved will forever haunt him. One snowy night Heathcliff responds to Cathy's phantom call and freezes to death out on the moors, searching for a person who isn't there.

Obsession for mere human love and worldly wealth bring death to both Cathy and Heathcliff. Their minds are set on things of this earth and not on God. Granted, his adopted brother mistreats Heathcliff, but Heathcliff chooses to play the victim, carrying hate into a single-minded, willful quest that can only end in tragedy.

It has been said, "Aim for heaven and you also get the earth. Aim for earth and you get neither." When we set our minds on things of this earth, we may get riches and our selfish way, but we won't achieve any happiness and we will probably die a death caused by our own choices. When we set our minds on heaven (that is, Christ and his kingdom), God will open up his blessings and give us all we need for life and happiness in this life and the life to come. Since we have been raised with Christ, our hearts are to be set on things above. We died and our life is now hidden with Christ in God.

Put to death your selfish ambitions before they put you to death.

PRAYER IDEA: Ask God to help you set your mind on heavenly, not earthly things.

NO GOD OF STONE

The Remains of the Day (1993)

MPAA: PG for themes

Read: Jeremiah 2:26–28

They have hands, but cannot feel. (Psalm 115:7)

James Stevens (Anthony Hopkins) is the emotionally crippled butler of Darlington House in *The Remains of the Day.* Bound to duty, he believes that a man cannot call himself contented unless he has done all he can to be of service to his employer. For Mr. Stevens, this means ignoring the presence of evil. Within the walls of Darlington House, Lord Darlington (James Fox) welcomes and sympathizes with the rising German powers of the late 1930s. When Miss Sally Kenton (Emma Thompson) joins the staff as housekeeper of Darlington House, she challenges Mr. Stevens not only on his veneer of servitude but also on his unfeeling response to the Nazi menace within the house. Jewish servant girls are fired and Mr. Stevens doesn't protest. Nazi spokespersons speak freely, but Mr. Stevens seems not to hear. The war comes and goes, but it isn't until twenty years later that Mr. Stevens realizes the error of his emotional responses. He finally renounces Lord Darlington and finds the will to reach out in love to the now-married Sally.

Don't be like Mr. Stevens. Resist the urge to keep a stiff upper lip when it comes to your relationship with God. Let your feelings show. God is our Father, and Christ is our Friend. Fathers and friends don't deserve cold and measured responses. God is not made of wood or stone. Raise your objections before God like Moses did. Like David, praise him. Like the women caught in adultery, fall at his feet. Like the disciples, eat with him and ask him questions. Go ahead.

He is not a wicked God that you should be ashamed of him (like the shame Mr. Stevens eventually feels for Lord Darlington). God doesn't have clandestine meetings, harboring the enemy. He exposes the enemy and has the power to contain him. Hence, your service to God should be marked by joy and gladness. Let your joy show.

You are not to serve God without thought or feeling, as if you were merely responding to a list of rules. You are made in his image, and so you can be sure that he has feelings like yours. Let God heal you of your emotional scars. Ask him to bring love where there has been neglect. Step out, like Mr. Stevens, and show love to those you have neglected in the past. God loves full, emotionally satisfying relationships.

PRAYER IDEA: Ask God to heal your emotional scars and let him open your heart to healthy responses.

MEN IN CAPES
Super Stories
of Superheroes

WEEK 26

June 25–July 1

SENT TO SAVE

Superman (1977)

MPAA: PG for peril, mild sensuality, and language

Read: Psalm 30

God sent his Son. (Galatians 4:4)

In *Superman* Jor-El (Marlon Brando) sends his infant son to planet Earth from the planet Krypton. Adopted by a kindly farming family, the boy known as Clark Kent (Christopher Reeve) slowly discovers super powers and abilities unique to himself. He can bend bars of steel, fly, melt metal with his laser vision, and more. Coming to understand himself and his place in the world, he uses his unique position to save humankind from deadly situations. All the while, a nemesis——Lex Luthor (Gene Hackman)——tries to destroy him and his ability to do good.

Christ never leapt buildings in a single bound, and he certainly didn't fly (except perhaps when he ascended into heaven). But he was super good and he performed miracles. He was sent from heaven by his Father, God, to perform a specific role here on Earth. Jesus obscured his identity to some mockers but told others openly who he was. His miracles pointed to his divinity, confirming his verbal assertions of his own nature.

God, taking the form of a man, makes it possible for men and women to be saved. We are helpless and in peril always, but when we cry out for a Savior, Jesus always comes to the rescue (Psalm 30:2). God is an ever-present help in time of trouble (Psalm 46:1). And that's more than super——that's awesome.

PRAYER IDEA: Thank God for sending his Son to rescue all humankind from death.

BLESSED ARE THE PERSECUTED

X-Men (2000)
MPAA: PG-13 for sci-fi action violence
Read: Matthew 5:43–48

Blessed are you when people insult you, persecute you and falsely say all kinds of evil against you because of me. (Matthew 5:11)

In the movie *X-Men* the world is partly populated by mutants—genetically altered, enhanced human beings with special powers. In this futuristic world it's tough to be a mutant. People are afraid of you. Others hate you. Legislatures want to lock you up so you can't use your powers for evil. Mind-reading mutant Professor Charles Francis Xavier (Patrick Stewart) knows persecution full well. So he starts a school, training mutants (or X-men) to use their powers for good. Professor Xavier hopes that normal people will someday treasure and value mutants. On the other hand, Magneto (Ian McKellen), a man who can levitate and control metal, wants to fight evil persecution with evil methods.

Christians can be a lot like mutants. The Bible calls us "peculiar" (Titus 2:14; 1 Peter 2:9, KJV). The Bible says we are not of this world. Some people are threatened by our love and our message of God's love. And so we are persecuted, discouraged with force from doing what God would have us do.

When we face persecution, we can do either one of two things: we can fight back with force, or we can bless those who persecute us. Fighting back encourages retribution because those who live by the sword die by the sword. When we bless those who persecute us, we are obeying the commandment to love our enemies.

Jesus says that we are blessed when we are persecuted (Matthew 5:11). He is pleased with us when we are active ambassadors for his name and kingdom. (People who are not vocal about his love and truth are not persecuted.) We can be glad that we share some of the same treatment that the great saints of old experienced. We will be rewarded in heaven when we face persecution.

When Christ and his love are within us so powerfully that we have to tell others about it, we become peculiar. We become mutants. Thank God for people like Professor Xavier, people who encourage us to use our faith for good.

PRAYER IDEA: Tell God you are blessed when you face ridicule and persecution.

SOLID AS A DIAMOND

Unbreakable (2000)

MPAA: PG-13 for mature themes, violent content, and a sexual reference

Read: Matthew 5:17, 18

The Scripture cannot be broken. (John 10:35)

David Dunn (Bruce Willis) is unbreakable. As a passenger on a train that wrecks, he emerges as the sole survivor. Furthermore, he doesn't even have one scratch. Slowly, David discovers that he has other abilities, such as super strength. In time he gets to know an odd, fragile man named Mr. Glass (Samuel L. Jackson). Mr. Glass explains to him that he is special. Mr. Glass helps David understand why he doesn't get sick, become injured, or break bones. Understanding his newfound abilities, he helps the weak and vulnerable.

David Dunn and God's Word share something in common. Both are unchanging and unbreakable. Like David Dunn, the Bible cannot be picked apart. One cannot believe some of it while disbelieving other parts of it. It's all or nothing. A collection of historical records, poems, allegories, and visions, "all Scripture is God-breathed and is useful for teaching, rebuking, correcting and training in righteousness" (2 Timothy 3:16). To disbelieve some of it does not shatter the truth of God. Its complete integrity makes it powerful to help those in need.

While complete trust in God's Word may seem hard to accept, it is actually a great source of peace and confidence. When we accept God's Word as truth, we can trust that all his promises are still in effect. We don't have to be on uncertain or shaky ground, not knowing if we are inside God's love or outside it. He is the same today, yesterday, and forever (Hebrews 13:8). His Word is unbreakable.

PRAYER IDEA: Thank God for his great and precious unbreakable promises.

ENDURANCE THROUGH SUFFERING

Spiderman (2002)

MPAA: PG-13 for stylized violence and action

Read: Romans 8:28–39

We . . . rejoice in our sufferings. (Romans 5:3)

The girl you secretly love dates somebody else. A spider has bitten you. You develop flu-like symptoms and then an armed thug guns down your Uncle Ben (Cliff Robertson). Life stinks if you are Peter Parker (Tobey Maguire) in *Spiderman*. But in the midst of his misery, Peter receives a wonderful gift: superhuman strength and the ability to spin super-strong webs. Before Uncle Ben dies, he tells Peter, "With great power comes great responsibility." Peter takes these words to heart and develops his skills to perfection as a crime fighter. He foils ordinary robbers and the extraordinarily insane Green Goblin (Willem Dafoe). Even as Spidey does good, he pays a price for his notoriety. The local paper paints him as a possible criminal, and the Goblin tries to murder people he loves. Nevertheless, Spidey endures valiantly.

God has made each person unique, with individual talents, brains, personality, and background. In this sin-stung world, we all must walk a trail of tears, enduring a series of sins and woes committed against us (and some that we commit against ourselves). Some never rise above their pain and never develop their potential. Others seize their potential but spend it on selfish gain. To those who hear God's call and decide to live a life of bold devotion to Christ, God promises victory, joy, and triumph, but also suffering.

The superhuman God-man Jesus Christ endured suffering and pain for the good of humanity. He didn't hide who he was but waited for the proper time to demonstrate his power. When the apostle Stephen took up his cross and followed Christ, he suffered through martyrdom. Most of the original twelve disciples also lost their lives because of their allegiance to Christ. Why? Because the alternative was worse: spiritual and eternal death. They had been given a gift they couldn't deny.

Peter Parker could have denied his calling and lived a life of quiet obscurity. But he realizes that, with his blessings, he can bless others. With the dynamic, life-giving Word of God and all its transforming power, we too have a blessing meant to be shared with others. Will you answer God's call and endure misunderstanding, shame, attack, and possible death for the sake of Christ? Someone's eternal life may depend on your decision.

PRAYER IDEA: Rejoice in God while you suffer and use his gifts for his glory.

DARKNESS INTO LIGHT
Batman (1989)
AA: Best Art Direction/Set Decoration
MPAA: PG-13 for action violence and thematic elements
Read: Psalm 139:11, 12

JUNE 29

There is no dark place, no deep shadow, where evildoers can hide. (Job 34:22)

The dark corners and shadowy alleys of Gotham City cannot shield its criminals when Batman (Michael Keaton) is on the prowl. Seldom seen by the upstanding public, he instills as much fear as he does peace into the hearts and minds of the city residents. Reporter Alexander Knox (Robert Wuhl) and prizewinning photojournalist Vicky Vale (Kim Basinger) intend to uncover the real story on this elusive caped crusader. Crime escalates when Jack Napier (Jack Nicholson) falls into a vat of toxic chemicals, transforming him into a lunatic who calls himself the Joker. With an ever-present silly grin, The Joker terrorizes Gotham City by tainting beauty products so they cause death. Billionaire Bruce Wayne watches the Joker with great interest, and in time we discover the link between the Dark Knight and the laughing murderer. D. A. Harvey Dent (Billy Dee Williams), Police Commissioner Gordon (Pat Hingle), the mayor (Lee Wallace), and the citizens of Gotham City come to trust Batman when they discover his powers and abilities to stop the Joker.

With seemingly superhuman vision and a keen awareness of when trouble will strike, Batman goes out at night and scours the darkness until it is clean. Like Batman, Jesus is a misunderstood hero who has no fear of the dark. Psalm 139:12 says of our Lord,

Even the darkness will not be dark to you; the night will shine like the day, for darkness is as light to you.

Our Lord is not afraid of the dark because he himself is light. His presence peels back the fear and mystery, causing the evil that dwells in darkness to be exposed.

Ephesians 5:11–14 says, "Have nothing to do with the fruitless deeds of darkness, but rather expose them. For it is shameful even to mention what the disobedient do in secret. But everything exposed by the light becomes visible, for it is light that makes everything visible." Batman exposes the Joker and destroys him. And Jesus exposes the deeds of the evil one, having destroyed his power on the cross.

PRAYER IDEA: Ask God to show you how can pierce the darkness with his light.

ANGER MANAGEMENT
The Hulk (2003)
MPAA: PG-13 for sci-fi action violence,
disturbing images, and brief partial nudity
Read: John 2:12–16

The LORD's anger burned against them. (Numbers 25:3)

Research scientist Dr. Bruce Banner (Eric Bana) bottles up his anger. Working closely with his girlfriend, Dr. Betty Ross (Jennifer Connelly), they hope to discover the formula for spontaneous cell regeneration after injury. Betty's father, General Thaddeus Ross (Sam Elliott), sees tremendous military applications. If soldiers could instantly heal, they could be kept on duty. But Dr. Banner has a secret: he has mutant DNA in his cells and his mad scientist father, David (Nick Nolte), killed his mother. After an accident in the lab, Dr. Banner's rage turns him into an oversized green monster, the Hulk. General Ross hides Betty and captures Bruce for research, but Bruce cannot be contained. Breaking free from his underground prison, the Hulk battles military choppers and bombs. Eventually Bruce meets up with his father for a major father/son tussle. Finally General Ross drops a big bomb on the duo to put a lid on these raging, muscle-bound freaks.

Like the Hulk, we sometimes bottle our anger until a moment when it all comes out in monstrous fury. Anger rears its ugly head all too often in our homes, at work, and on the streets. How should we deal with anger, biblically speaking? First of all, it's okay to be angry. Anger is an emotion that even our Lord experienced. When Jesus saw that the temple was being used as a marketplace, he got mad and turned the tables over. So it's okay to sometimes express anger, especially to expose sin. But Scripture also says the following: "His anger lasts only a moment" (Psalm 30:5). "Time after time he restrained his anger" (Psalm 78:38). "The LORD . . . is slow to anger, abounding in love" (Psalm 103:8). Our Lord kept his anger in check and so must we.

Anger should never lead to sin and devastation. The Bible also says, "In your anger do not sin" (Ephesians 4:26). Obviously, anger shouldn't involve hurting others. The more we rage, the more it limits our ability to constructively solve the problem we are facing. Some problems can't be solved (like slow traffic), and this calls for acceptance. Deep-rooted anger that we can't seem to shake may call for some deep spiritual healing or professional intervention. One thing is for sure: the joy, love, and peace that Christ wishes to impart to us can't coexist with anger, hate, and discord. They are like oil and water.

Submit to Christ, resist temptation, give thanks in all things, and ask God to set you free from the kind of anger that turns you into a Hulk.

PRAYER IDEA: Ask God to heal the rage inside of you and give you self-control.

LEADING WITH RIGHTEOUSNESS

Mr. Smith Goes to Washington (1939)

AFI: 29 • AA: Best Original Screenplay • MPAA: not rated

Read: Exodus 17:8–15

Righteousness exalts a nation, but sin is a disgrace to any people. (Proverbs 14:34)

U.S. Senator Jefferson Smith (Jimmy Stewart) has the Senate floor in *Mr. Smith Goes to Washington.* Angered by the injustices and political moves that go on there, he lets fly a speech that rivals that of any actual politician. Smith knows that he must stand and continue his filibuster, or else injustice will prevail. In the midst of his lengthy speech, he tells the other senators,

> Just get up off the ground—that's all I ask. Get up there with that lady that's up on top of this Capitol dome, that lady that stands for liberty. Take a look at this country through her eyes if you really want to see something. And you won't just see scenery; you'll see the whole parade of what man's carved out for himself after centuries of fighting. Fighting for something better than just jungle law, fighting so as he can stand on his own two feet, free and decent, like he was created, no matter what his race, color, or creed. That's what you'd see. There's no place out there for graft or greed or lies or compromise with human liberties.

These words define Smith as a noble and righteous leader. Today's leaders could take a cue from him. Again and again in Scripture we learn of righteous leaders and unrighteous tyrants. The health and prosperity of the nations they rule are in direct proportion to the honesty and righteousness of their rule.

We are powerless without God. As long as Moses' arms were spread out over the armies, God's power was demonstrated through Israel. If Moses had dropped his arms, the Amalekites would have prevailed. We need the power of God to help us. We need human helpers to hold up our hands in the pursuit of righteousness. We need the prayer and moral support of others to govern righteously, and so do our president, congressional representatives, and senators. We are indeed "one nation under God."

PRAYER IDEA: Ask God to fill our leaders with wisdom and strength to govern righteously.

OUR COUNTRY
'Tis of Thee: Hailing
the Spirit of America

WEEK 27

July 2–July 8

FIRST IN SPACE
The Right Stuff (1983)
AA: Best Sound Effects; Best Film Editing; Best Score;
Best Sound • MPAA: PG (previously rated R)
Read: Mark 9:33–37

Whoever wants to be first must be your slave. (Matthew 20:27)

With World War II over and the Cold War just starting, the Russians and the Americans race to be the first to put a man in space. American Chuck Yeager (Sam Shepard) breaks the sound barrier in the late 1940s, and other test pilots follow, flying even faster. The U.S. government recruits some of these men—including Alan Shepard (Scott Glenn), John Glenn (Ed Harris), Gordon Cooper (Dennis Quaid), and Gus Grissom (Fred Ward)— to be the first astronauts for the Mercury program. The U.S. government thinks these men have the right stuff. Run through a battery of mental and physical tests, these fellows charm American audiences and become heroes. Though the Russians beat us to the punch when Yuri Gagarin becomes the first man in space, Alan Shepard becomes the first American to enter space and John Glenn becomes the first to orbit the earth.

Being first in the space race was a matter of national pride, especially when America and Russia wanted to flex their muscle in a display of political and technological superiority. But Jesus gave a different view for spiritual superiority. He said, "If anyone wants to be first, he must be the very last, and the servant of all" (Mark 9:35). The cheering throng of heaven doesn't want to see you puffed up in personal pride. That throng delights in your taking a backseat and helping others along the way.

In *The Right Stuff* the other Mercury astronauts give the nickname Hot Dog to their member Gordon Cooper. Cooper himself always says he is the best pilot he ever saw. This kind of bravado doesn't play well in the kingdom of God. Confidence is one thing, but posturing is another. Greatness is service and love and compassion and putting others ahead of oneself. Giants of the faith, such as Mother Teresa and Billy Graham, have fame not because of their own claims about themselves but because of their humble service. Nobody is racing us to become a great human. There's enough space for us all to reach the skies and to be all God wants us to be.

PRAYER IDEA: Ask God to show you how to be the last and the servant of all.

BELIEVE IN MUSIC

The Music Man (1962)

MPAA: G

Read: John 11:38–44

Believe that you have received it, and it will be yours. (Mark 11:24)

Professor Harold Hill (Robert Preston) has some big trouble right there in River City, Iowa. The townspeople are counting on him to form a marching band, but Professor Hill doesn't know a lick of music, not one note. Exposed for the fraud he is, Hill must escape an angry mob bent on tarring and feathering him. Only Marian the librarian (Shirley Jones) sees the good that Professor Hill has brought to River City. Under the kindly but criminal Professor Hill, juvenile delinquents find purpose. Marian's little brother emerges from a funk. A barbershop quartet is even formed. Hill teaches them all the "thinking method," imagining the possibilities first and then watching the results come later. The people capture Professor Hill and are about dip him in tar when the band shows up ready to play. For weeks, they have imagined playing, and though they don't know any music, they play well enough to make the townspeople cheer. The band gets even better and Professor Hill's name is restored from crook to "the music man."

It's amazing what a little belief can do. Marian believed Harold could reform, and he did. The band believed they could play, and they did. Belief can transform bad situations into good. When we begin to believe the beliefs that God believes in—watch out. Miracles might occur.

Perhaps the most difficult thing to believe is that Jesus could raise a dead man from the grave. (Indeed, thinking that an untrained band could play music would take much less faith.) But Jesus said, "Did I not tell you that if you believed, you would see the glory of God?" (John 11:40). Then Jesus raised Lazarus from the dead.

God doesn't ask us to engage in wishful thinking. He asks us to believe. When we pray (about changing a sinner we know into a saint, about bringing order to chaos, or about deriving music from disharmony), let us not doubt in our hearts but believe that we have received it, and it will be ours (Mark 11:24).

PRAYER IDEA: Ask God to give you faith to believe in miracles.

Our Invisible Weapon

Independence Day (1996)

AA: Best Visual Effects

MPAA: PG-13 for sci-fi destruction and violence

Read: 1 Samuel 17:45–47

JULY 4

The weapons we fight with are not the weapons of the world. (2 Corinthians 10:4)

In *Independence Day* aliens from space arrive and hover their giant spacecraft over our major cities. But we cannot communicate with them. On July 2 David Levinson (Jeff Goldblum), a cable systems engineer, discovers that the aliens are going to attack major points around the globe in less than twenty-four hours. On July 3 the aliens obliterate New York, Los Angeles, and Washington. Some survivors, including President Thomas J. Whitmore (Bill Pullman), set out toward Area 51, where our military has kept one of the aliens' downed spacecraft since 1951. Through analysis of the old craft, David discovers that he can upload a computer virus and knock out the enemy's defensive shield. On July 4 Captain Steve ("Eagle") Hiller (Will Smith) and David fly the alien craft to the mother ship to deliver the virus, which shuts down the enemy's entire defense system.

In Area 51 the president asks an alien, "What do you want us to do?" The alien replies, "Die." The aim of this alien is nothing less than the annihilation of the human race.

Similarly, our foe, Satan and his demons, are not of this world. They seek our total destruction and separation from God. The terrible news is that, on our own, we cannot fight them. Nothing we have created, no amount of willpower, no amount of human strength can defeat them. We cannot reason or negotiate with our enemy. He is an unstoppable force of evil. He must be denied and thwarted, but how?

Jesus didn't bargain with Satan. He dealt with him through scriptural truth and by resisting him. True victory lies in the knowledge that we don't wrestle against flesh and blood but against spiritual, supernatural forces. We win through prayer. We win by speaking truth in the face of lies. We win through ejecting the enemy, using our authority in spiritual warfare. The unseen computer virus of *Independence Day* brings victory for humanity in this movie; the unseen power of the Holy Spirit brings us victory today.

PRAYER IDEA: Ask God to teach you how to do spiritual warfare.

"GONNA FLY NOW"

Rocky (1976)

AFI: 78 • AA: Best Picture; John G. Avildsen,
Best Director; Best Film Editing
MPAA: PG for boxing violence and themes
Read: 1 Corinthians 9:24–27

J
U
L
Y

5

Prepare your minds for action. (1 Peter 1:13)

In the late 1960s Sylvester Stallone saw boxing champ Muhammad Ali almost lose a fight to an unknown boxer. Inspired, Stallone wrote *Rocky* and pitched it to Hollywood, where it was received enthusiastically. Unfortunately, many studios didn't want to cast the unknown Stallone in the lead, and for a long time Burt Reynolds was considered for the title role. But Stallone stuck to his guns, prepared his acting chops and his boxing socks, and won the part in the role of a lifetime.

Rocky ("The Italian Stallion") Balboa is a part-time boxer in Philadelphia. Current world heavyweight boxing champion Apollo Creed (Carl Weathers) invites the unknown Rocky to fight for the title of world heavyweight champ. At first Rocky says no, but then he agrees, trains hard, and enters the ring for the highly publicized match. Creed vows to drop Rocky in three rounds, but Rocky battles through the whole fight, pummeling Creed and nearly taking the belt away from him.

To win the role of a lifetime, a heavyweight fight, or the battles of the Christian life, you must prepare yourself. Floating through life doesn't cut it; if you do, you will be brutally assaulted by your foe. Actors, dancers, doctors, lawyers, retail clerks, and people of all occupations must go through training and testing before their actual work begins. Living up to God's purposes is no exception. God calls us to train—hard!

Who can forget the image of Rocky running up the steps and raising his arms in triumph? The fight with Apollo hasn't even yet begun, but Rocky feels the thrill of victory because he knows he has done all he can to prepare for the fight. The apostle Paul asked us to "run in such a way as to get the prize" (1 Corinthians 9:24). Rocky beats his body and puts it into submission so that he will not be disqualified for the prize. Though Rocky eventually loses the fight to Apollo by the narrowest of margins, he wins the hearts (and box office) of the American people, leading to four *Rocky* sequels and colossal financial returns. It is one of the most successful movie franchises ever created.

PRAYER IDEA: Tell God that you accept the assignment he has planned for you.

A man reaps what he sows. (Galatians 6:7)

In 1776, near Charleston, South Carolina, widowed father Benjamin Martin (Mel Gibson) says, "I have long feared my sins would return to visit me, and the cost is more than I can bear." A veteran of the French and Indian wars, he vows pacifism against approaching British redcoats. Yet his son Gabriel (Heath Ledger) signs up for battle, anxious to fight. When Gabriel is caught and handed over for execution, Benjamin turns to action. He takes up arms, especially against the evil Col. William Tavington (Jason Isaacs), who heartlessly murders Benjamin's number-two son. After Benjamin rescues Gabriel in an act of terrible violence, Gabriel adopts the bloodthirsty ways of his father. When Tavington kills Gabriel's wife, Gabriel goes after Tavington with a vengeance. This time young Martin loses and is killed. Benjamin must once more return to his bloody beginnings and vows to kill Tavington before war's end.

Sin wreaks havoc over long periods of time. It is never an isolated act. The legacy of sin yields more sin in future generations. Children and grand-children often duplicate the sins of their parents. This sin must be identi-fied, repented of, and snuffed out. Some may say *The Patriot* is about caring for a family, about patriotism, or about retribution. But the real horror of this story is how a son observes the sins of a father, imitates his ways, and pays for it with his life. "All who draw the sword will die by the sword" (Matthew 26:52). The greatest tragedy of this story is that Benjamin sees this violent legacy on display as Gabriel trades blows with a foe and falls lifeless.

Our Father God passes down a legacy of love, forgiveness, mercy, and wis-dom. We never inherit anything but goodness from him. This is all the more meaningful since none of us is fortunate enough to have a perfect father on earth. All of us must reckon with the errors of our parents and make decisions to either go and do likewise or stand firm in opposition.

Patriotism is loyalty to a sovereign or a country. God is our Sovereign, his king-dom is our country, and love is his legacy to us. Our earthly nation may one day call us to arms, but our eternal nation calls us to a far greater cause: faithfulness.

To whom are you a patriot? Where do your allegiances lie? Begin now to teach your children to obey the one true God. That way, your children may never duplicate your sin.

PRAYER IDEA: Ask God to grant you the legacy of his mercy, instead of sin.

HOW TO BE THE BEST

Top Gun (1986)
AA: Best Song • MPAA: PG
Read: Mark 10:35–45

Whoever wants to become great among you must be your servant. (Matthew 20:26)

Hotshot Navy aviator Pete ("Maverick") Mitchell (Tom Cruise) longs to be the best of the best. He gets his chance when his lieutenant commander sends him and his partner, Goose (Anthony Edwards), to Flight Weapons School in Miramar, California. There the best of the best achieve top-gun status. Maverick says, "I am dangerous," to his teachers and fellow students, provoking their ire as much as their respect. Maverick struts his way through school, even romancing a flight instructor, Charlotte Blackwood (Kelly McGillis), until one day tragedy strikes. During a training exercise gone awry, Goose dies after incorrectly ejecting from the cockpit. Now Maverick doesn't even know if he can finish school. Humbled, he is haunted by the memory of his deceased fighter-pilot father as well as the loss of Goose. Although Maverick loses his bravado, he achieves greatness in combat. Subjugating his desire to be first, he provides wingman backup to Iceman (Val Kilmer) while confronting actual Russian MiGs over the Indian Ocean.

Those who are full of themselves can't be full of Jesus. Self-sacrifice isn't just about the grandiose idea of laying down your life for another. It's about laying down your attitudes, your will, and your agenda. If Maverick hadn't provided backup to Iceman, lives could easily have been lost. When everybody wants to lead and nobody wants to follow, space at the top gets crowded and people start bumping into each other. High in the air or down on the ground, those who serve others find the greatest rewards. Plus, a whole team of servants experiences greater efficiency and happiness.

James and John wanted to be wingmen to Jesus, but Jesus told them they didn't know what they were asking. If they had followed him to death, they would have been on either side of Jesus on crosses at Golgotha. Jesus told them, "Whoever wants to become great among you must be your servant, and whoever wants to be first must be slave of all" (Mark 10:43, 44).

Slavery to others isn't a popular idea today. But as the old Bob Dylan song says, "You got to serve somebody." You can serve yourself, you can serve God, or you can serve evil. There are no other options. Whom will you serve today?

PRAYER IDEA: Tell God that you recognize all good gifts are from him.

OUR UNRELENTING BUT DEFEATED FOE

The Terminator (1984)

MPAA: R for violence and sexuality

Read: 1 Peter 5:8–11

The thief comes only to steal and kill and destroy. (John 10:10)

A landmark science fiction movie, *The Terminator* perfectly exemplifies the nature of evil. Arnold Schwarzenegger stars in the title role as a half-man/half-machine cyborg that doesn't feel, doesn't pity, doesn't regret, and will not stop pursuing Sarah Connor (Linda Hamilton) until she is dead. In the future, after a nuclear war, artificially intelligent machines rule the world. Two men come back from the year 2029 to the year 1984. One is the Terminator (Arnold Schwarzenegger); the other is Kyle Reece (Michael Biehn), a soldier sent to protect Sarah Connor. The Terminator was sent by machines to kill Sarah because her yet-to-be-born son, John, will eventually lead a rebellion against the machines. If the Terminator can kill Sarah, than John will not exist either. Reece was sent by John to ensure Sarah's survival. After lots of close calls and brutal slayings, the Terminator is eventually destroyed and Sarah survives to give birth to a son.

Like the Terminator, Satan doesn't take a holiday. He is real, he seeks your harm, and he wants to see you dead. He takes no pity and has no feeling for you. When you think you've finally got him licked, he whispers in your ear, "I'll be back," and then returns at the most inopportune moments to tempt you to sin. God promises that if we resist the devil, he will flee. God also promises that after we endure temptation for a while, he will make us strong, firm, and steadfast (1 Peter 5:10). Apart from God, we have little hope of resisting the advance of evil. But because the Christian no longer lives in his or her own strength but has the life of Christ living within him or her, the Christian can endure.

Jesus was tempted in every way but never sinned. Since his Spirit lives within you, you have that same power. Sarah knows she has a life within her that will save the world, and therefore she knows she has to persevere. Unlike the Terminator, Satan knows he is ultimately defeated. Hence, he tries to inflict as much havoc as he can now, before Christ will forever and terminally vanquish him. The devil can seem like a scary foe, but he is defeated. Terminate his advances by resisting him in Christ, before he terminates you!

PRAYER IDEA: Thank Jesus for triumphing over the devil by his death on the cross.

SCI-FI
FILM FEST
Tales of Science
Gone Mad

WEEK 28

July 9–July 15

THE CHOICE IS OURS
The Day the Earth Stood Still (1951)
MPAA: G

Read: Deuteronomy 28

See, I am setting before you today a blessing and a curse. (Deuteronomy 11:26)

Klaatu (Michael Rennie) comes from another planet to give the people of earth an important message. Though he looks and acts like a man, he is considered a threat when he lands his flying saucer on the Mall in Washington, D.C. Klaatu attempts to give a peace offering to the president, but the military mistakes it as a weapon and shoots him. Klaatu is taken to a hospital but escapes and remains a fugitive from an increasingly suspicious and frightened government. Klaatu turns off the electricity of the world for half an hour to demonstrate his seriousness. This is the day the earth stands still. While he gets the attention of the world by this act, now people think he is an even bigger threat. Klaatu is discovered, shot, and healed before finally being able to deliver his message to representatives of the world: "Join us and live in peace or pursue your present course of violence and face obliteration. The decision rests on you."

During the 1950s, lots of people could relate to this movie in light of world conflicts. The Russians and Americans were deep in the Cold War, and wars and rumors of wars abounded. Naturally, people suspected that if our present course of aggression continued, annihilation would result. Today tyrants and presidents throw around ultimatums. Threats bounce back and forth. But many people call these words mere political posturing meant for control and dominance.

The supreme power of the universe, God, issued ultimatums frequently in the Bible. God is always in control and is always dominant. He doesn't need to flex his spiritual muscle; he just needs to tell it like it is. He doesn't threaten; he informs. He says, "I made you. I put you on this planet. You can make it easy on yourself and do it my way or you can make it hard on yourself and do it your own way. The choice is yours." We may think this is an unfair threat, but it isn't. If God made us, who are we to squawk back? The good news is that many blessings are found when we do it God's way. He is always good, and it is we who chose our own fate.

PRAYER IDEA: Ask God to help you always choose blessing over curses through obedience.

DINO-MITE!

Jurassic Park (1993)

AA: Best Sound; Best Sound Effects; Best Visual Effects

MPAA: PG-13 for intense sci-fi terror

Read: Genesis 6

Leviathan the gliding serpent, Leviathan the coiling serpent; he will slay the monster of the sea. (Isaiah 27:1)

What were they thinking—mix huge, ravenous beasts with insatiably curious, succulent human beings in a low-security theme park called Jurassic Park? That's a recipe for disaster. When visionary John Hammond (Richard Attenborough) genetically resurrects the reptilian beasts and invites dino expert Dr. Alan Grant (Sam Neill) and a team to check it out, the "oohing" and "ahhing" turn to running and screaming. Hammond realizes what a terrible mistake he has made when his capitalistic, scientifically foolish plan backfires, proving that people and the terrible lizards aren't good neighbors on planet earth.

Although the Bible does not specifically address dinosaurs among its pages, it does refer to enormous beasts of the deep, such as the leviathan. Evolutionists tell us that dinosaurs lived hundreds of thousands or millions of years ago and never coexisted with humankind. Many creationists contend that people and giant reptiles did indeed coexist and that dinosaurs were even brought aboard Noah's ark. Both positions require faith to believe since recorded history only goes back to about 2000 B.C. and modern science has its fallibilities.

What *is* known is this: God created every living being, including dinosaurs. Sometime long ago they died off because of natural causes, human efforts, or both. The true lesson of *Jurassic Park* is that we shouldn't play God. We shouldn't mess with science and history to bring back dinosaurs, because if we do, there will be terrible consequences. In the Old Testament era people became full of pride, ruling their own lives. God regretted making the human race and brought on the great Flood. Only the humble Noah, his family, and a handful of animals were saved.

God opposes the proud but gives grace to the humble. (James 4:6)

PRAYER IDEA: Recognize that all creative power comes from God, and God alone.

THE ULTIMATE SCI-FI

The Andromeda Strain (1971)

MPAA: G

Read: Genesis 11:1–9

The ark is to be 450 feet long, 75 feet wide and 45 feet high. (Genesis 6:15)

he Andromeda Strain puts the science back into science fiction. The first story to hit the big screen by *Jurassic Park* and *Congo* author Michael Crichton, it's jam-packed with technospeak, research, scientists, and highly advanced equipment. A satellite falls to earth and kills all the residents of a small New Mexico town. No explosion or radiation happens here. This satellite carries a microbe from space that immediately kills humans by turning their blood into powder. So a team of scientists in an underground facility race against the clock to identify and combat this menace before it spreads and kills the entire western United States.

---

s the story of *The Andromeda Strain* continues, the audience discovers that the U.S. government knew about the microbe from space already and that the satellite was possibly crash-landed in New Mexico on purpose to test its killing capabilities. In this situation human beings want to exploit science for selfish and destructive purposes. When humans misuse science, tragedy and sin and God's correction often result.

Genesis records that in earliest history of humankind, people wanted to build a tower so high that it would reach the heavens. No doubt, they organized the brightest minds of the day to figure out how to do it. But their efforts resulted in confusion. God entered in, saw the pride, and called off the project. Nevertheless, God loves big, ambitious projects and has orchestrated some of the most technically advanced man-made inventions of all time. God designed an ark to carry Noah and his family and a representation of all animals on the earth. God also designed the tabernacle with exact specifications. Science is best used to explore and defend God's glory, not to usurp it.

PRAYER IDEA: Thank God for the new products that science provides.

THE HIDDEN WORD

Fahrenheit 451 (1966)

MPAA: not rated

Read: Psalm 119:9–16

In the beginning was the Word, and the Word was with God, and the Word was God. (John 1:1)

In the heat of summer, firefighters sometimes have to rush to put out wildfires. In *Fahrenheit 451* firefighters rush to start fires and burn what is forbidden: books! This science fiction film adaptation of a Ray Bradbury novel portrays a scary future in which the owning and reading of books is banned. The authorities of the day say that books rile people up and make them sad. They say that everyone must be the same and that nobody must be influenced or challenged by the written word. Firefighter Montag (Oskar Werner) is transformed from a book burner into a book lover, eventually hiding away in a secret society where each person has committed a book to memory. In this secret place you can only hear books spoken by the residents. Those who live there hope that one day they will be able to write down the words of each book so that others can read again.

God knows the power of the written word. In fact, he calls himself the Word. The beginning of the Gospel of John says, "In the beginning was the Word, and the Word was with God, and the Word was God" (John 1:1). God says that his written Word is flawless, a lamp, and praiseworthy. No wonder it (and Christ) is a threat to those who don't understand it!

The apostle Paul once persecuted people of the Word (or Christians), only to one day embrace and hide the Word in his own heart. Are you hiding away God's Word in your heart? Or are you—through neglect or scorn—destroying its richness and purposes in your own life? God longs to dwell in you and through you. One of the greatest ways to enjoy his company is through his Word. When you read his Word and pray that he will speak, you can discover and be reminded of his fantastic love for you and for all humankind.

PRAYER IDEA: Ask God to hide his word in your heart for others to read and enjoy.

DON'T LET THE MONSTER IN

Alien (1979)

MPAA: R for sci-fi violence/gore and language

Read: James 4:7

Do not give the devil a foothold. (Ephesians 4:27)

Don't let the alien in the door." So says the third officer of the spaceship Nostromo, Lt. Ellen Ripley (Sigourney Weaver). Carrying tons of mineral ore and returning to earth, the Nostromo's crew of seven is under strict orders to explore signs of life in the far reaches of space. They land on a planet and discover a craft filled with egglike pods. One astronaut, Kane (John Hurt), gets too close to a pod and an octopuslike alien attaches itself to Kane's face. Scientific officer Ash (Ian Holm) wants to bring Kane into sick bay, but Ripley doesn't want Kane or the alien to enter the ship. She tells Ash that if that "thing" enters the ship, the lives of the whole crew could be jeopardized. Captain Dallas (Tom Skerritt) tries to cut the alien from Kane's face, but the creature has highly corrosive acid for blood. The space demon ultimately removes itself from Kane's face but later reemerges from Kane's abdomen, bursting out of his flesh and killing him. In short order the alien molts, grows, and systematically kills off the crew one by one until only Ripley remains. In giving the alien access to the ship, the whole crew suffers a cruel fate.

The unfortunate truth of spiritual reality is that Satan and his demons are looking for a way to enter your life, your home, your workplace, and your church. Like a cat looking to sink its claws into you, Satan looks for a way to repeatedly hurt you by anchoring in your heart. That foothold for evil is compromise and sin. Every time you hold a grudge, you're making a foothold. Every time you let anger fester, you're making a foothold. Every time you believe a lie that Satan whispers in your head, you're making a foothold. You've heard them before: "You're stupid." "You're not good-looking enough." "People don't really like you." When you agree with these lies, you set yourself up for a damaged heart, abused by an alien that wants nothing less than your total destruction.

Don't think you aren't in a battle for your heart, because you are. "Be self-controlled and alert. Your enemy the devil prowls around like a roaring lion looking for someone to devour" (1 Peter 5:8). When you put yourself in situations where you know that you are weak and vulnerable to attack, your best defense is resistance and standing firm in faith. Tell Satan the truth of Scripture. Refuse to give in to rage. Refuse to believe the lies. Guard your heart fiercely. Don't let the devil in the door.

PRAYER IDEA: Ask God to forgive you when you let sin gain a foothold.

CHOSEN TO SAVE
The Matrix (1999)
MPAA: R for sci-fi violence and brief language
Read: Matthew 3:13–17

He is the Christ of God, the Chosen One. (Luke 23:35)

By day, Thomas Anderson (Keanu Reeves) is a boring corporate worker. By night, he becomes an infamous computer hacker nicknamed Neo. Anderson always thinks he has a special destiny. He knows that something with the world just isn't right. An even more infamous man named Morpheus (Laurence Fishburne) shows Neo that reality is a lie. It's actually a computer construct called "the matrix," designed by evil artificial intelligence, which has human bodies enslaved in bio pods as mere power sources for their cruel schemes. Morpheus also tells Neo that he is "the One," a chosen person who will fight the agents of this evil A.I. and free humankind from oppression and enslavement. Neo accepts this call, is shot dead, and rises again more powerful than before.

The Matrix has many religious references and symbols within its plot, but the Judeo-Christian concept of Savior is perhaps most prominent. The Jews still await a Savior and make sacrifices for atonement. Christians accept Christ as their Savior and their atoning sacrifice for all time. Neo understands the truth, goes through training, and begins to fulfill his destiny. Christ understood his destiny as a young child, was baptized by water and the Holy Spirit, and began to fulfill his calling by teaching, gathering disciples, and performing the ultimate act of salvation by his death and resurrection.

Many of us know that something is wrong with the world. Many of us have a sense that we are not as free as we could be. Yet we are unable to free ourselves from sin. We are trapped in an illusion. We think that life might be good, but there is always a pervading sense of doom. Jesus said that he came to bring us abundant life. The name Neo means new. Jesus frees us from our old sin-wracked life and gives us new life. The abundant life begins not when we die but at the moment when we accept him as our Savior. He is the truth, and when he enters our life, the truth sets us free.

PRAYER IDEA: Thank Jesus for showing us the truth and giving us the abundant life.

THE PERILS OF POMPOSITY

Forbidden Planet (1956)

MPAA: G

Read: 1 Corinthians 8:1, 2

Whoever exalts himself will be humbled. (Matthew 23:12)

Before *Star Wars* and *2001: A Space Odyssey,* the landmark science fiction movie was *Forbidden Planet.* John Adams (Leslie Nielsen) is the commander of a spaceship that lands on the planet Altair-4 to find out why a colony of humans has suddenly become silent. The commander and crew discover that the only survivors are a brilliant hermit, Dr. Morbius (Walter Pidgeon), and his beautiful daughter, Altaira (Anne Francis). Upon further inspection, the commander ascertains that Dr. Morbius used his own invisible monster of the id, or subconscious, to kill all the former residents and that he is now after the commander and his crew. Dr. Morbius became full of pride in his own intelligence. He thought the other dimwit residents deserved to die. This pride, however, brings Dr. Morbius to his own destruction.

The Bible says, "Knowledge puffs up, but love builds up" (1 Corinthians 8:1). It also says that pride goes before a fall (Proverbs 16:18). When we think we are better than others, we begin to think we can judge and rule over them. In some cases, we might even have murderous thoughts toward others. Consider any megalomaniac, such as Adolf Hitler or Idi Amin, and you can see that pride unchecked is ruinous.

God says he gives grace to the humble. In fact, the apostle Paul asked us to be completely humble. Does this mean we are to let others walk all over us? Not at all, but "whoever exalts himself will be humbled, and whoever humbles himself will be exalted" (Matthew 23:12). We are all created in God's image, all sinners in need of a Savior. And if God places us in any position of authority or honor, we should be thankful that it gives us an opportunity to lovingly and faithfully serve those in our charge.

PRAYER IDEA: Ask God to forgive you when you are haughty and prideful.

MR. MONEY BAGS

Movies about Money

WEEK 29

July 16–July 22

THE COOKED BOOT

The Gold Rush (1925)

AFI: 74 • MPAA: not rated

Read: John 6:25–59

I am the bread of life. (John 6:35)

Charlie Chaplin was a master of making the miserable look hilarious. In *The Gold Rush* he plays a lone prospector, the "little fellow," looking for gold in Alaska. One day he is shacked up in a little cabin during a brutal winter storm. With no food on Thanksgiving Day, he resorts to cooking his own boot, which he shares with his companion, Big Jim (Mack Swain). Big Jim can hardly stomach the top leather, but the little fellow manages the laces and the sole just fine. In fact, he twirls the laces with his fork just like pasta and sucks the "meat" off the shoe nails. He almost seems to be enjoying the leather like it is a gourmet meal. Eventually the little fellow and Big Jim find their gold and return to the mainland as rich men.

The apostle Paul faced many hardships on his travels. He was shipwrecked, imprisoned, and hungry. But he endured it all for the cause of Christ. He wasn't a glutton for punishment, but he realized that his contentment and satisfaction were in God. In Christ, Paul was sustained.

When life gives you shoe leather to eat, do you complain? Do you curse God? Or do you give him thanks in all things? God doesn't always shield us from pain and hardships, but his promises of fulfillment abound throughout the Bible.

The Bible implores us, "Taste and see that the LORD is good" (Psalm 34:8). And the Bible promises us, "I am the bread of life. He who comes to me will never go hungry" (John 6:35). So when your spirit is hungry, seek Christ. He won't give you the boot.

PRAYER IDEA: Ask Jesus to help you realize that he is your satisfaction and sustenance.

IS GREED GOOD?

Wall Street (1987)

AA: Michael Douglas, Best Supporting Actor • MPAA: R

Read: Proverbs 30:7–9

A faithful man will be richly blessed, but one eager to get rich will not go unpunished. (Proverbs 28:20)

Young Bud Fox (Charlie Sheen) works on Wall Street as a stockbroker and makes a modest yet respectable $50,000 a year. Driven to greater success, he seeks out a relationship with the extremely successful (but ruthless) broker Gordon Gekko (Michael Douglas). After repeated attempts, Bud gets an audience with Gekko, and Gekko asks him for some insider information. Initially Bud balks, but then, not wanting to lose an opportunity, Bud does Gekko's bidding. Furthermore, Bud spies on an English power broker to gain information about an upcoming steel corporation. Bud delivers, and Gekko is impressed. Bud is swept up in illegal insider trading, making obscene amounts of money, and getting the best girlfriend and condo that money can buy. After Gekko buys out and plans to liquidate the airline where Bud's father works, Bud retaliates and regains his dignity but loses his job and faces possible jail time for insider trading.

At a shareholders meeting, Gordon Gekko says, "Greed is good, is right, it works, it clarifies, and it marks the upward surge of man." Nothing could be more wrong. God's Word says, "Greed . . . is idolatry" (Colossians 3:5). We are to be "not greedy for money, but eager to serve" (1 Peter 5:2). Is God saying this to keep us down? Doesn't God want us to "surge upward"? If "upward" is more of God, heaven, and his kingdom, then yes. But if "upward" is greater autonomy, pride, and personal achievement, then no. "What good will it be for a man if he gains the whole world, yet forfeits his soul?" (Matthew 16:26). Greed is not good, because it robs us of dignity, humility, reliance on God, and the joy of service to others.

How much is enough? Does he who dies with the most toys and the biggest bank account win? Sorry to say, you can't take it with you and nobody in heaven is going to care how big your bank account is. Gekko and others like him can never be content, because there is no amount of money that will make them satisfied. "Godliness with contentment is great gain" (1 Timothy 6:6). Wouldn't a more courageous and holy quest be to take a leap of faith and trust God for your every need? The "American dream" for you really should be about having the freedom to worship God and live life the fullest for him, not yourself.

Our reward is in heaven, where we'll walk not on Wall Street but on streets of gold.

PRAYER IDEA: Ask God to let his dreams be yours.

COMPOUNDING SIN
Bonnie and Clyde (1967)
AFI: 27 • AA: Estelle Parsons, Best Supporting Actress;
Best Cinematography • MPAA: M (equivalent to R)
Read: Proverbs 11:19

J
U
L
Y

1
8

The wages of sin is death. (Romans 6:23)

I t all starts rather innocently. A dapper young man named Clyde Barrow (Warren Beatty) stands outside the window of a pretty, blonde young lady named Bonnie (Faye Dunaway) until he gets her attention. Bonnie asks Clyde what he does for a living, and he says he robs banks. Doubting this, she calls him on it and he delivers cash and a shoot-out to boot. Together, they become the notorious Bonnie and Clyde. Soon they rope in a driver, Clyde's brother Buck (Gene Hackman), and Buck's wife. One bank turns into two and then three, and then an accidental murder really heats things up. Their spree spreads across state lines, and their notoriety splashes across the papers, fueling the resolve of the law to stop them. What starts out as a little sin grows into greater wickedness and an eventual tragic end in a hail of bullets.

B onnie and Clyde collect illegal wages from their heists. The more they steal, the bigger their sin debt racks up. You may not be an armed bank robber, but mounting, repetitive sin can only sink you into a deeper hole.

Thankfully, God's arms are never too short to pull you out of the deepest of holes. But physically you still may have to pay for your crimes. You'll pay in damaged relationships, fines, imprisonment, and loss of personal dignity. Accountability from friends, prayer, soaking yourself in God's Word, and pursuing healthier options can help you turn around from besetting sin. But the first step is repentance from your sin.

God doesn't want to take away your fun. He doesn't want to steal your thrills. The extreme fun of sin pales next to the extreme fun and joy of following Jesus. Consider the depths of his love. Consider the challenge of stepping out in faith through prayer for something you need but do not have. Consider the possibility of travel to another land to tell someone about Jesus. The wages of obedience to Christ are eternal, abundant life, not just in the hereafter but now.

Bonnie challenged Clyde to rob. Let yourself be challenged to give——your life, your heart, and your all to God.

PRAYER IDEA: Ask God to challenge you with the thrill of following him.

CRAZY FOR CASH

It's a Mad, Mad, Mad, Mad World (1963)

AA: Best Sound Effects • MPAA: G

Read: Job 36:18, 19

Whoever loves wealth is never satisfied with his income. (Ecclesiastes 5:10)

t's a mad, mad world. Why? Because people will do the darnedest things and act in the craziest of ways to get their hands on $350,000. Smiler Grogan (Jimmy Durante) is an old man who accidentally flies his car off a California cliff. In the throes of death, Smiler tells seven witnesses that they can have the money he buried years ago under a big "W" in a southern California park. With that news, the old man literally kicks the bucket and the race is on. From charter planes to stolen cars to pick-up trucks to kiddy bikes, the motley crew scramble to the park with hearts full of greed. It looks like the winner will take all—until they all arrive at their destination at the same time. Now they must contend with a disgruntled police chief, Captain C. G. Culpeper (Spencer Tracy) who also wants to get his hands on the money. In the end nobody but the public gets the cash and the whole moneygrubbing lot winds up in the hospital.

---

reed is human behavior at its worst. It makes you selfish. It makes money and things seem more important than people and relationships. It's the great divider of people. Those who are greedy are never satisfied. They aren't content. They look away from God as provider and look at theft, fortune, or their own efforts as the ultimate provider.

When we lose control of our better judgment to pursue money, it's mad. It's crazy. There's no guarantee we'll get it, and if we do, we'll always want more. Greed is a bottomless pit. Of course, using our skills and mind for profit is not wrong. Taking advantage of moneymaking opportunities isn't wrong. But when we do it for our own glory and pride, it is wrong.

Everybody in this movie who chases the money ends up bruised and bloodied. They reap what they sowed: estrangement from their family and a life of pain. There is a better way. It's God's way. As we look to him, he provides our every need.

PRAYER IDEA: Ask God to forgive you for never being satisfied with what you have.

MORE PRECIOUS THAN RUBIES
Romancing the Stone (1984)
MPAA: PG
Read: Mark 1:16–20

I tell you, whatever you ask for in prayer, believe that you have received it, and it will be yours. (Mark 11:24)

In *Romancing the Stone* romance novelist Joan Wilder (Kathleen Turner) buries herself in her work, never impressed with the men she meets in New York City. She wants adventure, excitement, and danger. One day Joan learns that her sister Elaine has been kidnapped in Colombia. Elaine calls Joan and tells her to drop what she is doing and bring her a rare map detailing the whereabouts of a hidden stone. Fearing for Elaine's life, Joan goes to Colombia with the map and, hours later, finds herself lost in the jungle. Joan comes under a threat by a thug, but a greasy American named Jack T. Colton (Michael Douglas) rescues her. Together, Joan and Jack go from one adventure to another as they seek both the stone and a way to rescue Elaine. Though in constant danger, Joan realizes she is having the time of her life. The stone is recovered, Elaine is saved, and Jack buys a boat and asks Joan to join him on a cruise around the world.

There's an old saying: "Be careful what you pray for; you just might get it." Joan wants a life of adventure, and she gets it through one long trial. She faces dirty bus rides, torrential rains, being fired upon, and having her clothes ripped. Yet in the end she tells Jack that she is loving it. Initially Jack sees only dollars, but he, too, finds something valuable in the trials of the jungle: love. There's another old saying: "Don't pray for patience. If you do, God will give you trials." Prayer is a dangerous thing. You just might get what you pray for.

Not all of us have sisters kidnapped in Colombia, but all of us have a Father who loves to put us to the test through various adventures. This Father doesn't mind sending us to the outermost parts of the earth, or to parts unknown domestically, so that we can find what we are really looking for. This Father wants us not to find things perishable, such as gemstones, but things imperishable, such as love and eternal life. Our comfortable city and suburban homes often cannot provide the trials we need to face in order to experience a new outpouring of God and his blessings. We need to be called out so that God can bring us into love and renewal.

PRAYER IDEA: Ask God for greater faith to believe that he will answer your prayers.

INNOCENCE LOST

Citizen Kane (1941)

AFI: 1 • AA: Best Screenplay • MPAA: PG

Read: Deuteronomy 15:7, 8

What good will it be for a man if he gains the whole world, yet forfeits his soul? (Matthew 16:26)

What is your Rosebud? What symbolizes your youth and innocence? Was there a moment in time when your innocence was stolen away from you?

Charles Foster Kane (Orson Welles) has everything that money can buy: a best-selling newspaper, a marriage to the president's niece, a colossal home called Xanadu, and the fear of all those who stand in his way. As citizen Kane, he lives a life that is full—full of himself! And boy, does he ever pay the price for it. He has wives, a child, and coworkers, but he doesn't have a partner, a family, or a team. He knows no love and shares no love. He dies wretched and alone, presumably to face an eternity of separation even from God.

It's amazing that this movie, often called the greatest movie of all time, is about a great failure. Though Kane is a fictional character (patterned after the life of newspaper magnate William Randolph Hearst), his story represents many lives across America.

Not everyone is as soulless and untouchable as Kane, but every one of us has areas in our lives that we try to control—things that we should surrender to God. We all have something that we hold closely to our vests. When the enemy stole our innocence from us, we put up walls and said, "I will not let anyone hurt me here again. Therefore, I'm going to fight you if you challenge me here." There is no greater physician who can heal the wounds of our hearts than the Great Physician, Jesus Christ. Jesus can and will heal the brokenhearted.

Kane himself becomes as a member of the living dead—a walking corpse without a soul. Yet he remembers that there was a time when he had a moment of innocence. When he was young boy, he skimmed across the snow on a sled called Rosebud. At that time he knew only love. But he was sold down the river by his mother for a few trinkets of gold, and he forever came under the influence of greed, selfishness, and power.

Don't raise Kane in your own heart. Let God come in and heal the broken areas.

PRAYER IDEA: Ask God to show you how to pray for the hard-hearted and materialistic.

GETTING TO GIVE
Rat Race (1999)
MPAA: PG-13 for sexual references, crude humor,
partial nudity, and language
Read: 2 Peter 1:3, 10, 11

We must help the weak, remembering the words the Lord Jesus himself said: "It is more blessed to give than to receive." (Acts 20:35)

In the tradition of *It's a Mad, Mad, Mad, Mad World* comes *Rat Race*, a starstudded, laugh-a-minute movie about a group of Las Vegas schmucks who race to claim a $2 million prize. A Las Vegas casino owner (English funnyman John Cleese) invents a simple game. Six lucky slots winners are all offered identical keys to a locker in Silver City, New Mexico. The first one to reach the locker is the winner of the cash stashed inside. A family, a young couple, a pair of conniving brothers, and a goofy Italian all take trains, planes, automobiles, and helicopters in their scramble southeastward to claim the prize. Meanwhile, back at the casino, Cleese and a group of big gamblers bet on who will get to the Silver City locker first. Eventually the racers give the whole stash to a group that feeds the hungry at a benefit rock concert. Some of the racers initially protest, but the joy of the roaring crowd and the smiles on the faces of the hungry children convince them all that it is "more blessed to give than to receive." (Acts 20:35)

Why would Jesus say, "It is more blessed to give than to receive"? Who among us hasn't enjoyed the blessing of getting a great gift? The child at Christmas marvels at the bounty under the tree with tags that spell his name. The bride-to-be cherishes her engagement ring. The sixteen-year-old rejoices at getting a used car to drive.

Giving has its own rewards. The giver enjoys watching the recipient experience a blessing. (Imagine the parents watching their boy open gifts on Christmas morning.) The giver takes satisfaction in having met a need or fulfilled a desire of the recipient. (The grateful parents don't have to shuttle their sixteen-year-old around anymore.) Finally, the giver gets to experience a little of the life of Christ. (Christ embodies giving in human flesh.)

The only way to experience the blessing of giving is to give. There's no way around it. The rat racers know nothing but greed and selfishness until the very end, when they give and it feels good. They see the children's faces. They hear the gratitude and become more Christlike by giving away their winnings.

Get out of the rat race of trying to grab the next buck. Be content with what you have—and give.

PRAYER IDEA: Ask God to show you how you can experience more joy through giving.

ANIMAL PLANET
Fur, Fang, and Feather Films

WEEK 30

July 23–July 29

POWER THROUGH ORGANIZATION
Chicken Run (2000)
MPAA: G
Read: Colossians 2:4, 5

May he give you the desire of your heart and make all your plans succeed. (Psalm 20:4)

British chickens Ginger (Julia Sawalha) and her friends lay eggs, day after day, in a confining chicken coop. Longing for a life on the free range, Ginger hatches plan after plan to escape, but she's foiled each time by the evil Mrs. Tweedy (Miranda Richardson). One day a smooth-talking American rooster named Rocky (Mel Gibson) crash-lands in the coop. Ginger and her friends think he can teach them all to fly. But he's too embarrassed to confess that he is only a circus performer who shoots out of a cannon. He abandons Ginger and the other chickens at their time of greatest need. But Ginger and the chickens hatch a plan, build an airplane, and fly the coop. At the eleventh hour, Rocky returns to help and the chicken run becomes a smashing success.

Throughout the story, dimwitted Mr. Tweedy catches the chickens "being organized." He tries to tell this to Mrs. Tweedy, but she says, "It's all in your head." How can anything as dumb as a chicken organize an escape plan? It doesn't matter if you are a birdbrain or a legal eagle, organization and planning are critical to success.

An old saying promises, "If you aim at nothing, you'll hit it every time." Lots of people complain about their prisonlike conditions, but they don't make any plan to get themselves out. God didn't even make the whole world in a single day; he spaced it out over six days, then took a break on the seventh. God is a God of order. We don't have all knowledge, so our plans sometimes come through trial and error or inspired thinking. Though Rocky can't fly, Ginger is inspired by flying to achieve her goal. Then, by working together, they get it done. Planning and implementing a plan may seem elementary, but you would be surprised by how few people actually do it. They live their lives, day in and day out, belly-aching and hoping that something will change but never acting for change. God wants us to work hard to apprehend all he wants to give us. Planning may mean the difference between soaring like eagles and sitting like ducks.

PRAYER IDEA: Ask God for a better plan and believe that it will succeed through his grace.

DOGGONE IT, PROTECT LIFE

Cats and Dogs (2001)

MPAA: PG for animal action and humor

Read: 2 Kings 20:1–11

He placed on the east side of the Garden of Eden cherubim and a flaming sword flashing back and forth to guard the way to the tree of life. (Genesis 3:24)

In *Cats and Dogs*, the Brody family holds the secret to domination over the pet world. Why? Because Dr. Brody (Jeff Goldblum) is inventing the antidote to dog allergies. If he succeeds, there will be no reason not to adopt a dog. So the evil cat population, led by fluffy white kitty Mr. Tinkles (Sean Hayes), try everything in their power to thwart Dr. Brody and his research. But the Brody dog, a beagle puppy named Lou (Tobey Maguire), protects the family with diligence, if not tact and poise. Trained by tough agent Butch (Alec Baldwin), a lab mix, Lou goes from flop to full-blown dog agent. The cats steal the formula, create a dog allergen, and even plan to distribute it worldwide by mice, but Lou stops Mr. Tinkles through courageously saving the Brody family.

After Adam and Eve sinned, diseases (including allergies) entered the world. These diseases would ravage and destroy people back then just as they do today. After God banished Adam and Eve from the garden, he sent a guard to protect the tree of life. God knew that if people were to eat of this tree and live forever, they would be faced with continual disease and trauma (as a result of sin). God continued to protect the tree of life both out of respect of his law and respect for the lives and wellbeing of those who might be tempted to eat of it.

Like Lou, it is the job of every Christian to protect and promote life. As the redeemed bride of Christ, we care for the sick, pray for their healing, and treat the infirm as if they were Christ himself. We also defend and protect those who defend and protect life.

There is so much you can do to help. Assist those who take care of the sick. Volunteer at hospitals. Pray for doctors and nurses. Pray for the healing of your friends, family, and coworkers. Support missionaries who go into countries where health care is scarce.

The tree of life may no longer be in Eden, but God still heals today.

PRAYER IDEA: Ask God how you can promote the legacy of life.

FOLLOW THE LEADER

Winged Migration (2002)
MPAA: G
Read: Acts 8:26–31

Train a child in the way he should go, and when he is old he will not turn from it. (Proverbs 22:6)

Nominated for an Academy Award in 2003 for best documentary, *Winged Migration* places you side by side with birds traveling hundreds of miles on their migratory patterns. From Iceland and Alaska to Senegal and Mali, with stops in Peru, Kosovo, the Falkland Islands, and lots of sites in between, these birds cover miles of territory, finding the same resting places year after year. The red-crowned crane covers a mere six hundred miles, while the rugged arctic tern flies 12,500 miles from the Arctic to Antarctica twice a year. How do they know where to go? The older birds teach the younger ones.

An Ethiopian man, in the midst of his travels back home, once asked the apostle Philip, "How can I [understand Scripture] unless someone explains it to me?" (Acts 8:31). Philip began with the same Scriptures the Ethiopian was already reading and told the man about the good news of Jesus Christ. The Ethiopian praised God because he began to understand. He came to rest at his spiritual home because someone showed him the way.

Way back in the days of Moses, God said, "These commandments that I give you today are to be upon your hearts. Impress them on your children. Talk about them when you sit at home and when you walk along the road, when you lie down and when you get up" (Deuteronomy 6:6, 7). Teaching our young where to go is of utmost importance. Moral and spiritual training gives children confidence and certitude. As they travel through life, they know that certain "migratory patterns" of life will lead to certain destinations. These routes are not only familiar but also true.

Those without a leader are certainly lost. Be teachable to those Christians who are older in the faith. Take others under your wing and show them where to go. In doing so, you will lead others to safe, holy ground.

PRAYER IDEA: Ask God to show you what you can learn from those older in the faith.

THE KIND SHEPHERD

Babe (1995)
MPAA: G
Read: Galatians 5:22–26

I am the good shepherd; I know my sheep and my sheep know me. (John 10:14)

A mother sheepdog named Fly takes orphan pig Babe into her family on Farmer Hoggett's (James Cromwell's) farm, much to the consternation of the adult male sheepdog, Rex (Hugo Weaving). On the farm Babe also meets Ferdinand, a quacky duck; Maa, an elderly ewe; a trio of singing mice; and other animals. Year after year, the sheep endure Fly and Rex, who bark and nip and make cruel demands with their shepherding techniques. After Fly and Rex are temporarily put out of commission, Babe undertakes shepherding duty. The sheep couldn't be more grateful. Unlike the dogs, Babe is kind and he politely asks the sheep to move. The sheep willingly comply. Farmer Hoggett is so impressed by Babe's shepherding ability that he enters Babe into the Grand National Shepherding Competition. Everybody laughs at Babe, but his loving powers of sheep persuasion win over the sheep, the judges, and the crowd.

Like Babe, Christ is a good shepherd. Christ is good because he lays down his life for the sheep (John 10:11). He puts the needs of his sheep before his own. Unlike Fly and Rex, whom the sheep call wolves, Christ goes after the real wolves and drives them away. Christ is good because he knows his sheep intimately, as individuals. He calls each sheep by name. Christ is also good because he is kind.

Kindness is often misunderstood as weakness or ineffectiveness. Nothing could be more wrong. Kindness usually requires great patience, strength, adept leadership skills, and bravery. How many times would Jesus go after lost sheep that have gone astray, only to lead them back with kindness? He could easily have been rude to lost sheep, but he always showed them the greatest respect and love.

The world says that to get ahead you must be dog-eat-dog (or dog-eat-sheep). This is not Christ's way. If you lead others in any capacity, let the Spirit of Christ fill you with kindness so that others may willingly follow your lead.

PRAYER IDEA: Recognize that Jesus is the good shepherd and ask him to lead.

BEST DOGGONE DOG IN THE WORLD

Old Yeller (1957)

MPAA: G

Read: Matthew 5:4

I will turn their mourning into gladness. (Jeremiah 31:13)

There's no dog in the world quite like Old Yeller. When Pa Coates (Fess Parker) goes off on a cattle drive in the 1860s, young Travis Coates (Tommy Kirk) is left to take care of the family farm with mother Katie (Dorothy McGuire) and younger brother Arliss (Kevin Corcoran). Along comes an old yellow dog that Travis reluctantly adopts. But in short order that dog proves his worth. Protecting the family from scrapes involving raccoons, snakes, bears, mad cows, and hogs, Old Yeller shows Travis that not all dogs are created equal. When a wolf attacks Old Yeller, the family dog comes down with rabies, a disease that turns animals crazy. Travis knows what he must do: put Old Yeller down. After Travis buries Old Yeller, his father comes home and tells him, "Life is like that. For no good reason, life will just haul off and knock a man so flat he'll hit the ground and all his insides will feel like it's busted. Don't waste the good parts of life fretting about the bad. That makes it all bad." Though he still feels pain, Travis walks home to accept one of Old Yeller's pups as the next family dog.

Death hurts, especially the death of a loved one. Mourning loss is good. In fact, Jesus says that those who mourn are blessed because they will be comforted (Matthew 5:4). Funerals, burials, and remembrance services are all part of the process of getting over the loss of one we love. But God doesn't want us to be stuck in grief. He wants us to move on and experience the joys of life. What good can be added to life by fretting over the bad parts?

Old Yeller helped the humans overcome their mourning by giving the Coates family a yellow puppy. Jesus took away mourning from the disciples by rising again. God doesn't promise continual joy and happiness to those who follow him. He does promise to wipe away tears and bring comfort. He doesn't always put things back the way there were. But he can bring in blessing and opportunity for us to love again.

Death hurts. It hurts even more when it happens to somebody who has been our friend and protector. But God is a father to the fatherless and a friend to the lonely and a big yellow dog to those who don't have one. Don't discredit new beginnings. If you've had a loss, don't turn away from a blessing that God might want to give you.

PRAYER IDEA: Ask God to show you how you can help turn others' mourning into gladness.

I will meditate on your wonders. (Psalm 119:27)

In *Never Cry Wolf* Tyler (Charles Martin Smith) seeks adventure. He signs up to study wolves in the Arctic to see if they are responsible for the steep decline in the caribou population. On the plane ride out, Tyler says to himself, "I want to find the basic animal in myself to find a new man." Left all alone on a frozen lake, Tyler nearly freezes to death, but a kind, mysterious Eskimo man pulls him to dry land and finds him shelter. The Eskimo disappears, and for three days Tyler hides away, alone, afraid, and wondering why he ever signed up for such a brutal expedition. In time Tyler ventures out again and begins to survey the land. He meets one wolf, then two, then puppies, and then a whole pack. After months in the Artic, Tyler says to himself, "I feel wonder again like I was as a kid, making me deeply happy." After Tyler encounters a herd of caribou, he's ready to go home, a changed man who has encountered the glory of God's creation.

Like lots of men, Tyler wanted an experience that would change his life. He wanted to find the animal within, but instead he found the animal without (that is, the wolf). The wolf pointed him to wonder. God's creation and the beauty of an uncomplicated life pointed him to wonder. And wonder reflects the glory of God.

You can never "find yourself" when on a trip to a foreign land. But you can find the God of wonders. It doesn't matter if you are in the United States, the Artic, or Timbuktu, finding yourself is not a proper objective. If you aim to find yourself, you get nothing. If you aim to find wonder and the God of wonders, you get both God and yourself. You are made in his image and for his glory. His wonderful creation (including wolves) points to his wondrous glory.

Wonder is astonishment or surprise. It's amazing admiration. Develop this characteristic in your life and learn to appreciate the awesome wonders of our God.

PRAYER IDEA: Meditate on God's creation and his wonders and thank him.

REDEEMED FROM SLAVERY

Black Beauty (1994)

MPAA: G

Read: Psalm 40:1–3

I will redeem them from death. (Hosea 13:14)

Wonderfully voiced by actor Alan Cumming, *Black Beauty* says in narration, "We don't get to choose the people in our lives." A magnificently beautiful quarter horse, Beauty is born into an environment of human love and kindness but lives most of his life as a beast of burden. When the mistress of the house at Bartwick Park comes down with a chronic illness, Black Beauty is sold off. Stable boy Joe (Andrew Knott) vows to one day buy Beauty back. First Beauty is a carriage horse, then a cab driver, then a horse for rent, and finally a cart horse toting heavy loads. All the while, Beauty never forgets Joe and the other friends he had at Bartwick Park. When Beauty is old and skinny and spiritless, Joe, now a young man, recognizes him and buys him for a single cent. Beauty spends the remainder of his days fattening up and enjoying the open field, just as he did as a foal at Bartwick.

Like Beauty, we were born to run free and live happy. But sometime in our life, probably early on, we were sold into slavery. When we gave in to temptation and developed a bad habit that took away our will, we entered into slavery. When this bad habit harmed our family life and relationships, we felt the sting of its whip. When we let a crime committed against us fester into anger and unforgiveness, we felt bridled by a bit. When we ignored our loving Creator and told him that we could do better on our own, we found ourselves alone in the world. Sin enslaves us, and we can't free ourselves from its grip.

Even if you are old and dirty and not worth much anymore, God is ready to redeem you from slavery. He wants to put your foot upon a firm and lovely spot. He wants to prepare a feast for you in the middle of your slave keepers. He wants to take off the bit and bridle and set you free in a wide-open space.

"To redeem" doesn't just mean "to pay for"; it also means "to buy back what was once ours." We belong to God, and he doesn't want to see us sold out to a counterfeit owner. He wants us for his very own. Our own sin puts a bit into our mouth and leads us away.

Let God set you free.

PRAYER IDEA: Thank God for his loving care and for setting you in a spacious field.

RIBBONS AND BOWS
Thank Heaven for Little Girls

WEEK 31

July 30–August 5

FLOWERY WORDS SINK SINGER

The Lizzie McGuire Movie (2003)
MPAA: PG for mild thematic elements
Read: Psalm 12

I will show partiality to no one, nor will I flatter any man; for if I were skilled in flattery, my Maker would soon take me away. (Job 32:21, 22)

Disney Channel teen sensation Lizzie McGuire (Hilary Duff) hits the big screen in *The Lizzie McGuire Movie*. Lizzie joins her freshman class on a field trip to Rome. While the other students are visiting historic sights, Lizzie meets a young Italian pop star named Paolo (Yani Gellman). Paolo butters her up, saying, "You shine with the light from the sun." This flattery encourages Lizzie to fake sickness, skip out on school tours, and join Paolo on private tours of Rome. Paolo says she looks just like his singing partner, Isabella (also played by Duff). Paolo wants Lizzie to join him on stage for the International Video Awards program and promises her fame. But he really wants to humiliate her on stage so he can advance in a solo career. Lizzie's best friend, Gordo (Adam Lamberg), warns Lizzie just in time. Paolo's scheme is revealed and he is exposed for the bad singer he really is. Isabella asks Lizzie to come on stage, and together they wow Rome and the television audience.

The message of this movie is very clear: beware of flattery. It often conceals a hidden agenda. Praise builds up and has no agenda other than to honor the person receiving it. (Praise honors the person giving it too.) Flattery manipulates and coerces the person receiving it into doing something he or she might not otherwise do. Any temporary boost from the words of flattery is undercut when the evil behind it is exposed. Who doesn't know a story of a teenage girl who was controlled by a flattering boy? All too often these girls compromise their values for the words of false praise.

The Bible doesn't mince words when it comes to flattery. Job's friend Elihu even said that God would "take [him] away" if he practiced flattery. Elihu feared God and used words that were "upright" and "sincere." We all need friends who are upright and sincere. We all need people who will speak the truth to us in love, not arm-twist us with controlling words. Flattery comes at a price. Those who practice it are setting a snare for their own feet. Just look at Paolo. He got laughed off the stage.

PRAYER IDEA: Ask God to forgive you for succumbing to flattery.

To Know the Father
What a Girl Wants (2003)
MPAA: PG for mild language
Read: Mark 1:9–11

I thought you would call me "Father." (Jeremiah 3:19)

Amanda Bynes teaches us "what a girl wants" in this light comedy about a teen traveling to England to find her long-lost father. Daphne (Bynes) and her mother, Libby (Kelly Preston), work as a mother/daughter wedding service. Libby sings in a band, while Daphne serves as a waitress. Daphne always grows sad when she sees the father/daughter dances. Daphne has never known her father, but she knows that he is prominent English politician Lord Henry Dashwood (Colin Firth). Seventeen years earlier Libby went to Morocco, met Henry, and was married to him in a Bedouin ceremony. On the couple's returning to England, Henry's advisers sent Libby away because she wasn't politically correct. In the summer between her seventeenth and eighteenth years, Daphne goes to England alone to find her father. Through some culture clashes and missteps, Henry and Daphne learn to love each other.

Each one of us is hot-wired to have a relationship with our Father. When we know our Father, we know our identity. Daphne tells her mother, "I feel like half of me is missing, and without the other half, how do I know who I really am?" This is a great question. How do we know who we are unless we know our Father? Unlike Henry, who abandons his daughter for seventeen years, and others who have done so for even longer, our Father in heaven craves a relationship with us. Christianity isn't about following rules or trying to shine up our morality. It's about loving and being loved by the Father. When we bask in the Father's love, we are complete—we learn our identity as children of the King. God is "a father to the fatherless" (Psalm 68:5). As our Creator, "he is the father of us all" (Romans 4:16).

In the end of this movie, Henry leaves England and comes to live with Daphne and Libby. God left heaven to join us on earth. "I will live with them and walk among them, and I will be their God, and they will be my people" (2 Corinthians 6:17). God is with us, loving us, teaching us—a perfect Father.

PRAYER IDEA: Recognize that you were made for relationship with your Heavenly Father.

EVERY GIRL A PRINCESS

A Little Princess (1995)

MPAA: G

Read: Esther 2

All glorious is the princess within her chamber. (Psalm 45:13)

ittle Sara Crew (Liesel Matthews) takes some hard knocks. Even after she thinks her father has died, even after she is forced into slave labor, even after she is forced to sleep in a cold attic, even after she is treated cruelly by the boarding school headmistress, Miss Minchin (Eleanor Bron), Sara says, "I am a little princess. All girls are princesses. Didn't your father tell you, Miss Minchin, that you were a princess? Well, didn't he?" Miss Minchin doesn't answer Sara because Miss Minchin's father did not. This enchanting movie dares to tell the audience that all girls are princesses, no matter what circumstances may come their way. Eventually Sara and the audience discover that her father wasn't killed in World War I, and he comes back to claim her and restores joy to the whole school.

---

ike Sara, our Father is a King. He meets our every need and more. Our heavenly Father wishes to give us beauty and joy. The first human princess, Eve, enjoyed fellowship with her Father in the garden, where she tasted all its delights. What horror she must have felt to be removed from fellowship with her Father and banished to live in a barren place. She felt the sting of death but not the sting of eternal punishment. Though her own sin removed her from the Father's provision and care, he made a way to save her through Christ's life-saving sacrifice.

In *A Little Princess* the father comes back and makes a way to bring joy again to the princess. Likewise, all the children of Eve can once again dwell in the joy of eternity with our heavenly Father through the work of Christ. The biblical Esther was adopted and was made not only princess but also queen. Through faith and grace, we are adopted and also made royalty, children of the King.

PRAYER IDEA: Ask God to help you understand your royal lineage as a child of the King.

GET IN THE GAME

National Velvet (1944)

AA: Anne Revere, Best Supporting Actress; Best Film Editing

MPAA: G

Read: Genesis 12:1–4

You stoop down to make me great. (Psalm 18:35)

The world needs more Velvet Browns: passionate, dedicated, visionary, determined, pure, and stouthearted. In *National Velvet,* Velvet Brown (Elizabeth Taylor) bucks convention. While other twelve-year-old girls flirt with boys or play with pets, she looks at a spirited local horse named Pie and sees a champion. Befriending a local vagabond and former jockey named Mi (Mickey Rooney), Velvet thinks that together they can shape Pie into a winner of the Grand National—England's greatest racing event. After Velvet acquires Pie in a raffle, she seizes the opportunity as manifest destiny. Velvet's mother (Anne Revere) looks into Velvet's eyes and sees promise and hope, so she fronts the money for the entry fee. Velvet and Mi train Pie day after day until the big race. But nearing race day, they lose their jockey. Velvet bucks convention again, races Pie herself, wins, and then is immediately disqualified. Though she is offered riches by endorsements, she refuses, contenting herself with the thrill of the journey and the unofficial victory.

Youth need not be wasted on the young. Idealism, vigor, and risk taking are for us all because God did not call us to safety but to go forth in boldness with a grand mission to share his love and good news. Are you willing to leave your nets, like the disciples did, to follow him and learn more, do more, and be more than you ever expected you could? God made us for a purpose. We should have a purpose-driven life.

What dream has God planted in your heart that you have never acted on? Do you need God to make new dreams for you? David was young, but he knew that God could use him to kill Goliath. Joseph was the youngest of all his brothers, but God promoted him to greatness. Greatness comes from consistently applying decisions toward achieving extraordinary goals. This system for greatness works for the meekest among us. Let God do great things in your life. Make yourself available to him for great works, no matter your age.

PRAYER IDEA: Ask God to mold you, make you, fill you, and use you for greatness.

Jesus immediately said to them: "Take courage!" (Matthew 14:27)

Mia Thermopolis (Ann Hathaway), an awkward San Francisco teenager, has just learned that her deceased father was the crown prince of Genovia, a small European country. The sole blood heir to the throne, Mia must accept her position as the crown princess, or else Genovia will come under foreign rule. Mia's grandmother, the Genovian queen (Julie Andrews), trains Mia in princess lessons, but Mia becomes increasingly afraid and unsure of her role. Classmates taunt her, people use her, the press hounds her, and all she really wants to do is make it to her sixteenth birthday. Ready to run away from it all, she discovers the princess diaries and a letter written by her father, which says, "Courage is not the absence of fear, but rather the judgment that something else is more important than fear." Strengthened by these words, Mia changes her heart and accepts her royal duties.

Entering into new territory and assuming a new lifestyle is always difficult. We often need a little encouragement to change. God admonished the Israelites to be strong and courageous when he led them out of Egypt and into the Promised Land. Their transition time in the desert was marked by lots of grumbling and fear. Some wanted to go back to Egypt. Others complained about the food. New rules and regulations were enforced. When Israelite spies checked out the land, they reported intimidating giants living there. But God knew this land would be wonderful, full of milk and honey. So he encouraged his people to square their shoulders, look fear in the face, and continue.

As we enter into and grow in the Christian life, God asks us to change. He asks us to "put on Christ" and follow him. Sometimes he calls us to different lands and asks us to leave what is safe and familiar. Our lives before Christ can also feel safe and familiar. But the future eternal grace that can be ours far outweighs the imperfect comfort of the past. We need encouragement to grow and change, and God is ready to offer it. Are you ready to offer it to those who are younger in the faith than you? The world tears us down, so let us continually encourage one another to good works, to holiness, and to love.

PRAYER IDEA: Ask God for encouragement to grow and change into his likeness.

BE ALL YOU CAN BE

Bend It like Beckham (2002)

MPAA: PG-13 for language and some sexual situations

Read: Exodus 15:15–19

Woman, you are set free. (Luke 13:12)

All that the young Indian-born Jess (Parminder Nagra) wants to do is play football (soccer) like pro footballer David Beckham. But Jess's traditionally minded parents think it is improper for a woman to play sports. A young player named Jules (Keira Knightley) spots Jess playing in the park one day and recruits her to play for a local women's team. When Jess's parents find out about her involvement with the team, they forbid her to play. Yet Jess sneaks out and plays anyway. An American scout hears of Jess and Jules and plans to make it to their final game, but Jess sits it out to attend her sister's wedding. During the wedding reception, Jess's father lets her go to play the second half. He says, "I cannot stand to see you so glum." Jess performs well in the game and is recruited to play professionally in America.

Today, more than ever, young women are breaking the bonds of tradition and pursuing life-changing goals. They are also entering territory traditionally reserved for men. Some Christians may shun such progress and quote Bible verses such as "A woman must not wear men's clothing" (Deuteronomy 22:5) and "Women should remain silent in the churches" (1 Corinthians 14:34). But do these verses really defend repression of women? No. The Bible mainly encourages kindness, wisdom, and inner beauty. The Bible tells the stories of many so-called "bad girls" who performed redeeming acts, boldly stepping away from traditional roles and behaviors. Even the "good girls" of the Bible stepped out of normal bounds and acted courageously, such as Mary defying Herod and giving birth to Jesus, the long predicted Messiah. The Bible doesn't discourage ambition or sports; it encourages radical thought and courageous action.

Jess holds on to hope even when discouragement comes her way. She doesn't listen to tradition (which can stand in the way of progress and happiness), but she pays attention to her God-given talents. She didn't ask to be good at football, but God gave her that ability anyway. So she steps out in faith and exercises her talents.

Encourage young girls to be all that God intended them to be. God is an equal-opportunity Savior and Liberator.

PRAYER IDEA: Ask God to bring peace, protection, and encouragement to young girls you know.

A CHILD SHALL LEAD THEM
Heidi (1937)
MPAA: G
Read: Isaiah 11:6–9

Children's children are a crown to the aged. (Proverbs 17:6)

The original lollipop kid Shirley Temple stars in the title role of Heidi, an Alpine orphan who charms everyone around her. At the start of the story, Heidi's cruel Aunt Dete (Mady Christians) drags Heidi up a Swiss mountain. The aunt has tired of caring for the child and takes her to live with her grandfather (Jean Hersholt). As the two are stopping at a mountain village on the way up, the townspeople warn the aunt that the grandfather is a strange, unkind hermit. The aunt doesn't care, drops off Heidi, and promptly leaves. An inattentive man of few words, Grandfather initially doesn't care for Heidi. But as Heidi unconditionally loves him, he opens up and comes to love not only her but God too. Heidi tells her grandfather that she wants him to teach her Bible stories. He, however, confesses to a pastor that he had a bad church experience in the past and doesn't want anything to do with God. One day he helps Heidi read the story of the prodigal son, a parable of Christ. This, combined with her zeal, kindness, charm and tenderness, breaks his tough exterior and he joins her one day at the village church, a changed man. Because she first loved him, he comes to her rescue after she is kidnapped and sold to a family with an evil governess, Fräulein Rottenmeier (Mary Nash).

A child's innocence and love is a powerful agent of change, able to melt the coldest of hearts. Lots of adults and church leaders think that a good children's program involves keeping them quiet long enough to tell them a few watered-down Bible stories. They think children are to be seen and not heard, unless you want them to come out once in a while and sing a simple song. This is not the children's ministry that God envisions. Their capacity to learn Bible truths and implement them in actual ministry is much greater than we might initially believe.

As a young boy, Christ taught religious leaders in the temple. By example, he showed that children can tell adults a thing or two about God's kingdom. God listens to children's prayers. Christ scolded adults and said, "Let the little children come to me" (Mark 10:14). As followers of Christ, we are to be like little children, full of faith, wonder, joy, and the innocence that comes with being born again in Christ.

Let little children minister. Let them love adults with their powerful innocence. Consider the young and their Christlike qualities, and go and do likewise. Like Heidi, they can resiliently and consistently bring joy to world-weary elders who need to return to faith in Christ.

PRAYER IDEA: Ask God to manifest his innocence and joy in your life.

THE HEAT IS ON

Tales of Sun, Surf, and Summer

WEEK 32

August 6–August 12

THE RAGING SEA
Jaws (1975)
AFI: 48 • AA: Best Film Editing; Best Score; Best Sound
MPAA: PG
Read: Mark 4:35–41

I will fear no evil, for you are with me. (Psalm 23:4)

We're going to need a bigger boat." So says police chief Brody (Roy Scheider) when he finally gets a look at the twenty-six-foot-long great white shark that terrorizes and kills residents of his little island community, called Amity. All Brody sees are the shortcomings of the *Orca*, the boat they are using to catch the swimming menace. The boat is old, the line and equipment are flimsy, and the smoke-spewing engine is in great need of repair. *Orca*'s captain, Quint (Robert Shaw), displays reckless bloodlust in pursuit of the shark. He destroys the radio (which could be used to call in a bigger boat or reinforcements), burns the engine out, and disregards the boat's taking on water. Brody rages at the seemingly suicidal Quint and tells him, "Don't you care if we live or die?" Later Quint's lunatic choices create his own demise, and Brody and fish expert Matt Hooper (Richard Dreyfuss) must fight the shark themselves.

Ravages of the deep are nothing new. One day, when the disciples were boating with Jesus, they saw waves about to crash down upon them. They lacked the faith that they could survive. They told Jesus, in effect, "We're going to need a bigger boat." They despaired for the future, saw a killer, and complained about not wanting to die. Jesus rebuked them for their lack of faith and dealt with the storm himself.

Police chief Brody wants a bigger boat, but ultimately he doesn't need one. He just needs a bigger solution to the threat. And he finds one. The disciples complained to Jesus, and he offered a solution: his own voice. Jesus spoke to the waves and they were silent. The disciples were amazed and put their trust in him. When we face troubles or life-threatening difficulties, Jesus is always with us. His word is our weapon and he can calm the wicked seas.

PRAYER IDEA: Ask God to give you tools to resist the savages of life.

Abraham said, "Now that I have been so bold as to speak to the Lord, what if . . . ?" (Genesis 18:31)

There's nothing like blue Hawaii. After serving in the Army overseas for two years, Chad Gates (Elvis Presley) returns to his home state of great beaches, surfboarding, beach buddies, and his girlfriend, native islander Maile Duval (Joan Blackman). Island living is great except for one thing: Chad's overbearing mother, Sarah Lee (Angela Lansbury), wants him to work in the family business at the Great Southern Hawaiian Fruit Company. Chad, however, wants to develop a career on his own merit and takes work as a tour guide at his girlfriend's agency. When Chad's parents continue to pester him about joining the company, Chad strikes a deal. He proposes to open his own tourist office and offer exclusive packages to quota-making Great Southern Hawaiian Fruit Company representatives from the mainland. Chad's parents accept this plan. Chad marries Maile, and everyone lives happily ever after.

Standing up to your parents and those in authority can be difficult. When you want one thing and the authorities want another, friction and strife often occur. Chad could have put his foot down and alienated himself from his parents, but instead he offered a compromise. *Compromise* is a word not often used in Christianity. On matters of God's morality and his commandments, his way is the final word. But God is willing to change circumstances if you are willing to intercede. God listens to prayers and God makes deals.

Abraham pleaded for the city of Sodom and convinced God to spare the city if ten righteous people were living there. Originally, God was going to destroy it if fifty righteous people couldn't be found living there. (The city was eventually destroyed because it was all wicked, but God was willing to listen to Abraham.) Likewise, God listens to Christ, who always intercedes on our behalf (Hebrews 7:25). Job claimed, "My intercessor is my friend" (Job 16:20). Be a friend to yourself and others by intercession to God on behalf of your causes and passions. God is full of mercy and grace and loves to bless those who call upon his name.

PRAYER IDEA: Call on the Lord and ask him to hear your plea for mercy.

THE LAND OF GIANT WAVES
Blue Crush (2002)
MPAA: PG-13 for sexual content, teen partying,
language, and a fight
Read: Numbers 13:26–33

The land we explored devours those living in it. (Numbers 13:32)

Hawaii resident Ann Marie Chadwick (Kate Bosworth) loves to surf. It is her passion. She dreams of winning the famed Pipe Masters competition and landing on the cover of *Surfer* magazine. All her friends know she can do it. Even pro football players know she's good and ask her for surfing lessons. Fear is Ann Marie's only problem. One time, as a young girl, Ann Marie fell off her surfboard and knocked herself out against a rock on the ocean floor. In this blue crush, she almost drowned. The power and size of the pipeline waves intimidate her. A budding romance with an NFL quarterback distracts her and lets her momentarily forget about the task ahead of her. Through encouragement from her friends and a realization that her entire life has prepared her for such a time as this, Ann Marie faces her fear and conquers the ferocious waves of the pipeline.

Fear always paralyzes and never energizes. It discourages obedience to God. It gets the blame for sin. But it is no excuse. Courage isn't the absence of fear but the will and determination to meet it face to face. When God says to do something, we must trust that he will give us the strength to do it. Fear also spreads like wildfire and causes other people to lose their faith in God, his provision, and his promises.

In the desert, the Israelites were always bellyaching. They were afraid of the Egyptians, but God routed the Egyptians at the Red Sea. They were afraid that they would starve, but God provided manna and quail. When it was time to enter Canaan, Israelite spies came back and said that the land was filled with giants. Fear spread among God's people. Caleb, however, spoke the truth and said that Canaan could be conquered. For his courage, Caleb was able to enter the Promised Land.

When giant waves or giant problems face you, step out toward them. Get your feet wet. Trust God that he will help you ride over them. Trust him to protect you and to keep your head above water. The very problem that causes you fear might be an opportunity for the ride of a lifetime.

PRAYER IDEA: Ask God to grant you the courage to face the "giant waves" of your life.

ALL ABOUT ME

Sunset Boulevard (1950)

AFI: 12

AA: Best Original Screenplay; Best Art Direction; Best Score

MPAA: not rated

Read: Romans 12:1, 2

AUGUST 9

In him we live and move and have our being. (Acts 17:28)

In *Sunset Boulevard* failed and broke screenwriter Joe Gillis (William Holden) says to a fifty-year-old former glamour queen (Gloria Swanson), "You're Norma Desmond. You used to be in silent pictures. You used to be big."

Norma Desmond responds, "I *am* big. It's the *pictures* that got small."

So begins this twisted tale of obsession, possessiveness, narcissism, and ruin. Alone except for her butler, Norma plans a comeback by playing the lead in her own screenplay, *Salome*. When Joe unexpectedly winds up in her home, she hires him to help her with the script. He moves in, but Norma quickly puts her talons into him and manipulates him into staying. She becomes depressed and suicidal when he leaves the house. Joe becomes overwhelmed and sneaks out at night to collaborate with an attractive young writer named Betty (Nancy Olson). Norma discovers these late-night working sessions and literally goes mad. When Joe finally walks out on her, she fires a pistol at him and he falls dead into the pool. Norma now must face the (newsreel) cameras one last time.

Norma is so full of her own importance and so personally needy that she can't tell right from wrong anymore. Her butler friend also propagates these lies. Norma thinks Hollywood and the world revolves around her comeback and will welcome her back. She is wrong.

Children throw temper tantrums when they can't get things to go their way. Norma is an extreme example, but all of us have areas of our lives that we find difficult to surrender to God. And some of us have friends that lie to us about our ill behaviors.

"No, Lord" is an oxymoron. In every area of our life, "Yes, Lord" is what pleases him. A contemporary worship song says, "It's not about me, as if you should do things my way." God wants to love us and make us great through his own terms. We can't trick him in prayer to go our way; we can't plead with him to do our will; and we can't fire bullets at him to stop him.

Our lives are not our own. Prima donnaism will always lead to death and separation from love.

PRAYER IDEA: Ask God to help you to be honest about all the areas of your life.

No Man an Island
Cast Away (2000)
MPAA: PG-13 for intense images and action sequences
Read: Hebrews 10:25

**The LORD God said, "It is not good for the man to be alone."
(Genesis 2:18)**

Chuck Noland (Tom Hanks) lives by the clock. As a FedEx corporate trainer, he must set an example of timeliness for all, even his beloved girlfriend, Kelly (Helen Hunt). Over the Christmas season, Chuck flies from Memphis to Asia. Bad weather strikes, and the plane goes down over the Pacific. All are lost, except for Chuck, who washes ashore on a small tropical island with nothing more than a few FedEx packages. For four years, this castaway lives by his wits, trial, lots of error, a few modern conveniences such as videotape and ice skates, and lots of hope to be reunited with Kelly. Over that time Chuck makes a friend out of a volleyball and names him Wilson. One day Chuck tells Wilson, "I'd rather take my chance out there on the ocean than to stay here and die on this island, spending the rest of my life talking to a volleyball." So Chuck makes a wooden raft to brave the ocean in hopes of restoration with Kelly and the rest of civilization.

It is not good for the man to be alone." Before humankind was created, God existed as three-in-one, the Father, Son, and Holy Spirit. Then Adam had Eve. Noah had his wife and sons and their wives. Abraham had Sarah. Connectedness didn't merely mean marriage, either. David had Jonathan for a dear friend. Moses had Aaron as an administrator and confidant. And Jesus had his twelve disciples. Even the Lone Ranger had Tonto. And Chuck Noland had Wilson. He had to have a friend. We all have to have friends—we need community.

The Christian word for community is *fellowship.* Fellowship is more than just communicating; it is understanding each other and appreciating each other on a profoundly spiritual level. It is not just sharing information but sharing God. Some Christians neglect this level of interaction, but the Bible says authentic community is to be practiced daily. Our emotional and spiritual health depends on it.

Get involved in the lives of others and let them get involved in yours. Join a Bible study or small group. Be willing to love and be loved in community. When Chuck comes home, he discovers that Kelly has gotten married to someone else. But Chuck knows he has to keep breathing, because one thing he hasn't lost is hope for another chance with someone else. Keep hoping. Keep reaching out and love others.

PRAYER IDEA: Thank God for community and ask him to place you in one if you aren't.

GIVE ME GRANDCHILDREN
The Long Hot Summer (1958)
MPAA: not rated
Read: Genesis 16

To us a child is born, to us a son is given. (Isaiah 9:6)

Southern businessman and landowner Will Varner (Orson Welles) wants nothing more than grandchildren. Former criminal and wanderer Ben Quick (Paul Newman) wants nothing more than a good job. When Will and Ben meet, it's a match made in heaven—or at least Mississippi. These egotistical men have a meeting of the minds. Ben will come on as proprietor of Varner's mercantile and marry Will's daughter, Clara (Joanne Woodward). Then the couple will have grandchildren, specifically boys. Will already has a married son, Jody (Anthony Franciosa), but Will doesn't like him. Problems compound when Jody feels threatened by Ben. And Clara doesn't cotton to Ben's advances, thinking that he is barbaric and uncouth. With all these predicaments, the long, hot summer seems particularly disagreeable. After Jody earns his father's respect and Ben learns to treat Clara like a lady instead of a piece of property, the summer cools and the romance between Ben and Clara heats up. The prospect of future grandchildren brightens.

Wanting children and grandchildren is a natural and wonderful aspiration. But God, not people, makes marriages. And when people try to join outside of God's natural order and timing, troubles elevate. God is love, and he wants children conceived out of love, not out of fear, anger, or worry. God promised Abraham and Sarah a son, but after a while, Sarah didn't conceive. So Sarah had Abraham sleep with her maidservant, Hagar. When Hagar conceived, Sarah grew resentful and started to mistreat Hagar. Hagar gave birth and named her son Ishmael, but it wasn't until Sarah gave birth to Isaac that God's promise and plan were truly fulfilled.

Today lots of people try to force the hand of God by hurrying marriage or having sexual relations outside of marriage. While a child might come from these unions, the circumstances are never within God's perfect plan. Such choices always create more trouble than marrying the right person and having children at the right time.

Every child is a blessing and every child is worthy of great love, but not every sexual act is holy. Marriage and childbearing are a reflection and representation of God's love for his church. Bearing and raising children should not be taken lightly, nor be done for spite or human pride.

Encourage godly families and be patient with God when it comes to children. He will uphold his promises.

PRAYER IDEA: Ask God to show you how to encourage godly marriages and families.

COMPROMISED TO DEATH

A Place in the Sun (1951)

AFI: 92 • AA: George Stevens, Best Director;
Best Original Screenplay; Best Cinematography; Best Editing;
Best Costume Design; Best Score • MPAA: not rated

Read: Exodus 32:7, 8

AUGUST 12

When the woman saw that the fruit of the tree was good for food and pleasing to the eye, and also desirable for gaining wisdom, she took some and ate it. (Genesis 3:6)

Poor George Eastman (Montgomery Clift). You couldn't really expect him to keep to the straight and narrow. After all, he is from the poor side of the family. Sure, they are street missionaries, but he has big dreams and big plans for a better life. He wants a place in the sun. To get there, he takes the road of compromise.

First, he goes against his Uncle Earl's wishes and starts dating a common girl named Alice (Shelley Winters) who works at the clothing factory that his uncle (Keefe Brasselle) owns. George works all day long, side by side with Alice, and takes her out at night. One thing leads to another and then . . . pregnancy.

Things get complicated when George gets a promotion and catches the eye of the well-bred, beautiful young woman named Angela Vickers (Elizabeth Taylor). Now George has two women to juggle, one of whom is pregnant. But George doesn't do the right thing and marry Alice. Instead, he begins to think about how he could quietly get rid of her so that he could marry Angela. When Alice is killed in a convenient boating accident, George is convicted as a murderer and sentenced to death. Raymond Burr delivers a stunning courtroom performance as the zealous prosecuting attorney.

The truth is, George compromises himself to death. His dreams of a better life are fine, but he disobeys his uncle, sleeps with Alice, lies to Angela, and creates circumstances that bring about Alice's death. Little decisions here and there add up to big trouble and big sins. The standards of George's upbringing fall away when he faces new challenges away from home.

Compromise can attack anywhere or at anytime. If we haven't predetermined what our response is going to be to temptations, then we can rationalize and compromise ourselves to death, just like George. God promises to meet our needs. Can we trust him when a more immediate, more enticing, less ethical option presents itself to us?

PRAYER IDEA: Predetermine with God a strategy to remain faithful to him.

MODERN DISNEY CLASSICS

Animation of the 1990s and Today

August 13–August 19

NEVER FORSAKEN

Toy Story (1996)

MPAA: G

Read: Psalm 16

He will not abandon or destroy you. (Deuteronomy 4:31)

Poor Woody (Tom Hanks—voice), the toy cowboy. When Woody's boy owner, Andy, has a birthday, Woody and all the other toys fear rejection and replacement. Board games and clothes are okay gifts, but not another toy. But Andy does get a new toy: a Buzz Lightyear (Tim Allen—voice) action figure. Woody cannot deal with this horror. Bickering turns to fighting, and fighting turns to danger. Buzz and Woody fall out a window and find themselves alone and separated from Andy in the cold, cruel world. On their quest to find their master, who has gone out for pizza, they face menacing traffic and Sid, a neighbor boy who likes to dismember and blow up toys. Eventually Buzz and Woody learn to trust each other in this delightful, modern, animated classic, *Toy Story*.

Woody never has to fear abandonment and rejection by Andy. The boy master naturally will welcome any new toy into the fold. Any kid knows that the more toys, the merrier. It's not a replacement-and-rejection system.

Though we might feel abandoned, God promises to never leave us nor forsake us. Unlike Andy, our eternal master, God, is with us wherever we go. God doesn't withdraw his kindness and love from us even if we sin or do wrong. Andy frequently tells his mother, "I can't find Woody and Buzz." Andy wants to know where his lost toys are. He looks for them when he can (even if his mother thinks he merely misplaced them.) Our God is constantly looking to find us.

Jesus was forsaken so we wouldn't have to be. He was despised and rejected by men. Yet even as he hung on the cross, Jesus said, "Father, forgive these people, because they don't know what they are doing" (Luke 23:34). His death allows us to face every horror, even our own death, by making a way for him to keep us near him always.

PRAYER IDEA: Thank God for always being near you and always accepting you.

May the God who gives endurance and encouragement give you a spirit of unity among yourselves as you follow Christ Jesus. (Romans 15:5)

Some call it better than the original. *Toy Story 2* adds unity to the themes of love, friendship, and salvation as found in the first *Toy Story.* At the start, the toys are a large, loving family in Andy's room. While Andy is away at camp, Woody (Tom Hanks—voice) is kidnapped by a toy salesman. Unbeknownst to himself, Woody is a highly valued collectible, even more valuable as the final piece in the Roundup Gang, which also includes Woody's horse, Bull's-eye, Jessie the cowgirl (Joan Cusack—voice), and Stinky Pete the prospector (Kelsey Grammer). Woody must decide whether to stay with the Roundup Gang and be sold off as a museum piece or go back home with Buzz, who shows up with a rescue team comprised of Andy's other toys.

Woody really must decide with whom he wishes to be united. At Andy's home he would be with his master and other toy friends. However, as Andy grows older, Woody's future becomes more uncertain. With the Roundup Gang, Woody and his new friends will be treasured and admired for generations of museum visitors forever. When Stinky Pete turns evil and forces Woody to stay with the Roundup Gang, Woody realizes that a loving, supportive community is what he, Jessie, and Bull's-eye really need.

God is big on the unity of his people. He calls his church a unit made up of many parts. He implores the church to be of like mind and spirit. Being a group of people with a common purpose doesn't necessarily make a unit; true unity occurs when we love one another. A worship song says, "They'll know we are Christians by our love." When we add Christ's love to our common theology, we become an extension of God to one another.

God is love, and when we love one another, we are sharing in his blessing and life forevermore.

PRAYER IDEA: Ask God to show you how you can love other members of his church.

No Fear

Monsters, Inc. (2001)

AA: Best Song • MPAA: G

Read: Isaiah 43:1–4

Our mouths were filled with laughter. (Psalm 126:2)

I n *Monsters, Inc.,* monsters Sully (John Goodman) and Mike Wazowski (Billy Crystal) work at a corporation that harvests the screams of children. These screams run the power of their monster city. The monsters are as frightened of the children as the children are of the monsters. If anything from the human world (such as a child's sock) enters the monster's world, it is immediately destroyed. If a monster comes into contact with a human item, the monster must be cleansed as if he were undergoing some kind of extreme disease control measures.

One monster, named Randall (Steve Buscemi), devises a scheme to force screams out of children through a mechanized instrument of torture. Sully and Mike uncover this plot and in the process realize that there is nothing to fear from the human children's world. Furthermore, they discover that the laughter of children is ten times more powerful than their screams. Though Randall tries to take the children captive, Mike and Sully expose this darkness and turns the children's screams into laughter. Love and goodness triumph over fear and pain.

T hings that go bump in the night aren't always what they seem. What we fear may, in fact, be afraid of us. Or what we fear may not really be threatening at all. People with unusual phobias, such as a fear of spiders, a fear of clowns, a fear of heights, or some other irrational fear, are bound by something that really isn't a threat at all.

God is in the business of turning our mourning and sorrow into laughter and joy. Satan wants to keep us in fear and doubt and will put thoughts into our heads to keep us in this bondage, even if the object of our fear is nothing to be afraid of at all. "Do not fear, for I am with you," says the Lord (Jeremiah 46:28). Fear can be described as an emotional reaction to something that we think might hurt us and that we have little or no control over. God is always with us, protecting us and shepherding us out of harm's way. In fact, he wants to lead us into delight and joy in him.

PRAYER IDEA: Ask God to fill you mouth with laughter and your tongue with singing.

Ants are creatures of little strength, yet they store up their food in the summer. (Proverbs 30:25)

The inventive and industrious ant Flick (David Foley) wants to bless his colony of fellow ants. Creating a mechanical grain combine, he hopes to speed up the harvesting and distribution of grain, meant not only for his ant brothers and sisters but also for the greedy grasshoppers. Led by the strong-willed, angry Hopper (Kevin Spacey), the grasshoppers intimidate the ants into collecting their food. Flick recruits a group of silly but talented performing-circus insects to come to the colony and help battle the grasshoppers. Together they create a bird made out of natural materials that will swoop down at the right time and scare the grasshoppers away. The bird works until the grasshoppers find out that it is fake. When a real bird shows up, the grasshoppers think the ants are playing another trick. When the grasshoppers stay to continue terrorizing the ants, the bird enjoys a fat, tasty dinner!

Hard work never hurt anyone. Hard work to solve problems for other people gets rewarded. Hard work that helps protect people's lives is celebrated. All hail hard work! It's biblical, it's rewarding, and it keeps us out of trouble while blessing others. Flick represents the perfect worker ant, an individual who not only does his job but even creates ways to do that job quicker and better.

Sometimes enemies try to steal the fruits of our labors. This could be an employer who doesn't pay us fairly, a thief who takes from us, or a bad habit that robs us of our earnings. We cannot get rid of these menaces alone. We need help from others. Flick gets help from the circus performers, and we need help from our friends, fellow church members, and others who care about us. A great way to care is to help others protect their assets.

Consider the ant—work hard, save what you make, protect yourself from bandits, and live content in your "colony" of friends and fellow coworkers.

PRAYER IDEA: Ask God to live wisely and industriously through you.

You were like sheep going astray, but now you have returned to the Shepherd and Overseer of your souls. (1 Peter 2:25)

Life on the Great Barrier Reef is great, but widowed clown fish Marlin (Albert Brooks–voice) could ease up a little on protecting his only son, Nemo (Alexander Gould—voice). On the first day of school, Nemo accepts a dare from his new buddies and swims past the drop-off point. Marlin calls him back, but Nemo refuses to return. In frustration Nemo tells his father, "I hate you." Seconds later, Nemo is scooped up by a scuba diver and taken away to be imprisoned in a dentist's aquarium in Sydney. Undaunted, Marlin enlists the help of a forgetful blue tang named Dory (Ellen DeGeneres–voice), and they embark on a mission of finding Nemo. Along the way, the duo face a ferocious deep-sea anglerfish, catch a ride with a surfer-dude turtle, almost become dinner to a flock of seagulls, and meet up with some lapsed vegetarian sharks at a Fisheaters Anonymous meeting. Through extraordinary circumstances, Nemo flushes out to sea and finally reunites with his grateful father. At their joyful reunion Nemo repents of his rebellion and tells his father, "I love you."

A funny little fish, this Nemo. He tells his father that he hates him, but the moment they are separated, all Nemo wants to do is to be reunited with his father. And all Marlin wants is to be reunited with his son. Apparently this hatred doesn't have much substance to it.

Nemo knows that great love and safety are found in the fins of his father. Marlin knows that true love always hopes, always perseveres, and always protects. Leaving the safety and familiarity of the reef, Marlin risks everything for one reason: reunion with his son.

Christ left the familiarity and safety of heaven for one reason too: reunion with humankind. God's desire is to bring the lost sheep home. Like Nemo, we have all told our heavenly Father at some point or another, whether consciously or not, "I hate you." We all have told him, "I can do it better my way," and that always gets us into trouble. We, like sheep (or proud little clown fish), have gone astray. We have all put ourselves in tiny little aquariums, but God wants us to swim freely and enjoy the beautiful reef, full of life and color.

Are you tired of swimming away? Return to God. He's looking for you, ready to embrace you. Do you have a lost child or loved one? Keep praying for that one and pointing him or her toward home. As the great hymn "Amazing Grace" says, "I was lost but now am found."

PRAYER IDEA: Pray for the lost children who have run away from home.

You do not belong to the world. (John 15:19)

Tarzan begins with a shipwreck that leaves a young couple and their infant son stranded on the shores of a hostile jungle. A leopard named Sabor kills the son of a female gorilla named Kala (Glenn Close) and then kills Tarzan's parents. Kala adopts Tarzan into the ape family and raises him as her own. After Tarzan matures into a skillful and athletic young man, he destroys Sabor. The ape family patriarch, Kerchak (Lance Henriksen), slowly begins to accept Tarzan. One day other human beings arrive in the jungle, including a primatologist named Professor Porter (Nigel Hawthorne), his beautiful daughter, Jane (Minnie Driver), and their charming but arrogant personal guardian, Clayton (Brian Blessed). Clayton tries to capture and exploit the gorillas, but Tarzan comes to the rescue. At the end Tarzan must decide whether to go to England with Jane and her father or remain in the jungle as a member of the ape family.

Torn between two worlds, Tarzan doesn't know if he should join his fellow humans in a developed (presumably better) place or stay with a species not his own in the beautiful yet dangerous jungle. This is the classic struggle of all humankind: the world or the kingdom of God. The world offers familiarity and even fellowship, but soulless creatures inhabit it. The kingdom of God is our true, eternal home. Heaven is full of blessing and people made alive in Christ, but it is unknown and somewhat scary.

Tarzan can't have it both ways: he can't live in England and in the jungle at the same time. He has to make a choice. Likewise, Jesus rebuked those who tried to straddle the fence between the world and God's kingdom. He said he will spit out those who are lukewarm (Revelations 3:16). Jesus wants us to get out of the woods and take the trip with him to a celestial city. He stands at the door and knocks. He also says that those who make the journey get to sit next to him on the throne at the royal palace.

Regrettably, in this movie, Tarzan misses the boat. His love for his ape family prevents him from seeing all the wonders of the civilized world. When Jesus knocks for you to come to him, will you also miss the boat? Are you trying to ride the boat and keep one foot in the jungle at the same time? If you are, you are likely to fall into the water. The momentary pleasures of the jungle do not compare with the unsurpassed, eternal joys of the kingdom of God.

PRAYER IDEA: Ask God to forgive you for choosing the jungle you're involved in.

MERCY, NOT LEGALISM
The Hunchback of Notre Dame (1996)
MPAA: G
Read: Psalm 57

Mercy triumphs over judgment! (James 2:13)

od help the outcasts," sings the gypsy Esmeralda (Demi Moore) within the walls of Notre Dame. There the hunchback Quasimodo (Tom Hulce) lives, imprisoned by the lies of his self-righteous stepfather, Judge Claude Frollo (Tony Jay). Quasimodo longs to enjoy the outside world, but Frollo forbids him to ever leave the tower, teaching him that the world is a cruel and horrible place. Longing for something more, Quasimodo escapes to the Festival of Fools but is lashed down, pummeled with fruit, and ridiculed by the townspeople. Frollo looks on smugly until Esmeralda comes to Quasimodo's rescue. Frollo pursues Esmeralda to condemn her, but she takes sanctuary within Notre Dame. Within the church, she looks to a statue of Mary holding the baby Jesus and exclaims, "You were outcast once." Because he was given grace and mercy, Quasimodo helps Esmeralda escape, and Frollo gets his comeuppance for all his wickedness.

---

egalism, haughtiness, anger, and condemnation mark Frollo's character. The Pharisees of Jesus' day also practiced these sins. Jesus, meanwhile, upheld and embodied perfect holiness, and he asked his disciples to pursue holiness as well, but with a spirit of humility and grace. The Pharisees thought life was all about fulfilling the law (and they even added a few laws of their own), but the law is powerless to change the character of a person. It can only point fingers and condemn. Jesus exposed the Pharisees' fraudulent thinking and rebuked them soundly. Through forgiveness, mercy, love, and grace, Jesus transformed lives and set them free.

So, what kind of a person are you? An Esmeralda or a Frollo? Are you a legalist, quick to condemn? Or are you full of grace, ready to love and forgive?

Jesus is both fully God and fully a man. He is fully holy and fully grace-full. Personally he is holy, but relationally he is forgiving and merciful. Thus we are called to love God through obedience (holiness) and love others through service, patience, forgiveness, and grace. Through God's grace, God writes the law on our hearts. Won't you free someone from a prison of lies by showing him or her the truth of God's love, mercy, and grace?

PRAYER IDEA: Thank Jesus that he didn't come to the world to condemn it but to save it.

BOYS
TO MEN
Dramas about
Growing Up

WEEK 34

August 20–August 26

ARE YOU CHILDLIKE?
Big (1988)
MPAA: PG
Read: Mark 10:13–16

You are the children of the LORD your God. (Deuteronomy 14:1)

Twelve-year-old New Jersey kid Josh Baskin (David Moscow) wants nothing more than to be big. This awkward youth wants to go on a ride at an amusement park with a tall girl, but he can't because he is too short. Dejected, Josh goes to a fortune-telling machine, inserts a quarter, and says, "I wish I was big." The next day he wakes up in the body of a thirty-two-year-old man (Tom Hanks). After his mother kicks him out because she thinks he's a kidnapper, Josh moves to New York City, where his best friend, Billy (Jared Rushton), puts him up at a cheap hotel. In time Josh gets a job as a consultant for MacMillan Toys. Mr. MacMillan (Robert Loggia) loves his childlike innocence, as does a cute coworker named Susan (Elizabeth Perkins). Meanwhile, Susan's sometime boyfriend, Paul (John Heard), acts childish and immature. Will Josh tell Susan who he really is? And will Josh ever get small again?

There probably isn't a twelve-year-old on the planet who hasn't said one time or another, "I wish I was big." Kids want to be teenagers, and teenagers want to be adults. It's good and it's natural.

God says that spiritual maturity is childlikeness. That's an attractive trait. Josh was so popular with his boss and Susan because he was innocent to the cares of the world. He thought like a child and reasoned like a child because he *was* a child. He never had any petty cares and squabbles, unlike Paul, but lived his life by loving play and people unconditionally.

Among his spiritual children, Jesus loves childlikeness and hates childishness. Jesus loves simple faith and simple ways. He loves people to come up to him without any fear or constraint brought on by cares of adulthood. Jesus does, however, want us to put away petty cares. He wants us to stop trivial squabbles. The apostle Paul said, "In regard to evil be infants, but in your thinking be adults" (1 Corinthians 14:20).

Lots of adults today have hard hearts because they have seen too much wrong and have done too much wrong. We should give all that up to God, allowing the Holy Spirit to cleanse our hearts and make us "born again" like little infants. "How great is the love the Father has lavished on us, that we should be called the children of God!" (1 John 3:1).

PRAYER IDEA: Tell your Heavenly Father you are his child.

THE GOOD SHEPHERD

Boys' Town (1938)

AA: Spencer Tracy, Best Actor; Best Original Screenplay

MPAA: not rated

Read: Matthew 18:10–14

When [Jesus] saw the crowds, he had compassion on them, because they were harassed and helpless, like sheep without a shepherd. (Matthew 9:36)

Spencer Tracy hits another home run with his performance as Father Flanagan in the Academy Award–winning *Boys' Town*. When Father Flanagan realizes that most of the adult men in the local Omaha, Nebraska, mission are beyond reform, preferring to continue their sinful patterns, he decides to open a home for boys. The priest holds strongly to his assertion that there is no bad boy and that all boys can be raised to be productive citizens if they are loved and given structure. Father Flanagan raises money to open a home for twenty boys, then fifty boys. Finally he purchases acres of land, which are developed into a whole town for five hundred orphaned and wayward boys. One boy, named Whitey (Mickey Rooney), is nothing but trouble, but through continual application of loving discipline, Whitey goes from town delinquent to town mayor.

Boys' Town offers many moral and biblical lessons: perseverance, kindness toward the poor, care for orphans, patience, and more. But the greatest lesson is unconditional love. Father Flanagan loves the devious and belligerent Whitey by choice. When Whitey runs away and is shot, Father Flanagan rescues him and treats his wounds. An even greater love toward Whitey is demonstrated by the cheerful Pee-Wee, a little boy who doesn't see Whitey's negativism or problems and follows him around like a puppy. Pee-Wee even follows Whitey into harm's way——the street.

Are you prepared to offer unconditional love to the undesirables who come into your life? When you are slapped in the face, are you prepared to offer the other cheek? Jesus loves his flock so much that he is willing to risk inclement weather, suspicion, and even death to bring in the one who wanders off. We cannot hope to see others change to Christlikeness if we are unable to meet them and engage them where they are. The Good Shepherd is good because his top priority is the safety and welfare of his sheep. Remember, we all were in need of rescuing. Thank God that the Good Shepherd came and found us.

PRAYER IDEA: Ask God to help you love others unconditionally, even delinquents.

FATHERS WITHOUT BACKBONES
Rebel without a Cause (1955)
AFI: 59 • MPAA: not rated
Read: Psalm 68:5, 6

Fathers, do not exasperate your children. (Ephesians 6:4)

Down at the police station, teenager Judy (Natalie Wood) tells a juvenile officer, "He hates me. He called me a dirty tramp. My own father."

That same evening, Plato (Sal Mineo) confesses to shooting puppies. He also explains that his parents have split up.

Drunken youth Jim Stark (James Dean) raves, "I don't want to be like him." Then he turns to his father and wails, "You're tearing me apart."

These three youth suffer from unloving, absent, or spineless fathers. No wonder they team up to form their own family after a fatal game of chicken at a seaside cliff. Jim wants to talk to the police, but his father doesn't want him to confess. Jim cries out to his father, "Stand up for me." But Jim's father does not.

When a police bullet strikes Plato down, Jim's father realizes that noninvolvement is no longer an option. In tears Jim's father tells his son, "I'll try and be as strong as you want me to be."

The movie that made James Dean famous is a landmark for its tale of teen disenfranchisement. Spawning a whole new malcontent youth culture, which carried into the rebellion of the sixties, *Rebel without a Cause* is actually full of causes—three bad fathers. Judy wants to show affection to her father, but he brushes her off and thinks she's being immature. Plato doesn't have any direction and is so needy that he calls Jim his best friend after knowing him a single day. Jim, likewise, wants to talk to his parents and get their honest opinions, but his parents only fret, worry, and come up answerless when questioned. All of these delinquents need firm but fair fathers. But all find their homes joyless and without value.

A home without firm love and guidance is emotionally and morally bankrupt. A strong house needs a firm head. Now, more than ever, kids need good role models who will listen to them and offer them straight talk and advice.

If you are a parent, teacher, relative, or older sibling to children or teens, be present, be genuine, and love sincerely. Hold kids accountable for their actions. Offer real answers and be prepared to stand by them. Children and teens need us to be strong. Don't cause a child to rebel.

PRAYER IDEA: Ask God to give you a strong backbone when nurturing young people.

A DUMB BUNNY

Swingers (1996)

MPAA: R for language throughout

Read: Proverbs 6:23–25

A fool's mouth is his undoing, and his lips are a snare to his soul. (Proverbs 18:7)

Hollywood wannabes Trent (Vince Vaughn) and Mike (Jon Favreau) are swingers. They like to attend swing dance clubs and meet girls. Trent seems to have no trouble finding and talking to beautiful girls, but Mike isn't over his old girlfriend from back east. Trent sweet-talks, charms, and demeans women. He has a few dates but no lasting relationships. Mike can't play that game. He tries to follow Trent's smooth moves, but it doesn't work for him. Trying the honesty route, he meets Lorraine (Heather Graham) and strikes up a genuine conversation with her. The promise of a new romance begins. Trent says, "My boy Mikey is all growed up." Mike displays honesty and gets the girl, while Vince continues his false, womanizing ways. He's cool and funny but ultimately alone and inauthentic.

Now is the time to get real. That doesn't mean giving up humor and lightheartedness, but it does mean putting an end to playing games and putting on an act. God doesn't want you to be foolish, and others don't want that either. If you have praise to God, say it. If you have a gripe, don't hold back. People need authentic people of faith now more than ever. No more phony baloney.

A real person looks at trouble and laughs. A fool looks at everything and laughs. The fool fails to make any distinction between what is praiseworthy and what is to be ridiculed. To him, it is all a stupid game. Have you ever been to a party and heard a loudmouth in the corner who thought he was God's gift to women? A few women fall for these types just because they are so audacious, but most know that one of these guys isn't worth a LTR (long-term relationship). A friend or romantic partner for the long haul has got to be real. Honesty, forthrightness, genuineness, and lightheartedness aren't reserved just for dating relationships; they are needed for *every* relationship.

PRAYER IDEA: Ask God to forgive you for your foolish talk and games.

TURN AND FACE THE STRANGE

AFI: 77 • *American Graffiti* (1973)

MPAA: PG

Read: Luke 9:57–62

Come, follow me. (Matthew 4:19)

In *American Graffiti* big changes meet up with Curt Henderson (Richard Dreyfuss) and Steve Bolander (Ron Howard) during one night in 1962. These two boys are scheduled to leave for college in the morning and both deal with their fearsome future by cruising in cars, listening to rock 'n' roll music, and otherwise rabble-rousing around town throughout the wee hours of the morning. Steve's girlfriend, Laurie (Cindy Williams), doesn't want Steve to leave and says, "It doesn't make sense to leave home to look for home, to give up a life to find a new life, to say goodbye to friends you love just to find new friends." In the end, after dances, romances, and a near-deadly car crash for Laurie, Steve decides to stay in town and attend a community college, while Curt courageously steps aboard the plane that will take him to his future.

Change is a big part of the Christian life. Both inward maturity and a willingness to go to new places and meet new people are commanded by Christ in the Gospels. When we see a person whose growth is stunted, we automatically realize that something unnatural has happened. But often we have a hard time facing change in our own lives. There is comfort in familiarity.

God is on the move. He cruises the planet looking for someone who will be his mouthpiece for his exciting, life-giving, invigorating gospel. He wants people like Curt who will be willing to leave home and hearth to become students of his good news, even if it hurts. When we speed out to new adventures in Christ, we aren't left choking on our own dust. God promises to be with us always, and he also promises homes, brothers, sisters, mothers, children, and fields (Mark 10:30) to those who leave their comfort for his sake. There may be periods of our life when we must tend to our fields and family, but Laurie's statement (above) seems to come from a position of fear. We aren't giving up new friends and family when we go, but we are seeking to add new members to God's family.

PRAYER IDEA: Ask God for courage to leave home, at the proper time, for his sake.

PRESSING TOWARD THE GOAL

October Sky (1999)

MPAA: PG for language, brief teen sensuality and
alcohol use, and thematic elements

Read: Romans 5:1–5

Blessed is the man who perseveres under trial. (James 1:12)

His father misunderstands him. His classmates laugh at him. His school principal calls him a menace and a thief. But Homer Hickam (Jake Gyllenhall) of Coalwood, West Virginia, perseveres, fights the scoffers, and makes a name for himself by building rockets.

In 1957 Americans watch the Russian satellite Sputnik fly over the October sky. Inspired by this ingenuity, Homer recruits three chums to form a rocket-building club known as the Rocket Boys. Encouraged by their teacher, the Rocket Boys build increasingly successful rockets through trial and error. Homer briefly works in the mines but quits and reemerges with more determination than ever to build rockets. The Rocket Boys go on to win the regional science fair, and Homer goes on to win nationals. Homer returns home, makes peace with his father, receives a college scholarship, and eventually becomes a noted NASA scientist.

Like patience, perseverance isn't often fun, but it is rewarding. The apostle Paul persevered through suffering and counted it all joy because he knew the gospel would advance. Jesus endured suffering because he obeyed God and knew what it would do for the whole world. Both these Bible heroes received a prize for their efforts: the salvation of men and women.

An old saying goes like this: "If you want something you've never had, you got to do something you've never done." Many people moan about their life, but few people do the work necessary to change their circumstances and win a prize. Reward always follows effort. Like inventor Thomas Edison said, "Success is 1 percent inspiration and 99 percent perspiration."

Unlike Homer's father, who frustrated his son, our heavenly Father asks us to endure hardship as discipline. He allows us to endure trials so we can share in his goodness and holiness. Therefore, let us throw off everything that hinders (including scoffers and naysayers) and the sin that so easily entangles (including laziness and unbelief) and let us run with perseverance the race marked out for us (Hebrews 12:1).

Homer takes hold of his passion and never lets it go. He rides it all the way to the greatest space program in the world. What is God calling you to achieve? To what end are you persevering?

PRAYER IDEA: Ask God to reveal what he is calling you to achieve.

BAND OF SKATEBOARD BROTHERS

Dogtown and Z-Boys (2002)
MPAA: PG-13 for language and drug references
Read: Luke 5:1–11

These things are excellent and profitable for everyone. (Titus 3:8)

One of the most memorable movie lines from the 1980s is surfer/stoner Tony Spicolli (Sean Penn) saying "Excellent" in *Fast Times at Ridgemont High*. Penn. brought this character to life and defined the California surf culture of a generation. In 2002 Penn narrates the story of the real-life surf culture on which Spicolli was based.

The Dogtown Zephyr skate team was a group of social misfits with an uncanny, unprecedented ability on surfboards and skateboards. They were a force to be reckoned with, both in the water and on the streets. Nurtured by surf-board builders Jeff Ho and Skip Engbloom, they achieved international fame. Each had his own style, but together they pushed the limits of what people could do on skates and redefined skateboarding, essentially creating the extreme sports movement of today.

These people had identity, purpose, and encouragement. Individually, they *may have* achieved excellence on wheels, but collectively they *proved* excellence to the world. In time the energy of the group could not be contained and each went off into separate parts of the world to share enthusiasm for skateboarding professionally or to break ground in other fields. One disappeared, another disgraced himself and wound up in prison, but all the others carry the torch and the love of skateboarding still.

Jesus' original team started out as twelve scruffy men, mostly fishermen. Before their star status as religious leaders, Jesus let them catch so many fish that the boats could hardly hold them all. Jesus showed them extreme fishing and then said, "Let's do this where it really counts. Let's do this with people."

Impressed, the disciples said, "All right, we're with you. Let's do it."

And together they created history. Jesus lost one (Judas), and another stumbled (Peter), but most went on to great exploits in his name.

Are you a part of a team that is willing to be extreme for Jesus? Are you willing to break new ground for him? When we let ourselves be spurred on by others to love and good deeds (Hebrews 10:24), we can be excellent for him.

PRAYER IDEA: Tell God that you are willing to break new ground for him.

CRIME FIGHTERS
Chasing the Bad Guys

August 27–September 2

Give me neither poverty nor riches. . . . Or I may become poor and steal, and so dishonor the name of my God. (Proverbs 30:8, 9)

Frank Abagnale Jr. (Leonardo Dicaprio) has been taught by his father all his life that the government has been cheating him and stealing from him. Frank Sr. (Christopher Walken) says, "Be like the mouse trapped in cream. Keep fighting and struggling until the cream turns to butter and crawl out." When Frank's mother and father divorce, Frank Jr. skips school and turns to a life of deception, forgery, and thievery. He pretends to be a pilot for Pan American airlines, a doctor, and a lawyer. Frank Jr. creates his own checks or gets himself onto the payroll of companies where he is entirely unqualified to perform the services for which he was hired. For years Frank Jr. is able to keep one step ahead of the law, particularly the FBI, represented by Agent Hanratty (Tom Hanks). When Hanratty finally does subdue Frank Jr., he ends up hiring him for the FBI's counterfeiting division. Frank Jr. eventually makes a great living from the government, the very institution that plagued his father years earlier.

Fraud, lying, cheating, and stealing aren't reserved for wicked, crafty criminals. All of us have practiced one of these sinful crimes to one degree or another, whether it was petty squabbles with our family members or criminal acts committed against our employers or against our government. And we all can give our reasons. We say, "Well, it's just not fair what (fill in offending party) has done to me" or "I'm just going through some tough times right now and I need to (fill in offense) in order to keep alive."

Justice would demand that we do hard time and pay back (with interest) everything we stole from another, no matter what circumstance we were in. Mercy, on the other hand, would offer leniency. God has created a way for mercy by placing the penalty for our sins upon the crucified Christ.

Hanratty could have left Frank Jr. in prison, but he had mercy on him and turned his skills of evil into skills for good. Let us likewise have mercy on one another.

PRAYER IDEA: Ask God to convert all your faults into acts of goodness.

SEEING IS BELIEVING

Witness (1985)

AA: Best Original Screenplay; Best Film Editing • MPAA: R

Read: Acts 1:1–8

He came as a witness to testify. (John 1:7)

Young Amish boy Samuel Lap (Lukas Haas) sees a murder in a Philadelphia train station rest room. This witness actually sees two bad cops knife a good cop to death. Upon the scene enters another police officer John Book (Harrison Ford) who questions Samuel, and Samuel identifies one of the murderers as a man from inside the police force. When John talks to his superior officer, he realizes how deep the police corruption goes. The next night John is shot at and hit in the gut by one of the murderers. Bleeding profusely, John nevertheless takes Samuel and his mother, Rachel, home to their Amish community. When John passes out, Rachel cares for him until he heals. In time the murderers find out where John is hiding and take their quarrel to him. A lethal shootout ensues in the quiet Amish community—all because a boy saw something violent and extraordinary.

A live witness is no good to a criminal. "A truthful witness gives honest testimony" (Proverbs 12:17), and honest testimony exposes the crime. The power of an eyewitness testimonial can sometimes be the turning point for a judgment. That's why, in the movie, the criminals want to kill John Book and Samuel. And that's why, even today, many witnesses for Christ are hunted down.

A witness for Christ is a powerful thing. No one can dispute a person who has had a personal encounter with the living God. A witness's statement is personal, profound, irrefutable, and useful for establishing evidence. Jesus told his followers to be a witness for him all over the earth (Acts 1:8). His disciples accepted this challenge, creating a threat to the spiritual and religious establishment. Many of the original disciples paid dearly for being a witness—but, my, has the world changed!

Like John and Samuel, are you willing to be a witness for the truth, even if it put your life at risk? Are you willing to say what happened when you met Jesus? Are you willing to talk about how Jesus has changed your life? When you do, you give powerful testimony. You provide compelling evidence of the truth and power of Jesus. You sway a scrutinizing jury in favor of God. If God asks you someday if you were a witness for him, will you be able to truthfully say, "Guilty"?

Jesus' death was violent. His resurrection was extraordinary. His life-changing power continues. Tell others about him and watch what happens.

PRAYER IDEA: Tell God you are willing to tell others your testimony of accepting Jesus.

JESUS RULES!
The Untouchables (1987)
AA: Sean Connery, Best Supporting Actor • MPAA: R
Read: 1 John 5:18–21

Do not be overcome by evil, but overcome evil with good. (Romans 12:21)

Al Capone (Robert DeNiro) thinks he rules the town of Chicago. He throws money at people to turn a blind eye to his illegal activities during Prohibition. If they don't cooperate, he kills them. But he has never encountered the likes of federal agent Eliot Ness (Kevin Costner) James Malone (Sean Connery) an old Irish beat cop, and Ness's gang of agents known as "the untouchables." Ness knows the town is corrupt and nobody can be trusted, so he uses unconventional pressure and sheer pluck to go after Capone. Capone's thugs rub out two of Ness's men, but Ness has the law and justice on his side and he eventually puts Capone away.

Al Capone and the devil are a lot alike. They both think they rule the town. Their rule is based on violence, corruption, and lies. They think that anybody can be corrupted if enough pressure is put on them. The overcoming power of goodness enforced with might is what brought down Capone; overcoming goodness brings Satan down too.

Satan thought he had touched Job with a crushing blow in the Old Testament story. But Job didn't give up on God, and so he prevailed.

Satan thought he could touch Jesus when Jesus was hungry after fasting forty days in the desert. But Jesus didn't buckle. Satan again thought he had touched Jesus when Jesus was crucified. No doubt, on that occasion, Satan thought, *Yes! I finally got him.* But Jesus showed Satan that he couldn't be touched when he rose from the grave. Jesus triumphed over all the plans of the devil.

We don't have to give in to Satan's bullying. We have power through God's Spirit to overcome the devil's schemes. Jesus rules in history and in our hearts.

PRAYER IDEA: Thank God that evil cannot take away his love for you.

It Suits You

The Tuxedo (2002)

MPAA: PG-13 for action violence, sexual content, and language

Read: Ephesians 6:10–20

I will put rich garments on you. (Zechariah 3:4)

Jimmy Tong (Jackie Chan) is just a normal New York cab driver, except he knows how to make his cab zip through traffic, turn on a dime, and navigate through alleys and byways like a cat. For these skills, he is hired to drive a top secret agent named Clark Devlin (Jason Isaacs), and his life is forever changed. When Jimmy's new boss is injured in an assassination attempt, Jimmy takes on his identity and wears a secret agent suit with special powers—a tuxedo. The garment can make its wearer dance with grace, fight with lightning-fast reflexes, and even scale buildings. In short, the tuxedo makes its wearer into a Superman. Because of this garment, Tong is able to foil the fearsome foe with finesse, flair, and fun.

If only we had a suit that would give us super powers! Wouldn't it be great to be able to put on something that could help us resist temptation? How about something to make us righteous? Or a helmet that would give us wisdom? Or a belt of truth? Wouldn't it be great to wear shoes that gave us peace? Yeah, that would be great. That's real Christian clothing— not just some cheap sentiment on a T-shirt but garments to change the inner person.

Such clothing *does* exist. It is called the armor of God. Helmets, belts, breastplates, and shoes are all in our wardrobe for use against the devil's schemes.

But God asks us to wear two more things: the shield of faith and the sword of the Sprit. With the shield of faith we can quench all the fiery darts that the wicked one throws our way. With the sword of the Spirit, which is the Word of God, we can thwart temptation and combat the enemy.

A tuxedo looks good, but a warrior's uniform looks even better. Young David didn't need King Saul's armor to fight Goliath. He only needed God's invisible armor of faith, peace, and truth, along with the assault weapon of a sling armed with five smooth stones.

God fights our battles. We just need to be wearing the right outfit for it, and he does all the work.

PRAYER IDEA: Ask God to remind you to put on your spiritual armor every day.

SIN NO MORE

Minority Report (2002)

MPAA: PG-13 for violence, mild language,
sexuality, and drug content

Read: Genesis 3

AUGUST 31

If we claim to be without sin, we deceive ourselves and the truth is not in us. (1 John 1:8)

Thanks to his pre-crime unit, Police Chief John Anderton (Tom Cruise) is proud of his murder-free city in *Minority Report.* The year is 2054 and the place is Washington, D.C. He and other police officers are able to "see" a murder before it happens due to the psychic efforts of "precogs," three genetically engineered and chemically enhanced humans. Anderton believes the system is flawless—until he sees himself as a murderer in one of the visions of the precogs. As the system is called into question, Anderton goes on the run from his coworkers. When Anderton faces his would-be victim, one of the precogs tells him that he has a choice: will he murder or will he not?

Nearly every day we face the temptation to think murderous thoughts or give in to sinful temptations. Are we always bound to sin, or is it possible to break free from sinful patterns? Before Adam and Eve gave in to Satan's temptation, the world and its two human dwellers were pristine. But through Adam's sin, all of his descendants—the entire human race—inherited sin. This included Adam's son Cain, who committed the first murder against Abel. Try as we might, we cannot be like God through our own efforts. We cannot be sinless on our own—it is just not humanly possible. "There is no one righteous, not even one" (Romans 3:10).

The paradox in this is that when we accept Christ's forgiveness for our sins, he asks us to be holy. Jesus told the woman caught in adultery, "Go and sin no more." (John 8:11) The apostle Paul said, "Count yourselves dead to sin" (Romans 6:11). Why would they ask us to say "no" to sin if we cannot help but sin? The answer is the divine power we receive when the Holy Spirit dwells within us upon our salvation.

When God enters our life, he makes a way for us so that we can escape temptation and avoid sin. Holiness is not something we can whip up through psychic phenomena, prescribe with drugs, or produce through genetic engineering. It is a complete spirit replacement. We are dead to sin but alive to Christ through his Spirit. We are given the same stuff that was in Christ to enable him to live a sinless life. God gives us back our freedom to make right choices instead of falling victim to the ravages of sin.

PRAYER IDEA: Thank God for giving you free will to make correct choices.

DISCOVERING THE TRUTH
The Fugitive (1993)
AA: Tommy Lee Jones, Best Supporting Actor
MPAA: PG-13 for a murder and other action sequences
Read: Luke 22:66–71

Do not put an innocent or honest person to death. (Exodus 23:7)

Deputy marshal Samuel Gerard (Tommy Lee Jones) always gets his man. When convicted wife killer Dr. Richard Kimble (Harrison Ford) escapes from a prison bus, Gerard and his team stubbornly give chase. Kimble keeps just one length ahead of Gerard's reach. Through lots of close calls and sleuthing on the streets of Chicago, Kimble slowly but meticulously pieces together the facts of the case. First, Kimble unearths the real killer: a one-armed man. Then he finds the motive: the thug was sent to kill Richard to cover up bad but profitable medical research, which Richard would have exposed if he had found out about it. As the evidence mounts, Gerard becomes convinced of Kimble's innocence and brings the true criminals to justice.

When they first meet, Kimble tells Gerard, "I didn't kill my wife."

Gerard replies, "I don't care."

But as the story draws to a close, Gerard tells Kimble, "I know you didn't kill your wife."

Sometime in between those two conversations, Gerard became enlightened. Gerard discovered the truth and believed. Everyone who comes to faith in Christ must do the same.

Author of the classic novel *Ben-Hur* and former Civil War general, Lew Wallace had no faith in Christ. But as he researched Christ to write the story, he became convinced of the validity and claims of Christianity. More recently, investigative journalist Lee Strobel examined the case for Christ in his book of the same name and found the evidence overwhelming. Jesus is who he says he is and he didn't deserve to die. This is basic theology, yet many Christians struggle with it and can't defend it.

Is your faith weak? Then look at the facts objectively. Do you have friends who casually disregard Christ? Challenge them to look at the facts. Our faith isn't a blind faith; it is based on evidence and records and witnesses. Those who are open to the truth often find themselves defending Christ, though they once accused him.

PRAYER IDEA: Ask Jesus to forgive you for ignoring the whole truth of who he is.

SOMETHING IN THE WATER
Erin Brockovich (2000)
AA: Julia Roberts, Best Actress • MPAA: R for language
Read: Exodus 17:1–7

S
E
P
T
E
M
B
E
R

2

Never again will they thirst. . . . He will lead them to springs of living water. (Revelation 7:16, 17)

She dresses in trashy clothes. Her manners are earthy and unrefined. A single mother with three children, Erin Brockovich (Julia Roberts) desperately searches for a job but is continually turned away. Topping it all off, she gets into a car accident and fails to win a lawsuit against the perpetrator. With no alternative, she successfully browbeats her lawyer, Ed Masry (Albert Finney), into giving her a job to compensate for her loss. Soon she discovers that the Pacific Gas and Electric Company is illegally dumping toxic chromium into the water table, causing irreparable physical harm to those who live nearby. Erin convinces her boss to take on the case, which grows and grows, leading to the biggest class-action lawsuit in American history. With justice and righteousness (and a little unconventional sassiness), Erin takes charge and wins the case.

Water refreshes, hydrates, cools, cleans, and nourishes. This David-and-Goliath story tells us just how valuable clean water really is. God knows that we need it for a healthy life. Way back in Exodus, we read how God instructed Moses to strike a rock, and water came out of it, quenching the Israelites' thirst. God calls himself "living water," (John 7:38) because he gives us life. The same David who killed Goliath said in Psalm 42:1,

As the deer pants for streams of water, so my soul pants for you.

God in his mercy plants us "like a tree . . . by streams of water" (Psalm 1:3) to restore our soul. When we give clean, refreshing water to those who need it, we give that cup to God (Matthew 25:35).

Will you let God use you to give clean water to others? Will you stand up for those who have been hurt by dirty water? Each one of us has been poisoned by sin. Some of us have been literally poisoned by impure water resources, such as many who live in Third World countries. Experience the thrill and privilege of giving water in the name of Jesus. This "water" can be love, kindness, legal advice, or actual water. When you give others something they really need, God says, you are giving to him. It doesn't matter if you are unrefined or uneducated like Erin. Anyone can give. And when you do, it will change your life.

PRAYER IDEA: Ask God to make you like cool, clean water, a refreshment to others.

THE GAVEL KNOCKERS
Tales from the Courtroom

WEEK 36

September 3–September 9

MERCY OVER JUSTICE
Les Misérables (1998)
MPAA: PG-13 for violence and sexual content
Read: Romans 9:14–18

Mercy triumphs over judgment! (James 2:13)

One of the greatest works of fiction ever written, *Les Misérables* by Victor Hugo has been adapted into many motion pictures. No wonder filmmakers are drawn to it. It offers one of the best examples of mercy and forgiveness in literature.

In revolutionary France released convict Jean Valjean (Liam Neeson) steals silver spoons from a bishop's house and is caught. The bishop tells the police that Jean was a guest, the spoons were a gift, and Jean should have also taken the silver candlesticks. Jean asks the priest why he is doing this. The bishop says, "I'm buying back your freedom. Now you belong to God." Jean vows to reform, and by nine years later he has become a benevolent businessman and the mayor of a small town. Yet Jean has a nemesis. The law-loving, unforgiving Inspector Javert (Geoffrey Rush) obsesses over Jean and wants nothing less than Jean's ruin. Jean continues to show mercy and grace to his pursuer and to those he meets, while Javert digs in his heels and relentlessly pursues his legalistic crusade. After a revolutionary uprising in Paris, Javert catches Jean. Yet Javert turns his gun from Jean to himself because he cannot fathom Jean's mercy.

This story remains powerful because it reflects the story of God and humankind. Because of our sins, we deserve justice and punishment. But God in his mercy took our punishment through Christ's death on the cross and has given us mercy. Legally, Jean deserves prison, but he finds mercy and therefore is able to give mercy to all those he encounters. When Christ grants us forgiveness for our sins, we in turn can grant it to others. We can show others the love we have received in Christ.

Do you love God's law? Good. But don't use it to abuse others. Law has no power to change the human heart; only love can do that.

Do you love God's mercy? All the better. But don't use it as a license for sin. Take God's love and mercy and show them to others. Apply yourself to the good work of helping others who need your help. Apprehend the grace of God, thank him for it, and go and do likewise.

God's Spirit lives in the heart of the redeemed person and is always looking for ways to reach out in love to others. So love your enemies. Pray for those who seek your ruin. And the God of mercy will watch over you forever.

PRAYER IDEA: Pray for your enemies that Jesus will be merciful to them.

WHERE'S THE JUSTICE?

Chinatown (1974)

AFI: 19 • AA: Best Original Screenplay • MPAA: R

Read: Luke 8:1–9

I, the LORD, love justice; I hate robbery and iniquity. (Isaiah 61:8)

The police do as little as possible in the Chinatown area of 1930s Los Angeles. When a murder happens there, J. J. Gittes (Jack Nicholson) knows that justice won't be served. Hired by Evelyn Mulwray (Faye Dunaway) to investigate her husband's extramarital fling, Gittes uncovers dead bodies, double-dealing, political scandal, incest, and more. Just when he gets to the bottom of the case, able to accuse the perpetrator, the police and justice officials ignore the bitter truth, resulting in more death and destruction.

Justice is often thwarted. Criminals go unpunished. Some of these criminals are in public service and in leadership positions. King David lamented in Psalm 43:1,

Vindicate me, O God, and plead my cause against an ungodly nation.

It seems that a failure of justice was as common in biblical times as it is today. Sometimes people who fight justice one day cause injustice the next. King David committed adultery with a married woman named Bathsheba. Then he put her husband on the front lines of battle so that he would be killed. David was called a man after God's own heart (1 Samuel 13:14), but even he committed injustice. "There is no one righteous, not even one" (Romans 3:10).

It's bound to happen—sometime or another, injustice will be happen to you, perhaps even caused by a close friend. When you are treated unfairly and not getting the justice you deserve, remember two things. First, remember that Christ himself was innocent, yet he was accused and condemned to death. Second, remember that the Lord loves justice. Jesus was sent to proclaim justice to the nations, and he will bring about justice for his chosen ones. Though we may fail him, he never fails us. He is always just.

PRAYER IDEA: Ask God to show you how you can be more just today.

RUNNING AWAY FROM RIGHT

Changing Lanes (2002)
MPAA: R for language
Read: Matthew 5:21–26

Jonah ran away from the LORD. (Jonah 1:3)

In New York City, attorney Gavin Banek (Ben Affleck) drives through traffic on the way to court. At the same time, troubled family man Doyle Gipson (Samuel L. Jackson) also drives to divorce court. Changing lanes on the expressway, Banek causes Gipson to steer his car into some safety barrels in the median. Gipson wants to keep everything aboveboard and wants an accident report. Banek wants to sweep the incident under the rug and offers Gipson a blank check for car repair. Both are late for their respective court sessions and both suffer greatly for it. Banek accidentally leaves an important document with Gipson, and Gipson loses custody of his children. Gipson doesn't return the document to Banek, so Banek bankrupts Gipson through a computer hack. The men continue to make each other's lives miserable until they develop a conscience for each other and work to right wrongs.

Sometimes an overwhelmingly stressful moment is needed for us to realize the error of our ways. Sometimes we can't go up until we've hit rock bottom. As Banek struggles with Gipson throughout the day, he realizes that his current court case, which will make him tons of money, is based on corruption and lies. When he tells his senior partners in the law firm about the missing documents, they encourage him to forge them and move ahead. Even Banek's wife wants him to forge the documents. But when Banek realizes that his deceitful decisions will have devastating implications in the lives of real people, he puts his reputation and job on the line and does the right thing.

Doing the right thing, even when it is unpopular, takes courage. This theme is continually expressed in the Bible. Jonah is a good example. He wanted to disobey God and not go to Nineveh to preach against it. Jonah tried to run away, but God made a big fish swallow him. Then Jonah changed his mind. He decided to go to Nineveh after all, and the fish spit him onto dry ground.

Funny how an unpleasant experience makes one see circumstances differently. When the heat is on and life is falling apart, maybe God is trying to tell you something about your thoughts and behaviors.

PRAYER IDEA: Ask God to show you what he is trying to tell you when the heat is on.

A TRUE TESTIMONY

A Time to Kill (1996)

MPAA: R for violence and graphic language

Read: Proverbs 8:6, 7

We know that his testimony is true. (John 21:24)

Is there ever a time to kill? That is the question that young Mississippi attorney Jake Brigance (Matthew McConaughey) poses to a mostly white jury in this cinematic version of a popular John Grisham novel. Jake defends black man Carl Lee Hailey (Samuel L. Jackson) for the murder of two white racist thugs who raped his ten-year-old daughter, Tanya (Rae'ven Kelly). The prosecuting district attorney Rufus Buckley (Kevin Spacey) thinks the case is open and shut. Rufus contends that Carl Lee was not insane but completely lucid and took the law into his own hands. As the KKK backs Rufus, and as the black community supports Jake, the trial stirs up strong social opinions. Jake builds his case on Carl Lee being momentarily insane. He also questions the possibility of justice for blacks in a still-racist South. Jake says to the jury in his closing remarks, "We have a duty under God to seek, find, and live truth." He then goes on to tell the story of Tanya's rape in vivid detail. The truth is too hard for the jurors to bear. They acquit Carl Lee and say he should not be sentenced for the murder of two men who so brutally violated his daughter. The testimony sets Carl Lee free.

Seemingly supporting vigilantism and revenge, the movie holds its power in Jake's closing statement. The truth always helps, even if it hurts to hear. When a true testimony is spoken, the facts speak for themselves. History is revealed, actions are told, and character comes forth. From these facts a just judgment can be rendered. In Carl Lee's case the jury hears the true horrors of the rape and finds Carl Lee innocent of wrongdoing. The testimony results in Carl Lee's acquittal.

Bearing false witness is so vile because it has lasting ramifications. Good people are imprisoned. Good character is smeared.

A true testimony is so important that God included it in the Ten Commandments. It's number nine: "You shall not give false testimony against your neighbor" (Exodus 20:16). A true story is all it takes to set the captive free. Something so fundamental shouldn't be difficult to grasp, but every day, little white lies crop up in our lives, clouding the truth and leading to improper judgments.

Seek, find, and live the truth. It is always the safest place to be. If you have sinned, 'fess up to it. If you can defend an accusation with truth, then say it. If you can implicate a criminal with the facts, share them. Don't let justice fall because you fail to speak the truth.

PRAYER IDEA: Ask God for opportunities to speak truth to serve justice.

WHAT EVIDENCE DEMANDS
The Verdict (1982)
MPAA: R
Read: John 8:12–20

This is the verdict: Light has come into the world. (John 3:19)

The plaintiffs are a young couple who have lost their sister due to medical negligence. Doctors at a Catholic hospital gave the young woman the wrong anesthesia, and so the victim is now brain-dead and in a coma. The defendants include a well-organized and well-heeled archdiocese, the Catholic hospital, and two very smart doctors. Down to his last cent and barely sober, Boston attorney Frank Galvin (Paul Newman) does the unthinkable. He turns down a $210,000 out-of-court settlement and says, "We're going to go to court." Nobody can understand him, not even the young couple he represents. Enlivened by a sense of justice, he knows he can win the case. But the chips seem stacked against him. He loses a respected expert witness and discovers a spy for the defense on his team. In court the judge even dismisses hard evidence. Yet Frank continues to do what he can to bring the truth to light, and when it is time to read the verdict, Frank and his cause prevail.

In the end, it doesn't matter who has more money or more clout. It doesn't matter what sins one might have committed in the past. What matters is the truth. Truth must prevail, and the evidence demands a verdict. Despite obstacles at every turn, Frank is able to present the truth, and the jury sees it and makes a judgment.

Today everyone must examine the case for Christ and render a verdict on this question: is he 'guilty' of divinity? Many don't want to open up this case, but on Judgment Day, God will ask us what we did with it. Many render the verdict "He was a good teacher." But in doing so, they aren't looking at the facts. The question remains: is Jesus who he says he is—God—or isn't he?

Is he God? If the verdict is yes, the implications and repercussions are colossal. The settlement will be enormous. Justice will prevail. If the verdict is no, then humankind should close all courts. Right and wrong no longer matter.

So much rides on that little question—is Jesus God? Won't you examine the facts and make a verdict?

PRAYER IDEA: Ask Jesus to teach you the facts about his case so that you may defend him.

THE GREAT "I AM"

I Am Sam (2001)
MPAA: PG-13 for language
Read: Exodus 3:13–17

God said to Moses, "I am who I am." (Exodus 3:14)

As a single dad, you give your young daughter extra special attention. You dote on her, throw her parties, and read her bedtime stories. She is your greatest blessing. You never want to lose her, but one day somebody thinks you are an unfit father. Somebody wants to snatch your daughter out of your arms and put her into the arms of strangers. Somebody wants to deprive you of the one real joy you have in the world. And why? Because you are mentally retarded and have the intelligence of a seven year old. Authorities say you couldn't possibly give your daughter what she needs.

Such is the conflict Sean Penn faces as Sam Dawson in *I Am Sam*. His case seems hopeless until a lawyer steps in to defend him. Performing the work pro bono (free), Rita (Michelle Pfeiffer) risks her reputation and gives up her valuable time for the case. Delivering solid arguments before the court, she proves that a father's greatest contribution to a family is not knowledge but love.

Many of those who would judge us are puffed up with degrees and higher education, and jaded in self-righteousness. They look down on our faith. They declare, "God, the great 'I Am,' is an unfit Father." The simplicity of his love and salvation plans seems incomprehensible when laid against disciplined man-made arguments honed by centuries of secularization. But God offers a better plan than any court or legislative body or college department could ever design. God says, "I am your provider. I am your caretaker. I am your Savior. I am your Creator. I am your teacher. I am your Father."

We are to have no other "I am" before God. God established governments, but they were never meant to replace him. They serve as agents of his justice and order. When challenged to trade in God for a counterfeit father, challenge your challenger to look at the facts: the case for Christ and Christianity. An honest judge who weighs the evidence should conclude the overwhelming validity of the great "I am."

PRAYER IDEA: Ask God to forgive you when you trust in human statutes instead of his.

DEFEND THE DEFENSELESS

Twelve Angry Men (1957)

MPAA: not rated

Read: Proverbs 31:8, 9

You have sat on your throne, judging righteously. (Psalm 9:4)

Quick to judge. That's what eleven jurors are in *Twelve Angry Men*. The murder trial they will decide seems like an open and shut case. A teenage boy is accused of murdering his father. The murder weapon looks exactly like the knife the boy had purchased earlier. A woman says she saw him do it. An old man says he saw him run down the stairs seconds later. Someone says he heard the boy shout, "I'm going to kill you." Eleven jurors in the deliberation room call him guilty, but one does not. Juror 8 (Henry Fonda) has a reasonable doubt that the boy didn't do it.

Juror 8 says he bought a knife just like the boy's a few blocks away from the murder scene. He proves the old man saw the boy run away much later than the actual time of the crime. He even discovers that a witness had glasses but wasn't wearing them. With the skills of a competent lawyer, juror 8 pokes holes in the prosecution's case until, one by one, the remaining jurors switch their votes to "not guilty."

Like juror 8, we are to defend the defenseless. This juror is quick to point out that the boy has a court-appointed attorney. Such an attorney probably isn't paid well and doesn't care if the boy lives or dies. God, however, has appointed each of us to "speak up for those who cannot speak for themselves" (Proverbs 31:8). Juror 8 also says that the boy lives a disadvantaged life and has little opportunity for financial or social advancement. In other words, the boy is persistently poor and needy. For such persons as this, God asks us to speak up and judge fairly.

Lots of people, even Christians, are quick to dismiss injustices toward the poor because defending them would be inconvenient. But human life should never be easily dismissed. Who among us today are the poor and defenseless? Inner-city families. The unborn. Orphans and widows. The elderly. The mentally and physically challenged. These are the people whom God calls us to defend, because these are the powerless people.

Naturally, whether a crime is committed by someone rich or someone poor, justice must be served. But all too often the disadvantaged are blamed for crimes they didn't commit. And it is at such a moment when we need to step in and say "No!" Even if we stand alone.

Juror 8 was added as twenty-eighth on the American Film Institute's list of the fifty greatest cinematic heroes of all time. If you do what juror 8 did, God will honor you as well.

PRAYER IDEA: Ask God to inconvenience you to defend the defenseless.

TRUE
DISTINCTION
Tales of Extraordinary Men

WEEK 37

September 10–September 16

FULFILLING A DESTINY

Lawrence of Arabia (1962)

AFI: 5 • AA: Best Picture; David Lean, Best Director;
Best Art Direction; Best Cinematography; Best Film Editing;
Best Score; Best Sound • MPAA: PG (previously G)

Read: Exodus 3:10–14

Father, if you are willing, take this cup from me; yet not my will, but yours be done. (Luke 22:42)

Rising above the mundane task of coloring maps, young British lieutenant T. E. Lawrence (Peter O'Toole) leaves the safety of the officer's club in Cairo and travels to observe and assess the Arab Prince Feisal (Alec Guinness). The British and Bedouin Arabs have united to rid the region of the Turks, who have allied with Germany during World War I. After Lawrence meets Feisal, he rallies an army to cross a desert and attack the Turk-held city of Aqaba. The takeover of Aqaba becomes legendary. Lawrence returns to his base in Cairo, where he is lauded as a hero. He is re-commissioned to take other cities, such as Damascus. This time the brutalities of war, the hot desert sands, and his reluctance to be a hero discourage him from continuing. Realizing that he is an important figure for the British army and has a destiny to fulfill, Lawrence leads a final attack on Damascus in a decisive campaign in the Middle East.

Reluctance in leadership is nothing new. Christ himself didn't want to die and asked the Father for a different way than the cross. But Christ knew the necessity and importance of the cross, and so he obeyed. Centuries before Christ, Moses was commissioned by God to lead the Israelites out of Egypt, but Moses hedged and wanted out. He made excuses and said he was unqualified. But God convinced Moses that everything was going to be all right, and Moses relented and obeyed.

Many of us are afraid to step into leadership positions. We make excuses and find reasons not to lead, because we are afraid. Courage to lead isn't the absence of fear but the willingness to take a position for which one is qualified.

Learn from T. E. Lawrence, Moses, and Jesus. Be willing to lead despite your fears. Be willing to say yes to God. Who knows how much history may change if you take the will of God seriously and assume the unique position that he has created for you?

PRAYER IDEA: Thank God for choosing you for a special position in his Kingdom.

NOT AN ANIMAL
The Elephant Man (1980)
MPAA: PG
Read: Colossians 1:15–20

Let us make man in our image, in our likeness. (Genesis 1:26)

He was no ordinary sideshow freak. A horribly disfigured nineteenth-century Englishman, John Merrick (John Hurt) was known as the Elephant Man. Legend has it that an elephant attacked John's mother as she was carrying John in the womb. Now, as a young man, John has tumors over 90 percent of his body, an enormous head, a useless right arm, and a crooked spine. Adding insult to injury, John is horribly mistreated, beaten, and caged like an animal by his handler. Dr. Frederick Treves (Anthony Hopkins) discovers John and steals him away to live at the London Hospital. There John lives out the rest of his days in dignity and happiness.

The power of *The Elephant Man* lies in the question, what is humanity? John certainly doesn't look human, and for most of his life, he doesn't live like one either. He is caged, mistreated, and fed poorly. But appearances and lifestyle do not define our humanity. God defines our humanity. Like Dr. Treves, God is our benevolent ringmaster. God loves us, fills us with his Spirit, and teaches us how to reflect his character.

We are made in God's image. Since no two of us look exactly alike, God's image reflects more a spiritual than a physical presence. His image consists of emotions and intellect. We were made for God's purposes. No other creature on this planet was made alive by the Spirit of God and asked to obey God the way humans are. Sadly, these simple facts are often lost today. College campuses and corporate boardrooms often look more like animal houses than heaven on earth.

Are you reflecting the image of God? Are you living for his purposes? Or are you pacing in your cage, giving full expression to your animal passions? John Merrick knew not to take for granted the image of God. He struggled hard to express his humanity, reciting the Psalms to tell others of his faith in God, and behaved as kindly and as gentlemanly as possible to reflect his Creator. No matter how ugly or disfigured you may think you are, you are God's image bearer.

PRAYER IDEA: Thank God that you bear his image.

A Better Product

Tucker: The Man and His Dreams (1988)
MPAA: PG
Read: 2 Thessalonians 2:13–17

Though the mountains be shaken and the hills be removed, yet my unfailing love for you will not be shaken nor my covenant of peace be removed. (Isaiah 54:10)

In *Tucker: The Man and His Dreams,* Preston Tucker (Jeff Bridges) plans to show up the big three automakers of Detroit with a better automobile. Shortly after World War II, Preston Tucker designs and manufactures a car with seat belts, pivoting headlights, disc breaks, and fuel injection. Teaming up with businessmen Abe Karatz (Martin Landau), Tucker secures steel and a factory to make his dream car. With masterful showmanship and promotion, Tucker fuels anticipation in the public and animosity from the big three automakers. But then, with only fifty cars off his lot, Tucker is subpoenaed to appear in court on charges of fraud and embezzlement. Though he is eventually acquitted, the controversy shuts down his factory and halts production. Tucker walks out of the courtroom with his head held high, bucking the establishment by keeping his pride, joy, and visionary spirit.

The quickest way to anger the establishment is to threaten them with a better product. The Pharisees and Sadducees of Jesus' day enjoyed superiority over the rest of Israel. They had a corner on spiritual authority and often told the common people of their accomplishments and adherence to the law. Jesus came in and threatened their stronghold. He told them about grace, mercy, and even breaking the law (such as by healing on the Sabbath) while surpassing them in personal holiness. He rocked their world and challenged them with a better spirituality, a better way to live.

Jesus also challenges us to live a life of faith led by the Holy Spirit. This Christian life is better than the alternatives, and the alternatives don't like it. Today materialism, humanism, New Age thinking, and legalistic philosophies try to squelch authentic Christianity, just as they did in Jesus' day. But Jesus warns us and equips us to stand fast during the trials. Tucker lost the chance to mass-manufacture his dream car, but he never lost his enthusiasm. Jesus did better than Tucker and rose from the dead, so that today he reigns with the same radical, life-changing spirituality he always had. Jesus makes new lives based on righteousness and truth, not legalism and lies!

PRAYER IDEA: Thank Jesus for having the guts to stand up to the Pharisees.

STANDING ON PRINCIPLE

A Man for All Seasons (1966)

AA: Best Picture; Fred Zinnemann, Best Director; Paul Scofield,
Best Actor; Best Adapted Screenplay; Best Cinematography;
Best Costume Design • MPAA: G

Read: Matthew 5:33–37

SEPTEMBER 13

I have taken an oath and confirmed it, that I will follow your righteous laws. (Psalm 119:106)

King Henry VIII of England (Robert Shaw) wishes to divorce his wife, Catherine, and marry his mistress, Anne Boleyn (Vanessa Redgrave), because Catherine cannot produce an heir. Yet being subject to the authority of the pope, who will not allow divorces, the king cannot legally end his marriage. So the king repudiates his allegiance to Rome and declares that he is the head of the Church of England. Free now to make his own laws, Henry divorces Catherine.

Wishing to offer no opinion on these matters, the "man for all seasons," Chancellor Sir Thomas More (Paul Scofield), resigns from his position and vows to remain silent on the matter. Yet the new chancellor, Thomas Cromwell (Leo McKern), throws Sir Thomas into prison and eventually brings him to trial on charges of treason. Before his execution, Sir Thomas says, "I am loyal to the king, but loyal to God more."

When he takes his office, Sir Thomas pledges allegiance to the church and to the law of the land. Regarding compromise, he says, "I think when statesmen forsake their own private conscience for the sake of their public duties, they lead their country by a short route to chaos."

Compromise for political gain is common today, and many politicians are guided not by law, conscience, value, or God but by political expediency. When public leaders place their hands on a Bible or sign a document saying they will uphold the law, it is not unreasonable to expect that they will do it. So, too, it is with us, for we are all commissioned by God to be honest and true.

Our word is our oath. If we sign our name to a document or speak our promises out loud, we should be bound to do what we vow. In these dark times, evil people will try to trap us in our words. That is why Jesus warned us to keep our oaths simple. "Simply let your 'Yes' be 'Yes,' and your 'No,' 'No'" (Matthew 5:37). Sir Thomas tries to extricate himself from legal harm, but evil men trap him with perjury and false accusation. Commitment to truth, God, and principle may not be popular, and it might even cost us our life, but fellowship with God in heaven is worth more than temporary fellowship leading to the fires of hell.

PRAYER IDEA: Declare you allegiance to Jesus Christ and ask him to help you keep your word.

A BROTHER'S A BROTHER
The Straight Story (1999)
MPAA: G

Read: Ecclesiastes 4:9–12

Go and be reconciled to your brother. (Matthew 5:24)

To what lengths would you go in order to be reconciled to your brother? Would you ride hundreds of miles through the elements on a lawn mower? That's what Alvin Straight (Richard Farnsworth) does.

The Straight Story is based on a true story about a man named Alvin who lives in Iowa. One day he hears that his brother, Lyle (Harry Dean Stanton), who lives in Wisconsin, has had a stroke. For over a decade, Alvin and Lyle haven't talked, due to pride, liquor, and fighting. But Alvin knows that before one of them dies, he must be reconciled to his brother, and so he decides to travel to Wisconsin. Alvin has poor vision, doesn't possess a driver's license, and won't let anyone else in the driver's seat. So he attaches a homemade trailer to a John Deere riding lawn mower and hits the road. Alvin tells a person he meets on the road, "I want to make peace. I want to look up at the stars together with my brother like we used to do."

God is in the business of reconciling. God reconciles the world to himself and reconciles brother to brother (or sister to sister). To reconcile means "to restore to friendship or harmony." God doesn't want us to be enemies with him or with our fellow human beings. Strife, drunkenness, pride, and other sins can drive a wedge between us and others. Reconciliation is achieved through repenting for our part in a rift and accepting forgiveness from the other party.

Alvin doesn't just wish things were better between him and Lyle. He takes steps, no matter how strange or difficult, to go to him. If Alvin Straight can ride hundreds of miles on a lawn mower to reconcile with his brother, you can reconcile with those people with whom you were once close.

On the way to Wisconsin, Alvin meets a runaway teen girl. He tells her, "My father told me to break a stick, which I could do easily. Then he tied a bundle of sticks together and told me to break that. I couldn't. My father told me that bundle of sticks is family."

We are all like sticks. Separately, we can break, but when we are together, we are strong. When we are together with God, we are stronger yet. "A cord of three strands is not quickly broken" (Ecclesiastes 4:12). If you have ill will against your brother, sister, father, mother, family member, or former friend, repent and be reconciled. It's God's way, and it's a whole lot healthier and freer than living with separation and ill will.

PRAYER IDEA: Ask God for strength to be reconciled to estranged friends and family.

THE GALL OF BITTERNESS

Amadeus (1984)

AFI : 53

AA: Best Picture; Milos Forman, Best Director; F. Murray Abraham,
Best Actor; Best Adapted Screenplay; Best Art Direction;
Best Costume; Best Sound; Best Makeup

MPAA: PG (director's cut is rated R)

Read: Matthew 5:43–48

Get rid of all bitterness, rage and anger. (Ephesians 4:31)

Court composer Antonio Salieri (F. Murray Abraham) hates Wolfgang Amadeus Mozart (Tom Hulce). Salieri wishes he were as good a musician as Mozart so that he could praise the Lord through musical composition. But he can't understand why God favors Mozart, whom he calls "a boastful, lustful, smutty, infantile boy." In a moment of jealous rage, Salieri burns a crucifix and shouts to God, "From now on, you and I are enemies. Because you are unjust, unfair, unkind, I will block you." Afterward, Salieri puts in motion a scheme to murder Mozart by anonymously hiring him to write a requiem for his own death. Through intense pressure and insincere friendship, Salieri works Mozart so hard that Mozart meets a premature end. In old age Salieri realizes that his crime has done nothing to end his mental, emotional, and spiritual torture.

Did God favor Mozart? Was God laughing at Salieri by giving him the desire to create great music but not the talent? The answer to both questions is a resounding no. God's Word says, "He causes his sun to rise on the evil and the good, and sends rain on the righteous and the unrighteous" (Matthew 5:45). In other words, God offers blessings indiscriminately to the redeemed and the unredeemed. It is our choice whether we will develop our talents to the best of our ability without comparing ourselves to others or letting jealousy and bitterness creep in.

Do you have envy, bitterness, or jealousy in your life? Are you mad that God apparently hasn't given you the tools to accomplish your dreams and goals? If so, perhaps you are actually seeking your own glory and not God's. Or perhaps you are seeking God's goals with the wrong motives. Or perhaps you have missed his assignment for you, ignoring talents he has given you and pushing yourself to achieve in ways you weren't wired for.

Know your strengths and limitations. Operate in your gifts cheerfully, even if someone else is better than you. And always give thanks to God, putting aside bitterness, envy, and strife.

PRAYER IDEA: Ask God to help you to be gracious to those who have greater gifts than you.

A FLAWED BUT CHOSEN WARRIOR

Patton (1970)

AFI: 89 • AA: Best Picture; Franklin J. Schaffner, Best Director;
George C. Scott, Best Actor (refused to accept);
Best Original Screenplay; Best Film Editing; Best Art Direction;
Best Sound • MPAA: PG

Read: Matthew 26:69–75

I tell you that you are Peter, and on this rock I will build my church. (Matthew 16:18)

The boisterous, larger than life, ferociously ambitious and determined World War II field commander General George S. Patton (George C. Scott) masterfully invades Germany and sees the fall of the Third Reich. The Germans fear him, and his allies sometimes resent and misunderstand him. A military historian and poet, he believes that he was a warrior in many past lives. He also believes that God has destined him for something great in this life. But his temper and habit of insubordination repeatedly get him in the doghouse with supreme allied commander Dwight D. ("Ike") Eisenhower. Despite Patton's many flaws, General Eisenhower believes in him and appoints him to lead the Third Army, which advances from France to Germany in rapid time with great success.

The apostle Peter was flawed and boisterous and denied Christ three times in one night, but Christ still believed in him and appointed him "general" of the disciples. In fact, Jesus appointed Peter as the foundation of the church even before Peter denied him. God didn't require Peter to clean up his manners or be completely fearless; he doesn't require us to be flawless to appoint us for a task either.

Many of us think we are inadequate to do anything important for God because we are well aware of our own faults and inadequacies. God knows of our faults and inadequacies and loves us no less. He wants us in the game, teaching, evangelizing, training, and helping others in the faith. Sometimes God holds us back or shapes us to keep us from doing something stupid (as Patton was held in check by Eisenhower), but all of us are commissioned to "go and make disciples" (Matthew 28:19).

Figure out your gifts and how best to use them in your assigned post. Don't worry about what you lack or the mistakes you might make. God is your Commander in Chief, and he'll watch your back.

PRAYER IDEA: Ask God to show you your gifts and how to use them.

CLASSIC DISNEY FESTIVAL
The Best from Uncle Walt

WEEK 38

September 17–September 23

NO DOG IS ABOVE THE LAW

Lady and the Tramp (1955)

MPAA: G

Read: Galatians 3:26—4:7

You are no longer a slave, but a son; and since you are a son, God has made you also an heir. (Galatians 4:7)

The golden cocker spaniel Lady (Barbara Luddy–voice) enjoys all the comforts of a domesticated lifestyle. Her human caretakers give her every luxury, including letting her sleep on the bed. One day Lady meets a charming, worldly-wise street dog named Tramp (Larry Roberts–voice). For a while, Lady is enthralled—until she learns of his womanizing ways. After a human baby is born in Lady's house, Lady feels neglected. Furthermore, a nanny treats her like a reckless mongrel. Lady runs away to the Tramp but is picked up by the dogcatcher and put in the pound. Frightened and dejected, Lady's gloom turns to joy when her masters take her out of the prison. Later, Tramp valiantly rescues the human baby from a rat bite, demonstrating his good character. So Tramp is invited into the wonderful human home too.

Lady and the Tramp teaches us that whether we are down-and-out or up-and-out, we all need to be cleaned up and taken into a good home. When God gets his hold on us, he cleans us up and puts an ID collar on us, and we become part of his family. Sometimes we may feel like he has left us alone in the house with a mean caretaker, but that doesn't change our position under God. In fact, when the Father takes us into his home, he asks us to continue this joyous way of life by inviting others to join us in our home (or as Lady and the Tramp do, by making babies who also become heirs).

You may think that life on the street has its thrills and moments of excitement, but remember its many dangers: hunger, attack, and constant hounding by the law. It is not until we have accepted God's grace and forgiveness for our sins through Christ's death and resurrection that we can live under grace. The stark reality is that our sin condemns us. Through accepting the work of Christ, we all become purebreds. We all are registered in his book and we all share in his glory. "There is now no condemnation for those who are in Christ Jesus" (Romans 8:1).

PRAYER IDEA: Ask God how you might be a shelter to the homeless and hurting.

When Bad Things Happen to Good Deer

Bambi (1942)

MPAA: G

Read: Psalm 30

Jesus wept. (John 11:35)

Bambi (Bobby Stewart) is like a lot of us. He is born, wobbles in his first steps, makes friends, and finds love . . . and then bad news hits home. In his case, hunters come. Panic ensues, everyone scatters, a shot rings out, and Bambi's mother is dead. Adding insult to injury, a fire comes to the forest and Bambi must "buck up" to lead to safety the other deer and his friends, including Flower the skunk (Stan Alexander) and Thumper the rabbit (Peter Behn). Throughout his troubles, he matures to become the "prince of the forest."

Many people have a hard time believing in a loving God when there is pain and suffering in the world. When a loved one dies, a fire takes away a home, or another calamity strikes, people give up their faith. They reason that if God is all loving, all powerful, and all knowing, then he can and should stop tragedies from happening. He should reach down and keep trouble at bay.

While there are no easy answers to this dilemma, God does promise to be with us always (Matthew 28:20). He also is a God who is closely acquainted with suffering (2 Corinthians 1:5). God saw his own Son die a terrible death on the cross and felt the loss deeply. And when eternity is kept in mind, a moment or even a lifetime of misery will fade away as a distant bad memory. The Bible promises,

> Weeping may remain for a night, but rejoicing comes in the morning. (Psalm 30:5)

We then can "buck up" and be glad, even in the face of sorrow.

PRAYER IDEA: Thank God for understanding your suffering and for wiping away your tears.

THE COMING PRINCE
Snow White and the Seven Dwarfs (1937)
AFI: 49 • AA: Walt Disney, Honorary Award • MPAA: G
Read: Genesis 3:1–6

Who will rescue me from this body of death? (Romans 7:24)

When *Snow White and the Seven Dwarfs* was released in 1937, audiences flocked to it and adored it. Now, generations later, young and old alike still treasure this Disney classic. People still fear for Snow White's safety, laugh at the seven dwarfs, and cry at the heroine's sleeping death.

The story goes back to the Brothers Grimm. A wicked stepmother, driven by jealousy, sends the fair Snow White (Adriana Caselotti–voice) into the forest to be killed by a huntsman. Yet the huntsman (Stuart Buchanan–voice) takes pity on her, spares her life, and sends her deeper into the woods. Animals guide her to the home of the seven dwarfs. There she cleans up the place and prepares dinner for them. They accept her, but the next day when they are off to work, the wicked stepmother (disguised as an old lady) offers Snow White a poisoned apple that brings her sleeping death. Snow White is fooled into believing that with one bite of the apple, her beloved prince will come to take her away. She takes a taste and falls fast asleep. Yet in true fairy-tale fashion, the young prince comes to Snow White and the rest, well, . . . they live happily ever after.

The biblical parallels to this story are rich. Satan promised Eve that she would be like God if she ate the forbidden fruit, but of course Eve experienced a far different fate: banishment from the garden and the ushering in of death. Like Snow White, Eve needed a Savior to rescue her from death. Thousands of years later, God himself showed up to rescue Eve and all her offspring from eternal death by dying in her place. God's death and resurrection is his love story, his kiss of life. David, Daniel, and Paul all wrote of the need for a rescue by God.

Savior, Prince, Rescuer—these names all belong to our Lord. When he comes, we can live in his kingdom happily ever after.

PRAYER IDEA: Declare the wonderful names of the Lord and thank him for his protection.

PRETTY AS A PRINCESS

Cinderella (1950)

MPAA: G

Read: Matthew 25:1–13

At midnight the cry rang out: "Here is the bridegroom! Come out to meet him!" (Matthew 25:6)

In modern times *Cinderella* has often been misinterpreted as a story of feminine weakness. But that is not true. In her weakness Cinderella is strong. Despite losing both her parents, despite enduring a wicked stepmother and two wicked stepsisters, despite a wardrobe of rags, and despite nuisances caused by a cat named Lucifer, she retains her beauty and dignity. Although her only friends are mice and birds, she offers them friendship, including much kindness and generosity. She works tirelessly and without complaint. In the end she is rewarded for her virtue. The glass slipper fits her foot, not because she crams it on, but because she was made for it. She's a princess of character and strength, through and through.

The Beatitudes say,

Blessed are the poor in spirit, for theirs is the kingdom of heaven. . . .
Blessed are the pure in heart, for they will see God. (Matthew 3:3, 8)

Cinderella is poor, but she eventually receives the kingdom through marriage to the prince. Though her skin and clothes are stained with the cares and trouble of her home, her heart is pure and she sees an opportunity to fulfill her royal destiny.

Though we may be poor and soiled by sin, God can give us pure hearts. With pure hearts Christ can take us to the wedding banquet. There we will be adorned with robes as white as snow. We do not know the day or the hour when he will come, but if we are prepared, he can receive us. And that's no fairy tale!

PRAYER IDEA: Thank God for your poverty and seek his blessing in the middle of it.

You Can Do It!

Dumbo (1941)

MPAA: G

Read: 2 Corinthians 7:2–16

Encourage the oppressed. (Isaiah 1:17)

Disney classic *Dumbo* encourages encouragement as much as it celebrates an oppressed little elephant that could fly. Mama elephant Jumbo (Verna Felton–voice) gets a visit from a stork carrying a baby elephant named Jumbo Jr., (Sarah Selby–voice). But little Jumbo has a big problem: enormous ears. All the other elephants in the circus make fun of him and nickname him Dumbo. Mama Jumbo goes crazy one day when Dumbo is teased by cruel boys. So circus officials lock her up. Now young Dumbo is all alone in the world, except for one little friend: a mouse named Timothy (Edward S. Brophy–voice). Timothy says, "Dumbo hasn't a friend in the world. Nobody to turn to. I'll do something about this." So Timothy makes a deliberate choice to encourage Dumbo every step of the way. He constantly affirms him, praises him, offers him practical advice ("pin your ears back"), and trains him in how to fly. Now the scorned elephant with a major weakness becomes a celebrated elephant with a major attraction!

Lots of us never got the encouragement we needed when we were growing up. Imagine what our lives would be like if we had a friend like Timothy. The apostle Paul had a friend named Timothy, and together they were able to encourage and strengthen many people during the early days of Christianity. If we all had rock-hard emotions and fully developed skills, encouragement from a buddy wouldn't be necessary. But God knew that we would need each other. God knew that our fragile spirits would need boosting from time to time.

Some of us don't think we have what it takes to be an encourager. Little Timothy the mouse doesn't have a lot of skills, but he does have a will. He makes a decision to encourage, and he acts on it. Throughout the New Testament, Paul talks about how he is encouraged by others, and he commands the church to encourage one another. Encouraging actually requires little effort, but it does so much both for the giver and the receiver.

Take time today to give an encouraging word to someone who is feeling oppressed. Praise him, mentor him—and be tenacious about it. Someday you might need to be encouraged too.

PRAYER IDEA: Ask God to let you encourage people and say, "You can do all things through Christ" (Philippians 4:13).

A WONDERFUL NANNY

Mary Poppins (1964)

AA: Julie Andrews, Best Actress; Best Editing; Best Score;
Best Song; Best Visual Effects • MPAA: G

Read: Mark 10:13–16

As a father has compassion on his children, so the LORD has compassion on those who fear him. (Psalm 103:13)

In 1910 English children Jane (Karen Dotrice) and Michael Banks (Matthew Garber) can't seem to hold on to a nanny. Everyone is frustrated. Mr. George W. Banks (David Tomlinson), a respectable banker, wants his home run with discipline and order. He advertises for a new nanny who will meet his qualifications. The children write their own advertisement and want a nanny who will "give them sweets and tell them stories." A stiff wind blows away all those who answer the father's advertisement, while the same wind brings in Mary Poppins (Julie Andrews). Strong and assertive but very loving, she introduces the children to song, wonder, enchantment, a vagabond friend named Bert (Dick Van Dyke), and a little bit of magic. One day she convinces Mr. Banks to take the children to work with him. Chaos ensues at the bank. Just when Mr. Banks is about to fire Mary, he realizes that he is to blame for exasperating his children.

Children need order and discipline, but most of all they need love. They also need a chance to explore wonder and imagination. Mary Poppins gives that to the Banks children, and she helps Mr. Banks recognize his inferior parenting skills. More than a few people have been raised in an exasperating environment, where religion and order were strictly enforced. Under these stifling conditions, the true relationship between parent and child and between God and child suffers.

Jesus said, "Let the little children come to me, and do not hinder them" (Matthew 19:14). Almost instinctively, children go where they are loved and shy away from danger. If God is made out to be a big "meanie," children won't want anything to do with him. Parents moan, "I trained him in the Lord, but he still rebelled? Why?" Perhaps the parents exasperated their children instead of teaching them the true nature of God.

Were you an exasperated child? Forgive your parents and discover the nature of our loving God. Are you a parent with children now? Teach them love and respect, but love them deeply. God is a wonderful nanny.

PRAYER IDEA: Ask God to teach you how to live and teach others as his child.

NOT OUR HOME

The Jungle Book (1967)

MPAA: G

Read: John 15:18–21

My kingdom is not of this world. (John 18:36)

Raised by wolves in the jungles of India, man cub Mowgli (Bruce Reitherman) wants nothing more than to live in the jungle and pal around with his friend Baloo the bear (Phil Harris–voice). In fact, Mowgli thinks he's a bear. But old, responsible Bagheera the panther (Sebastian Cabot–voice) knows better. He knows that the jungle is no place for a small boy. He know that animals like Kaa the snake (Sterling Holloway–voice) and Shere Khan the tiger (George Sanders–voice) want to kill and eat the vulnerable child. Through several close calls, Bagheera and Baloo protect and lead the child to human civilization. There Mowgli sees a young girl and follows her into the village. Saddened to see their friend go, Bagheera and Baloo know that now Mowgli has found his proper place——a safe place with his own kind.

The Jungle Book simply but beautifully tells us, "This world is not our home." Mowgli belongs in the world of humans, not the world of panthers, bears, snakes, and tigers. Mowgli doesn't belong in the jungle but the village. Thankfully, Mowgli has friends that know where he belongs and help him navigate through difficult situations to find his way out. They also have the good sense to let Mowgli go.

Our home is the kingdom of God, and this kingdom is a place where people live as they were meant to. Unlike Mowgli's village, God's kingdom isn't a place but a state of being, taught about by Jesus and received by grace through faith. Too many people continue to live in the jungle, scratched and bitten by the animals of this world. God doesn't promise complete safety, but he does promise protection, guidance, and weaponry to fight the battles this world brings against us. God also asks us to be like Baloo and Bagheera——he asks us to lead others to the place of safety and care found in Christ Jesus. He asks us to lead others to the kingdom of God.

The jungle is no place for a boy. This world of sin and dangers isn't our place either. That's why the Lord calls, "Come out from them and be separate" (2 Corinthians 6:17).

PRAYER IDEA: Ask God to show you how to live in the world but not of it.

TORTURED SOULS

Those Who Fought through the Pain

WEEK 39

September 24–September 30

THE PERILS OF VERBAL ABUSE

Who's Afraid of Virginia Woolf? (1966)
AA: Elizabeth Taylor, Best Actress; Sandy Dennis,
Best Supporting Actress; Best Adapted Screenplay
MPAA: not rated
Read: Matthew 12:35–37

Hatred stirs up dissension, but love covers over all wrongs. (Proverbs 10:12)

A harsh word stirs up anger," warns Proverbs 15:1, and there are plenty of harsh words in *Who's Afraid of Virginia Woolf?* Perhaps no on-screen couple before or since has spewed more poison than Richard Burton and Elizabeth Taylor in this maddening tale. Burton and Taylor play a sad middle-aged couple named George and Martha. All in one long night, they badger, berate, abuse, and love each other, both alone and accompanied by the naive young married couple Nick and Honey (George Segal and Sandy Dennis), whom they have invited over for a nightcap. As the cuts go deeper and deeper, an unspeakable void is revealed in the emotional center of the hosts.

G od knows our emotional aches and pains. He knows the frustration we face when we want intimate conversation with significant others but instead get insults and back talk. But the pain we feel cannot excuse the words we use to express our rage. We will have to give an account for every careless word we have spoken (Matthew 12:36).

We can't take back hurtful words we have said, but we can ask for forgiveness from God and from those we have offended. And we can determine to stop saying hurtful things in the future. We can begin to use apt and kind words. Sometimes it might be best to say nothing at all (Proverbs 21:23). When we use words properly, they are like "apples of gold in settings of silver" (Proverbs 25:11). Enough said!

PRAYER IDEA: Ask God for strength and healing from hurt so that you won't say careless words.

DESPERATE LIES

A Streetcar Named Desire (1951)

AFI: 45 • AA: Vivien Leigh, Best Actress; Karl Malden,
Best Supporting Actor; Kim Hunter, Best Supporting Actress;
Best Art Direction • MPAA: PG
Read: Proverbs 19:22, 23

They commit adultery and live a lie. (Jeremiah 23:14)

Blanche DuBois (Vivien Leigh) finds no relief on a streetcar named "Desire." She hopes the streetcar will take her to love and security, but instead it takes her into more heartache and trouble. Blanche is a fragile and neurotic woman who visits her brother-in-law Stanley Kowalski (Marlon Brando) and sister Stella (Kim Hunter), who live in the French Quarter of New Orleans. Immediately Blanche and Stanley butt heads. He concludes that she is deceitful and more than a little crazy. Blanche claims to have sold the family plantation, but the truth comes out that she lost it after she had an illicit affair with a seventeen year old. Blanche meets Mitch (Karl Malden), a card-playing buddy of Stanley's, and sparks of attraction ignite. But after Mitch learns the truth of Blanche's sordid past, she snaps emotionally and becomes a lying nervous wreck who lives in a fantasy world.

For some of us, our past actions are so terrible and our sins are so great that we can't accept and take ownership of them. We would rather sweep our skeletons under the carpet and pretend they never existed. But skeletons can stink after a while—or at least leave a big lump in the carpet that visitors can see. Inventing false realities to try to escape past sins and failures never helped anybody. Blanche invents lies and has a hard time keeping her stories straight. Her illicit romance with an underage man was never exposed, repented of, and dealt with, so it comes back to haunt her.

When God tells us not to lie or commit adultery, there's a good reason behind it. When he asks us to turn away from our sin, there is a good reason behind that, too. When we do what is wrong, relationships are strained, trust is severed, and healthy living is put at severe risk. Like Blanche, we are all desperate for love. But the solution is to fall on our faces before God in prayer, not fall on our faces before people in lies and deception.

PRAYER IDEA: Ask your heavenly Father to keep lies and deception far from you.

RUNAWAY MIND

The Seven Year Itch (1956)

MPAA: not rated

Read: Genesis 39

Drink water from your own cistern. (Proverbs 5:15)

Helen, I can explain everything—the cinnamon toast, the shower, everything," says Richard Sherman (Tom Ewell) in the Marilyn Monroe picture *The Seven Year Itch*. When Richard's wife, Helen (Evelyn Keyes), is away on a summer vacation, Richard's mind goes into a tizzy as he waffles on how to respond to the temptation offered by his alluring neighbor, played by Monroe. Thoughts of adultery and how to overcome them cause Richard to return to smoking and drinking. But they also cause him to flee into the arms of his loving wife by movie's end.

In the Bible story, Joseph had already made up his mind about adultery, so when he had an opportunity to engage in that sin, he fled. When Potiphar's wife grabbed his cloak, he didn't stop to negotiate for his return. He split—his shirt or cloak still in her hands! His mind wasn't unstable.

Jesus knew that thoughts of adultery on the mind of weak men mean trouble. He understood that even adulterous *thoughts* equate with unfaithfulness. So he called it a sin to think lustfully about a woman (Matthew 5:28).

We were made for intimacy with God, and we were made for a unique intimacy with our spouses. Marriage reflects the pure love of God for his church. When we entertain fantasies, we become unstable and operate not out of faith but out of doubt. We figure that some other person besides our spouse will give us the emotional and physical intimacy we crave.

When temptations crowd in and the mind wanders, don't walk but run to God and his holy answer to our needs. When it's too hot in the apartment, run for the hills!

PRAYER IDEA: Ask God to draw you into greater intimacy with him.

LOVE TAKES NO VACATION
What About Bob? (1991)
MPAA: PG
Read: Matthew 8:16, 17

[Love] always perseveres. (1 Corinthians 13:7)

Bob (Bill Murray) needs attention, manifests chronic phobias, and responds poorly to treatment. Therefore, his former psychiatrist wants nothing more to do with him. Successful analyst Dr. Leo Marvin (Richard Dreyfuss) decides to take on Bob as a patient and has one session with him before going on vacation for a month with his family. Bob feels great at first but then panics. He hunts down Dr. Marvin and relentlessly imposes himself on the doctor's family. Dr. Marvin goes from irritation to frustration to rage and then to lunacy. Meanwhile, his family embraces Bob. Dr. Marvin loses his mind just as Bob begins to feels better.

Jesus always had time for the undesirables of the world. Lepers, the blind, the poor, the lame, and even prostitutes were his frequent companions. He didn't start his ministry and then say, "Wow! I didn't realize how difficult these people would be. I'd better scram." He stuck it out it. Sure, he retreated occasionally to the mountains to pray, but even then his motivation was love for his flock and for the lost. Dr. Marvin, in contrast, retreats from love and practices impatience, envy, boasting, pride, and anger. He even delights in the evil practice of "death therapy," actually attempting to murder Bob. His consequence is personal destruction.

Christian love requires us to be open to interruption. Loving others always supersedes any other plan on our agenda. Noted author C. S. Lewis said, "Loving others doesn't require that we have to like them." Thank God for that. Love is a choice of the will to act as Christ does toward those who have no love. When you see an undesirable individual heading your way, do you want to turn and run away? Exercise your will over your feelings and stand firm. Predetermine in your heart to let the love of Christ flow through you when the undesirable one approaches. Smile and meet that person's needs, just as Jesus does.

PRAYER IDEA: When the outcast of the world say they need you, ask God to help you love them.

CUT UP THE ESTABLISHMENT
Edward Scissorhands (1990)
MPAA: PG-13
Read: Matthew 10:34-39

I did not come to bring peace, but a sword. (Matthew 10:34)

The eccentric creator of *Batman*, Tim Burton, fashions a modern-day fairy tale in *Edward Scissorhands*. In a pastel-colored suburbia, Peg Boggs (Dianne Wiest), "your friendly Avon representative," can't find a customer. So she goes up to a gothic mansion and there discovers a gentle young man named Edward (Johnny Depp) who has scissors where his hands should be. Taking pity on Edward, she takes him down to live in her house with her husband, son, and teenage daughter, Kim (Winona Ryder). Some in the neighborhood are threatened and scared by Edward, but most come to appreciate him and his topiary gardening skills and haircutting ability. Yet Edward's sword-like fingers have a way of getting him into trouble. The police think he carries a deadly weapon. Kim's boyfriend antagonizes him and eventually tries to kill him. One woman thinks he is from the devil. But Kim and Peg know that Edward is wonderful and special, though in the end they let him return to the mansion on the hill.

Like Edward, Jesus was gentle but carried a sword. From the day he came to earth, Jesus upset the existing order. Jesus challenged the thinking of the spiritual establishment. Jesus said you were blessed if you were "poor," "hungry," and "mournful" (Matthew 5). Later, Jesus said he came to turn "a man against his father" and "a daughter against her mother" (Matthew 10:35). Though he was all about love, Jesus came to upset the applecart and cut apart the normal, but flawed, way of living.

Letting Christ live in you is dangerous. God says his Word is "living and active. Sharper than any double-edged sword, it penetrates even to dividing soul and spirit" (Hebrews 4:12). When Jesus shows up, the real thoughts and attitudes of people come to the surface. With Jesus in our hearts, we are anything but pastel-colored, cookie-cutter, vanilla-flavored suburbanites. We are warriors who will threaten those who are comfortably wrong.

Are you willing to be sharp and dangerous for God?

PRAYER IDEA: Ask God to show you how you can change your neighborhood for good.

A TALE OF TWO TEMPTATIONS

Black Narcissus (1946)

AA: Best Cinematography; Best Art Direction • MPAA: not rated

Read: Romans 8:5–11

Each of you should learn to control his own body in a way that is holy and honorable. (1 Thessalonians 4:4)

Known for its stunning Technicolor photography, *Black Narcissus* is a story of how two women treat the same temptations: loneliness and desires of the flesh. Twenty-something Sister Clodagh (Deborah Kerr) is commissioned to start a convent in the Himalayan Mountains. The objective is to create a dispensary and a school for girls. Five nuns join her, including the equally young Sister Ruth (Kathleen Byron). At the nunnery, the wind is cold and clear and the natives are unlike any people the nuns have ever seen. The only other Westerner in sight is the dashing but sin-prone Mr. Dean (David Farrar). In time, when troubles mount and loneliness sets in, Sister Clodagh remains true to her faith, while Sister Ruth goes mad with lust after Mr. Dean. Deadly consequences result.

Sister Clodagh gets into trouble because, to her, following Christ is all about following rules and saying no to temptation. She doesn't practice understanding, mercy, or grace. She doesn't understand self-control. Sister Ruth understands holiness but she also understands that God is concerned about loving us and seeking our love in return. He wants relationship. The law points to our sin but cannot redeem us. Christ alone makes the way for us to have a relationship with God.

The cares of this world and the struggles of new and strange places can tempt us to place our hope and trust in other people instead of in God. Mr. Dean does not love Ruth, but she allows fantasies of their supposed mutual love to run rampant in her mind. Those lies dig her deeper and deeper into jealousy and rage. God wants us to nip our "stinking thinking" in the bud, not to take away our fun, but to protect us from further sin and self-destruction.

PRAYER IDEA: Ask God to help you control your thoughts and actions.

DISARMING BEAUTY

The Pianist (2002)

AA: Roman Polanski, Best Director; Adrian Brody,
Best Actor; Best Adapted Screenplay

MPAA: R for violence and brief strong language

Read: 1 Chronicles 6:31, 32

**You prepare a table before me in the presence of my enemies.
(Psalm 23:5)**

The pianist Wladyslaw Szpilman (Adrian Brody) entertains Warsaw high society in 1939, until one day Nazis rounds up him and his family and force them to live in the ghetto. As the war years continue, life becomes increasingly difficult for Wladyslaw. Almost shipped off to a labor camp, Wladyslaw is rescued by a fellow musician and smuggled from flat to flat in Warsaw, living undetected by the Germans. When his latest building is bombed, Wladyslaw sets up a home in the attic of a hospital. One day, when he searches for a can opener, he is caught red-handed by a German officer. The officer asks Wladyslaw what kind of work he does, and Wladyslaw says he is a pianist. The officer asks Wladyslaw to play something on the hospital piano, and Wladyslaw does—a beautiful piece by Chopin. Emotionally moved, the German not only doesn't shoot Wladyslaw but even gives him provisions until war's end. Once Poland is liberated, Wladyslaw returns to the orchestra, greater and more esteemed than ever before.

Music is powerful. It is a universal language that speaks to people even if they are enemies. Music is so important that God has required it to be played for many purposes and in many circumstances. He required it to be played before the tabernacle until Solomon built the temple. He required it to be played as a form of worship throughout the Psalms. David used music to minister to King Saul when the king was feeling low. In fact, the music of David drove away evil spirits from Saul.

Fine music is like a fine meal. It satisfies. Wladyslaw plays so beautifully and wonderfully that it doesn't matter that he is a Jew. The beauty overtakes the German officer and their differences melt. Music soothes the savage beast.

You don't have to have musical talent to use music to glorify God. Singing along in your own dissonant voice to a worship record or screeching out a song on an instrument may not sound like much to you, but God enjoys it. If you haven't praised God lately with music, begin doing it today. He inhabits the praises of his people. He reflects his beauty through music. He calms emotions with music. He wants you to enjoy its powers too.

PRAYER IDEA: Ask God to show you how to use music wisely.

90s
POTPOURRI
A Delightful Mix
from Recent Past

WEEK 40

October 1–October 7

HANDLING THE WORD

Mission: Impossible (1996)

MPAA: PG-13 for intense action violence

Read: 2 Timothy 2:14, 15

Kings and counselors of the earth, who built for themselves places now lying in ruins . . . (Job 3:14)

Mission: Impossible leader Jim Phelps (Jon Voight) assembles his team of covert operatives for their next project. They must trap a man in Prague who is trying to steal the top-secret NOC list, a tell-all directory of nonofficial coverts. In pursuit of this thief, most of the MI team lose their lives. Agency boss Kittridge (Henry Czerny) pegs Ethan Hunt (Tom Cruise) as a likely mole who engineered the NOC list theft. Now Ethan must stay away from Kittridge, steal the real NOC list, and deal with a crime lord named Max (Vanessa Redgrave) to draw the real mole to the surface. The device that helps Ethan through it all is the Bible, specifically Job 3:14. This verse serves as a password to Max and opens up new opportunities for Ethan to free himself from false suspicion.

Let's look at Job 3:14 more closely and see what it is really saying. This verse is part of a twenty-five-verse-long curse that Job spoke over the day of his birth. Remember, he had just experienced a series of terrible personal disasters. Job's children, livestock, home, and servants had all perished. Then painful sores sprang up all over Job's body. So Job had good reason to curse his birthday. He was mad. Job 3:14 is Job's claim that it would be preferable to be dead with former kings and counselors than to continue living in constant misery. God later spoke harshly with Job for his foolish talk, but still, in his goodness, the Lord blessed the latter part of Job's life more than the first.

Like Job, Ethan Hunt has lost much. He has lost his coworkers (who were his only family), his boss, and his reputation all in a single event. He could have rolled over and died (or let himself be prosecuted unjustly), but instead he uses the Word of God to extricate himself from harm.

God's Word is our shield and buckler. It is our safe haven. When trouble comes your way, do you hide in the Word and use it on the offensive? Or do you curse God and the day when he made you? Victory and restoration eventually came back to Job. Ethan finally finds favor with his boss. Handle your words and God's Word correctly so that it may go well for you through tragedy or in triumph.

PRAYER IDEA: Ask God to help you always handle his Word correctly.

JUDGE RIGHTLY

The Spitfire Grill (1996)

MPAA: PG-13 for thematic elements

Read: Matthew 7:1–6

God does not judge by external appearance. (Galatians 2:6)

Perchance ("Percy") Talbot (Alison Elliott) leaves her criminal life behind and begins a new life in Gilead, Maine. She ultimately finds work at the Spitfire Grill, owned by the cantankerous but harmless Hannah Ferguson (Ellen Burstyn). Percy is whispered about by many people, especially Hannah's judgmental nephew, Nahum Goddard (Will Patton). Nahum thinks Percy will crack and "go criminal" at any time. Nahum gets particularly antsy when Hannah amasses thousands of dollars in an essay contest recommended by Percy in an effort to raffle off the grill. When this money is lost, the townspeople assume that Percy stole it. A posse with dogs is formed to track Percy down, but Percy is only running to save an innocent man from danger. At a crucial moment, Percy sacrifices her own life to save another in a matter of mistaken blame.

At her funeral Nahum says, "I never knew Percy Talbot. I only thought I did. I thought she was a stranger that could bring no good to my family or to the town. I thought I knew her so well that I took that money out of the safe to keep her from stealing it. More than anyone, I am responsible for her death."

Judging by external appearances has caused countless errors and grievances. A person's past does not necessarily dictate how he or she will act in the future, especially if God has intervened and changed a person's heart. Someone who looks like a criminal isn't necessarily one.

Pharisees, legalists, prudes, and those who haven't encountered grace from the living God are the biggest purveyors of false judgment. Joining this bunch is a dicey business because, as Jesus said, "In the same way you judge others, you will be judged, and with the measure you use, it will be measured to you" (Matthew 7:2).

Don't let a tragedy, like Percy's death, cause you to see the plank of hypocrisy in your own eye. Percy serves coffee and meals and love and is merely trying to find hope and a future; someone you are quick to judge might be a person in similar circumstances. Stop condemning and start loving and forgiving and pointing others to the balm of Gilead.

PRAYER IDEA: Ask God to forgive you for judging others based on their appearance.

ONE-HIT WONDERS
That Thing You Do (1996)
MPAA: PG for language
Read: Matthew 13:18–23

You need to persevere so that when you have done the will of God, you will receive what he has promised. (Hebrews 10:36)

Drummer Guy Patterson (Tom Everett Scott) works at his father's appliance store but dreams of much more. Guy puts together a rock band called The Oneders (pronounced "wonders," but everybody calls them the O-Need-ers). Winning a local talent contest, they soon become well known around their hometown of Erie, Pennsylvania. They cut their own record of their hit song, "That Thing You Do," and meet a national agent, Mr. White (Tom Hanks), in Pittsburgh. Mr. White gets them big gigs, TV appearances, and movie bits. Just as the guys look like they will continue on with a successful music career and lots of hits, the band falls apart. Headstrong lead singer Jimmy (Jonathon Schaech) can't tolerate Mr. White's leadership; guitarist Lenny (Steve Zahn) runs off with a woman; and their bass player joins the Marines. Saddened by the breakup, but glad to be playing at a studio with one of his musical heroes, Guy realizes that few make it for the long haul in the music business.

The music business isn't the only place of "one-hit wonders." God's kingdom has its hits and misses too. Jesus talked about "one-hit wonders" with the parable of the sower. He said, "The one who received the seed that fell on rocky places is the man who hears the word and at once receives it with joy. But since he has no root, he lasts only a short time. When trouble or persecution comes because of the word, he quickly falls away" (Matthew 13:20, 21).

Jimmy, Lenny, and the bass player all fall away when things don't go exactly as scheduled. Band success and unity become secondary interests to them. Their flirtation with stardom is only that: a temporary thing until something better comes along.

Christianity isn't a fix-all, and it isn't about a series of big hits. In fact, God promises lots of troubles in this world. Guy stays in the music business because he loves music. He loves to be around music. He practices it. Likewise, those who stick with God through the tough times love him, want to be around him, and continually practice being in his presence. It's tough to stick it out, but those who do stick it out produce gigantic returns.

Are you a one-hit wonder or a repeat performer? Are you in with God for the long haul? He wants to be your love and joy forever and ever.

PRAYER IDEA: Tell God you are in it for the long haul.

UNITY OF PURPOSE
101 Dalmatians (1996)
MPAA: G

Read: Philippians 2:1–11

Ask the animals, and they will teach you. (Job 12:7)

Roger (Jeff Daniels) and Anita (Joely Richardson) and their two Dalmatians live happily in London. Both couples, humans and dogs, are expecting babies. Anita's boss, Cruella DeVil (Glenn Close), can't wait to get her hands on the Dalmatian puppies when they are born. Secretly, she wants to buy them all and make them into a fur coat. The pups are born, and when Roger and Anita refuse to sell, Cruella steals the entire litter of seventeen dogs. What ensues is a fantastic, madcap animal rescue brigade. Songbirds help the Dalmatian parents cross a dangerous electric fence. Raccoons booby-trap the getaway car used by Cruella's thieving thugs. A woodpecker creates a diversion. Sheep hide 101 Dalmatians under their wool. A crow steals Cruella's hat, and a horse kicks Cruella out of a window and into a vat of mud. Other animals do their part to thwart the evil plan. In time every one of the Dalmatians is rounded up and Cruella and her no-good team go off to jail.

We could learn a lot from the animals in this movie. Job from the Old Testament knew that the animals had messages and lessons to say. He knew that the Lord had his hand on them.

The animals of *101 Dalmatians* act more humanely than many humans do in real life. They don't fret, worry, or panic. They act decisively and without complaint. They work together, each having a part in a grand scheme to stop what would have been a mass killing. What they really practice is unity of purpose. Their compassion concentrates into a like-mindedness and a oneness of spirit. As Paul said in Philippians 2:3, "Do nothing out of selfish ambition or vain conceit, but in humility consider others better than yourselves." The animals set aside their own agendas to help 101 Dalmatians in need.

Are you willing to set aside your plans and look to the interests of others in a coordinated effort? It's biblical and it's called for in God's community. God's creatures may be counting on you—the two- and four-legged varieties.

PRAYER IDEA: Ask God to unite you with his church in attitude and deed.

THE GREAT HEALER

The Green Mile (1999)

MPAA: R for violence, language, and sexually-related material

Read: Luke 8:40–55

Heal me, O LORD, and I will be healed. (Jeremiah 17:14)

Death-row inmates in a 1935 prison must walk "the green mile," the distance from their cell block to the electric chair. Violent men with equally violent attitudes all face this awful journey. One man, however, is gentle and meek—an enormous man named John Coffey (Michael Clark Duncan), convicted of killing two young girls. Prison boss Paul Edgecomb (Tom Hanks) doubts that John Coffey really is a killer. When John miraculously heals Paul of a urinary tract infection and brings a squished mouse back to complete health, Paul is convinced that this man is blessed with healing power from God. Paul sneaks John out of the prison so that he can heal a woman suffering from a brain tumor. Coffey performs this wonder but still faces the electric chair. As an old man in the 1990s, Paul still remembers the miracles he saw in 1935.

Like John Coffey, Jesus healed people. Regularly throughout the Gospels, we read how Jesus placed his hands on people and healed them. Blindness, lameness, and leprosy were just a few of the diseased Jesus cured. Jesus also healed from a distance and raised people from the dead. Many called Jesus a great teacher, but he was much more. He was a great healer.

Jesus still heals today. The lame walk, the blind see, and cancer goes away. Some scoff and point out that not everybody who prays for healing receives it. True, but everyone who receives a miraculous healing has prayed for it.

If you have a disease, do not neglect to take a step of faith and ask God for healing. He is the Great Physician. As with John Coffey, some may dismiss Christ and his healing power, but don't let that dissuade you from seeking a healing. Nowhere does the Bible or church history say that Christ took back his offer to heal the sick. In fact, Christ told his disciples that they would go on to do even greater exploits than he did (John 14:12).

Believe in miracles from God. Believe in healing. If you don't receive one, don't blame yourself for a lack of faith, but praise God for the faith you do have and seek him for your good and the good of those around you.

PRAYER IDEA: Ask God to heal you and heal those you love.

LIGHT OF THE WORLD

Shine (1996)

AA: Geoffrey Rush, Best Actor

MPAA: PG-13 for nudity/sensuality and intense thematic elements

Read: Matthew 5:13–16

Arise, shine, for your light has come, and the glory of the LORD rises upon you. (Isaiah 60:1)

In German, Helfgott means "the help of God." With God's help, David Helfgott (Geoffrey Rush) rises from mental illness and returns once again to the international stage with brilliant, inspired piano virtuosity.

As a child in postwar Australia, David plays piano at the merciless prodding of his sadistic father, Peter (Armin Mueller-Stahl). After wowing judges in many competitions, David is given an invitation to continue his education in America, but Peter won't let him. In fact, Peter continues to verbally and physically abuse David. As an adolescent, David receives a scholarship to study at the Royal Conservatory of Music in London. David tells his father that he is leaving. Peter, in turn, tells David that if he goes, he will no longer be a son. David leaves anyway and learns a work by Rachmaninoff that is known as the most difficult of all piano pieces. However, during a performance, David suffers a brain aneurysm, which also triggers mental illness. For years, David languishes in obscurity and insanity. But slowly, with lots of love from others, he learns to shine again as both a survivor and a genius musician.

It doesn't matter how many knocks we might have had and how much abuse we endured as youths. We can still shine for God. Abusive parents and illness may try to steal our saltiness. People who don't understand us may try to keep us hidden "under a bowl." But our good deeds and talents and beauty must be put on display. Others must "see your good deeds and praise your Father in heaven" (Matthew 5:16).

Christ is light, and when you have accepted him into your life, his light shines out of you. As you fellowship with him, pray to him, and receive from him, his light will shine even brighter through you. This beauty shouldn't be squelched or hidden; it should be shared with others. A world with so much wickedness and sin needs your brightness and beauty. Don't be afraid to shine before others. Don't be afraid to show your beauty, talent, and light. With the help of God, you can shine bright truth and the love of God to a world that needs them so desperately.

PRAYER IDEA: Ask God to shine his light through you always.

THE PERSONAL TOUCH

Patch Adams (1999)

MPAA: PG-13 for strong language and crude humor

Read: Psalm 126

A cheerful heart is good medicine. (Proverbs 17:22)

Medical student Patch Adams (Robin Williams) angers the medical establishment with his antics and personal touches with the patients. His superiors have even cited him for "excessive happiness" and wish to kick him out of the fictional Virginia Medical University. The dean advocates maintaining a professional distance between doctor and patient. Patch, by contrast, says, "If you treat the illness, you may win or lose, but if you treat the patient, you always win." All in all, Patch advocates humanity and compassion as being as important as good medicine. Patch and some of his medical school chums open an unlicensed, unauthorized, free medical clinic called the Gesundheit Clinic. Through good grades and persistence, Patch graduates from medical school and insists that laughter can often be the best medicine.

Our Lord and Savior, Jesus Christ, is called the Great Physician. Is he great for his healing powers alone? No. He is also great because he provides a personal touch and compassion that no human doctor can duplicate.

One time some friends wanted to bring a lame man to Jesus for healing. Crowds surrounded Jesus, so the friends took the man up on a roof and lowered him to Jesus. Did Jesus say, "This isn't the way you should be admitting patients"? No, he commended the man's friends for their faith and healed him (Mark 2:5, 11).

On many other occasions, Jesus weaved through crowds to get to people who called on him for healing. Jesus didn't say, "Take a number"; he met them where they were and touched them.

Whether Patch Adams intended it or not, he tapped into the type of medicine that Jesus practices. Patch says it is far more important to care for people, get to know them, find out their dreams, and give them humor than to see them merely as case studies for illnesses. Patch touches his patients with humor, grace, and his own hands. He calls them by name.

Jesus told his disciples, including us today, that we will do far greater exploits than he did (John 14:12). Jesus commands us and predicts for us great feats of love, care, and divine medical practices. As you go forth in Christ's name and do his work, let the Spirit of Christ dwell richly in you so that all your "patients" see is love.

PRAYER IDEA: Ask God to give you a greater sense of humor for his glory.

IT CAME FROM SPACE

Space Oddities and Exploration

WEEK 41

October 8–October 14

WINKIN', BLINKIN', AND NOD

Invasion of the Body Snatchers (1956)

MPAA: not rated

Read: Matthew 25:1–13

Then he returned to his disciples and found them sleeping. (Matthew 16:40)

Panic in the streets! There's an invasion of body snatchers. Dr. Miles Bennell (Kevin McCarthy) doesn't know how it's happening, but friends and townspeople all over are dying and turning into emotionless shells of their former selves. Where is this threat coming from? And why is it attacking earth? Dr. Bennell first hears complaints of people not acting quite like themselves. Then the doctor sees the body of a man that doesn't look quite human. Next, he views giant pods hatching dispassionate humanoids. Finally, the doctor learns that sleep turns normal people into zombies without personalities, neither loving nor needing to be loved. When the doctor's girlfriend, Becky (Dana Wynter), loses her body to these invaders, he goes mad, running wild in the streets.

God's Word speaks of the dangers of falling asleep. Christ rebuked the disciples for not staying awake in the Garden of Gethsemane. He also told the parable of the ten virgins, some of whom missed meeting the bridegroom because they were asleep. In his criticism of sleep, Christ's meaning goes far beyond drowsiness (which we all experience) and rest (which we all need). He was speaking of heaven and hell, of life and death. He was speaking of spiritual readiness, which might seem minuscule in importance to some of us but may mean the difference between an eternity with Jesus or an eternity without him.

If you think that you are all right spiritually but you are lazy in some areas, beware. All may not be as well as it seems. Your good intentions and agreeable attitude toward following Christ's instruction may not fly when God is ready to move. When the disciples fell asleep in the garden, they weren't in danger of hell, but nevertheless Christ told them, "Watch and pray so that you will not fall into temptation" (Matthew 26:41). Let not these times, which praise entertainment and discourage dealing with real issues, lull you into spiritual laziness. Be alert and ready for God's call.

PRAYER IDEA: Ask God to place you on a prayer watch for the world falling asleep.

CALLING HOME FOR HELP

E. T.: The Extra-Terrestrial (1982)

AFI: 25 • AA: Best Score; Best Sound; Best Sound Effects;
Best Visual Effects • MPAA: PG for language and mild
thematic elements

Read: Romans 10:9–13

Call to me and I will answer you. (Jeremiah 33:3)

Everybody's favorite alien, E. T. exploded on the big screen in the early 1980s, becoming an indelible pop cultural icon. Popularizing Reese's Pieces and the catchphrase "Phone home," *E. T.* is the best boy-and-his-alien movie ever made. One night, while exploring the suburban California hills, E. T. misses his spaceship ride home. Young Elliot (Henry Thomas) finds the scared, lost little fellow in his garage and takes him in. Meanwhile, government thugs scour the area, looking for the space creature for research and experimentation purposes. As time goes on, Elliot begins to have the same feelings his alien friend has. Elliott helps E. T. create an intergalactic phone so that E. T. can tell his ride to come back and pick him up. After the government discovers E. T., the alien dies, rises again, and—with the help of Elliott—escapes to his meeting place in the forest to catch his ride back home.

Every one of us needs to call home. Heaven is our home, and God wants to pick us up and take us there. He is only a call away. God loves to answer our calls, and his line is never busy. He's always ready to listen and save us. In fact, God richly blesses all who call on him. Everyone who calls on the name of the Lord will be saved (Romans 10:13).

Those of us who are already citizens of heaven need to help others get home. We are to pray for those who aren't saved. We need to gently nudge others to call on God. As with Elliott, our job is to nurture the lost, protect them from evil, and encourage them to reach out to their home.

Unlike E. T., many people don't know they are lost. They know they are discontented, but they don't know why. The reason is that they are lost in a world that is not their permanent home. Sin has spoiled this planet and one day God will replace it with a new one. We'll travel from earth to heaven. Sound like science fiction? It's not. It's right there in the Bible. Phone home to God in prayer and ask him to save your friends who are lost.

PRAYER IDEA: Ask God to draw your lost friends close to him and rescue them.

A SUCCESSFUL MISSION

Apollo 13 (1995)

AA: Best Film Editing; Best Sound

MPAA: PG for language and emotional intensity

Read: Luke 10:1–16

He said to them, "Go into all the world and preach the good news to all creation." (Mark 16:15)

Jim Lovell (Tom Hanks) and his crew, Fred Haise (Bill Paxton) and Ken Mattingly (Gary Sinise), are anxious to go to the moon in *Apollo 13*. Days before the launch, Ken tests to be at high risk for the measles and so Jack Swigert (Kevin Bacon) fills his shoes. In 1970, when Apollo 13 launches, many consider the mission routine and the TV networks don't even air it. But after an accident with the oxygen tanks occurs on board, the moon landing is scrapped and the mission turns into just getting the three men safely back to earth. Houston flight commander Gene Kranz (Ed Harris), Ken Mattingly, and a whole team of specialists develop new contingencies to guarantee that failure is not an option. With creative plans and lots of prayers, the men come back home alive and well.

When Jesus sent out his disciples on the mission to make disciples of all people, he gave them marching orders. Among other things, Jesus told the disciples that they would be going into danger, like lambs among wolves. He told them to eat what was put in front of them and to heal the sick. They knew that the plan could work because God himself designed it.

Many disciples, in the course of carrying out their mission, have faced serious troubles. Paul, Peter, and John could have said, "Jesus, we have a problem." But instead they rejoiced in him and counted it all joy. They continued to praise God in prison and in the presence of enemies who sought to destroy their mission. But the plan Jesus gave them worked. They stayed on this planet doing the work of the Father as long as they were needed. They weren't destroyed before their time.

The crew of *Apollo 13* followed the plan, worked the plan, and got back safe. When we follow God's plan, we'll also get to our heavenly home safely.

PRAYER IDEA: Thank God that his plan always takes you safely home.

WATCH THE SKIES

Close Encounters of the Third Kind (1977)

AFI: 64 • AA: Best Cinematography, Special Achievement
in Sound Effects Editing • MPAA: PG for intense sci-fi
action, mild language, and thematic elements
Read: Acts 1:1–11

The heavens declare the glory of God. (Psalm 19:1)

Since the beginning of history, humankind has looked at the night sky and wondered, "Are we alone?" Well, God's Word answers with a resounding "No!". God and his heavenly hosts filled the skies long before people ever walked the earth.

In *Close Encounters of the Third Kind,* Richard Dreyfuss plays Roy Neary, a man who sees evidence of extraterrestrial life——UFOs. Adding to this wonder, he answers a strange call to meet the aliens at a mountain in Wyoming. Defying authorities and driving his family crazy, he makes it to the mountain and makes contact with creatures from another world.

The heavens declare the glory of God" (Psalm 19:1), and this is often one of the first reasons that people ponder whether God exists. Humankind sees the countless stars and the awesome wonders of God's handiwork and says, "This was designed by an awesome Creator." God then speaks to the heart of individuals and bids them, "Come, follow me" (Matthew 4:19). We ponder the question of God, and if we let our thoughts linger, we long for a personal encounter with God. When we do open ourselves up to meeting God, many describe it as a mountaintop experience.

God places great value on his heavens and skies. He knows of their overwhelming testimony of his glory. After Jesus rose from the dead, he ascended into heaven. But before he left, he told those around him that he would return again in the same way. "The dead in Christ will rise first. After that, we who are still alive and are left will be caught up with them in the clouds to meet the Lord in the air" (1 Thessalonians 4:16, 17). This may sound like science fiction, but it is in fact supernatural nonfiction.

Watch the skies for his return. We are not alone——and Christ is coming again!

PRAYER IDEA: Thank God for the marvelous creation of his constellations.

GUNG-HO GRAY

Space Cowboys (2000)
MPAA: PG-13 for language
Read: Genesis 12:1–4

Keep my commands in your heart, for they will prolong your life many years. (Proverbs 3:1, 2)

Space Cowboys tells the story of four hotshot test pilots who were grounded in 1958 from being the first men to go into outer space. Fast-forward to the present. An old Russian communications satellite, with technology designed by Dr. Francis Corvin (Clint Eastwood) is about to crash into earth's atmosphere. Because the old test pilots are the only ones who understand the outdated technology, Corvin convinces his former superior to let him and his gray-haired group of friends—including freelance pilot "Hawk" Hawkins (Tommy Lee Jones), astrophysicist Jerry O'Neill (Donald Sutherland), and retired Baptist preacher Tank Sullivan (James Garner)—save the day.

The Bible gives high praise to those who have racked up decades of living. God calls long life a reward for remembering his teaching and keeping his commands. He also says that gray hair is a crown of splendor and a symbol of wisdom (Proverbs 16:31). We could all learn much from our senior citizens.

Before sin entered the world, humankind was to live forever, but with the fall of humanity, death entered the world. For a time, people lived hundreds of years, but as centuries passed and presumably more consequences of sin accumulated, the human life span dwindled down to what Psalms says is "seventy years—or eighty, if we have the strength" (Psalm 90:10).

One of God's greatest works is creating his chosen people, the Israelites. Who did he choose to do it? An old married couple named Abraham and Sarah gave birth to Isaac when they were well advanced in years.

Despise not the lengthening of your days. God just might have something wonderful for you to do.

PRAYER IDEA: Ask God to bless the elderly with creativity, health and service opportunities.

THE END OF THE AGE

Armageddon (1998)

MPAA: PG-13 for sci-fi disaster action, sensuality,
and brief language

Read: Revelation 19:11–21

OCTOBER 13

They gathered the kings together to the place that in Hebrew is called Armageddon. (Revelation 16:16)

Meteors strike the earth and destroy a space shuttle as it flies through orbit. Then NASA official Dan Truman (Billy Bob Thornton) discovers a large blip on the radar screen. After more study, the awful truth emerges: a space rock the size of Texas is headed straight for planet earth. When it strikes, it will destroy all life on the planet. The only way to knock it off its course is to drill into its surface and detonate a nuclear weapon. So oil driller and daredevil Harry S. Stamper (Bruce Willis) and his crack team are brought in, given Astronaut 101 lessons, and sent up to the asteroid to do their jobs. Through determination, self-sacrifice, prayers, and lots of luck, the team comes through for the whole world and prevents Armageddon.

———————————

Through movies like these, pop culture conventional wisdom equates Armageddon with the end of the world. The Bible, on the other hand, labels Armageddon as the last battle, where good will finally vanquish evil. At this battle a white horse, whose rider is called Faithful and True, will lead the armies of heaven to crush the armies of kings of the earth, the beast, and the false prophet. Interpretations of this event are varied, and just where the destruction of earth falls on the time line of last-days events is unknown, but it *is* known that a new heaven and a new earth will come after the first heaven and earth pass away.

Unlike the case of the astronaut/drilling team of *Armageddon*, there is nothing people can do to stop God's plan as recorded in biblical prophecy. It is inevitable. Nor can we predict when it will happen. But it is not cause for fear or hysteria. God remains good. In the end Satan and his minions will be locked up forever and a glorious new heaven and earth will await God's faithful. Any momentary terror will certainly pass away, only to be replaced by eternal peace and joy.

PRAYER IDEA: Thank God that he has the past, present, and future firmly in control.

The letter kills, but the Spirit gives life. (2 Corinthians 3:6)

Based on a short story by Arthur C. Clarke, Stanley Kubrick's *2001: A Space Odyssey* launched a thousand interpretations. The question arose: what is this movie about? Many answers pointed to religion and humanity's place in the universe.

This largely incomprehensible movie does have an understandable plot in the middle of it—a story of man versus machine. A Mars-bound spacecraft is commanded by a talking supercomputer called HAL (Douglas Rain). Supposedly, HAL can do no wrong and has always operated without error. After a freak accident, human repairs are called for, but HAL disagrees. In fact, he is so adamant against human involvement that he leaves an astronaut to die out in cold space. HAL's human partner, Dave (Keir Dullea), must make a critical decision to turn HAL off before he, himself, becomes a casualty in the unforgiving, airless void.

In Bible times many of the Jews thought they were like HAL. They thought they were untouchable because they were God's chosen people and held God's perfect law. They thought they were a shoo-in for God's favor. They were wrong. The teachers of the law, the Pharisees, were often the brunt of Jesus' stern criticism. Calling them names and scorning their ways, Jesus frowned on their adherence to the letter of the law while having no love or forgiveness in their hearts.

Astronaut Dave could save his astronaut partner, but HAL refuses to see his error. HAL is convinced that he is right and doesn't agree to any allowances in the law.

Though Jesus is the fulfillment of the law, he broke the letter of the law by healing, feeding, and forgiving on the Sabbath. He demonstrated that loving and helping our fellow human beings is better than legal stipulations, which have no power to help. Jesus talked of a day when laws would be written on human hearts, when people would be guided by God's Spirit and not by a written set of rules enforced by spiritual police. If we love God and love our neighbors as ourselves, we fulfill all the requirements of the spiritual laws.

PRAYER IDEA: Ask God to show you how to love your neighbor as yourself.

IT'S A WONDERFUL LIFE

Miracles and Extraordinary Hope

WEEK 42

October 15–October 21

FAITH VERSUS SCIENCE

Contact (1997)

MPAA: PG for intense action, mild language,
and a scene of sensuality

Read: Hebrews 11:1–6

We live by faith, not by sight. (2 Corinthians 5:7)

Harvard-trained radio astronomer Ellie Arroway (Jodie Foster) obsesses over trying to discover intelligent life among the stars. One amazing evening, she receives contact from space, a message from the Vega system. The aliens have sent blueprints for a one-person spacecraft. Construction begins and an international committee is formed to decide who will go. Ellie is asked, "Do you believe in God?" She replies that she cannot believe in anything that cannot be supported by empirical research. Ellie's scientific rival, Dr. Drumlin (Tom Skerrit), is selected to go instead of her, but terrorists attack and destroy the craft and launching pad. An eccentric billionaire creates another craft, and this time Ellie goes. However, at launch, empirical data suggests that she never left earth. Ellie contends that she traveled through a wormhole and spent eighteen hours in space. With the tables turned, Ellie tells the world, "I can't prove I met extraterrestrial life, but everything in me tells me that it was real."

How ironic that Ellie denies a faith in God and yet asks the world to place faith in her when the evidence suggests that she has no out-of-this-world experience! Through having an encounter with something she cannot prove, Ellie transfers her belief system from facts to faith. If only all unbelievers in Christ could have such an encounter! An old hymn addressing the issue:

You ask me how I know he lives.
He lives within my heart.

Those who possess that old-time religion don't need proof, because they have had an encounter with the living God within their soul and hearts. "This is what the ancients were commended for" (Hebrews 11:2).

Faith needs no data to back it up other than the certainty within. That is why it boggles the minds of those who need proof. When God grabs you by the lapels of your heart and says, "Repent. I love you. Come and follow me," there is no squabbling over details. You don't ask, "Where did that voice come from?" or think, *I must be delusional.* God is not a fabrication of our own design. He is alive and continually calling humankind to repentance.

Do you stumble over the facts? Faith and science are not necessarily contradictory. The facts might even be pointing to God, not away from him. Step into the capsule of faith, if you dare, and take a trip to visit the living God. Reach out in faith and discover the Master of the universe.

PRAYER IDEA: Ask God to show you how science supports Creation.

ALIVE TO CHRIST
Awakenings (1990)
MPAA: PG-13
Read: Ephesians 5:15–21

Wake up, O sleeper. (Ephesians 5:14)

Socially awkward researcher Dr. Malcolm Sayer (Robin Williams) joins a care facility for mentally and physically challenged adults in 1969. Disturbed by the great number of comatose patients he finds there, Dr. Sayer wishes he could do something to bring them out of their imprisonment. When he notices that some have Parkinson's-like symptoms, he obtains permission to try a new Parkinson's drug called L-Dopa. After he administers massive amounts of L-Dopa to Leonard Lowe (Robert DeNiro), Leonard comes out of his fog and is able to move and speak. Many of the other patients also respond to the drug. Experiencing awakenings, these formally paralyzed people cherish all the wonders of life, some for the first time in decades. Unfortunately, the effect of L-Dopa slowly wears off. The patients return to their former paralyzed condition. Saddened, Dr. Sayer continues to research and experiment with drug therapies, but he never finds the success he enjoyed in the summer of 1969.

Becoming alive to Christ is a transformation as dramatic and bold as resurrection from the dead. In fact, Christ says we are "dead" in our sins and we must be "born again." Dead people cannot reflect the love and light of Christ. It is only when we are vertical and out in the light of day that we can feel the warmth of his love and give that love and life to others.

Unfortunately, the flawed science of L-Dopa wasn't able to create lasting change in the comatose patients. This is like some people who try on Christ for a while, only to shed his grace and mercy and return to their former dead and hardened ways. When Christ imparts his life into you, it is your responsibility to maintain and nurture it. God asks us to be wise and understanding of his will. He wants us to be filled with the Holy Spirit and to exercise a thankful heart. He asks us to take responsibility for our new life.

Rejoice every day that God has made you alive. Rejoice that he has awakened you to new life.

PRAYER IDEA: Ask God to show you how to live fully alive as long as you are on earth.

GOD MAKES TEACHERS

Mr. Holland's Opus (1995)

MPAA: PG for mild language

Read: Ephesians 4:11–13

Not many of you should presume to be teachers, my brothers, because you know that we who teach will be judged more strictly. (James 3:1)

In *Mr. Holland's Opus* musician Glenn Holland (Richard Dreyfuss) wants to compose one memorable piece of music that will last throughout the centuries. As a young man in the 1960s, he decides to teach music at a Portland high school for four years. He figures that in four years he can save enough money, let his wife work, and retire early to compose his opus. When his wife, Iris, becomes pregnant, Mr. Holland decides they need to buy a house. Months turn into years, and Mr. Holland discovers that "life is what happens to you while you're busy making other plans." Complications arise when he learns that his son, Cole, is deaf. In the mid 1990s the music program is cut, and Mr. Holland is forced into early retirement. Considering his life a failure, Mr. Holland hears his opus performed by his students of the past—students forever altered by his love and devotion to music.

Many of us would place our teachers at the top of the list of the people we respect and by whom we have been most influenced. The best teachers are the ones who are passionate about their subject matter and about educating their students. Those who don't love to teach should probably find something else to do.

Christ has been called the "Great Teacher." He is great because he is passionate to impart truth. Mr. Holland is great because he doesn't have pretenses to being a great teacher, but he sure is passionate about music. Even when his students cause him great frustration, Mr. Holland exercises patience and takes the time to make his students understand. Let us thank our teachers today and recognize the enormous responsibility they hold. God makes teachers "to prepare God's people for works of service, so that the body of Christ may be built up until we all reach unity in the faith and become mature" (Ephesians 4:12, 13).

PRAYER IDEA: Ask God to use you to teach others and to have the spiritual strength to do it.

MOST UNLIKELY GIVER
As Good As It Gets (1997)
AA: Jack Nicholson, Best Actor; Helen Hunt, Best Actress
MPAA: PG-13 for strong language,
thematic elements, and nudity
Read: Luke 6:37, 38

It is more blessed to give than to receive. (Acts 20:35)

Cranky, bigoted, obsessive-compulsive New York City writer Melvin Udall (Jack Nicholson) doesn't like his gay neighbor, Simon (Greg Kinnear), or Simon's dog, Verdell, very much. In fact, Melvin doesn't like anyone very much. He wonders, "Is this as good as it gets?" He tolerates waitress Carol Connelly (Helen Hunt) because she is the only one who tolerates him and his crazy demands at the restaurant where he eats his breakfast. After Simon is beat up and hospitalized, Melvin reluctantly takes in Verdell. This begins an upward spiral for Melvin in which he begins to do good. He pays for a doctor to treat Carol's chronically ill son. He gives soup to Simon when Simon returns. He even drives Simon to Baltimore so that Simon can visit his parents. Finally, he takes Simon into his own home to help him can get back on his feet financially. All along the way, Melvin complains and says outrageous things, but as he loves others, he discovers life does get a lot better. He becomes a better man—a giver who receives in return.

A crazy thing, this giving. The more you give, the more you receive in return. The most wonderful thing about this truth is that it works for spiritual and moral matters as well as for physical ones. Most people think that Jesus' promise "Give, and it will be given to you" (Luke 6:38) is about money. But let's look at Melvin. He gives money to Carol, but does he get money back? No. Does he get food back from Simon? No. When Melvin gives, he receives back friendship, joy, acceptance, self-respect, and love.

Christ said, "Do not judge, and you will not be judged. Do not condemn, and you will not be condemned. Forgive, and you will be forgiven" (Luke 6:37). There are lots of ways to give to others without forking over money. It's the small kindnesses or the words of encouragement that ultimately matter. Remember: you can't take money with you to heaven.

If you have been asking, "Is this as good as it gets?" then start asking yourself, "Am I giving as much as I can?" Chances are, you aren't. But if you start to, you will get back a "good measure, pressed down, shaken together and running over" (Luke 6:38). Give, and see just how good things can be.

PRAYER IDEA: Ask God to show you how good it can be to give.

GRACE OF MY HEART

Return to Me (2003)

MPAA: PG for language and thematic elements
Read: Ephesians 2:1–10

Were not our hearts burning within us while he talked with us on the road and opened the Scriptures to us? (Luke 24:32)

Chicago building contractor Bob Rueland (David Duchovny) grieves deeply when his beloved wife, Elizabeth (Joely Richardson), dies in an auto accident. Unbeknownst to Bob, at the time of Elizabeth's death, Grace Briggs (Minnie Driver), a waitress at a local Italian/Irish restaurant, lies in a hospital near death due to heart failure. Grace receives Elizabeth's heart and a new lease on life. A year later Bob eats at Grace's restaurant and instantly falls in love with her. Out of fear of rejection, Grace doesn't reveal her scar or her secret to Bob. One day, when she is at his house, she discovers a thank-you letter (for the heart of his deceased wife) that she had previously sent to him. Shocked to know where the heart came from, she runs off to Europe, but Bob's love for Grace and the new heart within her are too strong. He goes to Europe, and the two reunite in love.

Passions, longings, and emotions reside in our hearts. Bob is passionate about Elizabeth, and when she is brutally taken from him, part of him dies too. But a second chance at love and a reunion with the heart of his beloved comes in the form of the young woman Grace.

The disciples also had a passion for their Lord, Savior, and friend Jesus Christ. Through the spiritual realities of grace, forgiveness, and reconciliation, Christ became the living Word and opened himself up to humanity. Though he died tragically, Christ was resurrected by grace to continue demonstrating love to his beloved.

Christ's death and miraculous resurrection make grace and forgiveness all the more amazing. Does the grace of God that saved a wretch like you and me burn within your heart? Do you share the passion, longings, and emotions of Christ? If not, then serving him must seem like drudgery and a burden. Ask Christ to give you his heart. Ask for a heart transplant so that you may begin today to enjoy what he enjoys. This is the only way to truly live—out of genuine response to his love and grace. A heart quickened to Christ is a heart expectant to give and receive divine love.

PRAYER IDEA: Ask God to replace your heart with of passion for Christ and others.

THE SUSTENANCE OF REAL FOOD

Alive (1993)

MPAA: R for crash scenes too intense
for unaccompanied children
Read: Matthew 26:26–30

My flesh is real food and my blood is real drink. (John 6:55)

It really happened. A Uruguayan rugby team flies across the Andes Mountains, bound for Chile, and their charter plane crashes on a mountaintop. Many die, but the twenty or so survivors are confident that a rescue team will spot them and take them to safety. Some planes get close, but no rescue team arrives. Food becomes depleted and days turn into weeks. People starve to death. Everyone wonders, *Will I get out alive?* Eventually, an unthinkable choice is faced: eat the dead or join them. Strengthened on the nourishment, a small team led by Nando Parrado (Ethan Hawke) is deployed to find help.

Jesus told his disciples that they had to eat his body and drink his blood. Naturally, the disciples had a hard time accepting this and told Jesus, "This is a hard teaching. Who can accept it?" (John 6:60). Jesus told them that eating his flesh and drinking his blood were really about the Holy Spirit, who gives life. But some left him anyway. Later, on the night before he was betrayed, Jesus held the Last Supper with his disciples. He asked them to remember the significance of his broken body and shed blood as they broke bread and drank of the fruit of the vine. Today this meal is known in church services as Communion, the Lord's Supper, or Holy Eucharist.

Some Christians believe that Communion is a symbol, while others believe that the bread and wine literally transform into the body and blood of Christ. Either way, the meaning is clear: Christ lives in us and he is our sustenance. Communion is both a privilege and an obligation. It brings great joy in knowing that we don't have to walk out the Christian life on our own strength. If the rugby players had tried to walk out of their misery on their own strength, they wouldn't have gotten very far. Sustain yourself on the body and blood of Christ.

PRAYER IDEA: Ask God to show you the deep significance of Holy Communion.

REACH OUT AND TOUCH SOMEONE

About Schmidt (2002)
MPAA: R for language and brief nudity
Read: Matthew 18:10–14

Whoever welcomes a little child like this in my name welcomes me. (Matthew 18:5)

When Warren Schmidt (Jack Nicholson) retires, he discovers that his life is less than exciting. His wife, Helen (June Squibb), annoys him, he can't communicate with his only daughter, and he's bored. One day he answers a TV ad to sponsor a Tanzanian orphan child. He begins to write letters to this boy about his wreck of a life. Things go from bad to worse when Helen dies. Schmidt decides to take an RV trip from Omaha to Denver to break up his daughter's marriage to a waterbed salesman. But on arriving in Denver, he blesses the marriage instead. Warren considers himself a failure, but when he arrives home, he finds that the Tanzanian orphan child has drawn a picture of them together, holding hands. Warren cries at the beauty and tenderness of the picture, knowing his life hasn't been in vain.

Warren's life is only semi-tragic. Yes, he could have expressed his love and thanks in a more tangible way to his wife and daughter, but he did reach out and touch someone. And in return, love was given to him. He did not fail to touch someone with love, in spite of his awkward efforts.

We don't know how much time we have on this earth. We could die tomorrow. That is why we must always love. We need to show and tell our love to those closest to us: our family. And we need to show and tell our love to those we don't even know, like orphaned Tanzanian boys. A saying goes like this: "In a thousand years it will not matter what kind of house I lived in or what kind of clothes I wore, but it will matter if I made a difference in the life of a child." We are all children of God. Through the Spirit of Christ's love, let us strive to make a difference that will last for eternity.

PRAYER IDEA: Ask God to help you express love to others you don't know and who live far away.

HOW MONSTROUS

Ghouls, Goblins, and Things that Go Bump in the Night

WEEK 43

October 22–October 28

"DRINK MY BLOOD"

Dracula (1931)

MPAA: not rated

Read: John 6:41–59

In him we have redemption through his blood. (Ephesians 1:7)

Ooooh. Blood. The very sight of it sends chills up and down the spines of some. Others, like vampires, find it, well . . . delicious! Transylvanian count Dracula (Bela Lugosi) turns a real estate agent named Renfield (Dwight Frye) into a crazed servant. Together they board a ship, kill everybody on board, and travel to England. Once on firm land, the count kills a young woman named Lucy (Frances Dade) and nearly kills another named Mina. Finally, a learned man named Dr. Van Helsing (Edward Van Sloan) is able to resist the temptations of Dracula and puts him to death with a stake through the heart.

Perhaps no film character other than Tarzan has been depicted more times on celluloid than the not-so-gentlemanly count from Transylvania. This granddaddy of all horror movies from Universal Pictures has been praised and criticized by film fans through the decades, but it's hard to find a more perfect cinematic representation of a genuine anti-Christ. Count Dracula tries to woo and seduce others. He acts kind but intends evil. He gains immortality, not by giving his life, but by taking the lives of others. He does not shed his own blood for humankind, but he sheds the blood of others for his own selfish ends. He adds to his territory (through real estate purchases), not to expand the kingdom of light, but to expand the kingdom of darkness. Dracula casts no reflection because he is not made of flesh. He died long ago but did not rise again to new life. He walks the earth as one of the undead, a soulless, unredeemable force of evil. The cross of Christ and everything for which it stands repel him. He can only be stopped when a wooden stake pierces his heart.

It has been said that Bram Stoker, the author of the novel upon which *Dracula* was based, was actually a Christian and that he wanted to write about a character who embodied everything he wrestled with in his own life, namely lust and violence. And then Stoker wanted goodness and the cross of Christ to finally overcome this evil in his life.

We are called to partake of the blood of the God-man, Christ. The original disciples thought this was a hard teaching, and rightly so. They misunderstood the symbolic significance of the Lord's Supper. But the communion works its wonders to remind us of our eternal life in Christ. It tells us that we are made to please him and not ourselves. And it is confirmation that our sins are forgiven and washed away.

There is no alternative to Holy Communion. Accept no substitute.

PRAYER IDEA: Thank Jesus for shedding his blood to cleanse, save and empower you.

GOD BREATHED IN LIFE

Frankenstein (1931)
AFI: 87 • MPAA: not rated
Read: Psalm 139:13–24

The Spirit gives life; the flesh counts for nothing. (John 6:63)

Crazed Dr. Henry Frankenstein (Colin Clive) wants to distinguish himself from other medical students and dedicates himself to reanimating dead tissue. Giving concern to his friends and his fiancée, Elizabeth (Mae Clarke), Frankenstein sequesters himself to conduct his evil experiments. Not content with bringing dead animals to life, he creates an entirely new person out of cadavers (including one with an abnormal, criminal brain). The creature (Boris Karloff) turns into a monster who kills Henry's mentor and ravages the nearby Alpine town. Owning up to the error of his ways, Henry realizes the creature must be stopped. A torch-lit mob tracks the monster down. Henry finds his creation first and fights with him in an old wooden windmill. The townspeople arrive; the monster throws Henry down; and the windmill and monster are burned. As Henry convalesces in the days leading up to his wedding, his father raises a toast and says, "Here's to a son for the house of Frankenstein."

God doesn't make junk. He gives every person the exact brain he or she needs to fulfill God's purposes on earth. He doesn't make us out of spare parts; he knits us together as complete individuals. We aren't made alive by a spark of electricity (as if we were battery operated) but by the Spirit of God. Remember this: Adam came to life by God's breathing into him. Nothing man-made can bring us to life. Neither artificial chemicals nor even naturalistic remedies can do the trick. God makes us for his purposes.

The story of Frankenstein endures and fascinates us still today because it stands as a clear warning call to the dangers of playing God. Henry's father knows how new life is formed—God and God alone creates life. Doctors can study life, understand its mechanisms, and even help to preserve it, but they can do nothing to create it. Even cloning isn't creating life but merely copying it.

Since God is all good and all loving, you can trust that he has made you in a good and loving way. So don't abuse your body or think that it is somehow inferior. You are fearfully and wonderfully made.

PRAYER IDEA: Ask God to help you always respect human life as a special creation.

THE PHANTOM MENACE

The Invisible Man (1933)

MPAA: not rated

Read: 1 Peter 5:8–11

So we fix our eyes not on what is seen, but on what is unseen. For what is seen is temporary but what is unseen is eternal. (2 Corinthians 4:18)

Claude Rains plays an invisible man, and he lets his invisibility go to his head. He also lets it go to his hands and his feet and his face and, in fact, his entire body! He is altogether unseen and altogether evil. He wants to steal the country's gold reserves. He destroys precious property and he kills several men. The townspeople have seen his foul deeds on display and they band together to trap him, but he always escapes. The invisible man says, "I have the power to make the multitudes run, squealing in terror at the touch of my little invisible finger." Finally he is captured and contained, but only after causing great havoc.

We have an adversary who is just as bad as the invisible man. Often we let him wreak havoc in our homes and lives. Many people deny that this adversary even exists, because he cannot be seen. Others crouch in fear at this imperceptible foe who seems to have the upper hand. These people are stymied. They cannot flourish, because they fear impending terror. Our invisible foe is, of course, the devil.

Just because he is invisible doesn't mean we can't disarm him. Remember, first, that the devil can be in only once place at a time. He isn't behind every bush, nor are his demons. Second, if he does come, God says we can "resist the devil, and he will flee" (James 4:7).

The devil tried to tempt Jesus in the desert by misusing scriptures. He tried to steal Christ's loyalty away from his heavenly Father. But Jesus said, "Away from me, Satan! For it is written: 'Worship the Lord your God, and serve him only'" (Matthew 4:10).

When you resist the devil, "the God of all grace . . . will himself restore you and make you strong, firm and steadfast" (1 Peter 5:10). You can defeat the devil. Don't give in!

PRAYER IDEA: Ask God for the strength to resist and triumph over your invisible foe, the Devil.

WILD AT HEART

King Kong (1933)

AFI: 43 • MPAA: not rated

Read: Isaiah 11:6–9

The lion will eat straw like the ox. (Isaiah 65:25)

Moviemaker Carl Denham (Robert Armstrong) dreams of making the greatest adventure movie of all time. He knows of an island with primitive natives and a large mythical beast. Carl looks for a young female lead actress at a Woman's Rescue Mission but has no luck. Then he meets a beautiful girl named Ann Darrow (Fay Wray). Ann is accused of theft and tries to get out of it, so Carl sees her as a girl with some spunk. He asks her to act in the picture and she accepts. They travel by boat to the island, see natives chanting, "Kong," and start filming. The natives kidnap Ann and offer her as a sacrifice to Kong, an enormous gorilla. First mate Jack Driscoll (Bruce Cabot) rescues Ann, and the sailors capture Kong and take him back to New York. Kong escapes, grabs Ann, and climbs the Empire State Building, only to have his rule of terror ended in a hail of gunfire by flying aircraft.

In this movie an adventurous man wants an adventurous woman to join him on a grand journey to meet a beast greater than themselves. Yet this beast is untamed and dangerous. Similarly, God calls all of us to a grand adventure. When we follow him, we sometimes experience rough seas, high mountains, prisons, lion's dens, fires, and even death. The reward at the end is great, but the journey is both harrowing and full of excitement.

In the story *The Last Battle* by C. S. Lewis, one of the children speaks about the lion Aslan (representing Christ). The child asks, "Is he safe?"

The reply is "Oh no. He is not safe. But he is good."

God is enormous, all powerful, and certainly unsafe. He is in need of a bride, and that's us. Are we willing to lay down our lives to be carried off by an unpredictable but totally great God? Are we ready for God to climb to the high places and have him show us his awesome glory? King Jesus wants you in his grip.

PRAYER IDEA: Ask Jesus to forgive you for underestimating the adventure of the untamed Christian life.

I'M A BAD MAN

Dr. Jekyll and Mr. Hyde (1941)

MPAA: G

Read: Romans 7:14–20

There is only One who is good. (Matthew 19:17)

Is humanity essentially good, though with evil tendencies? Or are we evil and must overcome our evil tendencies with good? That is the question that the nineteenth-century Englishman Dr. Jekyll (Spencer Tracy) presents to a dinner party, which includes his fiancée, Beatrix (Lana Turner), her father, Sir Charles Emery (Donald Crisp), and other local members of high society. Dr. Jekyll says that he is working on a scientific solution to make people good, and this smacks of blasphemy to the local priest and other dinner companions. Sir Charles is so alarmed that he temporarily breaks off the engagement and takes Beatrix away on vacation. Meanwhile, Jekyll swallows his own medicine and transforms himself into a beast of a man that psychologically and physically tortures a young barmaid named Ivy (Ingrid Bergman). This alternate persona, Mr. Hyde, shows up at the most inopportune times. Hence, Jekyll breaks off his engagement, terrorizes Ivy some more as Hyde, and finally faces utter destruction himself.

Jekyll poses a serious question: is humankind basically good or basically evil? According to Scripture, humankind was created good, without blemish, spot, wrinkle, or stain. For a short period of time, we enjoyed unrestricted fellowship with God. But the first humans bought into a lie, went against God's command, and became tarnished by sin. In other words, the human race was created to be capable of evil (by choosing willful disobedience to God) and then chose to be evil, creating a condition in which all humans are now evil. But that can change.

Social convention, good parenting, and self-control can make us civil and even make us perform good acts, but these will never make up for our spiritually dead condition. Our righteous acts are as filthy rags to God, if we do them for our own glory or somehow try to earn our entrance into heaven. Salvation through faith in Christ washes us clean and makes us good. Putting to death the misdeeds of the body, plus continually reaching out to God for spiritual regeneration, helps us continue on in goodness. No potion or elixir will do the trick.

PRAYER IDEA: Confess to God that your own righteousness is as filthy rags and declare his goodness.

MONSTROUS ME

The Wolf Man (1941)

MPAA: not rated

Read: Romans 7:14–25

For from within, out of men's hearts, come evil thoughts, sexual immorality, theft, murder, adultery . . . (Mark 7:21)

In *The Wolf Man,* Larry Talbot (Lon Chaney Jr.) returns to his European home after a seventeen-year estrangement from his father. Larry learns this proverb: "Even a man who is pure in heart and says his prayers by night may become a wolf when the wolf bane blooms and the autumn moon is bright." Larry attempts to rescue a woman from wolf attack, but he is bitten and turns into a werewolf. Later, a wolf kills a gravedigger and the evidence points to Larry. Larry tries to attend church at the funeral for the man but cannot find the strength to stay. Larry's father, Sir John Talbot (Claude Rains), says, "Belief in the hereafter is a very healthy counterbalance to all the conflicting doubts man has these days." Furthermore, Larry's father tries to scientifically explain away Larry's delusions. But when Larry strikes again as a werewolf, Larry's father realizes the gravity of the situation and must stop Larry with his own hand.

Do you sometimes transform into a beast and commit unexplainable atrocities? Afterward, do you wonder why you did it? Do you become full of fear and guilt? Scientific solutions and "churching" are no answer to our spiritual problems today. Many people spend hours to receive therapy, trying to remove guilt over sin. Others try to cover over their sin by being more active in the church. These "Band-aids" don't bring the deep-down healing we need. We must take up the cross daily, putting to death the evil deeds of the body, and allow Christ to transform our lives from the inside out by the power of the Holy Spirit. Of course, this is much easier said than done, but one of Christianity's first leaders knew of this difficult struggle.

The apostle Paul was filled with doubts and conflicting behaviors. He said, "What I do is not the good I want to do; no, the evil I do not want to do—this I keep on doing" (Romans 7:19). Of course, Larry didn't want to commit murder. But he did. We don't want to lie, steal, cheat, lust, or envy, but we do. Psychiatrists can offer methods of healing, but they have no power, in and of themselves, to heal. Nor can activity in the church solve our problem. God is quick to give mercy and forgiveness. He longs to redeem us daily to be more like his Son, Jesus Christ. We are redeemed through faith in Christ. When we abide in him, he abides in us.

PRAYER IDEA: Ask God to transform you to do the things you should and to not do the things you shouldn't.

HOLD ON TO THE MAP

The Blair Witch Project (1999)

MPAA: R for language

Read: 2 Timothy 3:16, 17

**Your word is a lamp to my feet and a light for my path.
(Psalm 119:105)**

They're lost in the woods. They're cold. They're tired. They're hungry. And they're hunted by something they cannot define. Michael Williams, Joshua Leonard, and Heather Donahue presumptuously misunderstand the dangers they face as they journey into the Maryland woods. Though the team leaves home with a map and a plan, the deeper they go into the woods, the more confused they become. After one too many wrong turns, one enraged member sends their map down the river. They entered the woods to create *The Blair Witch Project,* a documentary video on a series of murders committed over the centuries. Instead, they become victims.

God's Word is our map. Discouraged by the trials of life or simply bored by sticking to the trail, many Americans today have sent the map down the river. Many Americans say, "Map out your own life" and "Find your own way." With or without a map, Americans face the same dangers as all humankind throughout time—temptations, setbacks, rugged terrain, hardships, and dark moments. Yet by having God's Word, guarding it, studying it, discerning and discovering what wisdom it speaks to you and to the circumstances around you, the road to eternal life is available.

American cannot save itself. Lost without a map, we haven't the tools, wits, resources, strength, or knowledge to do so. If you (or someone you know) are lost and afraid, don't abandon the map. Don't get mad at the mapmaker. Don't flail with anger or kick against your fellow human being when the attacker stalks you at night. Turn to the map. Turn to the Mapmaker (who actually joins you on every step of the journey). Rest in his love and protection, and let others know about the safety, joy, and confidence we can have in him as we navigate a scary world filled with things that go bump in the night.

PRAYER IDEA: Thank God for allowing us to have his eternal map—the Bible.

OF CLOTH
AND CLERGY
Stories of the Saints

WEEK 44

October 29–November 2

DOWN THE VIA DOLOROSA

Dead Man Walking (1996)

AA: Susan Sarandon, Best Supporting Actress

MPAA: R for a depiction of a rape and murder

Read: Luke 23:26–30

The crooked roads shall become straight. (Luke 3:5)

With death and hell staring him in the face, Matthew Poncelet (Sean Penn) knows that he is a dead man walking. Convicted killer Poncelet is sentenced to a punishment of death by lethal injection. Sister Helen Prejean (Susan Sarandon) comes to him, not to give temporary peace and comfort, but to lead him to Christ for everlasting peace and comfort in eternity. Helen Prejean also talks to the parents of the victim to understand their pain. Honestly facing himself and his crimes, Poncelet repents and turns to Christ, knowing that though his body will soon fail, his soul will dwell with God.

The ironic beauty of this story is that God paved the way to restore relationship to himself through Christ, the original dead man walking. Though he committed no crime, Christ was tried and convicted of a sin punishable by death. He was whipped and beaten and told to take his cross down a road, now known as the Via Dolorosa (way of suffering), to Golgotha. There he would die in our place so that we might have eternal life.

Our Christian faith is often compared to a journey down a road. As we follow him with our own cross (Luke 14:27), though the road may be rocky, and though it may be steep, we can take comfort that Christ walked it first. Making crooked paths straight, his act of supreme mercy is able to soften the most wretched and hardened of hearts. Though we were dead, in him we are made alive!

PRAYER IDEA: Tell Jesus you'll pick up your cross and follow him down the hard road.

NO PENANCE REQUIRED

The Mission (1986)

MPAA: PG for violence • AA: Best Cinematography

Read: Psalm 103:11, 12

My yoke is easy and my burden is light. (Matthew 11:30)

In the late 1700s the Spanish Jesuits reach the Indians of the South American jungles for Christ. Father Gabriel (Jeremy Irons) starts a mission in the remotest of regions above a raging waterfall. There danger hides in the leafy shadows. Captain Rodrigo Mendoza (Robert DeNiro) rounds up Indians as slaves and offers his services as a mercenary. Filled with bloodlust and greed, he is pushed over the edge to violence when his girlfriend is stolen away by his younger brother, Felipe (Aidan Quinn). Rodrigo kills Felipe and instantly is filled with contrition and shame. Hiding away in a prison, he is visited six months later by Father Gabriel. Rodrigo says, "There is no redemption for me."

Father Gabriel responds, "There is. Do you have the courage to choose your penance?"

Rodrigo does and carries a load of junk metal, old armor, and weaponry up the waterfall to the Indians, where they cut it away from him, setting him free from this burden.

Sin is a heavy burden. If we murder or enslave another, or even if we succumb to lesser sins like lying or unfaithfulness, we separate ourselves from God and put a heavy weight on our own back. Turning to God requires recognizing our sin, repenting of it (turning away from it), and letting God set us free from our sin through faith. Penance, on the other hand, is an outward act of showing grief or repentance of sin. It is often encouraged in the Catholic and Anglican churches to emphasize the redemption process. Christ takes away our burden instantly when we put our faith in him, and our repentance and contrition turn to joy and thankfulness. No extended period of penance is required.

Few movies pictorially describe the burden of sin, and the freedom that comes when it is lifted, as clearly as does *The Mission*. After the Indians cut away Rodrigo's heavy weight, which has been hanging around his neck, they send it down the river. They remove it from his sight, never to be seen again. When God takes away our sin and its guilt and consequences, he sinks it in the deepest sea and places it as far away from us as the east is from the west. We are new creatures—saints—able to join in community with God.

Redemption is always there for even the worst of sinners. And best of all, Christ will relieve the burden instantly by faith!

PRAYER IDEA: Thank Jesus for taking away the burden and punishment of sin.

ONLY SCRIPTURE

Luther (2003)

MPAA: PG-13 for disturbing images of violence

Read: Romans 4:1–8

The work of God is this: to believe in the one he has sent. (John 6:29)

U nless I am convicted by Scripture and plain reason, I will not recant," says Luther to the German and Catholic authorities accusing him of heresy. In the sixteenth century, the Roman Catholic Church in Germany is the *only* church. And at this time corruption is running rampant. Priests visit brothels. Priests sell indulgences and freedom from purgatory for deceased relatives to fund the building of St. Peter's Basilica in Rome. Martin Luther sees all this and is disgusted. He begins to preach at Wittenberg University that Scripture alone (*sola Scriptura*) should be the basis of our faith, not bizarre corruptions of the church as led by the pope. Just when Luther is about to be put to death, his friends come and rescue him. Luther translates the Bible into German and becomes founder of the Lutheran Church and the Protestant Reformation.

T he church (Catholic and Protestant) has come a long way since the days of Luther in the 1500s. But many people still think they have to jump through spiritual hoops in order to please God. Many people think they have to follow traditions or mandates that the Scripture clearly doesn't advocate. Icons, trinkets, superstitions, and idolatry don't help either. Trusting in these things and a works-based theology brings unnecessary condemnation and burden.

God came in the form of Jesus Christ to set us free, not to bind us in chains with petty rules and tradition-based religious acts. The Bible is meant to be our sole standard for life and belief. At the start of this movie, Luther anguishes over God's judgment. But as he digs into Scripture, he discovers that God is quick to forgive, full of mercy, and quick to impart to us the righteousness of Christ through faith. This is great news! He doesn't find out about these marvelous truths from some church official; he finds them in God's Word alone. Leadership and organized religion can be wonderful things when they are based on the Word of God. Let us celebrate God's truths as found in Scripture.

PRAYER IDEA: Thank God that you are saved by his grace and mercy alone and not works.

A PRODUCTIVE PRIEST

Going My Way (1944)

AA: Best Picture; Leo McCarey, Best Director; Barry Fitzgerald, Best Supporting Actor; Best Original Story • MPAA: not rated

Read: 1 Thessalonians 4:11

NOVEMBER 1

We work hard with our own hands. (1 Corinthians 4:12)

Father Chuck O'Malley (Bing Crosby) knows a little about living in the real world. A fan of the St. Louis Browns baseball team and a gifted singer/songwriter, he joins the elderly Father Fitzgibbons (Barry Fitzgerald) at the Church of Saint Dominic in the slums of New York. Secretly, the local bishop has assigned Father O'Malley to take over the financially ruined parish, but Father Fitzgibbons doesn't know it yet. The Savings and Loan demands payment, and if that doesn't happen, the church is going to be evicted. Through firm but loving pastoral care, Father O'Malley works hard to find a solution to the church's financial woes. First, he creates a boys' choir from a group of young delinquents. Next, he builds a friendship with a singer at the Metropolitan. Together, they wow a local song publisher. The publisher likes Father O'Malley's song and buys it, thus saving the parish and bringing in a little extra money, allowing Father O'Malley's mother to come from Ireland for a visit.

Like the apostle Paul and those under Paul's charge, Father O'Malley knows the importance of hard work. Also like Paul, Father O'Malley inspires productivity in others. Father O'Malley helps an aspiring singer financially and shapes thieving, reckless boys into a beautiful choir. At the same time, their efforts provide much-needed finances for the church.

Many people think there is the Lord's work and there is secular work and never the twain shall meet. The Bible says differently. It says, "Whatever you do, work at it with all your heart, as working for the Lord, not for men" (Colossians 4:23). If it's slinging a hammer, typing at a computer, or singing a song, all our efforts are unto God and for his glory. Furthermore, the money we earn doesn't belong to us. It's all his. Father O'Malley knows this and uses the money where it is needed most. Let God be the Lord of your work. He's a kind, generous, and forgiving employer.

Let God be the Lord of your finances. He blesses those who bless him.

PRAYER IDEA: Thank God for your wages and ask him to show you how to spend them wisely.

THE RELUCTANT LEADER

Joan of Arc (1948)

AA: Best Cinematography • MPAA: not rated

Read: Exodus 4:1–17

Father, if you are willing, take this cup from me; yet not my will but yours be done. (Luke 22:42)

I n 1492 English forces control France. The heir to the throne, the Dauphin (José Ferrar), languishes in seclusion. Nineteen years later, Joan of Arc (Ingrid Bergman) hears voices from heaven telling her that she will lead an army, expel the enemies of France, and crown the Dauphin as King. Resisting these voices at first, she finally accepts them as her duty from God. As she is on her way to the Dauphin, a French soldier tells her of a prophecy foretelling that a maid from Lorraine would one day save France. Joan smiles and continues on her way. After convincing the Dauphin that God sent her, she rallies the French armies and lays siege to English troops. Winning battle after battle, she eventually triumphs completely. The Dauphin, despite his reluctance to gain the throne, is crowned. Later, Joan falls into English hands and they convict her of blasphemy and apostasy. Now Joan must renounce the voices or face a fiery death. History records her faithfulness to God.

B oth Joan and the Dauphin have doubts about their duty, but both rally themselves and accept their personal challenges from God. Reluctance to accept one's duty isn't uncommon, and many great saints and leaders of the Bible initially balked. Moses complained of stuttering, but God said, "I'll give you help," and Moses became the great leader of all Israel. God told Jonah to go to Nineveh and preach against it, but Jonah ran away. God made a great fish to swallow him up, and Jonah quickly changed his mind about the job. God persuaded Jonah with a little display of force. Even Jesus was reluctant to go to the cross, but he, too, yielded to God's purposes.

There is no use fighting God when he says, "Go." You can put him off for a while and try to avoid his voice by filling up your mind with business, but he will not be denied. His agenda is bigger than yours, and if he wants to use you, he'll speak to you loud and clear. He calls all people to be saved, and he calls all his children to "Go and make disciples." These two charges are not negotiable, and many of us are still fighting God on one of these. But God is calling others to a specific task, and we know in our innermost parts that we are not accepting the call.

What is God calling you to do? Only you know the answer. Only you can make the decision to accept.

PRAYER IDEA: Ask God to forgive you for stubbornly avoiding his call on your life.

"THAT'S FANTASTIC!"
Fantasy Film Fest

WEEK 45

November 3–November 10

COME BACK TO ME

Somewhere in Time (1980)

MPAA: PG

Read: Ezekiel 34:11–16

"Return to me," declares the Lord Almighty, "and I will return to you." (Zechariah 1:3)

Return to me." These are the only words that the elderly Elise McKenna says to her young love, the playwright Richard Collier (Christopher Reeve), in the movie *Somewhere in Time.* Perplexed, Richard tries to find out all he can about her. He eventually discovers that Elise (Jane Seymour) was once a beautiful, vivacious actress on stage of the Grand Hotel in 1912. Finally determining that he must meet her somehow, he employs self-hypnosis and wills himself back to 1912. When he meets Elise, she asks, "Is it you?" Within hours, they fall in love, which does not make her manager, William Fawcett Robinson (Christopher Plummer), happy at all. Will their love survive Robinson's disapproval? Will Richard be able to stay in 1912? When Richard discovers a penny from the present in his pocket, these questions are answered.

Return to me," said God to his people in the Old Testament. With these words God urged his people, knowing that their stubbornness would be calamitous. When God calls you to return, be prepared to leave your fishing nets, like the disciples did, and follow him. The "fishing nets" of today are anything that hold us down to our daily grind. They are anything that keeps us ignorant of the love and mercy of God.

The God who transcends time looks down on the human time line and sees the past, present, and future. Yet he constrained himself to the limits of time to bring love to his people. Just over two thousand years ago, God entered time as a baby. As Jesus grew, he told others about the timeless, wonderful kingdom of God, which knows no end.

When Jesus comes around, are you prepared to ask, "Is it you?" Many don't recognize Christ as their Savior and eternal lover. But wise men and women still seek him and ask, "Is it you?" The answer, like Richard's, is always a resounding "Yes." The time is now to have a spiritual love affair with him.

PRAYER IDEA: Thank God for crossing the bounds of time to show his love to you.

Rule over the fish of the sea and the bird of the air and over every living creature. (Genesis 1:28)

Imagine crash-landing thousands of years into the future on a planet where apes rule and humans are treated like animals. Such is the case on the planet of the apes. Astronaut Taylor (Charlton Heston) is netted, prodded, and threatened by lots of rude gorillas and orangutans. The apes think all humans are unintelligent, mute, and only good for experimentation. When Taylor does speak, it shocks them all. A kindly chimpanzee couple, Cornelius (Roddy McDowall) and Zera (Kim Hunter), help Taylor escape. He travels with his intended mate, Nova (Linda Harrison), to the Forbidden Zone and discovers signs of intelligent human life. The final shocker at the end brings Taylor to his knees: he sees the Statue of Liberty and realizes this planet of the apes is actually planet earth!

This movie is shocking because it flies in the face of everything we know to be true about earth and its order among created beings. Christians who believe that humankind is specially created and filled with the breath of God might find this offensive. Genesis tells us that God made us ruler over all the animals, even apes. The word often used is *dominion.*

With dominion, however, comes a responsibility to treat the planet's animals with respect and care. We are their caretakers. Although the Old Testament talks of killing and using animals as sacrifices for atonement for sin, it also includes various laws that give respect to animals. "If you see your brother's donkey or his ox fallen on the road, do not ignore it. Help him get it to its feet" (Deuteronomy 22:4). Animals are a gift. Their beauty, grace, humor, strength, and delicacy are treasures to behold. When we are good stewards over them, we follow God's wishes. And that's no monkey business.

PRAYER IDEA: Thank God for animals and thank God for making humans in his image.

IT'S ABOUT TIME
Clockstoppers (2002)
MPAA: PG for action violence and mild language
Read: Luke 10:38–42

The sun stopped in the middle of the sky and delayed going down about a full day. (Joshua 10:13)

Run to the store. Pick up the kids. Take them to soccer practice. Pick them up again. Go to a Bible study. Go to your son's school play. Go to see your daughter's soccer game. Work forty hours a week, fit in dinner, crash into bed exhausted, get up bleary eyed, and do it again week after week for the rest of your life. This is called the rat race, and millions of Americans experience it all the time. Have you ever wanted to scream, "Stop the world. I want to get off"? Have you ever said to yourself, *There has got to be a better way*?

In the movie *Clockstoppers* a group of scientists develop a watch that enables the wearer to move at hyper-speed. The wearer of the watch moves so fast, in fact, that the world seems to have slowed to a stop. Imagine how much you could get done if the world did stop and you could move about it. Transportation would seem instantaneous. So much more work could be accomplished, not just in a single day but in a single moment. You wouldn't have to rush, because the world would no longer pass you by. You would be passing by the world. As the story progresses, though, we discover that nothing substitutes for good old-fashioned normal time, used wisely and practiced in peace.

Though Jesus enjoys doing the Father's business, he frowns on frantic busyness. He likes it when we are quiet enough to hear the voice of his Holy Spirit. When Mary and Martha were entertaining Jesus, Martha was running around like a spooked chicken, trying to meet Jesus' every need. Mary, however, relaxed by his side and enjoyed good conversation with him. Yes, there were things that could probably have been done, such as the dishes or other housework, but Mary knew there was a time for that and there was a time for enjoying the company of the Lord.

In the midst of your daily battles, don't forget to hang out with Jesus. And if there is never time for doing that, it might be good to ask yourself if you have too much to do. Frantic service to Christ is never a substitute for fellowship with him.

PRAYER IDEA: Ask God to forgive you for being too busy to hang out with him.

PANTS ON FIRE

Liar, Liar (1998)

MPAA: PG-13 for sex-related humor and language

Read: Proverbs 30:5–8

Each of you must put off falsehood. (Ephesians 4:25)

In *Liar, Liar* Fletcher Reid (Jim Carrey) is a fast-talking attorney and habitual liar. When his son, Max (Justin Cooper), blows out the candles on his fifth birthday cake, he wishes "that my dad would stop lying for twenty-four hours." When Max's wish comes true, Fletcher discovers that his biggest asset (his mouth) has suddenly become his biggest liability. He is soon telling his coworkers, boss, clients, son, and ex-wife, Audrey (Maura Tierney), lots of whoppers—brutally true statements that are shocking, to say the least. With this new pattern of truth telling, Fletcher just might convince his ex-wife and Max to stay in town and not move away.

Who among us hasn't told a lie and watched it grow into something terrible? God knows that when we lie, we break faith with those who are counting on us. If we are known as liars, it is much more difficult for others to believe us when we really are telling the truth. (Remember the boy who cried wolf?) God knows that when we run loose with our mouths, we can say things we don't mean and make promises we can't keep. To this, God says, "Simply let your 'Yes' be 'Yes,' and your 'No,' 'No'" (Matthew 5:37).

There is no falsehood in God. He is not a man that he can lie. By his mouth (words), God created the universe. And by our mouths, we can speak freedom (truth) or we can speak bondage (lies). Next time we are tempted to tell a lie to get out of trouble, or make a promise we cannot keep, let us seek the God of all truth to give us the right words to say.

PRAYER IDEA: Thank God for speaking truth into your life.

THE ORPHAN'S TRAVEL AGENT

James and the Giant Peach (1996)

MPAA: PG for frightening images

Read: Revelation 22:1–5

I saw the Holy City, the New Jerusalem, coming down out of heaven from God. (Revelation 21:2)

Merry old England treats James (Paul Terry) well in the early twentieth century. His parents love him and promise to take him across the ocean one day to visit a wonderful city called New York. But that day never comes. Alas, a rhinoceros kills James's parents and he moves in with his two horrid aunts. They slave-drive him all day long and feed him fish heads for supper. James goes from joy and hope to gloom and doom. Life can't get any worse—until an old man (Pete Postlethwaite) gives James some magical boiled crocodile tongues. These oddities cause a fruitless peach tree to produce a massive peach. Furthermore, James's only friend, a spider (Susan Sarandon), grows to the size of a human and talks to him. Together, James and the giant peach and the spider and other bug friends travel across the ocean to that city of promise, New York.

Many of us feel like orphans. We feel like we live with relatives who hate us. The poor orphan boy is a common character in the movies, but he's a good one. He communicates that all of us were created for joy but somehow lost the guidance and protection of our Father. We feel like we have come under the authority of false parents. What does it take to find joy again? What does it take to find elders who really love us? It takes a Savior.

The Promised Land, heaven, and the celestial city are all themes found in the Bible, but they are no fairy tale. They are true. God longs to take us from the desert lands to a place of milk and honey. He has done it throughout history; he does it today and will do it for us again in the future. You are not a settler but a traveler on a journey to a destination. Revelation tells us that the celestial city has a river with, on each side, a tree of life bearing twelve crops of fruit (Revelation 22:2). This celestial city is a brave new world across the sea, and God's grace is our magic crocodile tongues to take us there. Step out, O traveler, and seize the land the Lord is giving you today.

PRAYER IDEA: Ask God to always keep you moving forward to the Celestial city.

A LOVABLE MONSTER

Shrek (2001)

AA: Best Animated Feature

MPAA: PG for mild language and some crude humor

Read: John 10:1–6

What a man desires is unfailing love. (Proverbs 19:22)

A talking donkey (Eddie Murphy) is almost sold into slavery, but then a big green ogre named Shrek (Mike Myers) inadvertently helps him. The donkey pledges companionship and friendship for life to Shrek, but Shrek can't believe anyone would want to hang around him. "What am I?" asks Shrek.

"Really tall?" says the donkey.

"No, I'm an ogre. You know, grab your torch and pitchforks. Doesn't that bother you?"

"No," says the donkey.

"Really?"

"Really, really, man. I like you. What's your name?"

Lots of people think they need to clean up or get beautiful before God will have anything to do with them. They think that all God will see is their ugly parts. Well, God does see sin, which is ugly, but he also sees that we were made in his image. He sees that we were made for fellowship with him, and he is desperate to call us by name. He wants a relationship with us, warts, green skin, and all.

When you feel ugly, know that God loves you. When you're feeling mean and green, know that God is quick to forgive all your sins. When your friends push you away, know that God wants to draw you near. His love toward you is monstrous!

PRAYER IDEA: Thank God for loving you no matter what you look like, no matter what your disposition is.

A FALSE FATHER

Star Wars (1977)

AFI: 15 • AA: Best Art Direction; Best Costume Design; Best Visual Effects; Best Film Editing; Best Score; Best Sound; Best Sound Effects

MPAA: PG for sci-fi violence and brief mild language

Read: Revelation 12:7–9

I saw Satan fall like lightning from heaven. (Luke 10:18)

The granddaddy of the thrill-a-minute summer blockbusters has it all: laughs, romance, special effects, spaceships, bizarre creatures, and a mythical device that ties it all together called the Force. An imposing villain named Darth Vader (voiced by James Earl Jones) has built an ominous weapon called the Death Star and plans to use it as soon as he discovers where the rebel military base lies. So he kidnaps, tortures, and interrogates Princess Leia (Carrie Fisher) to find out the location of Alderan. A simple farm boy, Luke Skywalker (Mark Hamill), and his new allies—Han Solo (Harrison Ford), Chewbacca, Ben Obi-Wan Kenobi, C-3PO, and R2-D2—come to rescue Princess Leia from the clutches of Darth Vader. When they succeed, all Luke needs to do is take a team of crack pilots to shoot out a target that will trigger the death of the Death Star.

God is so big, and the earth is so old, that our existence almost seems like a mythic space opera. Long, long ago in a galaxy far, far away, a wonderful, perfect world existed where the Creator and his creatures coexisted in harmony and peace. The forces of our Creator God were all good. His power, thoughts, and creation were glorious. Then one day a powerful created being decided he could do better than the Creator and so rebelled. This prince became dark and established himself as a new ruler, taking a third of his kind with him, to tempt others to join his cause. Satan became a Darth Vader (Dark Father), guiding and tempting humanity toward darkness and separation from God.

Evil has a dark lord, and his name is Satan. The original author of rebellion against God, he continues his reign of terror today, promoting sickness, anger, and everything that is the opposite of good and true. Evil, hate, and malice are not of God. He has no light side and dark side. He is fully good, while Satan is fully evil. Satan sometimes poses as a surrogate father, but we have only one true Father. Good versus evil is a tried-and-true conflict in the movies. It is understandable because we face a fight against good and evil every day in our lives as we struggle to do the right thing and serve the right Master.

PRAYER IDEA: Ask God to forgive you for minimizing the reality of Satan, but thank God for victory over evil.

A-MAZING FRIENDS

Labyrinth (1986)

MPAA: PG

Read: Luke 1:76–79

I guide you in the way of wisdom and lead you along straight paths. (Proverbs 4:11)

Imaginative young actress Sarah (Jennifer Connelly) complains about another weekend night baby-sitting her baby stepbrother, Toby. In an act of defiance, she summons the goblins from her favorite book, *Labyrinth,* to steal Toby away. Amazingly, the goblins and the goblin king, Jareth (David Bowie), arrive to do her bidding. Jareth whisks Toby away to his castle. Jareth tells Sarah that she must rescue Toby in thirteen hours, or else he will turn Toby into a goblin forever. Guarding the castle is a labyrinth——a twisting, turning maze of rock and shrubbery, populated with outrageous characters and odd dangers. Unable to find the castle on her own, Sarah enlists the help of a cowardly, dwarflike goblin named Hoggle and a big, hairy, lovable goblin named Ludo. Sarah, Hoggle, Ludo, and a few more friends join together to find the baby and stop the goblin king.

Sarah needs friends to find the baby, and we, too, need loyal, kind beacons of hope to point us to Christ. Few find Christ by themselves. Most people need others to guide them through a maze of danger and confusion. The journey of life is just too difficult to not have supporting friends. Hoggle and Ludo never think they are friend material. Because they are ugly and subject to the evil demands of Jareth, Hoggle and Ludo never consider that friendship is anything they can offer. Before learning to love, Hoggle says, "Hoggle is Hoggle's friend." When Sarah comes along, she shows them a better way to live and, in turn, they show her a better path to take.

Tracts, television, video programs, and other communication tools can help point seekers to Christ, but the best guide is one made of flesh and blood. This type of guide can keep you company along the way. This type of guide can help you when you fall into a hole. This type of guide can share a meal and a song with you.

You don't have to be smart, pretty, or even well practiced in the gift of friendship to be a guide. You only need to know the pathway. As Christ expresses himself through you, make yourself available to be a guide to the lost. Show them the Christ child, the helpless babe whom Satan wanted to stop but never could. Make level the crooked paths.

PRAYER IDEA: Thank God for friends that point you to Christ.

TICKLE
ME NOW
Contemporary Comedy

WEEK 46

November 11–November 16

BROTHERLY LOVE

Stuck on You (2003)

MPAA: PG-13 for crude and sexual humor and some language

Read: 1 Samuel 20

There is a friend who sticks closer than a brother. (Proverbs 18:24)

Twins Bob (Matt Damon) and Walt (Greg Kinnear) Tenor do everything together. They have to—they are conjoined. Sharing a liver and a big flap of skin along their sides, they eat, date, sleep, and work side by side as owner/operators of the Quickee Burger in Martha's Vineyard, Massachusetts. Operating in synchronous harmony, they perform better together than they could separately. In fact, they guarantee meals in three minutes or less or it's free. Walt gets the acting bug and wants to move to California. Reluctantly, Bob agrees. There they meet actress/singer Cher, and Walt is invited to be her costar on a corny TV sitcom called "Honey and the Beaze." They blue-screen out Bob, and the show becomes a huge hit. But Bob's troubles with his girlfriend, May, along with his jealousy of Walt's success, bring strife. The brothers decide to have a surgical operation and separate. Successfully parted, they have more freedom but less joy. Wanting to be together again, Walt goes back to Martha's Vineyard, joins the local theater, and again works side by side with his brother.

Stuck on You humorously and sometimes tenderly demonstrates the beauty of brotherly love. Brotherly love celebrates the understanding and proximity of two people who help each other be more than what they could be alone.

Jesus sticks closer to us than a brother because, unlike a human, fallible brother, Jesus never leaves us nor forsakes us. Jesus always wants us to be more than what we can be without him. Jesus is closer to us than Eve was to Adam, even though Adam said of Eve that she was "bone of my bones" and "flesh of my flesh" (Genesis 2:23).

Jonathan (the son of Saul) and David (the future king of Israel) shared a bond of brotherly love. When Saul persecuted David, Jonathan shared in his pain. "Jonathan became one in spirit with David, and he loved him as himself" (1 Samuel 18:1).

Do you have someone with whom you are one in spirit? Do you love another as yourself? If not, ask God for such a friend. And seek Jesus as your brother. The rewards are an unparalleled intimacy.

PRAYER IDEA: Thank Jesus for sticking closer than a brother.

Love must be sincere. (Romans 12:9)

In the 1980s a button appeared on the public scene that read, "Obviously you've mistaken me for someone who cares." In the 1990s the rock group Nirvana sang, "If you need any help, please don't hesitate to ask someone else first." Such is the attitude of Will (Hugh Grant) in the movie *About a Boy*. He has lived all his life in the shallow end of life, having no job, no responsibilities, and no relationships with women that have lasted more than two months. Will tries to care, but he says, "You have to mean things when you help people." And since he has no sincere feelings of charity or love, he drops out. Yet when a single-parented boy named Marcus (Nicholas Hoult) drops by Will's house unannounced, Will must decide whether to care and to venture out into the deep, risky end of practicing sincere love.

Love is a choice, not a feeling. If we say to a cold, hungry man, "Be warm and well fed," but don't back it up by giving him a shirt and some food, then we have not practiced love. Offering sincere love has its risks. You may not get love in return. Those who think they are unlovable might even get angry with you. But refusing to love others is not an option in the Christian life. We cannot content ourselves with merely working, reading the Bible, and keeping our noses clean. And our love must be more than throwing money at a problem or doing some good works. Sincere love means not doing something out of obligation but responding to the love that God has given us by loving him in return through loving others.

Start getting involved in the lives of others and start meeting their needs, and you will begin to care. A desperate world in need of godly love needs you.

PRAYER IDEA: Ask God to forgive you for confusing love as a feeling instead of a choice.

KEEPING GOD'S HOUSE
The Cat in the Hat (2003)
MPAA: PG for mild crude humor and double entendres
Read: Psalm 84

We will not neglect the house of our God. (Nehemiah 10:39)

Children Sally (Dakota Fanning) and Conrad (Spencer Breslin) create an awful mess, all because they disobeyed their mother, Joan (Kelly Preston). When Joan was away at work, the children let in a stranger, the Cat in the Hat (Mike Myers). They gave this trickster cat an inch and he took a mile. Their lawbreaking started with jumping on the couches, but soon the dog escaped, the walls and floors became stained with purple paint, and then the walls and floors started falling in. As their mom came home, the children realized the error of their ways and the Cat rode in with a multi-handed contraption that cleaned up and restored the house in the nick of time.

Are you God's doorkeeper, or do you dwell in the tents of the wicked? These are the options the psalmist lays out in Psalm 84. God's house is a house of praise, refuge, joy, and comfort. It stays that way because a doorkeeper guards the entrances to it, keeping it holy. The doorkeeper has an important job, because if he or she fails, the house becomes corrupted.

Sally and Conrad aren't good doorkeepers. They want to play a little bit in the tents of the wicked. They give in to the Cat, and the Cat takes advantage of their home by turning it into a dump. Thankfully, the Cat cleans up after himself when he realizes the children repented of their evil ways. Our spiritual enemies aren't so gracious, and God himself must come in and clean up our messes.

Our bodies are dwelling places of God. Scripture refers to our bodies as temples. Likewise, our actual homes should be places where God and his Spirit are welcome.

How lovely is your body and your home? How orderly and pure are they? Are they a little messy inside because you haven't been keeping a good eye on the door and you have let in destructive forces? It's not too late to redecorate. It's not too late to call on the Lord to come in and clean up your home and temple. Psalm 84 says,

O LORD Almighty, blessed is the man who trusts in you. (verse 12)

Blessed are those who dwell in your house. (verse 4)

PRAYER IDEA: Ask God to order your body, his temple, and your home.

REBELLING, GOD'S WAY

School of Rock (2003)

MPAA: PG-13 for some rude humor and drug references
Read: John 11:45–57

They would not confess their faith for fear they would be put out of the synagogue; for they loved praise from men more than praise from God. (John 12:42, 43)

Let there be rock! Dewey Finn (Jack Black) loves to rock, but his bandmates can't stand him and his mediocre guitar playing, so they kick him out of the band. Broke and in need of rent money, Dewey pretends to be substitute teacher Ned Schneebly (Mike White) and accepts a job at a prestigious prep school. With nothing but a passion for rock 'n' roll, "teacher" Ned transforms his class of ten-year-old kids into a real rock 'n' roll band. There is the band itself, plus roadies, designers, security, and groupies. Dewey teaches them that rock 'n' roll isn't about fans, fame, or money but about "stickin' it to the man"— basically, rebellion. By the time principal Mullins (Joan Cusack) and the kids' parents find out that Dewey is no teacher, he has already whisked them away to a Battle of the Bands competition. Though Dewey never returns to the school as a teacher, he sets up a popular after-school program called School of Rock.

Rock 'n' roll and rebellion have always gone hand in hand. Making your parents mad, bucking the establishment, and making guitars wail have all mixed together since the days of Elvis. Believe it or not, there is a holy way of rebelling. In fact, Jesus practiced it regularly. Rebellion can be godly when God mandates it as a means to demonstrate true holiness against a facade of pretend holiness found in the religious establishment.

"The man" that Jesus "stuck" was the Pharisees, Sadducees, chief priests, and elders of the law. These people weren't interested in a relationship with God as much as they were interested in their own appearance and respect. They didn't like Jesus, because he exposed their petty vanity and he did things that didn't appear holy, like "work" on Sunday by healing others. Jesus rebelled against bogus religious behaviors and thoughts, and he encourages you to do the same. One warning, though: if you become a rebel for God, be prepared for the establishment to fight back. But God is our rebel commander and our shield. He brings a revolutionary message of love, salvation, and relationship.

PRAYER IDEA: Thank Jesus for exposing fruitless deeds and leading the way to true holiness.

HE'S GOT THE POWER!

Bruce Almighty (2003)

MPAA: PG-13 for language, sexual content, and crude humor

Read: Acts 1:1–8

Great is our LORD and mighty in power. (Psalm 147:5)

TV reporter Bruce Nolan (Jim Carrey), in Buffalo, New York, hates doing fluff pieces for the local news. He wants the job of news anchor. When he's passed over for the job, Bruce throws a fit and curses God, saying, "You're a mean kid with a magnifying glass." Since Bruce tells God that God is doing a poor job, God calls Bruce up and gives him almighty powers and responsibilities. At first Bruce thinks this is all a joke, but he realizes that he can create miracles and cause anything to happen (except bend a person's will). Bruce orchestrates events to get the anchor position he craves, and for a while he enjoys playing God. But Bruce also is overwhelmed with noises in his head—the prayers of the people of Buffalo. When Bruce loses his girlfriend to momentary unfaithfulness, he realizes that wielding supreme power is very difficult. After a near-death experience, Bruce realizes that loving others, loving God, and being who we were created to be is all that God requires of us.

Jesus himself said, "Love the Lord your God with all your heart and with all your soul and with all your mind and with all your strength" and "Love your neighbor as yourself" (Mark 12:30, 31). Jesus never said anything about our having to manage all the prayers of our city (let alone the world). Nor does he let us use his power to perform parlor tricks for our own amusement. God alone holds all power. God performs the miracles, and sometimes he lets us in on a little of the action. He gives us his power by sending us his Holy Spirit. He gives us power to live for him and to serve him.

But some people get mixed up. Some people accept too much responsibility or wield their power so strongly that they think they are God on earth. These kinds of people think they don't need God because they can handle anything that comes their way. Others curse God when trouble strikes, thinking God is ineffectual, weak, or indifferent. The truth is that God is sovereign on his throne, sees all of history, momentarily allows troubles to come into this world because of our sin, and continues to love us and provide for us, despite our pride and foibles.

If you want God to move in your life, humble yourself and pray. Realize that you are powerless to affect the circumstances of your life, and fully rely on God's power to see you through. How refreshing it is to know that he has everything in control!

PRAYER IDEA: Ask God to forgive you when you think you can do your work better than he can do it.

BEAUTY FROM THE INSIDE
Shallow Hal (2001)
MPAA: PG-13 for language and sexual content
Read: 1 Peter 3:3–6

Man looks at the outward appearance, but the Lord looks at the heart. (1 Samuel 16:7)

As Reverend Larson (Bruce McGill) lies dying, he tells his young son, Hal, that the most important thing in life is to marry a beautiful young woman. At the reverend's last breath, Hal tells his father, "I won't let you down." From that moment on, the boy turns into Shallow Hal. Now, as a young man, Hal (Jack Black) will not date any woman unless she is a knockout beauty, even if she's as dumb as a box of rocks. One day Hal is stuck in an elevator with self-help guru Tony Robbins. Tony hypnotizes Hal so that he will only notice a woman's heart. If she is beautiful on the inside, she will look beautiful to him on the outside too. Likewise, if she's of bad character, she will appear hideous. Then Hal meets the grossly overweight Rosemary Shanahan (Gwyneth Paltrow), though to him she looks like a model. Hal falls in love with Rosemary, but when the spell is broken, he sees her massive scale. Hal must now decide if he can look past the fat to the heart.

At one point in the movie, Tony Robbins tell Hal's shallow friend Mauricio (Jason Alexander), "Don't you think you're brainwashed? Everything you know about beauty is programmed from television, magazines, and movies. They all tell you what is beautiful and what isn't." Isn't that the truth? America leads the world in fashion, beauty, and health consciousness. Thin is in and fat is out. Supermodels aren't paid big bucks for buckteeth and pimples. But this funny little movie puts it all into perspective, because physical beauty really is only skin-deep.

Jesus wasn't much of a looker either. It says so in the Bible.

He had no beauty or majesty to attract us to him,
nothing in his appearance that we should desire him. (Isaiah 53:2)

Apparently he didn't want his face to get in the way of his mission. In fact, he let himself get bruised, battered, and disfigured for our sake. He was "marred beyond human likeness" (Isaiah 52:14). First, God made him homely, then God let him get torn up. That's humbling. It leaves little room for grumbling about our own appearance.

Focus on your beauty inside. It's the kind that never fades.

PRAYER IDEA: Ask God to give you an appreciation for true beauty.

BOGART BONANZA
"Here's Looking at You, Kid"

WEEK 47

November 17–November 23

A DOVE AMONG BIRDS OF PREY

The Maltese Falcon (1941)

AFI: 23 • MPAA: not rated

Read: Psalm 119:97–104

**Stand firm and see the deliverance the LORD will give you.
(2 Chronicles 20:17)**

Private eye Sam Spade (Humphrey Bogart) sure knows how to juggle crime and criminals. After Spade's partner, Miles Archer, is killed while trailing a thief, the police try to pin the murder on Spade. Then the trailed man is also murdered and the person who hired Archer—a woman named Brigid O'Shaughnessy (Mary Astor)—turns out not to be the woman she says she is. Added to all this are a murdered boat captain; a crime boss named Mr. Gutman (Sydney Greenstreet), who sends his thugs after Spade; and the Maltese Falcon, a gold-encrusted life-sized statue of a falcon, the only one of its kind. Spade plays every side and shifts his loyalties as he tries to get to the bottom of who murdered whom, and when he does, exposes them and their crimes to the police for pickup.

Exposing sin without being overcome by it requires self-restraint and a respect for God and his justice. Gutman offers money to Spade for the Maltese falcon, but Spade turns the little money he got for it over to the police. Brigid offers Spade love, and he is tempted to return it, but he eventually shuns her, too. Perhaps Spade merely wants to save his own skin, but he doesn't let himself err as he rubs shoulders with liars, killers, and thieves. He walks and works among them but doesn't let himself be overcome by them.

It's virtually impossible to go about our business in this world without rubbing shoulders with those who wish we would join them in their crimes. To many people, bad women (or men) and big money are mighty big temptations. How do we avoid them? One way is to predetermine our response to temptation. Before it comes, we vow to not give in to it. Another way is to develop a love of God and his law. Through daily worship of God, we conform more and more to his likeness and allow his Holy Spirit to strengthen our resolve. God is always our partner for truth, justice, and goodness—even in the middle of lies, injustice, and evil.

PRAYER IDEA: Ask God for a greater love of him and his law.

POWER IN WEAKNESS

The African Queen (1951)

AFI: 17 • AA: Humphrey Bogart, Best Actor • MPAA: not rated

Read: 2 Corinthians 11:24–29

My grace is sufficient for you, for my power is made perfect in weakness. (2 Corinthians 12:9)

English missionaries Rose (Katharine Hepburn) and her brother, the Reverend Samuel Sayer, dutifully and stoically serve the native people of German-occupied East Africa. In 1914 war arrives at their remote village. German soldiers burn and pillage their tiny village. Samuel dies and Rose is at risk of becoming a POW. So she hitches a lift down the Uganga River aboard the *African Queen*, captained by the salty, gin-soaked Charlie Allnut (Humphrey Bogart). Together, Rose and Charlie encounter heavy rains, dangerous rapids, German gunfire, extreme heat, leeches, mechanical failure, and more. Finally, they face death by hanging—until grace intervenes, saving them to fight, live, and love another day.

God will sometimes use danger and calamity to get our attention when we've gone off track. Rose and her brother aren't preaching Christianity to the natives as much as they are offering English culture. The locals can't follow the strange melodies of the English hymns. Rather than adapt to the situation, Rose and Samuel sweat it out in heavy, proper British clothes. It isn't until pressure is applied that Rose's resolve, ingenuity, and strength are revealed. (A grape cannot produce wine until it is crushed.) Rose strips off binding and unnecessary clothes, performs underwater repairs to the propeller, slugs through the mud while towing the boat, and becomes more fully alive than she ever has been before.

The apostle Paul boasted in his sufferings. He knew (1) that God would take care of him as long as he had a mission on this earth, and (2) that God's power would be made perfect in weakness. Paul boasted about his weaknesses and troubles because he knew that God would pick up the slack. If we let him, when the challenges come, God can give us supernatural courage, power, strength, and ingenuity. What excitement we'll see in our own lives when we offer ourselves up to him and his true purposes. It's hard for God to use a pew sitter. When we throw up our hands and say, "Okay, God, I give up," God will say, "Okay, child, I'll give to you."

PRAYER IDEA: Boast to God about your weakness and declare your trust in his strength.

HELPING THE NATIONS
To Have or Have Not (1944)
MPAA: not rated
Read: Luke 10:25–37

Nations will know that I am the LORD. (Ezekiel 36:23)

I n *To Have or Have Not* singer "Slim" (Lauren Bacall) romances Bogart's Captain Steve Morgan in 1940s Martinique. As France falls to the Nazis, this French port in the Caribbean also turns over to German rule. Most days, Steve minds his own business as a boat captain for pleasure fishermen, but he gets a call to do a dangerous job for his French loyalist landlord. Steve must sneak his boat past harbor patrols to an offshore island and there pick up two French resistance leaders and transport them safely back to Martinique. Initially, Steve balks, but after he gets in a hole and needs some money, he agrees. Complications arise and guns are fired. Now one of Steve's guests has a bullet wound. Going beyond the call of duty, Steve not only holds off the inquisitive enemy-controlled police but also checks up on the injured French leader as he heals in hiding. In a final bit of derring-do, Steve arranges one more trip of safe passage for the Frenchman while shooting it out with the police.

L ike most of us, Steve initially doesn't want to get involved. We think, *It's not my war. It's not my problem. Why should I help?* We see problems overseas on television or in the newspapers and think, *Poor people,* and then go about our own agendas. But when the problem hits home (or more specifically, hits our pocketbook), we might be moved to action. Whatever reasons we may have to help people from other lands, the most important necessity of our care is follow-through.

Steve followed through on seeing his French guests to safety. The story of the good Samaritan also talks about follow-through. The Samaritan (a man very different from the Israelites) cares for the man from Jerusalem, puts him up in a inn, gives the innkeeper money to care for him, and checks back on him in a few weeks. His care is immediate, consistent, and persistent.

When you give, don't just give once but continually. When you serve, keep showing your care over the long haul. God is love, and his love doesn't take vacations. Be willing to help the foreigner in need when the occasion arises. And see that he gets help until he doesn't need it anymore.

PRAYER IDEA: Ask God to challenge you to love people from other nations.

RESPECT FOR AUTHORITY
The Caine Mutiny (1954)
MPAA: not rated

Read: 1 Samuel 24:8–15

Obey your leaders and submit to their authority. (Hebrews 13:17)

During World War II, nobody wants to crew the battered, substandard minesweeper the U.S.S. *Caine*. Nevertheless, Ensign Willard Keith (Robert Francis) agrees to join the *Caine* for duty at Pearl Harbor. Also boarding for duty is Captain Queeg (Humphrey Bogart). Soon Keith, Executive Officer Steve Maryk (Van Johnson), and Communications Officer Lieutenant Keefer (Fred MacMurray) hate Queeg for his paranoid manner and excruciating attention to detail. Officers and crew of the *Caine* insult Queeg and sing disrespectful songs about him. During a typhoon, Maryk and Keith think Queeg endangers the ship and its crew, and so Maryk defies Queeg's orders by starting a mutiny. A tense court-martial drama ensues, with the resolution of justice under question.

Maryk and Keith's lawyer, Barney Greenwald (José Ferrar), chastises the two and says, "You don't work with the captain because you like the way he parts his hair. You work with the captain because he's got the job and you aren't no good." Obedience to and respect for authority aren't negotiable based on personality preferences, likes, and dislikes. English author and theologian C. S. Lewis once said that he found great comfort in realizing that you don't have to like someone to love him. When God asks us to respect and obey authority figures, he isn't asking us to like them. There is freedom in this, because we don't have to demand anything of our emotions that isn't there. Giving obedience and respect is an act of the will, not of the heart.

David of the Old Testament had good reason to hate King Saul, since Saul wanted to kill him. David told Saul, "May the LORD avenge the wrongs you have done to me, but my hand will not touch you" (1 Samuel 24:12). In *The Caine Mutiny* it's questionable whether Queeg actually endangers the *Caine* and its crew. As we know and may have experienced, when we treat our leaders well, it will ultimately go well with us. The Lord is in a position to reward us. Who knows? Someday we might have to exercise authority too, and others may have to serve under us.

PRAYER IDEA: Ask God to show you how you can build up your leaders and not tear them down.

ONE AGAINST MANY

Key Largo (1948)

AA: Claire Trevor, Best Supporting Actress • MPAA: not rated

Read: 2 Samuel 8:3–6

Saul has slain his thousands, and David his tens of thousands. (1 Samuel 18:7)

Stopping on his way to Cuba, Chicago gangster Johnny Rocco (Edward G. Robinson) and his goons hole up in the Key Largo Hotel in the Florida Keys. Retired World War II major Frank McCloud (Humphrey Bogart) visits proprietor Mr. Temple (Lionel Barrymore) and his daughter-in-law, Nora (Lauren Bacall), but winds up in the middle of a murderous plot. As a hurricane bears down on Key Largo, the mobsters kill a police officer, mislead the police chief, and force Frank at gunpoint to take them on a small boat to Cuba. Nora and Rocco's girlfriend, Gaye (Claire Trevor), urge Frank to run, but Frank won't back down from a fight. On the boat through the foggy night, Frank single-handedly bumps off Rocco and his goons, freeing Temple and the world from his lethal terrors.

One against the many. The few against the masses. God loves to bring victory in spite of long odds. The story of David and Goliath is a story of one man against another. But what about one man against a troop? After God used David to wipe up Goliath, God used David and small battalions to wipe up whole armies. The people sang, "Saul has slain his thousands, and David his tens of thousands." In fact, the Lord gave David victory everywhere he went (2 Samuel 8:6).

When the Lord tells you to move, even when the deck looks stacked against you, step out in faith and do the thing he tells you to do. God gives strength to his obedient ones, but he also allows his enemies to become confused and disoriented, making victory easier for the faithful. God is good, but he is not necessarily safe. He leads missionaries into hostile territories. He puts evangelists on drug-ridden, gang-filled city streets. He leads law enforcers and attorneys into the heart of organized crime, and with his Holy Spirit power, he brings down the likes of Al Capone and Johnny Rocco. Evil never has the upper hand when God's truth and power lead his people forward.

PRAYER IDEA: Thank God that you never have to look at the odds to know there's victory.

GENEROSITY AND GREED

The Treasure of the Sierra Madre (1948)

AFI: 30 • AA: John Huston, Best Director; Walter Huston,
Best Supporting Actor; John Huston, Best Screenplay
MPAA: not rated
Read: 1 Peter 5:1–4

A greedy man brings trouble. (Proverbs 15:27)

Americans Dobbs (Humphrey Bogart) and Curtin (Tim Holt) try to eke out a living as laborers in Mexico. Cheated by a corrupt employer, they eventually beat the money out of him and pool it to hire an old gold prospector named Howard (Walter Huston). Howard claims, "There's gold in them thar hills," and all three go after the treasure of the Sierra Madre. They strike it rich, but their luck runs thin. Howard tells his younger crew that gold does strange things to a man's head. It makes him want more and more beyond reason. This thought infects the mind of Dobbs, and he goes crazy with fear, mistrust, and murderous jealousy. After Howard goes off to help a sick Mexican boy, Dobbs ambushes Curtin and bandits ambush Dobbs. After the gold is lost, a member of the trio is shot at, another is killed, and all three end up penniless.

God's Word says you cannot serve both God and money (Matthew 6:24). If you serve money, then God's Word, his will, and his plan are ignored. Respect for human life gets flushed down the sluiceway. In fact, all three gold diggers decide to kill a man in order to protect their gold. If you serve God and predetermine to obey him, moral questions, when presented, will answer themselves. Money will always be subjugated to morality.

Money and gold aren't necessarily evil in themselves. God doesn't say, "Money is the root of all evil"; he says, "The love of money is a root of all kinds of evil" (1 Timothy 6:10). Greed is wanting more than we need. God promises to meet all our needs, so any thought beyond that is greed. God is our provider. He even feeds the birds of the air and clothes the lilies of the field. Lots of Americans are tempted to collect material treasures. God says, "Store up treasures in heaven, where moths and bandits can't get at them" (see Matthew 6:20). We can't take gold with us when we die, but there are streets of gold waiting for us in heaven!

PRAYER IDEA: Ask God how you can store up treasures in heaven.

LOOKING AT YOU, KID
Casablanca (1942)
AFI: 2 • AA: Best Picture; Michael Curtiz, Best Director;
Best Original Screenplay • MPAA: PG
Read: 2 Corinthians 8:1–7

The gift that came by the grace of one man. (Romans 5:15)

During World War II, Richard ("Rick") Blaine (Humphrey Bogart) operates Rick's Café Americain, the most popular nightclub in Casablanca. A former freedom fighter, his cynical demeanor fits in perfectly among the hopeless refugees looking for a plane to Lisbon and a ticket to America. Rick comes into possession of two valuable letters of transit. Czech underground leader Victor Lazlo (Paul Henreid) arrives at Rick's with his wife, Ilsa (Ingrid Bergman), hoping for safe passage. But Captain Renault (Claude Rains), prefect of police, holds them for the Nazis. Both Victor and Ilsa beg Rick for the letters, but Rick doesn't give them up. He can't. He's jealous. Earlier in Paris, Ilsa thought she had lost Victor and threw herself into Rick's arms. But when she found out that Victor was alive, she left Rick alone at a train station. Now Rick must decide whether to run off again with Ilsa or give the letters to Ilsa and her husband. Through a conscious choice, Rick fights off the Nazis and puts Ilsa and Victor on a plane for Lisbon.

At the critical moment, Rick chooses grace. He chooses the welfare of his beloved over his own feelings. He chooses love over punishment. Rick could have hurt Victor by running off with Ilsa, but he chooses to demonstrate the greatest act of love toward her by sending her off with her husband. At first Ilsa tries to refuse Rick's grace, but he tells her she will regret it. As Ilsa and Victor soar off into freedom, Rick continues to fight on the ground for their safety. His grace is immediate, sustained, and permanent.

The mercy and grace of our God through Christ is like that. It is immediate because he offers instant forgiveness for those who call on his name. It is sustained because it always available. It is permanent because he finished the work called for him to do, through his death on the cross and resurrection. Some people, like Ilsa, find it hard to accept grace. People reject grace because they are too comfortable with second best. To Ilsa, Rick is second best. Christ gave his all so that you could be your all. Just before Ilsa accepts Rick's grace, he tells her, "Here's looking at you, kid." God says the same to us when he gives us our ticket to freedom.

PRAYER IDEA: Ask God to help you never settle for second best but trust in his permanent grace.

I'M FOREVER GRATEFUL

Stories Celebrating a Thankful Spirit

WEEK 48

November 24–November 30

THANK GOD AND BOW BEFORE HIM

The King and I (1956)

AA: Yul Brynner, Best Actor; Best Art Direction;
Best Costume Design; Best Score; Best Sound • MPAA: G
Read: Psalm 145

You shall not bow down to [idols] or worship them; for I, the LORD your God, am a jealous God. (Deuteronomy 5:9)

Arrogant, egotistical, and called a barbarian by the British government, King Mongkut of Siam (Yul Brynner) demands that all bow before him. But teacher to his children, Englishwoman Anna Leonowens (Deborah Kerr), refuses to bow. Not only has the king broken his promise to provide her with a home apart from the palace, but also he has challenged her and called her difficult many times. He claims he wants to learn Western ways, and indeed he is trying (by reading the Bible, for example), but he constantly reverts to making his subjects bow and grovel before him. When the king almost lashes one of the women in his harem, Tuptim (Rita Moreno), for insubordination (loving another man), Anna says she has had enough and plans to leave on the next boat. But news of the king's impending death draws her to his side. She stays to see the king's eldest son take the throne, and this son issues a new proclamation: "No person will bow before me."

Bowing has always been an act of submission and worship. Many people in the Bible have performed this gesture. God demands that we don't perform it before idols. Idols are anything that takes the place of God in our lives. Today idols aren't necessarily made of stone and wood. They can be called Hollywood stars, musical stars, television in general, work, hobbies, or anything else that consumes our attention and pulls us away from the one true God.

Our King is in heaven. He is worthy of praise and honor and glory. Unlike the king of Siam, he is faithful to *all* his promises and has compassion on all. He is righteous and loving to all as well. We have a King who is truly worthy of our bowing before him. If you have false kings in your life, stand up to them like Anna and tell them you bow only to Christ.

PRAYER IDEA: Ask God to forgive you for all the times you have bowed to false kings.

A GREAT COACH

Miracle (2004)

MPAA: PG for language and rough sports action

Read: Luke 5:5–7

All hard work brings a profit, but mere talk leads only to poverty. (Proverbs 14:23)

Herb Brooks (Kurt Russell) has a good reason to want to coach the 1980 U.S. Olympic hockey team. He got cut from the 1960 Olympic team just one week before opening ceremonies, and he needs to prove to himself and to the world that he can be a winner. So in June 1979 he assembles a group of twenty-six recently graduated college students and puts them through a grueling regimen. He tells them, "We might not be the best team at the Olympic games, but we'll be the best conditioned." A few months before the Games, the U.S. plays Norway. Coach Brooks is so disappointed in the lack of effort during the game that he makes his players skate sprints to the point of exhaustion. Slowly, the team bonds as a family. In Lake Placid, New York, as they face the dreaded Russians, Coach Brooks tells his team, "They might win nine of ten games, but not tonight. Tonight we are going to win." That night they beat the Russians 4–3, a miracle on ice.

Two principles operate in this story of great achievement. First, there is the concept of predetermination. Coach Brooks determines his outcome before he starts and sticks with the plan. The Olympic committee, the Russians, and most of America doubt they can beat the Soviets. If he listened to their talk, it would have led to failure. Second, the players listen to their coach and do what he says. Sometimes they don't like it, and sometimes they don't understand what he is trying to do, but they do it anyway. They put their faith in him and get great results.

When Jesus was first putting together his team of disciples, he proved that he could deliver results. Simon and some others were fishing, and they told Jesus that they weren't catching much. Jesus told them where to fish, and when they followed his directions, they caught so many fish that their nets were beginning to break.

Jesus is a reliable coach, and we can trust in his word. He has a better grasp of history and what it takes to succeed than anyone else on earth. He will never steer us wrong or put us on thin ice. Sometimes he seems like a hard taskmaster, and sometimes we don't know why he wants us to do some things, but he will give us a miraculous victory.

PRAYER IDEA: Ask Jesus to coach you and determine your steps.

THANK GOD AND REPENT
Willy Wonka and the Chocolate Factory (1971)
MPAA: G

Read: Genesis 3:1–24

Jesus replied, "If anyone loves me, he will obey my teaching." (John 14:23)

Charlie Bucket (Peter Ostrum) hopes against hope to find a golden ticket and gain access to Willy Wonka's chocolate factory. Only five golden tickets are available in the whole world, and selfish, rude, and disobedient children have already found four. Yet Charlie does find the last ticket, and off he goes with his Grandpa Joe (Jack Albertson) to visit a world of pure imagination. One by one the disobedient children disappear through freak accidents. One falls into a chocolate river and is swept away. One turns into a blueberry. Another falls down a chute for bad eggs. Charlie also disobeys by stealing a drink of Wonka's soda pop, but in the end Charlie repents and wins not only a prize of chocolate but also the entire chocolate factory.

The Garden of Eden must have been a lot like Wonka's chocolate factory. Imagine flowers, animals, trees, streams, and lots of things to eat! In the beginning, the human race had won the lottery—a free pass to a land of enchantment with God as the master tour guide. Just as Wonka has rules about his factory, so God had a rule: Don't eat from the tree of the knowledge of good and evil. But Adam and Eve were disobedient children. They ate from the tree and were banished. They had the opportunity to repent, but they made excuses and were dismissed.

Today we have the same option. God invites us into his wonderful kingdom if we would only repent. Wonka could have disqualified Charlie entirely, but he had mercy on him and allowed him to change his ways. God said to the Israelites in the Old Testament era, "I'll give you blessings if you obey me." Jesus said to his disciples, "You are my friends if you do what I command" (John 15:14). It's all about trust and having a great relationship with the Lord through our obedience.

God wants to give you his kingdom. He wants to know whether he can trust you with it. Can he?

PRAYER IDEA: Thank God for his kingdom, filled with pure imagination.

THANK GOD FOR OUTRAGEOUS FAITH

Secondhand Lions (2003)

MPAA: PG for thematic material, language, and action violence

Read: Luke 8:11–15

Stop doubting and believe. (John 20:27)

Walter (Haley Joel Osment) sees old people in *Secondhand Lions*—two old uncles, to be exact. Emotionally battered by his lying, unstable mother, Mae (Kyra Sedgwick), Walter goes to live with Hub (Robert Duvall) and Garth (Michael Caine) in the 1960s. Eccentric and quick to fire shotguns, the uncles reportedly have hidden millions of dollars somewhere on their Texas farm. Garth tells Walter a series of incredible tales involving the French Foreign Legion, a fabulously wealthy sheik, and an Indian princess named Jasmine. Walter doubts these stories but loves the life and passion of his uncles. Walter's mother returns and makes the uncles out to be nothing but ordinary criminals. But Walter decides to stand in faith with his uncles, rejecting his mother's plan to take him back. Walter doesn't care whether his uncles are lying or not. Their passion and life are worth more than life with his petty, vain mother. Years later Walter discovers that his uncles were right all along.

Like the uncles of *Secondhand Lions*, the Gospels tell stories of mystery, romance, and intrigue. These tales are so incredible that, to some, they are hard to believe. Jesus understood that his parables would be hard for some to grasp. He knew that many would find his claims of divinity to be sacrilegious and untrue. But Jesus also knew that those who believed on him and stayed with him, no matter what he said, would eventually claim a colossal reward. "Faith is being sure of what we hope for and certain of what we do not see" (Hebrews 11:1).

If faith were easy, everyone would practice it. Many people put their trust in things that are visible but are transient and ultimately worthless. Do you have the courage, patience, and strength to believe in the claims of Christ? Are you willing to temporarily be thought a fool to gain what you do not yet see?

Walter believes his uncles because their stories not only are exciting but also are life transforming. Walter bets and wins because he sees evidence of greatness in their claims. Search out the claims of Christ. Understand that their mythic nature only makes them more persuasive. As C. S. Lewis stated, Christ must be a liar, a lunatic, or the Son of God.

PRAYER IDEA: Thank God for claims so extravagant that they must be true.

Lead us not into temptation. (Luke 11:4)

New York City junior advertising executive Darrin Fox (Cuba Gooding Jr.) never has a problem with temptation. He always gives in to it. He lies and fritters away his money regularly. When he learns that his aunt from a small town in Georgia has died and left him a sizable inheritance, he goes down South. However, on arriving, he hears that he cannot collect the money unless he forms a church choir and enters it into the fourteenth annual Gospel Explosion choir competition. Undaunted and still lying, he tells the townspeople that he is a record executive and pulls together anyone he can find who has a good voice, including drunks and convicts. Also included is the lovely single mom Lilly (Beyoncé Knowles). While in Georgia, Darrin's employers offer him a raise and a forgiveness of his debts. He returns to New York but discovers that the simple faith of his Southern friends and the blessing of singing to the Lord are greater than the shady business deals of the big city. Darrin returns to Georgia, dubs the choir "The Singing Temptations," repents of his lying ways, wins the competition, finds out there isn't any inheritance after all, doesn't care, and lives happily ever after, married to Lilly.

Gospel music and the love of a good woman cause Darrin to resist temptation and become a new man. Indeed, being filled with the Spirit and genuine love are two great ways to be so filled up with God that you don't feel like you want to sin in order to meet a perceived need.

But the Bible also talks about other ways to avoid temptation. Twice in Luke 22, Jesus tells his disciples, "Pray that you will not fall into temptation." Apparently God can orchestrate situations for you that minimize your desire to sin or maximize your ability to say no to temptation. Jesus combated temptation by claiming the power of biblical truth over it. When Jesus fasted forty days in the desert, Satan tried to tempt Jesus, but Jesus claimed the Scriptures and the devil departed. "Whatever is true, whatever is noble, whatever is right, whatever is pure, whatever is lovely, whatever is admirable—if anything is excellent or praiseworthy—think about such things" (Philippians 4:8). This isn't just a temptation-fighting tool. It's a great way to fill up your brain. If you fill your mind with thanksgiving, beauty, and greatness, it will be hard to think about sin.

PRAYER IDEA: Pray to God that you won't fall into temptation and trust he will answer.

THANK GOD FOR FORGIVENESS

A Charlie Brown Thanksgiving (1973)

MPAA: not rated

Read: Luke 11:1–4

Forgive, and you will be forgiven. (Luke 6:37)

It's Thanksgiving, and Charlie Brown is depressed. Lucy pulls a football out from under him, Sally complains about extra schoolwork, and now Peppermint Patty invites herself and Marcy and Franklin over for Thanksgiving dinner. Being his wishy-washy self, Charlie Brown just can't tell Patty that he and his family are going over to his grandmother's house for dinner. Linus suggests that Charlie Brown make an early dinner for his friends and afterward go to his grandmother's. Charlie Brown thinks this is a good idea and recruits Linus, Snoopy, and Woodstock to prepare a table and a meal of popcorn, toast, and jelly beans. Peppermint Patty takes one look at this meal and complains, driving Charlie Brown away. She instantly regrets the harsh words she said and goes into Charlie Brown's house to ask for forgiveness. Charlie Brown accepts her apology and invites her over to his grandmother's house for a real Thanksgiving dinner of turkey, mashed potatoes, cranberries, and pumpkin pie.

Forgiveness is a real lifesaver. It releases others (including God) to bless you. If Peppermint Patty didn't rush in to apologize, and if Charlie Brown didn't forgive her, she and Marcy and Franklin would never have made it to Grandma's house. Charlie Brown would have dismissed her and the rest of the party. He would have gone alone to Grandma's house with just his immediate family, licking the wounds that Patty had caused him. When we forgive one another, we bring spiritual and emotional healing and restoration.

Forgiveness also releases God to forgive you. "If you forgive men when they sin against you, your heavenly Father will also forgive you. But if you do not forgive men their sins, your Father will not forgive your sins" (Matthew 6:14, 15). Forgiveness, then, is not just a nice thing to do; it has everlasting significance. God believes in restored relationships that much. We must forgive so that God will forgive us.

PRAYER IDEA: Ask God to help you forgive others when they have attacked you with words and deeds.

THANK GOD FOR HUMILITY
A Christmas Carol (1984)
MPAA: not rated
Read: Matthew 16:24–28

What good will it be for a man if he gains the whole world, yet forfeits his soul? (Matthew 16:26)

Bah, humbug!" says Ebenezer Scrooge (George C. Scott) of his most hated holiday: Christmas. The 1984 made-for-TV version of *A Christmas Carol* is a fine remake of the Dickens classic. The theme of the story remains the same as always: generosity.

The ghost of Jacob Marley (Frank Finlay), Scrooge's former business partner, visits Scrooge on Christmas Eve. Marley tells Scrooge that three more spirits will haunt him before the night is through. The ghost of Christmas past shows Scrooge where he began to slip into selfishness. The ghost of Christmas present takes Scrooge to the home of Scrooge's employee Bob Cratchet (David Warner). There Scrooge sees how meagerly Cratchet and his family live. Plus, Scrooge sees the frailty of Cratchet's youngest and crippled son, Tim (Anthony Walters). The ghost of Christmas future points Scrooge to a Cratchet family without Tim and also to a group of robbers who care nothing for a man who died rich but alone: Scrooge himself. In the morning Scrooge buys the Cratchet family the biggest turkey in the neighborhood, doubles Cratchet's salary, and makes amends with his only nephew.

These ghosts give Scrooge great gifts: hindsight, current perspective, and foresight. They let Scrooge see things as they were, how they really are, and how they could be if he doesn't change. Scrooge doesn't like what he sees and ultimately changes his ways.

Wouldn't it be great if we had a view of the bigger picture: keen hindsight, current perspective, and foresight? In Christ, we do.

In God's Word, Christ warns his followers of the dangers of a selfish life. He offers three "spirited" truths, bringing clarity and perspective to the selfless life. First, we must pick up our cross and follow him. We must die to self and live for Christ. Second, Christ promises good news. If we lose our life for him, then we will find it. Third, he gives us really good news. When we live our life for him selflessly, we will be rewarded. Wow! Rewards for generosity. Sounds good, doesn't it?

Scrooge sets aside his selfishness and finds joy, happiness, fellowship with estranged family members, a contented employee, and more. Join Scrooge and say, "Bah, humbug" to selfishness. And join Tiny Tim in saying, "God bless us, everyone." It's a real life with real benefits.

PRAYER IDEA: Thank God for understanding the big picture and thank him for rewarding generosity.

DYNAMIC DUOS
Stories of Highly Effective Couples

December 1–December 7

TOO STUBBORN TO CHANGE

The Odd Couple (1968)

MPAA: G

Read: Luke 10:38–42

Lord, if you are willing, you can make me clean. (Matthew 8:2)

I n the lonely town of New York City, neat freak Felix Ungar (Jack Lemmon) has just broken up with his wife. Despondent, he tries to kill himself but is saved by his slovenly friend, Oscar Madison (Walter Matthau). With nowhere else to go, Felix is urged by Oscar to move in with him, at least for a little while. Soon their differences cannot be ignored. Felix goes around the house cleaning everything with nervous compulsion. This drives Oscar crazy, and he tells Felix, "Why do you have to control every single thought that comes to your head? Why don't you let loose once in your life? Stop controlling yourself." Eventually Oscar throws Felix out, but both men begin to learn how to change.

T he real issue between Felix and Oscar isn't cleanliness versus slovenliness. It's stubbornness—resistance to change. Felix needs to learn to relax and enjoy life. Oscar needs to learn how to accept more order and cleanliness. Both have something that the other needs, but both are unwilling to budge, and that's what causes the sparks to fly.

The normal Christian life is one of change. First, Christ asks us to follow him. He may take us places where we have never been and ask us to leave family, friends, and patterns with which we have grown comfortable. Second, he asks us to be more like him. He asks each of us to be his disciple.

One day Jesus visited the home of two women, Martha and Mary. Mary enjoyed Christ's company, while Martha was busy preparing and ordering. Martha (like Felix) wanted to control her life, while Mary (like Oscar) wanted to enjoy the company. The Lord told Martha to relax.

Some of us need to relax in Christ, and some of us need to have Jesus clean us up. In either case, we need to let change into our life. Christ is always willing to help us change, if we are willing to let him do the work.

PRAYER IDEA: Ask God to change your heart and life.

YOU'D BETTER RUN

Butch Cassidy and the Sundance Kid (1969)

AFI: 50 • AA: Best Original Screenplay; Best Cinematography;
Best Score; Best Song • MPAA: PG

Read: Jonah 1

DECEMBER 2

Where can I flee from your presence? (Psalm 139:7)

Legendary bank robbers Butch Cassidy and the Sundance Kid (Paul Newman and Robert Redford, respectively) find that their line of work isn't smiled upon by the local law enforcement. After this thieving duo robs one too many banks, a posse of expert trackers is formed against them. Over deserts, hills, rocks, and streams, Butch and Sundance flee their pursuers. After narrowly escaping through sheer luck, the two decide to pack up and leave the country, going all the way to Bolivia, where the banks are overflowing with money from the local gold rush. There again, with Butch full of ideas and Sundance all action and skill, banks fall open one by one. Eventually a whole army of Bolivians forms against them, cornering them in a little village square. Butch and Sundance shoot it out to the death.

Fleeing justice. Resisting change. These are the behaviors of many a Christian who holds on to a sin and says, "No, Lord. Don't make me give this up." We try to outrun the voice of the Lord, who doesn't really want to punish us but only give us a better option than the one we are holding on to with all our strength.

Sundance and Butch talked about cleaning up and even tried it, but they couldn't make it stick. All they knew was thieving, and it was just too easy to fall back into that lifestyle. Jonah was told by God to go to the great city of Nineveh, but Jonah ran away. God pursued him and Jonah couldn't escape. Eventually Jonah's sin found him out and he was thrown overboard and left for dead. Sundance and Butch experience a similar fate. Their sins find them out.

An old saying tells us, "Your arms are too short to box with God." Well, your legs are also too short to outrun him. Have faith that God has a better option for you than the sin you are clutching with all your strength. Trust that he has your best interests in mind. Jonah, Butch, and Sundance would not have had to face their fates if they had only responded to wisdom's call.

PRAYER IDEA: Ask God to forgive you for trying to run away from him.

DO YOU TRUST ME?
Batman and Robin (1997)
MPAA: PG-13 for strong stylized action and innuendos
Read: James 5:1–9

Trust in the LORD with all your heart and lean not on your own understanding. (Proverbs 3:5)

There's trouble in the Bat Cave. Lately, Batman (George Clooney) has had to restrain an overzealous Robin (Chris O'Donnell) in their pursuit of villains Mr. Freeze (Arnold Schwarzenegger) and Poison Ivy (Uma Thurman). Robin resents the paternalism and thinks Batman wants all the glory in capturing this evil duo. Robin says, "How are we supposed to work together if you won't trust me?"

Batman, in turn, asks Robin, "Will you trust me?"

The butler, Alfred (Michael Gough), offers words of wisdom, saying, "Trust is the nature of family."

So Batman and Robin learn to trust each other, and their crime-fighting abilities improve. When Batgirl (Alicia Silverstone) joins the caped crusaders, Bat and Bird learn to trust her and finally vanquish the threat against Gotham City.

Trust is difficult because we often feel helpless when practicing it. When we trust another, we are making ourselves vulnerable and letting another have power over our welfare. But trust is essential in a family, in the workplace, and in our relationship with God. We need to count on those who count on us. We need to know that each member on our team will be loyal and do what they say they are going to do.

God is completely trustworthy. He never lies and never fails. He's with us in the darkest times and always loves us, no matter what. Money can be lost, guards and forces can be slain, and governing powers can turn corrupt. A lack of trust in God results in instability. A person with an unstable mind is like a boat blown and tossed about in the wind. God can't give that kind of person anything. But the one who trusts in the Lord finds refuge, strength, wisdom, and might. Trust is a conduit for God to move.

Holy crime fighting, Batman! When we trust in God's holiness for our lives, sin doesn't have a fighting chance.

PRAYER IDEA: Tell your heavenly father that you place your trust in him.

GOD USES DIRTY DOGS

Turner and Hooch (1989)

MPAA: PG

Read: Philippians 1:1–11

Even a live dog is better off than a dead lion! (Ecclesiastes 9:4)

Neatnik police officer Scott Turner (Tom Hanks), in Monterey, California, looks forward to a cushy new job off the force. In one week he'll turn in his badge. Meanwhile, he trains the new guy on the rounds, Detective David Sutton (Reginald VelJohnson). They visit an old man who lives on the docks with a bullmastiff named Hooch. Hooch is dirty, slobbery, disrespectful, and disorderly and knocks Turner down with a single leap. After the old man is mysteriously killed, Turner takes in Hooch as an unlikely partner in solving the case. At first Hooch has no regard for Turner's home or property, but in time they form a close friendship. Turner and Hooch go on a visit to a nearby fish-packing plant and discover drug money hidden in the ice and the suspect to the crime. The bad guys fire guns, and Turner seems doomed, until Hooch again takes a flying leap, immobilizing the shooter.

Turner doesn't have many clues to stitch together this case. All he has is Hooch, a dirty, mangy, unruly animal. But like the writer of Ecclesiastes says, "Even a live dog is better off than a dead lion!" (Ecclesiastes 9:4). A little bit of something is better than a whole lot of nothing. Hooch doesn't have much to offer, but he has a good nose and a good memory and he knows who the killer is. He witnessed the killing. Turner has the courage to take a live dog and use him to capacity (despite all the messes) to solve a murder mystery.

Many times we think God gives us dirty, mangy mongrels. We think, *What good are these?* We look at our resources and find they come up short. But look deeper. Perhaps some people we are paired with have hidden talents and qualities that aren't obvious at first glance.

Paul leaned on untrained, unglamorous sinners to advance the gospel. Paul rebuked them and put them in the doghouse when they got out of hand, but he also praised them and discovered new wonders that God had placed within them as they were used to their potential.

In your church and in your life, praise the underdogs you know. Stick with the dirty bullmastiffs with whom you are partnered. Find out their talents and utilize them to their full potential. "Even a live dog is better off than a dead lion!"

PRAYER IDEA: Thank God for the "dirty dogs" in your life and ask God to clean them up.

WE ARE FAMILY
Lilo and Stitch (2002)
MPAA: PG for mild sci-fi action
Read: Mark 3:31–35

Am I my brother's keeper? (Genesis 4:9)

What are you to do when your little sister bites her classmates? What are you to do when your sister's dog is actually an evil alien from outer space? What are you to do when the social worker looks in on you just when your home life is falling to pieces? Scream into a pillow? Well, maybe initially, but if you are Nani (Tia Carrere), living in Hawaii in the movie *Lilo and Stitch,* you soldier on, making the best of a rotten situation. After all, Nani says, "*Ohana* means family, and family means never giving up on each other or leaving anyone behind." Eventually Nani, Lilo, and Stitch learn to get along as family and support each other as they should.

Often our family members cheat us, embarrass us, hurt us with words, and let us down. Living in a family can be a difficult thing to do, especially if it is nontraditional, changed by divorce or death. Sometimes the challenges can seem insurmountable. Being a Christian is a lot like joining a big family. There may be trouble and squabbles, but there is no greater bond than our mutual love and fellowship. It is a bond that will last for eternity.

The Bible frequently talks about treating each other with love as brothers and sisters. "Be devoted to one another in brotherly love" (Romans 12:10). "Love the brotherhood of believers" (1 Peter 2:17). We siblings in Christ have a bond through our mutual acceptance of Christ's death and resurrection. This eternal bond ties us together in ways that no mere club or social organization could ever duplicate.

We must love one another as brothers and sisters because we will be together forever. But we must also love each other because Christ lives within us. We love each other because we love Christ. In *Lilo and Stitch,* even the evil, space-alien dog learns the value of loving family. In Christ, we are "Ohana."

PRAYER IDEA: Ask God to help you to be devoted to your brothers and sisters in Christ.

FROM THE TOP DOWN

From Here to Eternity (1953)

AFI: 52 • AA: Best Picture; Fred Zinnemann, Best Director;
Frank Sinatra, Best Supporting Actor; Donna Reed,
Best Supporting Actress; Best Screenplay; Best Cinematography;
Best Editing; Best Sound • MPAA: not rated

Read: Psalm 27

[If a man's gift] is leadership, let him govern diligently. (Romans 12:8)

In 1941 Robert E. Lee Prewitt (Montgomery Clift) requests a transfer to Schofield Base in Hawaii. His officer, Captain Holmes (Philip Ober), wants him on the company boxing team, but "Prew" doesn't want to fight. So Holmes rides him mercilessly, hoping that he'll break down and agree to be on the team. Meanwhile, First Sergeant Milton Warden (Burt Lancaster) begins an affair with the captain's wife, Karen (Deborah Kerr). As Prew avoids the captain, he begins a romance with a social club employee named Lorene (Donna Reed). Furthermore, Prew's buddy Maggio (Frank Sinatra) gets thrown into the stockade and is ruffed up by the sadistic Sergeant "Fatso" Judson (Ernest Borgnine). All the men seek authentic relationships, but all suffer consequences from the misguided leadership of Captain Holmes. Unexpected by all, the Japanese begin their attack on Pearl Harbor.

Drunkenness, loneliness, infidelity, anger, and other woes mark the lives of the leading characters in *From Here to Eternity.* Although each character is responsible for his or her own behavior, lots of the trouble can be traced back to Captain Holmes and his inability to lead properly. If Holmes truly loved his wife, her affair with Sergeant Warden might have been avoided. If Holmes curbed Fatso's sadistic tendencies, Maggio might not have wound up dead. If Holmes cared more about his men than about boxing, Prew might not have been driven to violence. If Holmes fostered authentic communication and comradeship, perhaps drunkenness would have been kept to a minimum.

Every day we have the power to affect life and prosperity or death and destruction. Obedience to God and holy, joyful leadership give life. Disobedience to God and corrupt, hard-hearted leadership give death. We are all leaders because we all influence others with our attitudes and actions. Our choices create a ripple effect for good or bad. Jesus, our Good Shepherd, leads us to green pastures and still waters. Holmes the bad commander leads his men to sin and personal destruction.

PRAYER IDEA: Ask God to fill you with the Holy Spirit to bring goodness to others.

ARE YOU READY?

Pearl Harbor (2001)

AA: Best Sound Effects • MPAA: PG-13 for intense war sequences, images of the wounded, brief sensuality, and language

Read: Ephesians 6:10–19

Be prepared in season and out of season. (2 Timothy 4:2)

They don't see the warning signs. Earlier that December day, a Japanese sub is detected and fired upon outside the mouth of Pearl Harbor. Furthermore, Navy personnel see approaching Japanese Zero fighters on radar, but they mistake these planes as our own from the U.S. mainland. The enemy is approaching to attack, but we do nothing. A serious breach in intelligence and readiness causes a lack of preparedness on that day of infamy, December 7, 1941. Two fighter pilots, Rafe McCawley (Ben Affleck) and Danny Walker (Josh Hartnett), strike back but can do little to stop the Japanese aggressors. Amid the wreckage, America is thrown into war.

As we go about the Lord's work in our daily lives, are we ready for battle? Can we see the warning signs? Do we have our guard up and are we fully protected? God's Word tells us to put on the full armor of God so that we might be ready to stand firm on the day of battle (Ephesians 6:11). When we don't put on our armor, we ignore the warning signs in our spiritual lives and expose ourselves to attack and injury.

What does it mean to put on the full armor of God? It means knowing God's truth and applying it in our lives when we face temptations and problems that come our way. It means keeping watch over our minds and spiritual lives, taking assessment of how we are thinking and behaving. Laziness in spirituality can breed error and sin. When we watch our lives and doctrine closely (1 Timothy 4:16), we stay spiritually fit and prepared to face our challenges.

PRAYER IDEA: Ask God to give you sharp discernment so that you might always be prepared.

WHAT A THRILL
Famous Thrillers
that Took Our
Breath Away

WEEK 50

December 8–December 13

THE FIERY FURNACE

The Sum of All Fears (2002)

MPAA: PG-13 for violence, disaster images,
and brief strong language
Read: Daniel 3:8–30

Do not fear, for I am with you. (Isaiah 41:10)

For Washington insiders, politicos, and most of America, the sum of all fears is nuclear war between the U.S. and Russia. This movie takes us to the brink of nuclear war but stops just short of it, thanks to greenhorn CIA agent Jack Ryan (Ben Affleck). When a new Russian president takes power, the CIA and the U.S. president don't know what to make of him. A bomb explodes in Chechnya and the Russian president claims responsibility, prompting the U.S. to think that the Russian president has an itchy trigger finger. Then the unthinkable happens. A nuclear bomb explodes in Baltimore and the U.S. prepares to retaliate against Russia. The flames of war are stoked. As the heat intensifies, will Ryan be able to make the U.S. and Russia stand down?

Fear of fire didn't keep the Old Testament's Shadrach, Meshach, and Abednego from ultimately facing it. Nothing short of being burned alive was reserved for all those who didn't bow down to King Nebuchadnezzar's golden idol. Shadrach, Meshach, and Abednego did not bow but stood tall. Were these men impervious to flames? Did they know something about the fires of Nebuchadnezzar that others didn't know? Not at all. But they did know that the God who created fire was able to save them from it. They also knew that if God didn't save them from the fire, they would be with him in paradise. It was a win-win situation. They had already made up their minds on how to respond to such a crisis.

What is your biggest fear? Loss of health, job, home? What about war or nuclear attack? Fear can be debilitating and overwhelming. When others threaten you with fiery bombs because you don't do things their way, who will you trust? God is with you always, even in the hottest trials. He can save you from destruction or he can walk through it with you. Either way, you win. So the hotter it gets, the cooler your head and spirit can be because God is with you always.

PRAYER IDEA: Ask God to walk with you in the midst of fiery trials.

WHO ARE YOU?

The Bourne Identity (2002)

MPAA: PG-13 for violence and some strong language

Read: Isaiah 62:4–12

A good name is more desirable than great riches. (Proverbs 22:1)

Jason Bourne (Matt Damon) does not know who he is, where he came from, what his occupation is, or why men are chasing him with guns. Jason is rescued from a fishing boat in the Mediterranean with two bullet holes in his back and a Swiss bank account number implanted in his leg. When he comes to, he suffers from amnesia. He remembers several languages and fighting skills but nothing else. When he opens his safety deposit box, he discovers wads of cash from many countries, a few guns, and many different passports. He hires a girl named Maria (Franka Potente) to take him to Paris, where he thinks he might be able to fill in some of the gaps. Along the way, he is chased, shot at, followed, and almost arrested on charges of attempted murder. In the end, the shocking truth is revealed: Jason is an undercover CIA assassin who failed a job and must be brought down.

Do you ever feel like you're minding your own business when someone labels you as someone you aren't? You are called a no-good, dirty, rotten, lying thief, and you don't understand why. Well, the devil is in the business of applying names, lifestyles, and identities that aren't our own. Lonely, outcast, afraid, fearful, angry, alcoholic, loose, and stupid are some of the many names the devil gives us to trap us in dangerous circumstances. With these names, the "moral authorities" of this world come down hard on us to punish us or make us keenly aware of our faults. Some even come after us to rub out our existence. "Let's get rid of the undesirables," they say.

God finds you desirable. The awful truth is that you are pretty messed up by sin. But God wants to give you a new identity—a great identity. He wants to call you his bride, his beloved, his church, his chosen people, the elect, sons and daughters redeemed, the renewed, and the transformed. He doesn't want to chase you with guns but to pursue you and capture you with love. He wants to give you an eternal feast of blessing, not an endless cycle of tiring moves just to keep yourself alive. At salvation God takes mislabeled names you had in the past and writes his name on your heart. There is no identity crisis in him when you are reborn.

PRAYER IDEA: Thank God for changing your name and for writing his on your heart.

CLONING EVIL
The Boys from Brazil (1978)
MPAA: R
Read: Jeremiah 1:1–8

God made man. (Genesis 9:6)

Twenty years before the appearance of Dolly the sheep, and about fifteen years before *Jurassic Park, The Boys from Brazil* dramatized the possibilities of cloning. In this story Nazi doctor Josef Mengele (Gregory Peck) gathers colleagues in South America for a horrifying project. Famed Nazi hunter Ezra Lieberman (Laurence Olivier) begins to piece the puzzle together. Across the world, ninety-four fathers aged sixty-five are to be murdered. Each father has an identical, adopted, black-haired, blue-eyed son. Soon Lieberman discovers the awful truth: each boy is a clone of Adolf Hitler.

Science and experimentation can be used for good or evil ends. Human cloning, however, poses a dilemma, and arguments against it can be made on more than mere humanitarian grounds. The Bible talks about the uniqueness of each individual and about God's plan of human conception.

Male and female, we are made in God's image (Genesis 1:27). We are also told to "be fruitful and increase in number." (Genesis 1:28). Natural reproduction is part of God's original plan. God told Jeremiah (and presumably tells the rest of humankind),

> Before I formed you in the womb I knew you,
> before you were born I set you apart. (Jeremiah 1:4)

This tells us that God places further importance on natural conception and childbirth. Cloning says we are replaceable; God's Word says we are unique and special.

PRAYER IDEA: Thank God for placing importance on natural conception and childbirth.

LOSING LIFE TO FIND IT

The Game (1997)

MPAA: R for language, violence, and sexuality

Read: Matthew 10:37–39

He learned obedience from what he suffered and, once made perfect, he became the source of eternal salvation for all who obey him. (Hebrews 5:8, 9)

Corporate control freak Peter Van Horton (Michael Douglas) doesn't like people very much. An investment banker, he is divorced and living alone in the family mansion. He begrudgingly joins his brother, Conrad (Sean Penn), for a birthday lunch. Conrad offers him a present: a gift certificate to Consumer Recreational Services. This gift entitles Peter to the Game, a tailored set of unexpected experiences designed to "fill in what's lacking." Peter takes the extensive psychological tests and undergoes a physical. Soon his game begins. Peter experiences one trouble after another, including nearly drowning, being chased by dogs, being shot at, and suffering from paranoia. When he accidentally shoots his brother "to death," he decides to end his life by jumping off a building. But this, too, is part of the game. He falls not to his death but into a big air bag. And there on the ground his brother, coworkers, and business associates greet him. The game is over. Peter has discovered that in order to gain a life, he needed to learn to lose it.

Lots of times, we think that God is putting us through a game by letting us experience pressure and suffering. Troubles, sickness, disease, and ruin happen, and we think that God is cruel. What he is really doing is shaping us to be more dependent on him. Jesus said, "Whoever loses his life for my sake will find it" (Matthew 10:39). A biblical writer said Jesus himself "learned obedience from what he suffered" (Hebrews 5:8). Becoming a Christian doesn't insulate us from suffering, pain, and trouble. It merely allows us to give it a context when it happens to us, and it helps us learn obedience to God.

God doesn't want part of you; he wants all of you. He wants to put to death your old self and make you into a new creation. He asks you to pick up your cross and follow him. The cross represents death to our sinful and selfish nature. When we have new life in Christ, we have joy and peace, despite our pain and sorrow. His life is one of uncertainty and lack of control. He asks us to change and he lets us go through some harrowing experiences, where we must cry out, "God, I need you. I am completely dependent on you." Our life in Christ is not by might, nor by power, nor by vain ambition, but by faith. And when we exercise that faith, we'll have God's power to do the impossible.

PRAYER IDEA: Ask God to teach you obedience through suffering.

DEFECT FROM EVIL
The Hunt for Red October (1990)
AA: Best Sound Effects Editing • MPAA: PG
Read: 1 Peter 3:8–12

Turn from evil and do good. (Psalm 34:14)

In this fictional tale, the Russians create a virtually undetectable submarine called *Red October* in 1984. Captained by the famed Marko Ramius (Sean Connery), the sole purpose of this ship is to sneak up on the American shoreline and launch nuclear missiles at our major cities. CIA agent Jack Ryan (Alec Baldwin) discovers the submarine and is convinced that Captain Ramius intends to defect. Nevertheless, both American and Russian forces go on the hunt for *Red October* to stop it on its renegade and misunderstood mission. Through incredible events, Ryan boards the *Red October* with American commander Bart Mancuso (Scott Glenn). They meet Captain Ramius, confirm their suspicions, and provide him asylum while convincing the Russian Navy that the *Red October* has been destroyed.

Turning from evil is difficult. Evil digs its talons into its victims and holds on tight. When victims free themselves through defection, evil gives chase. In the spiritual realm, our satanic foe labors to keep us in sin and death. When a person turns from evil and does good through repentance and receiving of God's grace, feathers are ruffled, old friends don't understand, old enemies mistrust the change of heart. Some of the evil gang might try to hunt us down and convince us to return to our old ways or merely try to kill us for our disloyalty.

Captain Ramius turns from the evils of communism and is pursued by both his mother country and the Americans. But through grace, he is received by those sympathetic to his cause. He endures momentary peril and enters into asylum.

If you have lived a life apart from God in the past, don't be surprised if the old evil gang tries to drag you back down. Hold fast. Seek help and pray,

> For the eyes of the Lord are on the righteous and his ears are attentive to their prayer. (1 Peter 3:12)

God doesn't turn anyone away who wants to find rest and peace in his mercy.

PRAYER IDEA: Thank God for giving you asylum from sin and death.

A KENTUCKY CONUNDRUM

Goldfinger (1964)

MPAA: PG

Read: Job 22:21–30

I love your commands more than gold, more than pure gold. (Psalm 119:127)

Criminal mastermind and megalomaniac Goldfinger (Gert Fröbe) loves gold, and this inordinate greed becomes his undoing. Not content with his own considerable pile of the precious metal, Goldfinger intends to detonate a nuclear bomb in Fort Knox, Kentucky, the U.S. gold repository. With this gold destroyed, the value of his own gold will increase. But cool British agent 007, a.k.a. James Bond (Sean Connery), is on the case. After romancing Goldfinger's private jet pilot, Ms. Galore (Honor Blackman), James sways her allegiance and alerts the proper authorities. The bomb is stopped with 007 seconds on the timer, and Goldfinger meets a terrible fate. He is sucked out the window of a moving jet piloted by Ms. Fort Knox is saved and James seizes for himself a golden opportunity of more romance with the lovely lady.

Gold continues to fascinate and stir up greed in the hearts of men and women worldwide. Still, enjoying its color and brilliance isn't necessarily wrong. In fact, one of the first gifts Jesus received was gold, given to him by one of the wise men. Units of currency change names from nation to nation and from year to year, but gold means wealth in any time or language. Over the centuries, many have found themselves in sin, in danger, or in death's throes because of gold.

God's Word says the way to prosperity is through submission to him and his commands (Job 22). God himself is our gold, our delight, our answer to prayer, and our light. He is our sustenance and provider, able to deliver on more promises than storehouses of gold. Goldfinger doesn't content himself in the Lord but lets his greed become his downfall. He submits to his own lusts and desires. The message is simple but true: greed for gold will haunt and harm you, but contentment brings great gain. Better to crave the words and provision written by the finger of God than gold around the finger.

PRAYER IDEA: Thank God for creating gold and ask him to remind you of your own value, brilliance, and preciousness.

THE TWELVE DAYS OF CHRISTMAS

Twelve Movies that Point to Our Coming King

WEEK 51

December 14–December 25

YOU GOTTA HAVE FAITH

Miracle on 34th Street (1947)

AA: Edmund Gwenn, Best Supporting Actor; Valentine Davies,
Best Original Story; Best Screenplay • MPAA: not rated

Read: Galatians 2:15–21

DECEMBER

14

Who do you say I am? (Matthew 16:15)

Macy's Department Store special events director Doris Walker (Maureen O'Hara) tells her lawyer boyfriend, Fred Gailey (John Payne), "I think we should be completely truthful and not have the children believing in legends and myths like Santa Claus." Her beliefs are challenged when Macy's hires a man named Kris Kringle (Edmund Gwenn), who claims to be the real Santa Claus. Doris's daughter, Susan, begins to notice something special about Kris and his magical ways. Others want to lock up Kris in the loony bin, so Fred represents Kris in court, trying to prove that Kris is the real Santa Claus. When the U.S. Postal Service sends thousands of letters from children to Kris, the judge calls the case closed. He figures that if the U.S. Postal Service believes Kris is Santa Claus, then he can't rule otherwise. A final miracle on Thirty-fourth Street occurs when Susan receives a real home for Christmas, cementing her faith in the old man.

At the trial Fred Gailey says, "Faith is believing when common sense tells you not to." This is close to the biblical definition: "Faith is being sure of what we hope for and certain of what we do not see" (Hebrews 11:1). We live two thousand years away from Christ's time on earth, yet we trust that he did walk the earth and that his claims about himself are true. We trust that the written record of him, as found in the Gospels, is also true and worth believing in. Historical records validate the case for Christ.

When Christ says, "Come, follow me," why should we? On what grounds is faith in him necessary, practical, or justified? Faith in him makes sense because he answers these age-old questions:

1. Why are we here? (Answer: Because God made us.)
2. What are we to do on this planet? (Answer: Give God pleasure.)
3. What must we do to get our lives right with God? (Answer: Place our faith in him and his atoning power.)

All of the other religions either have holes in their answers to these questions or have improperly made humankind too important or too unimportant. God's Word says, "Taste and see that the LORD is good" (Psalm 34:8). Continue to discover his love and goodness in the coming year.

PRAYER IDEA: Agree with God and believe that he is who he says he is.

HOW TO HONOR A GENERAL
White Christmas (1954)
MPAA: not rated

Read: Psalm 84:11, 12

Those who honor me I will honor. (1 Samuel 2:30)

On the front lines in Europe, 1944, outgoing General Waverly (Dean Jagger) allows Bob Wallace (Bing Crosby) and Phil Davis (Danny Kaye) to perform a song-and-dance act on Christmas Eve. After the war, Wallace and David team up to become a top traveling act. On the road, they meet Betty and Judy Haynes (Rosemary Clooney and Vera-Ellen), another top song-and-dance act. Intrigued by their beauty, Davis drags Wallace along and follows the girls to a Vermont ski lodge for the holidays. There they discover that the innkeeper is none other than old General Waverly. The joy of reunion fades quickly when a lack of snow threatens business failure. Wallace concocts a scheme to call in as many of the troops from the division as possible to honor General Waverly and save the inn with a really big show.

Our military veterans deserve honor. Anybody who has fought in the trenches through years of service to God and humanity also deserves honor. Our senior citizens have plowed a road before us on which we now smoothly travel. The Bible admonishes us, "Honor your father and mother" (Exodus 20:12)—and the same goes for grandparents. "Is not wisdom found among the aged?" (Job 12:12). When we give honor, we position ourselves to receive it in return.

Honor must also be given appropriately. In a case of misunderstanding, Betty thinks Wallace is going to broadcast the show on television, making a spectacle of the general and his financial plight. But Betty is wrong. Wallace isn't going to broadcast the show but merely announce it on television to the troops. If our honoring embarrasses or exploits our subject, then it is not really honoring at all.

Lots of glasses will be raised this holiday season. Lots of gifts will be given too. Let us honor and celebrate one another respectfully. Let us thank God for those who have given so much to us. Let us encourage others to come and honor our elders. And let's do it all in a way that also honors God.

PRAYER IDEA: Thank God for the elders and leaders in your life.

All the people left, each for his own home, and David returned home to bless his family. (1 Chronicles 16:43)

Los Angeles–based college student Jake (Jonathan Taylor Thomas) doesn't want to come home to New York for Christmas this year. He doesn't like his new stepmom and he'd rather go to Mexico with his girlfriend, Allie (Jessica Biel). A conniver, a liar, and a cheat, Jake becomes interested in home only when his father bribes him with a new Porsche. If Jake can get home by 6:00 p.m. on Christmas Eve, the Porsche is his. This is an offer Jake can't refuse, and he says, "I'll be home for Christmas." After a prank goes foul, he finds himself stranded in the desert with a Santa suit glued to his body. Furthermore, his girlfriend has hitched a ride with another would-be boyfriend, Eddie (Adam LaVorgna). Through a series of misadventures on the road with crooks, cops, and a visit to a fake Bavarian village, Jake becomes more and more authentic. At a breaking point, Allie tells Jake, "I don't want a fake boyfriend with fake remorse from a fake Santa suit making fake apologies." By the time he gets to New York, Jake gets real.

Stuck in Wisconsin, Jake has no money and no help. He enters a Santa 5K Run, where all the runners must wear Santa suits and the grand prize is $1,000. As he rounds a bend, a nun holds up a sign reading, "Jesus loves Santa." Think about that for a moment. Jesus loves this conniver, liar, and cheat named Jake as well as all the other fakers dressed up to run that race. Jesus loves fakers. This love is so powerful that it turns fakers into winners. Jake goes on to win that race, but he doesn't use the money to fly home. He's changing inside, and he gives the money to charity. Jake realizes that the real prize is love and honesty and goodwill and selflessness.

Childish at first, Jake wants a special gift for Christmas: the Porsche. But as he matures, he wants something less material. He wants to see his family and reunite with his girlfriend. He wants to live honestly, with love and patience and authenticity. The love of Christ (and a few hard knocks from life's journey) changes us that way.

Are you estranged from your family? Grow up, go home, and love on them. Do you feel estranged from God? Jesus loves you just as you are, dirt, fake beard, and all. He's calling you home.

PRAYER IDEA: Ask God to help you live more authentically for him.

A MATTER OF TRUST
Jingle All the Way (1996)
MPAA: PG for action violence, mild language, and thematic elements
Read: Numbers 23:19

Trust in the LORD and do good. (Psalm 37:3)

Howard Langston (Arnold Schwarzenegger) loves his wife, Liz (Rita Wilson), and his son, Jamie (Jake Lloyd). But frankly, he loves his work more. Howard makes promises to his family but breaks them repeatedly. He vows forgiveness, but his relationships crumble. When Howard fails to make it to Jamie's karate class, Howard tell Jamie that he will buy him a Turbo Man doll for Christmas. The problem is, it's December 24 and Turbo Man dolls have been sold out all over town since Thanksgiving. Howard makes a deal with a corrupt Santa, fights off a crazed mailman named Myron (Sinbad), and plays the real Turbo Man at the "Wintertainment Parade." After jetpack rides and unexpected brawls with costumed cartoon villains, Howard fulfills his promise to his son and rebuilds his wife's trust.

Jingle All the Way isn't so much about gift giving as it is about restoring trust. Jamie doesn't believe his father, because his father always lies. Essentially, Howard needs to repent of his workaholic, lying ways and spend more quality time with his family and fulfill his promises. Excuses and long explanations don't cut it. The only way to restore trust is to be trustworthy. That's why Howard is so determined to get the Turbo Man doll. It means so much more than just a Christmas gift—it means the health and welfare of his closest relationships.

To restore his relationship with humanity, God delivered his Christmas gift right on time. Hundreds of years before Christ, the prophet Isaiah promised,

To us a child is born, to us a son is given. (Isaiah 9:6)

Later, God used Isaiah again to tell us about the coming king.

He was pierced for our transgressions, he was crushed for our iniquities; the punishment that brought us peace was upon him, and by his wounds we are healed. (Isaiah 53:5)

Some doubted the Messiah would ever come, but in the fullness of time, a babe was born in Bethlehem. God's gift to the whole world wasn't a token gesture but rather his own flesh and blood. Similarly, Jamie realizes that the best gift isn't a trinket or a toy but a living, breathing man: a trustworthy father and true hero.

If you haven't placed your trust in God, fully and for every area of your life, what is holding you back?

PRAYER IDEA: Tell God that you place your whole life in his hands and will.

BELIEVE IN HIM
The Santa Clause (1994)
MPAA: PG for a few crude moments
Read: John 9:35–41

I do believe; help me overcome my unbelief! (Mark 9:24)

Young Charlie (Eric Lloyd) doesn't believe in Santa. His mother and stepdad tell him Santa is not real. Yet Charlie's boorish father, Scott Calvin (Tim Allen), wants Charlie to believe in the man in red. When Charlie spends Christmas Eve with his father, things don't go so well—until they see the actual Santa on the roof. Scott calls out to the housetop intruder, and Santa falls down into a snowbank, unconscious. Alarmed that he has killed Santa, Scott reads a small card that says, "If Santa is unable to fulfill his duties, put on the suit. The reindeer will know what to do." Excited, Charlie convinces his father to try on the suit. When he does, they do all the wonderful things Santa does every Christmas Eve, including going on a visit to the North Pole. The next day, Charlie tells his mother that Scott is Santa Claus. The mother and stepfather become concerned. Yet Scott begins to get fat and his hair turns white and his beard grows out hours after he shaves. Scott literally transforms into Santa. It's not until Charlie's mother sees him with her own eyes that she accepts Scott's claim to be the true "jolly old elf."

Like Charlie's mother, many people today have a hard time with belief. They don't believe there is a Savior who is alive today and who makes house calls and changes lives and provides spiritual gifts. Even in Christ's own day, he continually confronted unbelievers. The Pharisees questioned him and tried to undermine him. Some accepted his words, but in a time of testing, they fell away. The earliest disciples of Christ believed in him so much that they dropped what they were doing and followed him when he called. True believers are what Christ wants.

Those who produce a crop of righteousness, faith, and prominence in God's kingdom do so by persevering in belief. They believe in God and his saving power, even if they keep messing up. How deep is your faith in Christ? Is it a mental consent that merely recognizes Christ as Savior but doesn't know him? Or is it a deep, growing, active, penetrating faith that always wants more and more of Christ? Santa Claus is a sneaky fellow, always leaving just after he arrives. But Christ comes to stay. He wants to make a home in your heart and walk with you and be friends with you and use you mightily for his kingdom. Believe in him deeply because he deeply believes in you.

PRAYER IDEA: Ask God to forgive you for merely giving him mental consent instead of faith.

403

WHAT DO YOU WANT FOR CHRISTMAS?

A Christmas Story (1983)

MPAA: PG

Read: 1 Corinthians 12:1–11

Follow the way of love and eagerly desire spiritual gifts. (1 Corinthians 14:1)

In *A Christmas Story* all nine-year-old Ralphie (Peter Billingsley) wants for Christmas is a genuine Red Ryder two-hundred-shot carbine-action air rifle. But in the conservative Indiana of the 1940s, his mother, father, teacher, and even Santa Claus tell him, "You'll shoot your eye out." Yet, for Ralphie, no other gift will do. Ralphie calls this gift "the holy grail of all Christmas gifts." He fantasizes about a robber attack on his home in which he dons a cowboy outfit and drives the perpetrators away with his gun. On Christmas morn, Ralphie receives zip-up, full-length pink bunny jammies. Yuck! But the old man has one more gift waiting behind the desk. That's right—a genuine Red Ryder two-hundred-shot carbine-action air rifle. Now Ralphie can shoot away (outdoors, of course) to his heart's content.

Children love to receive Christmas presents, especially ones they really want. God wants us, his children, to crave gifts too. But the gifts God asks us to crave are spiritual, not material. The gift that God wants us to crave the most is prophecy. "Everyone who prophesies speaks to men for their strengthening, encouragement and comfort. . . . He who prophesies edifies the church" (1 Corinthians 14:3, 4).

Ralphie wants a Red Ryder two-hundred-shot carbine-action air rifle, but his little brother is happy with a toy fire truck. God gives out different gifts to different people. These gifts build up the church in different ways, but it is the same Spirit working behind them all. Wisdom, knowledge, faith, healing, miraculous powers, prophecy, and more are all listed in Scripture. God has wired us each differently and given to us different abilities. Ralphie gets what he wants, but the greatest gift in his home is a loving family. Be glad for the gifts God gave you and faithfully use them for Christ and his kingdom. But also remember that love is the greatest gift of all.

PRAYER IDEA: Ask God for a deep eagerness for spiritual gifts.

ADOPTED TO BE A SON

Elf (2003)

MPAA: PG for mild rude humor and language

Read: Romans 8:22–25

In love he predestined us to be adopted as his sons through Jesus Christ. (Ephesians 1:4, 5)

Buddy's (Will Ferrell's) single mother doesn't think she can raise him alone, so she drops him in Santa's sack and hopes for a miracle. Santa finds the child and gives him to Papa Elf (Bob Newhart), who raises Buddy like he is an elf. But as the years go on, Buddy's large size and awkward nature get the better of him. Papa Elf has to tell Buddy the truth: "You are not an elf but a human." Crushed, Buddy goes to New York City to look for his biological father, Walter (James Caan). Full of new sights, sounds, and sensations, New York almost gets the best of the naive and blissfully cheerful Buddy. In this strange new world, Buddy feels he can do no right. But when Santa comes to town, Buddy rediscovers his elven skills and saves Christmas by encouraging Christmas cheer.

When nobody wants Buddy, Santa (the fictional, secular saint of Christmas) takes him in. The living, true, real representation of Christmas—Christ himself—also is an adoptive father. Christ takes us in, cleans us up, gives us purpose, and joyfully engages in relationship with us each and every day.

One of the joys of Christmas is family. We celebrate reunions with family members we may not have seen in a while. Every year Christmas is an excellent time to remind ourselves that we are members of God's family. When we were born anew into God's family, Christ paid all the hospital bills. He signed the adoption papers and took us in, taking full responsibility for our formation into the likeness of Christ. At the end of *Elf*, Buddy whips everybody up into a Christmas spirit so Santa's sleigh can fly. In Christ, all we have to do is believe and receive the blessings of his kingdom. Our Father in heaven is the real Father Christmas—the Father of Christ and all who believe in the real reason for the season.

PRAYER IDEA: Thank your heavenly father that he is the real Father Christmas.

WHERE ARE YOU, CHRISTMAS?

How the Grinch Stole Christmas (2000)

AA: Best Makeup • MPAA: PG for some crude humor

Read: Matthew 2:13–23

Herod is going to search for the child to kill him. (Matthew 2:13)

Who can forget how the Grinch stole Christmas? The furry, green curmudgeon hates the day Christ came to earth. Despised and rejected by the residents of Whoville as a child, the Grinch (Jim Carrey) resides in a cave in the mountains, thinking ugly thoughts. A little Whoville resident, Cindy Lou Who (Taylor Momsen), looks at all the commercialism of the holiday season and wonders, "Where are you, Christmas? Did Christmas change, or just me?" Attempting to find a deeper Christmas spirit, she tries to befriend the Grinch, but no luck. She nominates him Holiday Cheermiester of the Year, but he ruins the ceremony with bombastic chaos. On top of it all, the Grinch creates a fake Santa costume and comes down to Whoville on Christmas Eve and steals every present from every Who. Just as the Grinch is about to dump all the Christmas booty over the side of the mountain, he hears the residents of Whoville singing. That gets his puzzler puzzling and he realizes that Christmas isn't about presents but about family, friends, and love.

If the Grinch had a first name, it would be Herod. When Christ came into the world, King Herod tried to take the baby's life. Herod pretended to be an ambassador of goodwill when he sent the Magi to "go and make a careful search for the child" (Matthew 2:8). But Herod was jealous of Jesus and wanted to rub him out. Thankfully, God warned the Magi and Joseph to be wary of this evildoer. The Magi returned to their country by another route, and Joseph took Jesus away to Egypt. Then Herod did the unthinkable: he killed all the boys under two in Bethlehem and the surrounding area.

Unlike the Grinch, Herod never repented for wanting to kill Christmas. Herod died in his sins. The death of Christ was reserved for a later date and for a richer purpose. Christmas didn't die; he lived to redeem the whole world.

Not everyone who hates Christmas is doomed to a life of evil. Look at the apostle Paul. He persecuted the church but became one of Christ's greatest ambassadors. When you see people who show animosity to Christ, do you pray for them and love them, like Cindy Lou Who did with the Grinch? Or do you avoid and despise them? Let Jesus and the true spirit of Christmas reign so strongly in your heart that the unredeemed are compelled to come to Christ.

PRAYER IDEA: Ask God for the ability to love those who hate his name.

MISFIT FINDS HIS PLACE
Rudolph the Red-Nosed Reindeer (1964)
MPAA: not rated
Read: Luke 19:1–6

Weakness was turned to strength. (Hebrews 11:34)

Of course you can recall the most famous reindeer of all. Though not a movie, this stop-motion animated TV special is a perennial favorite and never loses its charm or its message. Burl Ives shimmies across the snow as Sam the Snowman to tell the story of Rudolph the red-nosed reindeer. At Rudolph's birth, Father Donner says, "His beak blinks like a blinking beacon." Mother encourages him to "overlook it," but everybody, including Santa, sees that shining snout as a colossal freak. All the other reindeer laugh and call him names, so Rudolph (Billie Mae Richards) runs away with an elf dentist wannabe named Herbie. The two join a gold prospector named Yukon Cornelius, tame an abominable snowman, and discover an island of misfit toys. One foggy Christmas Eve, Santa recruits Rudolph to lead the deer team. Christmas continues and Santa places the misfit toys in happy homes.

Santa doesn't really see any value in Rudolph until he needs some help. But Jesus immediately and always calls the weak, the outcast, and the misfit people of this world valuable. Jesus loves, disciples, heals, and teaches arrogant people, prostitutes, lepers, demon-possessed people, foreigners, epileptics, the blind, and the lame, and even short people.

Zacchaeus was a wee little man, but he climbed high up into a sycamore tree and Jesus saw him. Jesus could have walked right past him. Jesus could have laughed at him. Jesus could even have hurled rocks at him to knock him down. But he went up to Zacchaeus and said, "Come down immediately. I must stay at your house today" (Luke 19:5). People murmured that Jesus was going to the home of a sinner, but these people didn't know that Jesus came into this world to transform lives. He came to call the poor and the rich, the mournful and the comforted, the meek and the strong.

If you feel too short or too strange, or if you wake up one day with a big red pimple on the end of your nose, rejoice! God loves you just the same and wants to come to your house and fellowship with you.

PRAYER IDEA: Ask God to use your imperfections for his glory.

FACE YOUR FEARS

Home Alone (1990)

MPAA: PG

Read: Isaiah 41:10

I sought the LORD, and he answered me; he delivered me from all my fears. (Psalm 34:4)

Eight-year-old Kevin (Macaulay Culkin) and his family plan to fly to Paris for the Christmas holiday. But the day before the trip, Kevin is sent to the attic for troublemaking. The next morning, Kevin discovers he is home alone. Only when she is in the air on the way to France does Kevin's mother realize that he is not among them. Meanwhile, back at home, Kevin confronts his fears in three ways. First, he tells his scary, noisy furnace to shut up. Second, he befriends the scary neighborhood recluse, Old Man Marley (Roberts Blossom). Finally, Marley tells Kevin that he is afraid to talk with his only son. Together, Old Man Marley and Kevin challenge each other to face their fears. Marley goes on to reunite with his estranged family, while Kevin battles burglars bent on robbing his home. By the time his mother comes back home, Kevin has become courageous, and Marley finds quality family time once again.

Christmastime often challenges us to face old family feuds and broken relationships. Some people deal with this by choosing to be uninvolved. But these fears should be faced. It takes courage to admit fault with family members. It takes courage to forgive others. It takes courage to restore broken relationships. But if not at Christmas, when?

The story of the Christ child is all about restoring our relationship with God. God has good reason to hold a grudge against us, but he sent his one and only Son to earth to bring us back into a right relationship with him. God wants us to take courage and place our faith in Christ. When we find Christ, we find the strength to confront whatever holds us back from having the best that God intends.

If you are afraid of forgiving someone this holiday season, why not take advantage of the spirit of the season and face your fears? You may also be afraid of being alone this Christmas, but there are others just like you who want to be with someone this Christmas. Overcome your fears and invite somebody over for conversation and some food. God sent his Son so that you wouldn't have to be alone. God loves parties and people loving each other in his name. Don't get caught home alone this Christmas.

PRAYER IDEA: Ask God to show you who you can love this holiday season so that they may have a loving home.

KEEPING IT REAL

A Charlie Brown Christmas (1965)

MPAA: not rated

Read: Luke 2:8–14

Go out quickly into the streets and alleys of the town and bring in the poor, the crippled, the blind and the lame. (Luke 14:21)

One of America's most beloved annual television programs, *A Charlie Brown Christmas* distinguishes itself with jazz music, real kid voices, and a simple message of the meaning of Christmas. Charlie Brown mopes and tells Linus, "I think there must be something wrong with me. Christmas is coming, but I'm not happy. I don't feel the way I'm supposed to feel." His troubles continue. Lucy thinks he's psychologically disturbed. Snoopy enters a house decorating contest and wins, while Sally wants a long list of Christmas presents. After Charlie signs up to be the director of the school play, Linus tells Charlie Brown about the birth of Christ. Moved by this true story, all the *Peanuts* characters clean up and decorate a barren little Christmas tree, transforming it with love into a lush, beautiful holiday tree.

It's easy to lose the real meaning of Christmas. There is so much shopping and party going, so much cooking and running around, that the real, miraculous, but humble story of Christ's birth gets buried in ribbons, tape, and eggnog. For many people, Christmas is a sad time. Some don't have family to love or they don't have the money to buy gifts. In many areas of America, the weather outside is frightful. The best gift given at Christmas, however, is free. It's the gift of love. This gift warms and enlivens all who receive it. Charlie Brown is told the real meaning of Christmas: God's love for the world through the giving of his Son. This encouraging and wonderful news motivates the *Peanuts* gang to nurture a twig of a tree into a full, vibrant showpiece for Christ.

The implications of this story are obvious. Love one another. Share the good news of Jesus Christ. Love others so much that it transforms their lives into a showpiece for Christ.

One final admonition. Be creative in sharing the good news. By mixing jazz, cartoons, a good dose of reality, and a lot of humor, this little Christmas gem from Charles Schultz has not only been shown every year on television but has also been embraced and celebrated. The good news hasn't changed. It remains as radical and powerful, as challenging and intriguing, as on the day when it was first lived, just over two thousand years ago. It deserves to be told well. Our post-Christian culture needs Christ and his love more than ever.

PRAYER IDEA: Ask God to show you how to creatively spread the good news.

WHAT IF HE NEVER CAME?

It's a Wonderful Life (1946)

AFI: 11 • MPAA: not rated

Read: Isaiah 9:6, 7

To us a child is born, to us a son is given. (Isaiah 9:6)

Try as he might, George Bailey (James Stewart) can't get out of Bedford Falls. Just before an overseas trip, George's father dies and George must take over the family building and loan business. For years George stays on, even letting his younger brother go on ahead to college. George can't even leave town for a honeymoon with his wife, Mary (Donna Reed)——a business crisis holds him back. One Christmas Eve, George is so broken over misplacing an $8,000 loan that he almost commits suicide. His guardian angel, Clarence (Henry Travers), comes down and shows George the unthinkable: a vision of what life would be like at Bedford falls if he were never born. Sadness, corruption, and civil unrest mark a Bedford Falls without George. Even the name of the town is different. Begging for his old life, George gratefully returns to his family. Just as George is about to be arrested for misappropriation of funds, the whole town shows up and offers money for the debt. This town loves George Bailey, and he realizes it really is a wonderful life.

Our lives are important, no matter how small we may think we are. George Bailey made a tremendous difference to the sons and daughters of Bedford Falls. The difference he made was immediate, extensive, and important.

Just over two thousand years ago, a child was born on this earth in a little town called Bethlehem. That baby made the greatest difference this planet has ever seen. What if Jesus never came? What would Bethlehem and the whole earth look like if he never came? Would we even be around today? People complain about how bad the world is today, but if Christ hadn't come, would sin already have snuffed us out? In light of Christ's birth, we should respond with nothing less than falling to our knees in gratitude.

Imagining life without Christ is unthinkable. He has made all the difference. This season and in the coming year, let Christ make all the difference in your life as you let his light shine through you to all.

PRAYER IDEA: Ask God to give you a glimpse of what this world would be like without Christ.

ALL'S WELL THAT END'S WELL

Movies with Great Finishes

WEEK 52

December 26–December 31

VEHICLE OF DELIVERANCE

The Prince of Egypt (1998)

AA: Best Song • MPAA: PG for intense depiction
of thematic elements
Read: Matthew 6:9–13

From the LORD comes deliverance. (Psalm 3:8)

Born a Hebrew, Moses (Val Kilmer) is raised in privilege and honor in the Egyptian courts of Pharaoh (Patrick Stewart). But Moses has an appointment with destiny. Moses discovers his Hebrew nationality, flees from his Egyptian home, and goes to live in Midian. There God speaks to Moses from a burning bush and gives him a great assignment: go to Pharaoh and tell him, "Let my people go." At first Moses hedges, but then he accepts the call and goes. After many plagues—including the Passover, in which God passes through Egypt and strikes down every firstborn man and animal—Pharaoh lets the Israelites go. Through the Red Sea, God leads the Israelites and delivers them. The Egyptian army pursues them, but God faithfully fights the battle for his people and lets the sea close behind them, vanquishing Israel's enemy.

God is in the business of delivering his people from evil. He is our great Liberator, freeing us from oppression and sin. Pharaoh trusts in court magicians, but they are no match for an almighty God. Pharaoh thinks he can overtake the Israelites with horses and chariots, but God delivers Israel from further captivity. One psalmist wrote, "He will deliver the needy who cry out" (Psalm 72:12). Jesus asked us to pray, "Deliver us from evil" (Luke 11:4, KJV).

Moses was used by God as a vehicle of deliverance because Moses was obedient. When God calls us and we say yes, we can be instruments of his deliverance too. Already God has asked us, his people, to go into all the world and share the good news of Jesus Christ. When we obey this call, we are allowing ourselves to become a vehicle of deliverance, just like Moses. But if we disobey this call, we are acting like Pharaoh, hardening our hearts, keeping others and ourselves in bondage and slavery. The kingdom of God is a spacious land of milk and honey and God's blessing. Will you help to deliver the lost to this spacious place?

PRAYER IDEA: Ask God to use you as a vehicle of deliverance for the oppressed.

RISE ABOVE THE PAIN

Antwone Fisher (2003)

MPAA: PG-13 for violence, language, and
thematic material involving abuse

Read: Matthew 26:36–38

Carry each other's burdens, and in this way you will fulfill the law of Christ. (Galatians 6:2)

A man named Antwone Fisher really exists and his story, depicted in this movie, is true.

Before Antwone is born, his father is shot dead. After he is born, Antwone's mother turns him over to the state and never inquires about him again. A Mrs. Tate adopts Antwone (Derek Luke) and repeatedly abuses him. An older step-sister sexually assaults him. His only escape from this living hell is to join the Navy. When Antwone lashes out at his fellow shipmates with his fists, he begins regular counseling sessions with Lieutenant Commander Jerome Davenport (Denzel Washington). Slowly, the two unpack Antwone's terrible past. They form a lasting friendship, and Antwone finds healing and eventually a loving family.

Each and every one of us has had people hurt us—some more than others. Each one of us has a reason to be angry over something terrible that has happened to us in the past. Expressing these pains is one step toward overcoming the damage. David wrote in the Psalms that his enemies were continually assailing him, and yet he was called a man after God's own heart. In the Garden of Gethsemane, Jesus revealed his pain and then asked his disciples to be with him. Then he fell to the ground and asked God to take away the pain.

Keeping your pain bottled up inside you is no way to get over it. It's great to have a loving friend with a listening ear or even a professional counselor in whom you can confide. When a hurting friend comes to you to express grief, will you listen to what he or she has to say? As this year ends and a new year begins, make yourself available as a sounding board for a person who needs to unload some pain. Make yourself available to carry another's burdens, so that when you need to express some grief, someone will be there for you.

PRAYER IDEA: Thank God for the gift of counselors and those who speak truth into your life.

BEAUTY COMES FROM WITHIN

Beauty and the Beast (1991)

MPAA: G

Read: 1 Peter 3:1–6

The king is enthralled by your beauty; honor him, for he is your LORD. (Psalm 45:11)

Once upon time, a handsome young prince behaves selfishly toward a disguised enchantress. She turns him into a hideous Beast (Robbie Benson–voice) and tells him that he must find true love by his twenty-first birthday or he will never be human again. (Plus, his staff will forever be changed into household utensils.) Brooding in his castle, the Beast lives in quiet, hopeless desperation. Not far away, in a French village, young beauty Belle (Paige O'Hara–voice) avoids the advances of the dashing but dim suitor Gaston (Richard White–voice). When Belle's father gets lost out in a storm, he seeks shelter in the Beast's castle. The Beast takes him prisoner, but Belle rescues him and takes her father's place as the Beast's prisoner. The Beast learns to behave beautifully toward her, hoping she might fall in love with him and break the spell. One day the Beast releases Belle so she can help her father. Gaston comes to the castle to kill the Beast, but Belle and her father come to stop the murder. Gaston delivers a few blows, but as the Beast lies wounded, Belle tells the Beast, "I love you." This true love breaks the spell, and the Beast and all his servants transform back into humans. Everyone lives happily ever after, except Gaston.

The lesson here is obvious: true beauty comes from within. That's hard to accept when you're a teenager with an acne problem. That's hard to accept when you see the sports hero get all the attention and praise. That's hard to accept when you've got lots of pent-up anger and feel like a trapped animal. But it's true. Physical beauty fades, angry couples live miserably or divorce, and sports heroes get replaced when they wear out. Beauty for the long haul comes from within.

God loves beauty. He made a beautiful world and called it good. He transforms ugly hearts full of sin and confusion into hearts full of goodness, love, joy, and peace. Too bad there isn't a mirror we can look into that would show our beautiful hearts, right? Ah, but there is: God's Word. It tells us, "If anyone is in Christ, he is a new creation; the old has gone, the new has come!" (2 Corinthians 5:17). It also says, "The unfading beauty of a gentle and quiet spirit . . . is of great worth in God's sight" (1 Peter 3:4). Inner beauty doesn't tarnish or fade. It has great value to God. It has great value to those you love the most.

Inner beauty, given to us by God, transforms the ugliest beast into royalty.

PRAYER IDEA: Ask God to show you truth, beauty, comfort and strength in the coming year.

THE INNER MAN ALIVE

The Core (2003)

MPAA: PG-13 for sci-fi life-and-death situations
and brief strong language

Read: Proverbs 20:27

DECEMBER 29

**Count yourselves dead to sin but alive to God in Christ Jesus.
(Romans 6:11)**

The earth's core has stopped spinning, and if it isn't fixed in six months, we will all burn to death because of out-of-control microwaves. The adventure begins when failed pacemakers and disoriented birds puzzle geologist and college professor Dr. Josh Keyes (Aaron Eckhart). After looking into the matter and checking with his esteemed colleague Dr. Zimsky (Stanley Tucci), they realize the awful truth. They ask, "How can we get to the core and restart it? How can we save planet earth?" Well, Keyes and Zimsky gather a crack team of scientists, geologists, and astronauts, dig in with the latest equipment, and drop a carefully planned series of nuclear weapons to restart the core. Piloted by Major Rebecca ("Beck") Childs (Hilary Swank), the earthship Virgil digs deep and accomplishes its mission just in the nick of time.

Each one of us has a dead inner core in need of jump-starting. We are dead in our transgressions and powerless to make ourselves alive (Ephesians 2:1). Some try to be made alive by good works, but apart from Christ, these works matter little to our eternal life. Christ calls our self-righteous works "filthy rags." (Isaiah 64:6) We need to be made alive or we will remain dead in our sins. But there is a rescuer who can penetrate deep and make our core alive again. Jesus restores us to life. Our spirit, soul, and body are lined up in perfect synchronization, operating by God and for God. We cannot make our inner self alive by good works or a force of will. Only God can turn us from death to life.

When God makes us alive, it's called grace. It is by grace that we are saved (Ephesians 2:5). When God raised Jesus from death in the grave, he made a way for us to rise up again to new life. We rise with Christ to forever rule and reign with him. In *The Core,* the earth can't make itself right; it needs a helper. We also need the help of Christ to make us alive. We can't do it alone and therefore there is no room for boasting. Anybody who boasts about how good they are and therefore deserves to go to heaven is misguided and wrong. All we need to do is receive God's forgiveness and acceptance. And that is a great feeling—to the very core!

PRAYER IDEA: Ask God to kill off your old man and make you into a new creation.

415

RECONCILED AS BROTHERS

Final Solution (2000)

MPAA: R for violence and brief language

Read: 2 Corinthians 5:16–21

We also rejoice in God through our Lord Jesus Christ, through whom we have now received reconciliation. (Romans 5:11)

Winner at many film festivals and exhibited on PBS television stations throughout America, *Final Solution* dramatizes the true story of how racist white South Afrikaner Gerrit Wolfaardt (Jan Ellis) comes to Christ, changes his ways, and reconciles himself to those whom he had previously persecuted. In the early 1990s Gerrit comes up with a massive plan for ridding his country of all blacks. Inspired by Adolf Hitler, Gerrit doesn't even think black people have souls. But after he meets Celeste (Liezel van Der Merwe), a young college student who will one day become his wife, he begins to question his beliefs. She challenges him to read the book *Cry, the Beloved Country*. He reads it. Then he reads the Bible. One evening Gerrit tries to shoot and kill a black pastor, the Reverend Peter Lekota (John Kani), but he can't go through with it. Love has penetrated his hardened heart. A changed man, Gerrit asks forgiveness from those he had previously beaten, including one black man from the township named Moses (Mpho Lovinga).

Reconciliation means "to restore to friendship or harmony." Reconciliation cannot occur without repentance, and repentance cannot occur without a change of heart. The Holy Spirit changes Gerrit's heart and he repents. Gerrit understands that he is not the same man he was before but rather is a new creation. Because God reconciles Gerrit to himself, Gerrit is able to participate in the ministry of reconciliation to his fellow human beings. Through Christ's death on the cross, the penalty of sin is removed and we can stand before God and those we have sinned against and say, "Now, there is no reason for hating each other. Let's be friends."

If you have not reconciled to God, now is the time of God's favor, now is the day of salvation (Romans 6:2). If you are already reconciled with God, why not join in the ministry of reconciliation? Ask those you have wronged to forgive you and encourage them to receive forgiveness from God through salvation. Hatred isn't simply a racial issue or an issue between warring nations; it's a personal issue between you and God and between you and others. The final solution is to receive the blessing of God. This is the only solution where he will not count our sins against us. Receive God's love and mercy and go and do likewise.

PRAYER IDEA: Ask God to reconcile you to those who are estranged from you.

. . . so that you may know the certainty of the things you have been taught. (Luke 1:4)

It hasn't won a Golden Globe or an Oscar. It doesn't have a single Hollywood star. Yet, since it was created, the *Jesus* film has been translated into over 660 languages and has been seen by more than 4 billion people. Why have the distributors of this low-budget movie worked so hard to translate it into so many languages, so that the whole world can watch and understand it? Because it is the true story of Jesus. He is a man so important and revolutionary that he just has to be introduced to as many people in the world as possible. Jesus admonished his disciples, "Go into all the world and preach the good news to all creation" (Mark 16:15). As far as we know, this command has never been retracted.

Based on the book of Luke, the *Jesus* film tells the entire history of Christ on earth. First, it speaks of the birth of Christ. Then it talks of Jesus as a youth in the temple. He grows to manhood, is baptized by John the Baptist, and calls his first disciples. A sinful woman anoints Jesus, and he forgives her sins, proving his divinity. He raises a girl from the dead and heals the eyes of a blind man. Jesus drives out a legion of evil spirits from a man, and the spirits enter a herd of pigs. Children approach Jesus and he welcomes them. Finally, Jesus eats the Last Supper and is betrayed, tried, crucified, and buried. On the third day, he rises from the dead and appears to his disciples, then ascends into heaven. The entire Gospel of Luke is not recorded on film in this movie, but it clearly tells his story.

Those who distribute the *Jesus* film receive reports every day from people who have given their lives to Christ and become believers after watching it. Are you preaching the good news to all creation? Many people are afraid to speak out about Christ, or they are confused as to how to begin. Perhaps you need to "record" his Word and the testimony of how he saved you onto your heart and mind. The actors of the *Jesus* film practiced their words and actions, then repeated them to be recorded on film. Take time now to practice your testimony. Take time to read and learn Scripture. Then, when you have an audience, "play back" the message you practiced earlier. Learn the good news, practice telling it to others, and then go out and do it. The world is dying to hear this fantastic message.

PRAYER IDEA: Ask God to give you a ready answer so that all who ask may know about your hope.

MOVIE ORGANIZATIONS

here are many organizations at the intersection of movies and faith. They include fellowships, classes, networking opportunities, and more. Here are a few of my favorites:

The Christian Film and Television Commission began in 1978 as a Christian advocacy group in Hollywood. They speak to Hollywood executives, producers, directors, and writers in support of redemptive, Christian content in movies and entertainment. In 1985 they began *Movieguide* magazine. *Movieguide* does a complete content analysis of every theatrically released movie in America. They list the worldview and objectionable content and give you a quality and morality rating on each movie. Go to their website www.movieguide.org.

The First Presbyterian Church of Hollywood offers many opportunities for Christians in Hollywood. First, they have their weekly worship services. Second, they sponsor Actor's Co-op, an award-winning professional theater company. Third, they sponsor Act One, a writing-for-Hollywood seminar designed specifically for the Christian writer. Fourth, they sponsor Inter-Mission, a Christian fellowship and support group for entertainment industry professionals. Last, they sponsor MovieTime, a family friendly movie time followed by a panel discussion. Go to their website www.fpch.org/arts.

Christian Filmmaker Ministries has a fantastic network that combines film distribution, Bible study, Christian film news, a Christian actors network, and much more. Go to their website at www.christianfilmmaker.com.

One of my favorite Christian film schools is located at **Regent University**. They have a graduate program that has up-to-date equipment and lots of opportunities. Many of their alumni are doing great work in Hollywood and across the country. Go to their website at www.regent.edu. **Biola University** in La Mirada, California, also has a great undergraduate program in film and mass communication. Go to www.biola.edu.

The City of the Angels Film Festival grew out of a dialogue between filmmakers and theologians who believe that spiritual perspectives are indispensable to the filmmaking process. They are dedicated to screening quality works that not only celebrate film as art but also raise vital religious and social issues. Go to their website at www.cityofangelsfilmfest.org.